A Study of the Sacred District Scene in Private Tomb Decoration

Kelly-Anne Diamond

GHP Egyptology 37

GHP

This title is published by
Golden House Publications

A catalogue record for this book is available from the British Library

ISBN 978-1-906137-83-0

Printed in the United Kingdom

London 2023

Table of Contents

ACKNOWLEDGMENTS

This work is the outcome of the field research that was conducted on the west bank of Luxor and at Elkab in the winter and spring of 2009. The post-doctoral fellowship that funded my research was granted by the United States' Department of State, Bureau of Education and Cultural Affairs and administered through the American Research Center in Egypt.

I would like to begin by thanking the Supreme Council of Antiquities for allowing me access to the individual tombs, without which my work would not have been possible. I would like to thank Dr. Zahi Hawass, Mr. Mansour Boreik, Mr. Mustafa Waziri, and my inspector Hassan Ramadan for facilitating my project. Chicago House graciously allowed me to use their library facilities while I was living in Luxor and conducting research. I would like to thank the late Dr. Lanny Bell who made my transition to Luxor so easy; Reis Ali Farouk and Reis Omar Farouk for making ground transportation simple; my inspector Hassan Ramadan for navigating the tombs on the west bank during and after the demolition of the Gurna village houses.

Additionally, I am thankful to the many people who helped me complete my research and writing in numerous ways. I am thankful to the late Edwin Brock and to Lila Pinch Brock for providing me with photographs of the remaining fragments of the Sacred District scene in Theban Tomb 120. Ted Brock was a friend to me both during my fieldwork and after, and I will miss having a Stella with him at the roof top restaurant of the Saint Joseph Hotel. Ted was a fountain of practical information on how to efficiently navigate Luxor (both ancient and modern), and his expertise in the field helped make fieldwork much more manageable. John Shearman and Dr. Andrew Bednarski of the American Research Center in Egypt (Luxor) generously allowed me to visit Theban Tomb 110 during their conservation work, which allowed for a better understanding of the placement of the Sacred District in that tomb. I would also like to thank Khadija Adams, Conservation Manager in Luxor for the American Research Center in Egypt, and Dr. JJ Shirley for providing me with photographs of the left wall of the passage of Theban Tomb 110 that greatly enhanced the remaining images. Dr. Peter Brand, from the University of Memphis, has kindly shared with me his wonderful photographs of the Elkab tombs and has allowed me to include them in my work. Dr. José Galán of the Spanish National Research council has graciously shared photographs of what remains of the Sacred District scene taken during his current archaeological investigation in Theban Tomb 12. I am also grateful to the late Dr. Ramadan Hussein for his time and patience in answering my many questions about working in Egypt, and without whose help I may not have had the courage to begin this project. Dr. Melinda Hartwig of Georgia State University generously provided me with a line-drawing and a detailed description of the left wall of the passage of the tomb of Menna, for which I am very appreciative. I would also like to thank Dr. Janet Richards from the University of Michigan for taking the time to correspond with me via email to answer questions about the processional route at Abydos and the Mysteries of Osiris. I would also like to thank Dr. John Baines for sharing with me his new manuscript on "Watery Egyptian Landscapes and Performances Within Them." Thank you to Dr. J. R. Pellini for corresponding with me about Theban Tomb 123 and to Thierry Benderitter for helping with images of Theban Tomb 100. Emily Carson was a great help in editing the final draft of this work, but any errors that still remain are entirely my own. I would also like to thank Dr. Lanny Bell for providing constant encouragement for my research and for being a wonderful sounding board for my ideas. And finally, I am most grateful for the loving support and the unrelenting reassurance of my husband Jeffrey Moore, who has championed my cause and encouraged me for many years while I finished my manuscript, and for my mother Diane Diamond who helped with my children while I was working in Egypt.

INTRODUCTION

Rites in the Garden, the Holy Place, or the Sacred Temenos are all names given by scholars to a particular scene found in numerous private tombs from ancient Egypt (Figure 1). The Sacred District, as I refer to it, is a map-like illustration that depicts a landscape with trees, ponds, shrines, and garden plots, among other elements. However, this scene differs from so many other tomb scenes because it shows few people performing understandable actions. Most tomb scenes show images of daily life or depictions of funerary rituals and activities. The Sacred District scene shows none of these. It also differs because of the plethora of basins, ponds, and pools that the artists have illustrated in calculated measure. It portrays a landscape and locations that were rarely recorded in ancient Egypt. In fact, beginning in the dynastic period, examples of settings in art decrease dramatically, and the background of scenes is regularly rejected in place of the foreground. This situation changes at the end of the seventeenth dynasty when the Sacred District exemplifies a recurring topographical setting in tomb art, but without any indication of precise locations. Generally, when locations do appear in tomb art, they are included for what they produce, not how they looked. Yet, there are no production scenes in the Sacred District. In fact, decoration in tombs tends to reference the lived world of the tomb owner, but this scene suggests something else and is therefore an anomaly. Because of these many differences the Sacred District scene has remained an enigma that has perplexed researchers, or at the very least, has been a point of intrigue to scholars who want to better understand its significance.

What is known is that this illustration began to appear in the decoration created within private tombs during the Second Intermediate Period, the era when the Ahmosid family in Thebes began to rule Egypt. There are also a few instances of the Sacred District scene south of this region at Elkab and Hierakonpolis. The scene is found in the tombs of elite officials who worked for the king, particularly during the joint reign of Hatshepsut and Thutmose III of the eighteenth dynasty (*c.*1479–1425 BCE). Yet, more work needs

Figure 1: The Sacred District scene in the eighteenth dynasty tomb of Reneny at Elkab. Photo by author.

to be done to understand what this scene's uniqueness truly means.

With this study, I explain the Sacred District: when it appeared, where it appeared, which people included it in their decorative programs, and what it might have meant to those who employed it. I catalogue which micro-scenes, or episodes, were consistently depicted within the Sacred District and suggest meanings for each selection. I also discuss why these particular elements were useful in life and why they were chosen for inclusion in this significant tomb scene. At the same time, this work discusses the liminal nature of this scene and how it interacted with adjacent tomb scenes, the architecture of the tomb, and the passing of the deceased into the hereafter.

This work offers a significant contribution to our understanding of New Kingdom tomb art in general, and specifically of organizational patterns of individual funerary scenes in reference to aspects of the architecture of the tomb. This study also elaborates on developments within the cult of Osiris during the New Kingdom, the relationships that might have existed between private cemeteries in Upper Egypt, the artistic patterns visible in contemporary tombs, and the network of professional relationships among tomb owners. This study is important because there has not been a comprehensive study of the Sacred District scene since Settgast's publication in 1963.[1] In the last sixty years there have been significant advances in the understanding of Egyptian history, archaeology, and religion, not to mention the myriad of tombs exposed, studied, published, and conserved on the west bank. This study promises more up-to-date information and the inclusion of additional primary and secondary sources.

One of the challenges that comes with studying the Sacred District scene is that it has been referenced in many different ways across scholarly publications. Thus, the problem has been that it is difficult to understand if it is this scene that scholars refer to in their work unless an actual illustration is published. Likewise, it has been challenging to gather together the results of similar lines of research because of this distinct terminology. My aim is to streamline and collate past studies on the district by bringing together works that should be studied in tandem. I have also made choices as to which micro-scenes to include in the Sacred District and which ones to leave out. In these cases, I take into consideration previous scholarship, but also make new suggestions by following my own intuition and experience with the material.

Another pain point is the fact that most of the available evidence about landscapes or environmental settings comes from the vast eastern and western deserts that flank the Nile and the low desert and escarpments near the Nile floodplain, and yet the desert is not visible in the Sacred District, at least not as a focal point. I might contend that all the micro-scenes of the Sacred District are foregrounded to a desert landscape as a backdrop, making the desert itself inarticulate and in the distant background. Because of modern settlement patterns there is an imbalance in the archaeological record when it comes to material closer to the Nile in the fertile area.[2] This pattern affects this study because the current record is not informative about where the main cultural centers were in antiquity, and it is quite feasible that some of the environments shown in the Sacred District reflect these centers; at least that has been the opinion presented in several past studies.

One of the arguments I make is that the Sacred District scene is an imaginative rendition of the journey of the deceased who travels from this life to the next. What we see is not truly a map as we know it, but a visualization of something that no one has ever seen, of a place that everyone will eventually go. The style of the illustrations resembles ancient Egyptian maps in some ways (although we have very few ancient maps for comparison), but the Sacred District is not a real place. It incorporates real places from the Theban area that were familiar to the artists and to the deceased and their families, but we also see other elements that were not indigenous to the Thebaid. This is why this landscape should be considered a conglomeration of the known and unknown, a place that harks back to the past, incorporates the contemporary religious traditions and evokes the wishes of the deceased. The historicity of these episodes is based on the collective memory of the society. We do not know exactly why these places were important, or in fact which locations are actually shown. But several settings have a long history in Egyptian art, and we find precursors to the Sacred District in the art as early as the Naqada Period. The Scorpion mace head (*c.*3100 BCE) is the earliest known detailed image of an environment which bears some resemblance to the Sacred District scene, in that the shrine depicted on the former is pervasive in the

[1] In 2011 Christoffer Theis made a significant contribution to the study of funerary ritual with his work, *Deine Seele zum Himmel, dein Leichnam zur Erde: zur idealtypischen Rekonstruktion eines altägyptischen Bestattungsrituals* (pp. 203–98).

[2] Baines 2020: 177.

latter. One of the most significant points I want to make is that these scenes are not analogous to other garden scenes or pool scenes that feature the deceased relaxing outside. They are special and relatively limited. They date to a specific time and appear in particular places.

My argument is that the significance of the Sacred District scene lies in its ubiquity (during its specific time of employment) and the need to include it even when wall space was at a premium. Its uniqueness lies in its static renditions of landscapes with little action and no sense of movement. I must approach these scenes primarily through the images, as little text remains, excluding the captions in the tomb of Rekhmire (TT 100) and a handful of other tombs. Unfortunately, many of the rituals that are shown as taking place in the Sacred District cannot be interpreted in detail, specifically for the reasons listed above.

The way the ancient Egyptians imagined this scene seems to resemble a segregated plot of land and suggests that the illustrators were thinking of, or perhaps trying to imitate the local Theban landscape. Yet, it was mythologized as the route the deceased should traverse to meet the god Osiris in the west. By this, I mean that the area has imagined qualities that materialize at the edge of the desert. There are no tombs depicted in the Sacred District, so it was not considered to be the cemetery proper. The Sacred District scene conjures up the image of a holy landscape on the west bank of Thebes, possibly as it was being imagined during the late seventeenth and early eighteenth dynasties. The god Osiris has a prominent position in most of the Sacred District scenes, which means that by the time of the seventeenth dynasty, a scene that some argue originated in a Lower Egyptian context, had become Osirianized. This is not a daily life scene but a setting liminal in nature and set up for the performance of rituals that concerned the passing of the deceased from this life to the next. It represents an area that must be traversed by the deceased as he moves from death to new life.

Chapters one through five present and categorize the evidence, while chapters six through nine analyze and discuss these descriptions and characterizations. In chapter one I present my methodology for examining the Sacred District and how this line of research emerged from a study on the ancient Egyptian word *ḥ3i*. Chapter two summarizes the past research on this scene and documents the evolution of thought regarding several individual micro-scenes, namely, the *Mww*. With chapter three I discuss the history of the private Egyptian funeral, the ritual voyages, and the Osirian afterlife, and how these areas provide context for understanding the tomb scenes of the Sacred District. Within the Sacred District there is little ritual action illustrated in the garden representations, and there is no activity taking place in the gods' shrines. The entire district gives the impression of peacefulness and serenity. Chapter four examines the artists' renditions of the Sacred District and considers the location and date of these illustrations, the type of tomb in which they appear, and the nature of the surrounding scenes in which they are embedded. In chapter five, I assess the garden in ancient Egypt and look at the symbolism of each micro-scene within the Sacred District, present the artistic conventions employed by the artists, reveal the types of vegetation and watery landscapes that appear, and identify the stylized reproduction of the arrangements that create a model or view of a location.[3] Chapter six explores the relationships between the officials who owned these tombs, and clarifies patterns that existed in terms of the tombs' locations and dates. In conjunction with this, the mobility of the artists in relation to these patterns is considered. Chapter seven analyzes the placement of the Sacred District scene in relation to other funerary scenes and demonstrates how its position augments the function of the tomb as a place of transition. Chapter eight focuses on two eighteenth dynasty tomb inscriptions, the label *t3 ḏsr*, and how this term might be connected to the quality and nature of the Sacred District. The last chapter focuses on those examples of the Sacred District from the private New Kingdom tombs at Elkab, a site located about eighty kilometers south of Thebes.

In terms of the bigger picture, this study of the Sacred District scene illuminates one of the ways the ancient Egyptians chose to express their understanding of the process of rejuvenation and explains how it was employed in tomb art. My hope is that this study will serve scholars in furthering their research on funerary rites, rituals, tomb art, and architecture, and that it will be a contribution to the research of those working on the Butic Burial and its descendants. Lastly, this study finally resolves the issue of the nature of this garden scene and establishes that it should be considered a map-like illustration of a mythologized realm ostensibly located on the west bank, and not a typical tomb garden.

[3] Settgast 1963: 48.

CHAPTER ONE: CURRENT APPROACH

This chapter outlines the origin of this project, how it emerged from my previous research, and what connections it maintains with my previous work on funerary ritual. I present the objectives I had at the beginning of this project and explain how they changed as my work progressed. Following, I elaborate on my fieldwork and methodology, in order to clarify why and how I approached this topic. Several challenges that I faced are outlined below, and I extrapolate on the solutions I found to overcome them. One of the biggest obstacles I encountered at the outset of this project was deciphering the terminology used by modern scholars in their published works to describe this scene.

This work on the Sacred District scene emerged from my doctoral research at Brown University under the direction of the late Lanny Bell, which focused on the ancient Egyptian term *ḥ3i*.[4] *ḥ3i* has the connotation to "ritually transform," with the express purpose of revivifying or rejuvenating the deceased. This word study arose from a more general study of "mourning words," in that while collecting the citations for words meaning "to mourn" (a deceased individual), the word *ḥ3i* stood out as an anomaly. Because it is accompanied by Alan Gardiner's A 28 sign as a determinative (a man with upraised arms), this word has strong ties with the act of rejoicing. This same determinative is used to write both *ḥ3i* and *ḥ*ꜥ*i* ("rejoice"), which renders the two words similar, both visually and aurally.[5] According to Raymond Faulkner, the ancient Egyptians believed that there was no such thing as coincidence in their language, and that if one word resembled another there was an innate relationship.[6] In fact, different modern translations of the same ancient text employ either "rejoice" or "mourn" as the English translation of *ḥ3i*. The fact that these are two contrasting emotions was intriguing. Even the earliest attested example of *ḥ3i* is initially puzzling, in that it is included in a caption accompanying a funeral scene in which women are dancing. Unfortunately, this confusion has made its way into the most modern dictionaries, where women with this label have been categorized as mourners. Females who perform the *ḥ3i* ritual in other sources also appear in the Sacred District in some New Kingdom private tombs. Moreover, in the tomb of Amenemhet (TT 82), the ritual of *ḥ3i* occurs in a scene adjacent to the Sacred District. Thus, this is how I chanced upon the Sacred District scene.

Beginning at least as early as the fourth dynasty, the rite of *ḥ3i* was an important element in the resurrection process—a process that magically enabled the deceased to reach the hereafter. This was a necessary process for helping the deceased to become a spirit—a transition that did not happen automatically.[7] In the mid to late Old Kingdom, in the royal sphere at least, the ritual of *ḥ3i* was part of the procedure to transform Horus into Osiris. The Osirian resurrection was potent and had mass appeal, because if Osiris could be revived, so could anyone.[8] After the Old Kingdom, the rite of *ḥ3i* occurs only with reference to the mythological realm.[9] The nature of this rite reveals its jubilant character, as the arrival of the deceased in the afterlife was a time to celebrate and rejoice. This *ḥ3i* ceremony was not originally Osirian but was adapted by the royal cult at some point during the first five dynasties. In the early Old Kingdom, evidence suggests that royalty had more access to the cult of Osiris. Private people participated in other funerary traditions, namely those that existed prior to the advent of the cult of Osiris. Griffiths attributes this transformation of tradition to a change in regime:

> It is not hard to understand why this ceremonial (Butic tradition) would not always be given prominence in the royal funerary cult of the early dynastic period. This regime reflected an Upper Egyptian supremacy, which would not be anxious to follow Lower Egyptian traditions. Their funerary cult had its origin in Abydos.[10]

The rite of *ḥ3i* may have belonged to the Butic ceremonies in that it developed from a Lower Egyptian tradition and had spread among private persons. The cult of Osiris eventually absorbed the Butic traditions and reinterpreted them. Hence, the result is a new understanding of the old ceremonies, a phenomenon that may be revealed in illustrations

[4] Diamond 2007 and 2010a.

[5] The word *ḥ3i* resembles both *ḥ*ꜥ*i* and *ḳ3i*; all three words use the A 28 sign as a determinative.

[6] Faulkner and Goelet 1994: 146.

[7] Breasted 1959: 59.

[8] Griffiths 1980: 3.

[9] The exception is Gardiner's Funerary Liturgy that was found in a Middle Kingdom context but may date back to the third dynasty (1955).

[10] Griffiths 1980: 60.

of the Sacred District in the New Kingdom private tombs. Therefore, an account of the Sacred District ostensibly commences in the Old Kingdom, if not earlier, with the appearance of rows of Delta shrines on several artifacts and in private tomb scenes— but it does not yet appear in its fully realized artistic form. Barry Kemp warns that by "carefully following the sources backwards in time from the better understood later ones to the more fragmentary and elusive earlier ones" we assume that the meaning remained the same.[11] His point is meaningful even though the case of the Sacred District is slightly different. Instead of using later sources to understand earlier sources, we have an intricate New Kingdom scene from which we are trying to find vestiges of early knowledge. The meanings behind whatever we are examining may have changed since its first appearance in the Early Dynastic Period or Old Kingdom. We must keep this in mind as we study the Sacred District.

The Old Kingdom evidence connects to the New Kingdom scenes through the actors involved in this ritual. One of the ritualists who performed the rite of *ḥ3ỉ* was the *dmḏyt*, a ritualist whose title can now be translated as "bone or limb collector."[12] Her appearance is rare in the historical record, but one of the places where she appears is in the Sacred District, as shown in Theban Tombs 82 and 100. It is through the various Sacred District scenes presented in the private New Kingdom tombs on the west bank of Thebes, Elkab, and Hierakonpolis that reminiscences of these older rituals remain.[13] They function as indirect hints at past traditions. Yet, there is more to these scenes than just being copies of outdated ceremonies. As our evidence for private funerary rituals in the New Kingdom is indeed sparse and exists mainly in the form of tomb decoration, understanding the significance of the Sacred District scene can greatly expand our knowledge of funeral rites and rituals, among other things.

In the following pages, I present the objectives of this study, the methodology I use to establish my conclusions, the challenges I encountered during my field work and beyond, the limits the materials necessarily imposed on my study, and a discussion on the modern terminology previously used to identify the Sacred District in scholarly works.

Objectives

When initiating this project in 2009 my first objective was to determine a basic set of terms to describe what the viewer sees in the Sacred District scene. Within modern scholarship there has been an inconsistency in the terminology, not only for the name and nature of the complex as a whole, but also for the individual episodes, or micro-scenes that appear within the different compilations of the Sacred District. I wanted to systematize the terms so that discussions about the Sacred District could be more streamline and uncomplicated. Thus, my approach to this subject was twofold: to elaborate on the functions of the various female participants within the district whose titles were associated with the performance of the rite of *ḥ3i* and to decipher patterns among the micro-scenes for a better reading of the scene as a whole. The latter endeavor seemed necessary if I were going to understand the function of the female performers. However, the end result is quite different. This work evolved into an analysis of the Sacred District and its constituent parts, with the aim of understanding what it meant to the Egyptians who chose to have it depicted on their tomb walls. What began as a journal article, quickly developed into a full manuscript as I realized that I could not understand the Sacred District in isolation—it was inevitably connected to myriad concepts that took me well beyond the tomb walls.

Fieldwork

Another principal task at the outset of this project was to use the available published sources to create a database of those tombs known to have an example of the Sacred District depicted among the funerary scenes. One of the first sources I consulted was the scene index in *The Topographical Bibliography* by Porter and Moss, which offers a list of tombs that include the "Rites in Garden."[14] I then compared this list to Jürgen Settgast's 1963 work *Untersuchungen zu altägyptischen bestattungsdarstellungen* and expanded my database. Additional tombs were then added throughout the research process, with the total number of tombs eventually reaching thirty-nine.[15]

Fieldwork was conducted from January 2009 through May 2009, when I investigated twenty-three tombs on the west bank of Thebes and at Elkab.[16] For

[11] Kemp 2018: 141–143.
[12] Diamond 2015a and 2017.
[13] Seyfried 2003: 64.

[14] Porter and Moss 1970: 472.
[15] This study includes thirty-nine tombs from Thebes, Elkab, and Hierakonpolis. However, this study also discusses two additional tombs, TT 60 and Elkab TC 10. This brings the total to forty-one tombs.
[16] Theban Tombs: 100, 81, 21, 179, 125, 69, 71, 224, 110, 127, 112, 122, 123, 82, 53, 96B, 17, 69, 41, 275. Elkab Tombs: Reneny (TC 7), Paheri (TC 3), Setau (TC 4).

each tomb fundamental information was recorded, including the date of entry, tomb number, name of the tomb owner and his profession, and location of tomb. Attributes that were of particular significance were the wall where the Sacred District appears (ex. left wall passage, right wall passage, etc.), the register in which the scene appears, the cardinal location of the scene within the tomb's architecture, the female appellations, the orientation of the participants, and the scenes which precede and follow the Sacred District scene. Whether the tomb was plastered and painted or carved and painted was also recorded, as well as the general state of the tomb, considering the fragmentation of the decoration and any blackened or discolored walls. Any other anomalies, or curious features, were also duly noted.

There was some confusion about which micro-scenes were *expected* to appear in a tomb's decorative program, because the name given to specific micro-scenes by secondary sources was inconsistent. Due to the lack of attention previously given to the Sacred District, it was unclear, for example, if the rites to the mooring-post took place within the Sacred District or adjacent to it. Or should the pool and pond (garden scene) be considered as separate from the Sacred District, or as its core component? Was the garden scene inclusive of what has sometimes been called the sacred Delta localities? Or were these two separate micro-scenes?

The tomb of Rekhmire (TT 100) is often the answer to all questions funerary, it being the most recognized and most elaborate example. Rekhmire offers a large composition that includes almost all of the documented micro-scenes, with the slaughter scene in the dominant position. Yet, Rekhmire is not truly a comparative for other Sacred District representations and at times has proved to be misleading, as the majority of the micro-scenes in this tomb are missing from the others. In fact, the size of the Sacred District scene and the number of micro-scenes within it varies substantially from tomb to tomb.

After I recognized and defined the Sacred District in each tomb, photographs were taken, and sketches were created. It was important to capture not only the details of the Sacred District scene, but also the larger context in which the Sacred District scene occurred. Any inscriptions were carefully recorded, although inscriptions turned out to be rare, either because the paint was worn away, or because they were never added in the first place.

During the execution of the fieldwork, entry to most tombs proved feasible; however, there were extenuating circumstances that prevented visitation to the following Theban tombs: 15, 39, 84, and 120. In these cases, published reports or notes and photographs by the excavators were utilized. As the research continued post-fieldwork, additional tombs were incorporated into the study, especially once I realized that a row of closed shrines could act as a substitute for a full Sacred District when wall space was limited.[17] This increased the number of Sacred District scenes included in this study, and these additional tombs were informative in several ways.

Methodology

I distinguished seventeen unique micro-scenes for inclusion in this study, of which six can be sub-divided into multiple variants.[18] However, in the end there are several micro-scenes that I believe should not be considered part of the Sacred District. Yet, I decided to leave them in the list because they have been discussed together in several modern studies, so it is now necessary to explain how they are separate. There is no required sequence for these micro-scenes, and a tomb can contain any number of them. Thus, it was not necessary for the Egyptian artists to depict every episode for the identification of the Sacred District to be clear to viewers. However, some micro-scenes are more widespread than others and various patterns emerge with further analysis. The following is a complete list of the micro-scenes that could be included with a Sacred District scene:

1. The *Mww*
    a. Hall of the *Mww*
    b. *Mww* with conical headdress welcoming deceased
    c. Men doing the dance of the *Mww* (*ḫbt*-dancers)
2. Pool with palms
3. Two obelisks
    a. Standing alone
    b. Accompanied by two men (not included in the Sacred District)
4. Garden plots
5. Two sycamore trees

---

[17] For example, TT 161.

[18] Settgast distinguishes the following micro-scenes or episodes: The Hall of the *Mww*, the Women's Tent, the Garden Pond, Gods of the Great Gate, the Gods' Shrines, the Three Ponds, the Slaughterhouse, the Four Basins, and Rites performed for the Mooring Post (1963: 49–50). Other studies have recognized sixteen or seventeen episodes (Seyfried 2003; Altenmüller 1975a).

6. Anubis shrine
7. Three pools
8. Gods' shrines
    a. Open
    b. Closed
9. Women's tent
10. Kneeling women:
    a. Before four basins
    b. Before Anubis in his shrine (not included in the Sacred District)
11. Guardians of the great gate
12. Osiris shrine
13. Braziers
14. Delta Shrines: (not included in the Sacred District)
    a. *Pr-nw* shrine and palm tree combination
    b. Saite shrine
    c. Unnamed structure
15. Rites to the mooring-post
16. Slaughtering area
    a. Typical
    b. With sycamore-pool
17. Cattle

Using my list of micro-scenes, I have isolated each of them within the larger Sacred District scenes, recorded their variations from tomb to tomb, and tracked their appearances over time. I have detailed repetitive combinations of micro-scenes to establish patterns in their placement, and I have attempted to discern if certain episodes appear at random. With this, the intention was to discover how to read the Sacred District scene more accurately. Other elements I considered were the absolute and relative positioning of each micro-scene, the level of the register in which the Sacred District is found, the orientation of the participants, and any embedded directives for viewers.

In reference to my original query, several examples of the Sacred District scene feature appellations for female performers that function as captions. These titles include *mn/knwt*, *dmḏ(y)t*, and *mnỉt wrt.* Each of these titles has been conceived of previously as "mourning woman," a definition that evidently pertains to her funerary context. The two most recognizable examples of these titles occur in Theban Tombs 82 and 100. One of my tasks was to try to locate more examples of these titles and to discover illustrations of other women who also perform the same rituals. Unfortunately, most of the tombs that I examined either did not have extant inscriptions or their scenes were not given labels in the first place. Fortuitously, several additional examples of these women, some accompanied by inscriptions, have been located and are included in the current archive. However, often these female ritualists bear the titles "Greater Kite" or "Lesser Kite" which have been studied previously.[19]

Challenges

There were several obstacles that I encountered when documenting the tomb decoration. Once the fieldwork began it was quickly realized that my original line of research was not going to be as productive as I had hoped. The reason for this was simply that there were not enough preserved inscriptions (or perhaps they never existed) to provide much additional evidence for female ritualists. I did, however, see that the title *mn/knwt* had yet a further variation: *ktnw*.[20] The same signs are employed but they were inscribed in a different order, which perhaps amounts to scribal error.

Another significant impediment was the blackened walls that were present in several tombs, such as TT 110 and 224. In some cases, the walls were so black from smoke it was impossible to even locate a general outline for the Sacred District scene, let alone articulate the individual micro-scenes. The most striking example was perhaps in Theban Tomb 110, which belongs to the royal butler and royal herald Djehuty, which in 2009 needed to be accessed through the rear of the tomb via TT 42. Since this time, TT 110 has been conserved and documented by the American Research Center in Egypt, so this example of the Sacred District scene is now partially visible.[21] In other cases, for example TT 123, the tomb of the scribe, overseer of the granary and counter of bread, Amenemhet, chunks of stone and plaster had fallen, and large portions of the scenes were missing. R. J. Pellini is now making significant headway on this project.[22]

Additionally, as noted earlier, several tombs could not be accessed because of on-going excavation and conservation work. These challenges make aspects of this research more difficult and in certain areas put real limits on the outcomes of this study.

Terminology

At the onset of the study, researching this scene was problematical because of the variety of names assigned to this scene by modern scholars. There has been no standard term used in modern scholarship

[19] Fischer 1976: 39–50.
[20] Diamond *In progress.*
[21] Personal communication with JJ Shirley.
[22] Pellini 2022a and 2022b.

to refer to the Sacred District. It has been variously labeled as *der Heilige Bezirk*,[23] the sacred *temenos*,[24] the holy place,[25] the holy district,[26] the sacred district,[27] and rites in the garden.[28] For the purpose of this research, it is necessary to have a standardized way to communicate about the material. For instance, each of the aforementioned terms, when used in scholarly publications, refers to a series of individual micro-scenes within a composition, thus it has not been clear what these terms have actually been referencing. There has also been an overwhelming effort in past scholarship to connect the Sacred District scene to the Butic Burial of the ancient kings of Lower Egypt.[29] This correlation is based on the Old Kingdom tomb scenes where the *Mww* appear in conjunction with the shrines of the Sacred Delta localities.[30] This trend has elucidated certain episodes within the repertoire of Sacred District micro-scenes, but it has also overshadowed other traditions that this image may reflect. What is more significant than the terms modern scholars employ, is the term the ancient Egyptians used to describe this place. In two cases the Sacred District has been identified in Egyptian texts as *tꜣ ḏsr*, a phrase that has been generally translated as "necropolis."[31] As James Hoffmeier has shown, the literal translation is "segregated land."[32] One attestation comes from the Middle Kingdom tomb of Senet (TT 60), where a caption to a funerary scene reads, "Putting down (the coffin) at the Hall of the *Mww*, toward the opening of the *tꜣ ḏsr*."[33] A second example appears on the south wall in the upper scene in the early eighteenth dynasty tomb of Tetiky (TT 15). Therefore, the Egyptian term employed for the place where the Hall of the *Mww* is situated is at the entrance to the *tꜣ ḏsr*. Even though this means literally "the segregated land," over time the term *tꜣ ḏsr* became synonymous with necropolis.[34] These two scenes associate the *tꜣ ḏsr* with the Hall of the *Mww* and indicate that the space the *Mww* guard (the Sacred District) is called the *tꜣ ḏsr*. It is clear from the New Kingdom examples of the Sacred District that this Hall is situated at its entrance.

Hence, it is accurate to assert that the architectural features and natural elements inside this space comprise the *tꜣ ḏsr*. The Hall of the *Mww* is regularly the first episode in the series of micro-scenes that constitute the Sacred District. From an analysis of these scenes, it is clear which micro-scenes were included within the Sacred District and which ones were separate scenes, and it is evident that "Sacred District" is an appropriate English term for this location. Hopefully it can be used by all moving forward.

---

[23] Settgast 1963: 48–74.
[24] Assmann 2005: 305.
[25] A. Wilkinson 1998: 106.
[26] Hodel-Hoenes 2000: 165.
[27] Hodel-Hoenes 2000: 168.
[28] Porter and Moss 1970: 472. Scene Index. *Rites in Garden with Pool* and *Garden Pool* are also found throughout text.
[29] Junker 1940; Brunner-Traut 1938; Altenmüller 1975b; A. Wilkinson 1994a. This list includes only some of the publications that support this identification.
[30] Junker 1940: 6, *Abb.* 4.
[31] Faulkner 1991: 293.
[32] Hoffmeier 1985: 85-89.
[33] This is my translation. Norman de Garis Davies describes this scene as "the coffin is set down at the booth of the *mww* dancers before the gates of the necropolis" (1920: 21). He does not offer a translation of this passage, but clearly his commentary is based on the hieroglyphic inscription that appears in his plate 21. See also Settgast 1963: 48.
[34] Hoffmeier 1985: 85–87.

CHAPTER TWO: PREVIOUS SCHOLARSHIP

The Sacred District scene has been recognized by scholars for decades and has received some academic attention. Most of the past research done by Egyptologists has been published in German and is in reference to the funerary rituals. What attracted the earliest scholars to this scene was the appearance of the *Mww* and their seemingly bizarre headdresses and unique footwork. They have elicited many curious explanations by researchers and have thus furthered the study of this landscape as a whole. My intention is to use these past studies on the *Mww* to better understand the Sacred District in its entirety. Even though many of these earlier studies did not have the objective of clarifying the substance or import of the Sacred District, does not mean that they cannot provide a strong footing for it when considered collectively.

One of the earliest studies related to the Sacred District was written by Emma Brunner-Traut in 1938. *Der Tanze im Alten Ägypten* examines dance in ancient Egypt, and it is within this context that the *Mww,* who perform within the Sacred District, are discussed. In this work, Brunner-Traut focuses on the dance of the *Mww* as an integral part of the Sacred District and groups them into three categories: those who intercept the funeral procession at the cemetery and use a particular hand gesture; those who stand in the Hall of the *Mww*; and the *ẖnw*-dancers who she associates with the People of Pe.[35] Brunner-Traut believed the deceased private person visited the city of Buto, located in the Delta, and was greeted by the *Mww*. She further interpreted this scene as deriving from the royal funeral and the voyages that past kings took to Buto, and also to Abydos to visit Osiris. Brunner-Traut saw the *Mww* as demi-gods acting as agents from beyond.[36] Her work established a framework for interpreting the *Mww* as representatives of Lower Egypt and the Butic burial, and she inaugurated how to conceptualize their context.

More recently scholars have modified Brunner-Traut's ideas. Beginning in 1940, Hermann Junker published *Der Tanz der Mww und das Butische Begräbnis im Alten Reich*. As his title suggests, Junker concentrated his efforts on clarifying the Butic rituals that permeated the Old Kingdom funeral scenes.[37] He incorporated recent finds from the necropolis at Saqqara and argued that the *Mww* have appeared in tomb decoration since the Old Kingdom.[38] Junker elaborated on Brunner-Traut's work and provided the first comprehensive description of the Sacred District through his interest in the *Mww*. To establish his claim, Junker used early examples of the *Mww* from the private tombs of Ptahhotep, Ptahhotep II, Idwt, and Nebkauhor, among others. He also believed that the *Mww* and the rituals they performed were fashioned after the prehistoric royal funerals from Buto.[39] He coined these rituals "*Butisch*/Butoesque" and claimed that they involved the dead king journeying by boat to Buto and to other sacred Delta localities, such as Heliopolis and Sais, and that it was these *Totenfahrts* that were depicted on the walls of these Old Kingdom private tombs. This seemingly established the Sacred District's location in and around the areas of Buto and Sais. Junker fine-tuned his theory by further stipulating that these voyages were done on sacred waterways and that the *wrt*-canal directly connected Buto and Sais in the western Delta. Another feature of these Old Kingdom tomb scenes, he noted, was the rows of *pr-nw* chapels that were ubiquitous in Lower Egyptian iconography. In these cases, Junker associated them with the royal cemetery at Buto, citing their similarity to the royal palace and the kings' sarcophagi.[40] It is these *pr-nw* chapels (coupled with the Saite shrine and another unnamed structure) as well as the *Mww*, that would surface again in New Kingdom iconography.[41]

Fortunately, Junker moved beyond the *Mww* and commented on the most typical elements of the Sacred District: the pool and sycamore trees. He interpreted these elements as reminiscences of the "holy island of Osiris." And Junker classified the pair of obelisks that appear in some of the New Kingdom scenes as memories of Heliopolis. The three sites of Buto, Sais, and Heliopolis, he believed were pilgrimage destinations for the deceased king during the *Totenfahrts.*[42]

---

[35] Brunner-Traut 1938: 43; 53–59. These correspond to episodes 1.a.–c. respectively in chapter one.

[36] Brunner-Traut 1938: 59.

[37] Junker 1940.

[38] Junker 1940: 1.

[39] Junker 1940: 12.

[40] Junker 1940: 20. Junker distinguished two different crowns worn by the *Mww,* one of which was shaped like papyrus growing out of the wearer's head. He believed this crown was symbolic of Lower Egypt (1940: 1).

[41] An early example of this shrine is found on a tag of king Aha from the first dynasty (CG. 14142) (Baines 2020: fig. 9.3).

[42] Junker 1940: 22.

Furthering his case, Junker viewed the *Mww* as the ancestors of the king and the Souls of Pe. With this suggestion, Junker expanded Brunner-Traut's idea of the *Mww* as demi-gods greeting the dead. He invoked PT §1005 to illustrate that the Souls of Pe dance to greet the dead king, "The Souls of Pe clash (sticks) for you, they smite their flesh for you, they clap their hands for you, they tug their side-locks for you, and they say to Osiris: ...."[43] He considered this ritual to be the moment when the spirits of the deceased kings arrived to meet the funeral cortege. His theory becomes slightly complicated when he attempts to reconstruct the relationship between the north and the south of Egypt; yet the essence of his argument is that the Sacred District rituals derived from the funerals of the predynastic rulers of Buto and that these rituals were usurped by the southern kings when they united Egypt.

What is most important to take away from Junker's work is his assertion that the Butic royal death journeys did become Osirianized and that it is this form of the ritual that is illustrated in the New Kingdom private tombs on the west bank of Thebes, Elkab, and Hierakonpolis.[44] Likewise, Junker perceived these ceremonies as being just that: ceremonies to be performed at the entrance to the tomb in the cemetery. This means that Junker understood the Lower Egyptian shrines within the Sacred District as symbolic elements only that represented locations in the north. Yet, the wrt-canal does not appear in any rendition of the Sacred District.

Inspired by Junker's work on the Mww, Jacques Vandier published a study in 1944, where he set out to investigate the pilgrimage to the Delta sites undertaken by the deceased as part of the funeral.[45] He cites Hermann Kees' work, *Totenglauben und Jenseitsvorstellungen der alten Ägypter*, first published in 1926, pointing out that these pilgrimages were also associated with the cult of Osiris as early as the Old Kingdom.[46] A new edition of Kees' work has been published since that time,[47] and one of the changes made in the new edition is his interpretation of the scenes on Louvre stela C15 as Butic, instead of Osirian.[48] At the very least, this attests to a complex entanglement of funerary traditions visible in the later sources.

Jürgen Settgast has written the most comprehensive study on the Sacred District scene, which in 1963 made a significant contribution to its interpretation.[49] In Settgast's study of burial portrayals he distinguishes two categories of tombs: those belonging to an early group (tombs dating from the Middle Kingdom until the reign of Amenhotep I and slightly beyond) and those belonging to a later group (tombs dating from the reign of Hatshepsut until that of Thutmose IV).[50] His work is presented both chronologically and by scene type. The Sacred District scene begins to appear at the end of his early group and continues into his later group. Although Settgast acknowledges a significant decline in examples of the Sacred District scene post-Thutmose III, this did not noticeably affect his grouping of tombs. He also includes tombs that date to later periods, for example, Theban Tomb 36, from the time of Psammeticus I (*c*.664–610 BCE). In his chapter seven, Settgast groups the micro-scenes into eight subcategories: Hall of the *Mww*; Women's Tent; Garden Pond;[51] Gods of the Great Gate; Gods' Shrines; Three Ponds; Slaughtering; and Four Basins. His chapter nine explores the crossing to the west bank and the rituals performed in the Sacred District.

Settgast acknowledges the close connection between the various buildings, chapels, ponds, and gardens, which have been preserved in numerous examples, that made all these elements part of one large complex. He remarks that this *temenos* is attested at the beginning of the New Kingdom, but not yet in its fullest form, because the district is elaborated under Hatshepsut and Thutmose III.[52] Individual micro-scenes can be traced back to before the New Kingdom: the three ponds appear in the eleventh dynasty; the crowned *Mww* date back to the fifth dynasty; the shrine of Sais first appears in the fifth

[43] Junker 1940: 24. Translation by Faulkner (1998: 169).

[44] Reeder 1995: 73 (following Junker).

[45] Vandier 1944.

[46] Vandier 1944: 36.

[47] Kees 1956.

[48] T. Allen 1958: 148. See Gayet 1889: 12 and pl. LIV; Louvre Museum, "Abkaou stela."

[49] Settgast 1963: 48–74.

[50] This author prefers to see early tombs as those dating to the reigns of Ahmose-Amenhotep with the core group of tombs dating to the reigns of Hatshepsut and Thutmose III. Any tomb decorated post-Thutmose III can be considered to be late. Of course, there are varying degrees of lateness, but as the scene climaxes during the reigns of Hatshepsut-Thutmose III any utilization of the tomb after these reigns is no longer in high style.

[51] Within the title "Garden Pond" Settgast includes the following elements: the pool surrounded by multiple palm trees, the sycamore trees, two obelisks, and parcels of land (Settgast 1963: 51).

[52] That this arrangement of micro-scenes has existed since the beginning of the New Kingdom—starting with Theban Tomb 15, that of Tetiky—from the time of Ahmose, is clear, but not in its complete form.

dynasty; and the gods' shrines date back to the annals of the first dynasty.[53] Settgast acknowledges that these are not the only elements in a Sacred District but that they are some of the main ones.[54]

One of the key areas Settgast attempts to clarify is the function of the Sacred District within the funerary proceedings. Establishing its function is complex because there is no understandable action in this area, except for the dedications at the four basins, and even this scene has been interpreted in a variety of ways. When actors do appear, they are the *Mww*, women inside a booth, and the armless guardians who stand cautious and waiting within their gate. The many gods who appear do not engage in ritual activity either, but instead sit (or, on occasion stand) motionless.

Settgast concedes that the whole district gives the impression of a quiet, peaceful atmosphere, and suggests that this was the artists' intention. Yet, he points out that a description of the entire district cannot be found in conjunction with the New Kingdom illustrations. He thus brings attention to an important piece of evidence in the tomb of Senet (TT 60), a Middle Kingdom tomb, that provides a name for this area. As noted in chapter one, this reference appears as a caption to the dragging of the coffin to the necropolis. Settgast suggests that this description, which names a particular part of the complex, may also refer to the district as a whole, "Lowering (the coffin) at the Hall of the *Mww*, at the entrance of the *tꜣ ḏsr*."[55] His label, "*Heiliger Bezirk*" refers to the whole complex or arrangement of scenes, a term that is based on the ancient Egyptian word *tꜣ ḏsr*. It is undoubtedly correct that the Hall of the *Mww* in TT 60, is the same *Mww* building seen in the New Kingdom versions of the Sacred District.[56] In the caption, this *sḥ n Mww* now appears parallel to *r(w).ti tꜣ ḏsr*, whereby the place where the coffin is set on the ground is more narrowly defined. With this, Settgast rightly asserts that the relationship between these two phrases is even deeper, in that it can be said that the Hall of the *Mww* represents the entrance into the *tꜣ ḏsr*.[57] He employs the illustrations in the early tombs (TT 15, Reneny, TT 81, and TT 21) and the illustrations in the later tombs (TT 342, TT 110, TT 112) to prove his case. He suggests that in TT 53 and TT 123, there was an attempt to emphasize the Hall of the *Mww*. In these tombs, the Hall of the *Mww* is depicted in the middle of the district, but it is symmetrically aligned with the women's tent, which is especially noticeable in these two tombs.[58]

Considering Settgast's initial acknowledgement that the Hall of the *Mww* was the entrance point to the *tꜣ ḏsr*, he concludes that the district should be regarded as only a section of the actual necropolis, a section that was not a burial place.[59] What is not clear to Settgast is if the name *tꜣ ḏsr* is a generic term for the cemetery, or a name for a ritual enclosure in close proximity to the cemetery. He does, however, assume the Sacred District was located on the west bank, that it was a ritual district of the cemetery, that no tombs existed in this area, and that it was located between the embalming place and the tomb. Overall, Settgast makes many significant conclusions that have furthered our understanding of the Sacred District as a whole.

Following Settgast's work, Hartwig Altenmüller made his first attempt to break down the complete "Butic" ritual in a published work from 1972.[60] In 1975 he revised his original work for the *Lexikon der Ägyptologie* and organized the funeral scenes into sixteen sections.[61] That same year Altenmüller also wrote an article, entitled "*Zur Frage der Mww,*" where he further modified the work of Brunner-Traut and Junker, in that he perceived four scenarios in which the *Mww* could occur: in the Hall of the *Mww*, at Sais, by the gates of Buto, and greeting the funeral procession with the *tekenu* and canopic chest.[62] Altenmüller distinguishes the *Mww* by their costumes and rejects the *ḫnw*-dancers as "real *Mww*."[63] He also discards Junker's theory that the *Mww* were the Souls of Pe, as there are no inscriptions that directly equate the two.[64]

Another key idea emphasized by Altenmüller was the symbolic nature of the voyages to the sacred Delta localities during the New Kingdom, and he denies the connection that Junker made between the Delta shrines and those illustrated in the Old Kingdom tombs. Altenmüller takes his examination one step further and suggests that the *Mww* were ferrymen,

[53] Settgast 1963: 48. The shrine on the Scorpion macehead dates back even earlier.

[54] This study establishes that the shrine of Sais is outside of the Sacred District.

[55] N. Davies 1920: pl. 21.

[56] Settgast 1963: 48; N. Davies 1920: pl. 21.

[57] Settgast 1963: 49.

[58] Here Settgast states that the *Mww* hall is symmetrical with the *Mww* tent, but I wonder if he means the Women's Tent, as it is the Women's Tent that stands to the left of the hall of the *Mww* and appears comparably sized (1963: 49).

[59] Settgast 1963: 49.

[60] Altenmüller 1972: 112 ff.

[61] Altenmüller 1975a: 745–765.

[62] Altenmüller 1975b.

[63] Called *ḫbt*-dancers in this study. See Altenmüller 1980.

[64] Altenmüller 1975b: 2.

invoking *Pyramid Text* Utterance 310 as evidence:

> O you whose vision is in his face and whose vision is in the back of his head, bring this to me!
> Which ferry-boat shall be brought to you?
> Bring me 'It-flies-and-alights.'[65]

Altenmüller asserts that the *Mww* as ferrymen cared for the deceased as they travelled along the waterways.[66] Furthermore, he suggests that *Pyramid Text* Utterances 220-222 identify four crown-gods who are spirits who greet the deceased and introduce him to the sun god. *Pyramid Text* Utterance 263, also cited by Altenmüller, reveals that the king is ferried over the sky to Re:

> The reed-floats of the sky are set in place for Re
> That he may cross on them to the horizon.
> The reed-floats of the sky are set in place for Harakhti
> That Harakhti may cross on them to Re.
> The reed-floats of the sky are set in place for me
> That I may cross on them to Harakhti and to Re.[67]

Altenmüller thus identifies the *Mww* of the funerary ritual with the ferrymen of the Heliopolitan mythology. He furthers his argument by incorporating *Pyramid Text* Utterance 520 where the ferrymen are described as having, "dancing tresses which are on the top of [their] heads like lotus-buds in the swamp-gardens."[68] This passage is reminiscent of the *Mww* from the Old Kingdom tomb scenes who are shown with lotus blossoms for their hair and of ships' crews who also wear floral head-decorations.[69] It should be noted, that there are no examples of this type of headdress in the Sacred Districts from the New Kingdom; however, these same headdresses are found on the late eleventh dynasty stela of Abkaou from Abydos (Louvre stela C 15) and in the tomb decoration of Sobeknakht II at Elkab.[70] Therefore, Altenmüller understands the *Mww* and the rows of shrines depicted in the Old Kingdom tombs to be of a solar nature and connected to the theology of Heliopolis. His study represents a decisive divergence away from previous theories about the *Mww* that focused on their supposed connection to Buto.

Jumping forward to 1984, M. F. Moens published an article, entitled "The Ancient Garden in the New Kingdom: A Study of Representations," where he discusses schematic garden illustrations and remarks on New Kingdom images of the Sacred District.[71] Moens restates some conclusions made by Junker and Settgast, such as the Sacred District is part of the funeral procession and is located between the embalming place and the necropolis. This author appears to agree with these earlier scholars as to the identification of this district as a holy area where ritual dramas were performed and to the garden pond and palms as analogous to the curved *wrt*-channel. Moens also reiterates that in the New Kingdom an area as such was no longer in existence, but the images simply paid homage to the earlier tradition—a tradition that ceased to exist in the early fifth dynasty. Moens' own opinion is that the Sacred District represented an ideal necropolis garden.

Moens also utilizes the work of Ingrid Gamer-Wallert and, contrary to Junker and Settgast, remarks that the sycamore trees surrounding the pond are not indicative of a Delta locale and thus complicate the picture.[72] Also following Gamer-Wallert, Moens further contemplates why the ritual boat pilgrimages are not actually illustrated in the Sacred District. This is an intriguing point when considering that in tomb paintings there are many representations of items being drawn across pools; examples are found in TT 80, TT 87, and TT 100.[73] If the garden pond was intended to represent the sacred voyages, it would have been easy for artists to incorporate a barque into the design.

Alix Wilkinson has also contributed to the study of the Sacred District. She produced two articles in 1994, entitled "Landscapes for Funeral Rituals in Dynastic Times" and "Symbolism and Design in Ancient Egyptian Gardens."[74] As the titles suggest, Wilkinson is primarily concerned with the garden elements visible in these scenes, and her former article includes a succinct section on what she calls the "Holy Place of the Butic Burial." Her latter article deals with the religious considerations that might have motivated the choice of certain garden plants and garden arrangements, which is useful for understanding why particular elements might have been chosen for the Sacred District. Wilkinson, heavily influenced by Altenmüller's earlier works, interprets the "Holy Place of the Butic Burial" as representing both the

[65] Faulkner 1998: 97.
[66] Altenmüller 1975b: 20.
[67] Faulkner 1998: 72-73.
[68] Faulkner 1998: 194.
[69] Altenmüller 1975b: 22, 36; Reeder 1995: 75.
[70] Louvre Museum, "Abkaou stela"; Tylor 1896: pl. III.
[71] Moens 1984: 48.
[72] Moens 1984: 48–49.
[73] Moens 1984: 49.
[74] A. Wilkinson 1994a: 391–401; *idem*. 1994b: 1–17.

eastern and western horizons of heaven, as described in the *Pyramid* and *Coffin Texts*.[75] She describes this landscape as one of three different types of funerary landscapes. Noting both the New Kingdom and Saite examples of the Sacred District, Wilkinson concludes that it is a site for rituals on the way from the embalming place to the tomb, and she infers that it is the place where the deceased is identified with the sun god, and by means of symbolic objects participates in his daily regeneration.[76]

Wilkinson provides a brief overview of the different components of a typical Sacred District, and using Altenmüller's work, applies several *Pyramid Texts* and *Coffin Texts* to the rituals. For example, she cites *Pyramid Text* §289, which mentions various Delta localities in conjunction with the excavation of a pool in the Field of Reeds and equates it with an inscription from the tomb of Paheri at Elkab that is associated with the Sacred District.[77] Paheri's inscription reads, "Proceeding in peace to the horizon to the Field of Reeds, to the Duat." Wilkinson suggests this was not a burial place at all, but instead the place where pre-burial rites were performed for the Butic Burial, an idea previously suggested by Settgast and others.[78] As will be demonstrate in the succeeding chapter, the shrines that represent the sacred Delta localities make up a separate scene, and do not appear within the confines of the Sacred District.

In her 1998 book on Egyptian gardens, Wilkinson fine-tunes her previous assessment and describes the Sacred District as an Offering Place. Noting the scene's uniqueness, she remarks, "This scene shows a mythical place, containing religious symbols, trees, and pools."[79] She reiterates the district's association with the eastern and western horizons and states that it is the pool with palms where the sun god purified himself before he journeys across the sky. As in her earlier article, she associates certain features with the east and others with the west and asserts that the context for the scene is the burial ritual, which is taking place in the adjacent scenes.[80] This theory presupposes the availability of a solar afterlife for the deceased private individual, for which there is evidence as early as the First Intermediate Period, but it does not consider the scene's Osirian overtones.[81]

A wholly different approach to the Sacred District emerged in 1994 when Manfred Bietak published an article on a possible archaeological context for the Sacred District at the site of Avaris.[82] To the south of an early thirteenth dynasty palace two strata of gardens were discovered, the older one consisting of squares lined by trees with an unfinished pool in the middle, with another square of trees and a regular pattern of flowerbeds.[83] The layout suggests that it was most probably a vineyard.[84] At a later date, these gardens were used as a cemetery for the functionaries of the palace, where six tombs were discovered with parallel tree-pits at a distance of about nine meters to the east. Bietak proposes that each pit belonged to a tomb and that this arrangement reflects an archaic Egyptian funerary feature.[85] He compares this composition to the sacred localities of Buto and Sais, where he claims the tombs of the predynastic Lower Egyptian kings were most likely located.

The parallel elements that Bietak refers to show a palm tree in front of a structure with a vault-like roof. These structures are of the *ḫm*-type and were regularly employed to represent shrines. Bietak appears to be describing the micro-scene that occurs *adjacent* to the Sacred District in the private New Kingdom tombs (micro-scene 14a), not the Sacred District itself. Furthermore, Bietak's description of the structures begs the question: Are these structures shrines or tombs? My understanding of Beitak's suggestion is that the tomb/palm combination seen in the archaeological record at Avaris is the same as in micro-scene 14a, which appears in funerary scenes in the New Kingdom. Thus, he interprets the latter illustrations as depicting a predynastic burial ground dedicated to the kings of Lower Egypt and located at Buto and Sais.

According to Barry Kemp, designs of gateways were regularly used as symbols of places, and thus it is as such that we should view these facades in the

[75] A. Wilkinson 1994a: 391; Altenmüller 1975a: 745-765; A. Wilkinson 1994a: 391 and 396, note 2; Junker 1940.

[76] An idea suggested by earlier scholars (A. Wilkinson 1994a: 391).

[77] This utterance reads, "...she sets up my two standards in front of the Great Ones, she excavates a pool for me in the Field of Rushes, she confirms my land in the two Fields of Offerings, and I give judgment in the heavens..." (Faulkner 1998: 64).

[78] A. Wilkinson 1994a: 391–392; 396, note 14; Tylor and Griffith 1894: 20, pl. v.

[79] A. Wilkinson 1998: 105.

[80] A. Wilkinson 1998: 105–106.

[81] Smith 2017: 166–270.

[82] Bietak 1994. He also published a short book in 1996, entitled *Avaris: The Capital of the Hyksos. Recent Excavations at Tell el-Dab'a.*

[83] Bietak 1996: 22.

[84] Bietak 1996: 22.

[85] Bietak 1996: figs. 18-19 and pls. 8a-c.

Sacred District (and micro-scene 14a).[86] As concerns early monumental buildings, Kemp asserts that the royal tomb was the principal public statement of kingship at this early period, and that at this time celebrating human leaders took precedence over finding homes for gods.[87] Thus, we might assume that any early monumental architectural remains/illustrations might be attributed to royal tombs. This was certainly true for the early kings buried at Abydos, but did this also apply to Lower Egypt? Large sites like Tell el-Farkha and Tell el-Fara'in (Buto) probably came under the control of the south *c.*3350 BCE, at least culturally. Sometime within the period of dynasty 0 all of Egypt was under the political control of a single kingdom based out of the south.[88] Early in the first dynasty a large, well laid-out structure with a complex internal plan was constructed of mud bricks at Buto and Kemp is tempted to call it a palace. He states that this is "the most obvious connection between a Lower Egyptian place and later myths of kingship."[89] Yet, Bietak is not discussing evidence for a palace. Mudbrick became the normal material used for building by the Early Dynastic period and it was used for all sorts of structures, but not for temples.[90] A parallel architectural tradition consisted of buildings with wooden frames covered with wooden panels, woven matting, or bound reeds. The façades of the buildings depicted in the Sacred District appear as though they are products of the latter tradition. The crisscross pattern that appears to cover a number of these shrines is most likely a pattern in matting or binding. So, at this early date, most shrines were collapsible, temporary, and portable structures. Kemp points out that once brick architecture did emerge tent shrines were probably not as common as one might think, despite their ubiquity in illustrations. Buildings based around wooden posts have been found at many predynastic sites, especially in the Delta.[91] Two examples from the Old Kingdom persist: the cabins on the funerary boat of Khufu and the cube-shaped tent of Queen Hetepheres.[92] Likewise, an illustration of one is preserved on an ivory tablet from the tomb of King Den at Abydos.[93] Hence, during the latter part of the Predynastic period this type of structure gave way to architecture of brick, but some survived as temporary buildings, as protection for portable images, and as Kemp states, "in the imagination as the ideal type of building set in an imaginary primaeval world in which the gods dwelt."[94] Therefore, the history of temple architecture confirms that these structures are indeed shrines, which is corroborated by the fact that gods sit inside many of the *ḥm*-chapels that appear in rows in the Sacred District. These are not tombs. Despite this, Bietak concludes that within the palace necropolis at Avaris, the Butic tomb tradition persisted. However, he notes that the proximity of the tombs to the palace is an Asiatic tradition.[95]

In 1995, Greg Reeder published an illuminating article, also on the *Mww*, where he outlines past research on the subject, debunks old assumptions, and speculates further about their function.[96] Previous scholars have noted that the *Mww* must hurry and meet the deceased to allow entry into the necropolis, but Reeder uses the tomb scenes of Senet (TT 60) (published as the tomb of Antefoker) and Tetiky (TT 15) to expound more fully on the details of this encounter. He describes the lead priest of the funeral cortege as stopping and offering a gesture of invocation to the *Mww*, and the priest calling out, "Come O *Mww*."[97] What Reeder rightly acknowledges is that the *Mww* are not "hurrying" to intercept the procession, but instead are greeting the cortege as they cross over from the Other World and appear before the priests.[98] This is why the *Mww* appear as though they are stepping into the "necropolis."

Reeder utilizes Richard Wilkinson's work in *Symbol and Magic in Egyptian Art* to connect the *Mww*'s hand gestures with those used by ferrymen in some Old Kingdom tomb scenes.[99] Accordingly, the two-fingered hand gesture is one of protection, which helps the deceased pass safely along the waterways of "Paradise."[100] Reeder refers to the Sacred District as "Paradise," and when discussing the Hall in which the *Mww* appear, he describes it as their house, situating it at the edge of "Paradise, the gardens of peace."[101] Reeder's synopsis of the Sacred District is appealing, as he recognizes the divine aspect of the area through the appearance of the gods' shrines and the presence of

[86] Kemp 2018: 78.
[87] Kemp 2018: 97, 104.
[88] Kemp 2018: 83.
[89] Kemp 2018: 83–85, fig. 2.13.
[90] Kemp 2018: 146.
[91] Kemp 2018: 146, 149.
[92] Kemp 2018: 146.
[93] Petrie 1901: 25, pl. VII.8.
[94] Kemp 2018: 149–151.
[95] Bietak 1996: 25.
[96] Reeder 1995.
[97] Reeder 1995: 76; Gardiner's sign list A 26 (1957: 445).
[98] Reeder 1995: 76.
[99] R. Wilkinson 1994: 195. Reeder does not mention that PT Utterance 519 recounts the four spirits giving two fingers to the deceased as an act of protection.
[100] R. Wilkinson 1994: 195.
[101] Reeder 1995: 77.

Osiris. He succinctly notes that the most recognizable geographical locations within the broader collection of scenes are Buto, Sais, and Heliopolis, but in this author's opinion he fails to see the importance of Abydos and the Osirianized landscape, despite the fact that he acknowledges, "Osiris is king." Reeder specifies that this "Paradise" was modeled on the environs of the Nile Delta, a theory that contradicts a statement made earlier by Moens that the sycamore trees are particularly Theban.[102]

Reeder makes the point that the Sacred District can be interpreted in two ways: what is imagined taking place in the hereafter and what is actually taking place during the funeral in the cemetery. In following Junker's assertion that the *Mww* are the Souls of Pe, Reeder suggests that the people of Pe and Dep (Buto) played a leading role in the funerary rituals (real or symbolic), perhaps lining the waterways as the procession passes, or possibly only representing the people of Pe at the tomb. He categorizes the *ḫnw*-dancers as the people of Pe as well, and remarks that they do the dance of the *Mww* but are not actually *Mww* themselves. Following the work of Altenmüller, Reeder suggests they do a ferryman's dance.[103] What remains obscure is, how much of the original rites were retained, how much influence the Upper Egyptian culture had on the rituals, and what was brand new.[104] Finally, he postulates that the characters in this drama were patterned on the common folk of the Nile Delta, men who lived and worked within the confines of the Delta canal system, and that the wickerwork of the Delta skiffs was the origin for the conical headdress.[105]

In 2001, Jan Assmann published *Death and Salvation in Ancient Egypt*, which was subsequently translated into English in 2005. Assmann describes the Sacred District scene as a "cult drama in the sacred *temenos* and rituals in the garden."[106] In the sequence of events of a typical elite funeral, Assmann places the Sacred District scene after the embalming but before the actual procession to the tomb, as scholars have done before him.[107] Assmann considers the sacred *temenos* to symbolize various places in Lower Egypt, and he reasons that by the New Kingdom the journeys depicted were purely symbolic, meaning that the deceased did not actually visit those locales during their funeral procession. Assmann further suggests that it might have been possible in remote prehistory that such journeys were undertaken to the sacred Delta localities during the funerals of the Lower Egyptian chieftains or kings, yet he describes the scenes in the private tombs of the early eighteenth dynasty as only representations of an archaic cult drama.

Assmann created a level system whereby he evaluates a scene's content in terms of its relationship to reality. Level One includes "old scenes" stored in the cultural memory, which refer to an antiquated cult drama from early in the historical period. Level Two consists of "new scenes" that represent the funeral ritual as it was actually performed. And Level Three includes representations of the afterlife that do not refer to rituals performed at the funeral, but to events in the world of the gods.[108] He categorizes the Sacred District scene as Level One. Yet, Assmann differs from previous scholars in that he thinks the journey to Abydos *was* actually carried out during the funeral ceremony, unlike those to the Delta.[109]

Like previous scholars, Assmann also describes the Delta shrines as being inside the Sacred District. Rows of *ḥm*-chapels do appear inside the Sacred District, but they cannot be equated with the sacred Delta localities with any certainty. There is, however, a separate scene among the funerary illustrations that explicitly depicts shrine façades from the sacred Delta localities, namely Buto and Sais. It is this scene that symbolizes the pilgrimage to the Delta sites and is located after the embalming workshop and before the tomb itself. An amalgamation of these two scenes has persisted for decades in the scholarly literature, yet the independence of these two episodes is evident in Rekhmire's tomb (TT 100), Paheri's tomb (TC 3), and Amenemhet's tomb (TT 82). Consequently, the question arises: How does the journey to Lower Egypt relate to the Sacred District? In the tomb of Rekhmire, the Sacred District is located at the very top of the funerary scenes, while the sacred Delta localities are found in the third register from the bottom. In the tomb of Paheri, the Delta shrines appear two registers above the Sacred District scene, and in Theban Tomb 82 they appear one register above. In other compositions the sacred Delta localities are left out entirely.[110] Because

[102] Moens 1984: 48–49.
[103] Reeder 1995: 77.
[104] Reeder 1995: 73.
[105] Reeder 1995: 80–83.
[106] Assmann 2005: 305.
[107] Assmann follows Settgast and cites inscriptions from Theban Tombs 82 and 100 (Amenemhet and Rekhmire, respectively). Assmann 2005: 305 follows Settgast 1963: 101–102; see also Settgast 1963: 49; Moens 1984: 48; A. Wilkinson 1994a: 391.
[108] Assmann 2005: 300.
[109] Assmann 2005: 305.
[110] Examples include TT 15, TT 81, TT 21, and the tomb of Reneny at Elkab.

there is no significant action displayed in the Sacred District scene, it is not obvious that any pilgrimage by boat is undertaken. There is no boat and there is no waterway. As a result, Assmann's suggestion—that the cultic drama performed in the sacred *temenos* was above all a symbolic journey by boat to various places in Lower Egypt—is speculation and is based on the statements of several earlier scholars, going back to Junker, who, it would appear, conflated the two scenes.

In 2003 Karl-J. Seyfried published an article on reminiscences of the Butic Burial in the Theban necropolis during the New Kingdom in an attempt to elucidate the purpose of the double-burial evidenced there. Inside some tombs Seyfried has identified a space he calls the "Butic place of the dead," and he suggests that this is the point of contact with home for the ancestors in the afterlife (relatives of the deceased), that is physically located in the tomb beyond the vertical shaft.[111] For Seyfried, this space is a home beyond life and a place where all those who are deceased can go. Likewise, it is an area used by the deceased to enter and exit the hereafter. Seyfried integrates the Sacred District scene into his analysis of these private tombs by commenting on the form and function of the *Mww*, who he sees as performing in this world on behalf of the ancestors and greeting the deceased at the entrance to the tomb. The ancestors themselves are those shown standing in the Hall of the *Mww* in scenes of the Sacred District. Seyfried's theory supports my premise that the Sacred District is other-worldly, but he does not go so far as to suggest the superimposition of the divine realm onto an actual physical landscape.[112]

Seyfried recognizes several sequences of micro-scene as burial rites of an ancient Lower Egyptian character, and he separates them into seventeen micro-scenes and four general categories.[113] Following Assmann, he claims that these micro-scenes remain relevant in the decoration of private New Kingdom tombs until the Amarna Period, at which time tomb art develops to reflect the changing ideology of sacred space.[114] The episodes that Seyfried classifies as Butic are the following: The journey to Sais, the procession to Buto, the reception by the *Mww*, and the journey by shrine-boat to Heliopolis.[115] Noting that the Sais/Buto/Heliopolis cycle is both ancient and associated with Lower Egypt, Seyfried remarks that these localities are represented in the tomb decoration in the forms of kiosks, shrines, and obelisks, and suggests that these architectural features may have actually stood at these particular sites in antiquity.[116] Because he also conflates the scene of the sacred Delta localities with the Sacred District scene, he connects the Sacred District with the north of Egypt. Seyfried also considers the pool as integral to the ritual voyage and interprets its appearance as reminiscent of the *wrt*-canal, paralleling Assmann's opinion (and others). Similarly, he views the *Mww* as ferrymen as reiterations of this connection. Water features prominently in the scenes of the Sacred District, but not in the form of a river—at least not in the New Kingdom. Hence, Seyfried's position resembles past scholarship on many points, but it also incorporates more recent studies.

Another crucial point that Seyfried makes is that the ceilings in some of the private New Kingdom tombs at Thebes are reminiscent of these symbolic shrines of the sacred Delta localities. He suggests that these different ceilings in the tombs are attempts to equate them with the archaic shrines and that they should be interpreted as relics, like the illustrations of the shrines in the pictorial art. Seyfried is careful to mention that he does not necessarily believe that the illustrations or the ceiling architecture can confirm that an actual ritual practice took place in this form.[117] This opinion conforms to that of earlier scholars in that ritual voyages to Lower Egypt probably did not take place as part of the funeral proceedings in the New Kingdom.

Among the most recent publications on the Sacred District is Christoffer Theis' work on ancient Egyptian burial rituals, which includes a short section on the Sacred District.[118] Most of what he includes has already been published elsewhere, but not necessarily in one place. He includes several points worth considering. Theis points out that there have not been any archaeological discoveries that could be considered identical to the area depicted in the Sacred District, and no *pr-nw* chapel has ever been found. Theis also brings attention to the tomb of Ipwia at Saqqara and suggests that it might also

[111] Seyfried 2003: 62.

[112] See also Assmann 2005: 306.

[113] Seyfried 2003: 64.

[114] Seyfried follows Assmann 2003.

[115] Seyfried 2003: 64.

[116] It is worth noting that according to Ulrich Hartung, the on-going excavations at Buto and Sais have revealed large settlement mounds with early occupation. Unfortunately, both sites' prehistoric layers are below the current water-table and are covered by numerous meters of late dynastic and Ptolemaic/Roman remains (2017: 63).

[117] Seyfried 2003: 64–65.

[118] Theis 2011: 139–149.

depict a Sacred District. In my opinion, there are too many discrepancies between this illustration and the numerous examples of it farther south, such as the enclosure wall, the ducks and fish, and the graves and ships. Thus far, the Sacred District is known only from Upper Egypt. Another point Theis supports is that the Sacred District is not the necropolis, or the tomb itself, but a type of station on the way from the embalming tent to the tomb. He interprets the district as a kind of gateway to the necropolis, and thus to the tomb, and thinks it constituted another rite of passage.[119]

Most recently John Baines has provided some useful insights on the Sacred District scene in two studies: *High Culture and Experience in Ancient Egypt* and "Watery Egyptian Landscapes and Performances Within Them."[120] Baines' work offers new ideas for interpreting pictorial representations of settings, and he carefully articulates how locations are repeatedly vague, generalized, or abstract. He also states that specific details are rarely given away through location unless there is an inscription or caption. Although Baines' article focuses on the first millennium BCE, his work is particularly relevant to studying the Sacred District because he focuses his attention on northern Egyptian landscapes and the site of Buto. He discusses how such environments were integral to architectural forms and ritual settings. Baines' ideas about the importance of water and the river can be applied to the ubiquity of pools and basins seen in tomb art.[121] Baines also makes clear that scenes like the Sacred District possess topographical content to convey a sense of setting, but of no place in particular. It was the associations that were important, not the simple idea of a place.[122]

Baines specifically looks at the Sacred District compositions in the tombs of Tetiky (TT 15) and Ineni (TT 81) where he finds that the employment of mixed conventions derives from models in ritual books.[123] He also correctly notes that several micro-scenes in the Sacred District are representations in plan or map mode.[124] With its "catalogue-like presentation," Baines describes this place as lacking emotional charge and as semi-abstract, but he connects it with cultivated land and an ideal environment. Lastly, Baines sees the use of temporary structures as symbolizing renewal and transition, which I, too, believe is the primary function of this illustration.[125]

Scholarship has offered many theories identifying and interpreting the *Mww*, the most recognizable characters from the Sacred District scene, and therefore the Sacred District has often been interpreted in light of those theories. Yet, the *Mww* are only one micro-scene within a much larger composition that in its entirety represents a liminal space linking this world to the next. This work explores each of the micro-scenes individually and it considers the Sacred District as a whole. The great research of previous scholars has provided a strong foundation on which to move forward.

[119] Theis 2011: 143.
[120] Baines 2013: 73–83; *idem*. 2020: 177–197.
[121] Baines 2013: 75.
[122] Baines 2013: 76.
[123] Baines 2013: 78, citing Hofmann 2011: 42–55.
[124] Baines 2013: 79.
[125] Baines 2013: 81.

CHAPTER THREE: FUNERARY RITUAL AND ACCESS TO THE AFTERLIFE

The Sacred District cannot be studied in isolation. There are four areas of study that together help to better contextualize the Sacred District scene: the traditional proceedings of a private funeral, the ritual voyages made by both royal and private individuals to various sacred cities, the mysticism surrounding the deceased's passing from this life into the afterlife, and the interaction of the deceased with Re and Osiris. Each of these areas has been studied by scholars, but there are points of controversy and questions that still remain. This next section discusses the Sacred District scene in relation to these four broad topics.

The Private Funeral

Much of what is known about the private funeral in ancient Egypt comes from the study of the scenes that are preserved in elite private tombs. However, the selection of scenes is not the same in all Egyptian tombs. In fact, no tomb contains all the episodes of a complete funeral.[126] Nevertheless, an entire funeral can be reconstructed through the preserved scenes from various tombs.

Funeral scenes begin to appear in tombs in the fourth dynasty during the reign of Khafre, first at Giza and then at the other Memphite sites of Saqqara and Abusir. In the provinces they begin during the fifth and sixth dynasties.[127] The earliest large-scale funeral scene is in Room Two of the rock-cut chapel of Debehni at Giza.[128] The most fully developed Old Kingdom scenes are in the late sixth dynasty chapel of Pepiankh: Heny the Black, at Meir.[129] Andrey Bolshakov has studied the scene content in some of the Old Kingdom tombs and notes that only the last stages of the funeral are shown in the earliest tombs.[130] These rites include the transferring of the body toward the tomb, the mastaba itself, and the rites performed on the roof. All these rituals took place on the last day of the funeral after the body had been embalmed. However, the situation changes in the sixth dynasty when transfer scenes and ritual scenes at the mastaba no longer appear. Now the earlier events of the procession are illustrated instead, and funeral scenes in general are more abundant.[131] The funeral procession begins at the home of the deceased where the ritual of mourning takes place. Then the corpse is taken to the water for transport. At this point the coffin is ferried in a boat, which is either towed by a barge or dragged by men on the shore. As noted above, this voyage is thought by some to be of a purely ritualistic nature[132] because there was not always a need to cross the river since both the home of the deceased and the cemetery were located in the Memphite region or on the west bank at Meir, for example.[133] Perhaps it was not necessarily the crossing of the river that was illustrated in this nautical scene, but possibly the traveling up or down stream. This alternative makes more sense when considering that men and women drag the boat.

A reconstruction of a funeral based on Old Kingdom tomb scenes might look like the following. The first stop in the procession was the *ibw*, the purification tent, followed by the *wꜥbt*, the embalming workshop, where the body was left for possibly seventy days.[134] When the corpse was retrieved on the day of burial, it was taken to the tomb.[135] Then, men on the shore can be seen dragging the boat for the ritual ferrying to Sais.[136] After this, the statue within the naos (or the coffin) was dragged to the tomb by a team of oxen to prepare it for burial. When the procession had reached the tomb, there were customary rituals that took place on the roof of the mastaba or in the courtyard in front of the tomb.[137] Over the course of several hundred years new ideas and customs would certainly have affected the course of events of a funeral, not to mention that at all times there would have been geographical variants in ritual performance and topographical differences to take into considerations. There is less information

[126] Kantor 1957: 46. The one exception to this might be the funeral scenes in the New Kingdom tomb of Rekhmire (TT 100) at Thebes.

[127] Harpur 1987: 254.

[128] Hassan 1943: 176.

[129] Harpur 1987: 113.

[130] Bolshakov 1991: 43.

[131] See both Harpur (1987) and Bolshakov (1991) for general descriptions and patterns in Old Kingdom funerary scenes.

[132] Contrast Taylor 2001: 187 with Assmann 2005: 305.

[133] Bolshakov 1991: 38.

[134] See Dawson (1927) and Smith and Dawson (2002) for more information on mummification. The seventy days in the embalming workshop is first encountered in the New Kingdom.

[135] Most scholars believe the *wꜥbt* was a collapsible structure located near the tomb.

[136] As for it being a symbolic journey, the same applies to the Sais pilgrimage as to the Abydos pilgrimage.

[137] Settgast 1963; Harpur 1987; Bolshakov 1991.

Figure 2: Scene showing ritual voyage to Abydos from the tomb of Amenemhet (TT 53). Photo by author.

preserved for the funeral procession in the Middle Kingdom, with the site of Beni Hasan being one of the best sources. There is an abundance of unspoiled tomb decoration for the New Kingdom, specifically in the Valley of the Nobles on the west bank of Thebes, at Elkab, and at Memphis. A New Kingdom private, elite funeral appears to have followed in much the same fashion as an Old Kingdom funeral, but with some minor developments.[138]

Funeral scenes were a staple for the decorative programs of private New Kingdom tombs at Thebes and Elkab. Until the reign of Amenhotep III, the funeral scenes appear regularly on the left wall of the passage. For the remainder of the eighteenth dynasty, these scenes appear on the left wall of the first hall. In nineteenth and twentieth dynasty tombs, the funeral scenes appear on both sides of the walls in the first hall; however, there are very few Ramesside tombs included in this study.[139] During the New Kingdom, episodes of the funeral that take place at the home or during the purification and mummification processes were rarely, if ever, represented.[140] One of the standard episodes displayed in New Kingdom tombs is the pilgrimage voyage to the site of Abydos (Figure 2).[141] The cult of Osiris was paramount during the early New Kingdom and Abydos had surpassed the older sacred Delta localities (Buto, Sais, and Heliopolis) as the destination for the funerary voyage. However, the latter sites were sometimes still illustrated in the tombs, where they appear separate from the Sacred District. The scene of the voyage to Abydos is also a distinct scene that appears among the funeral scenes but is usually adjacent to the Sacred District scene.[142] The funeral procession itself is one of the most significant parts of the decorative programs for private tombs during the New Kingdom, and it is within this context that the Sacred District appears. The funeral procession included the crossing of the river, the walk to the cemetery, and the arrival at the tomb entrance. It usually involved the dragging of the coffin on a sledge by both men and oxen. The general scene arrangement of the procession comprises the priests, the burial goods, the *tekenu* (when present), followed by the coffin and mourners. The burial rites follow, but the interment is never included. When it appears, the Sacred District scene was placed at the end of the procession and occupies the space the deceased must transverse before arriving in the hereafter with Osiris. Marking the end of the Sacred District, Osiris sits

[138] Seyfried suggests that there was much continuity between the Old Kingdom private funeral and the New Kingdom private funeral, at least until the reign of Amenhotep II-Thutmose IV (2003: 63).
[139] Assmann 2005: 299–310.
[140] Muhammed 1966: 161.
[141] For example, TC 1 at Elkab, TT 17, TT 39, TT 69, and TT 82.
[142] For example, TT 39 and TT 17.

on his throne, or stands inside his shrine and faces toward the entrance of the tomb ready to receive the deceased.

The most elaborate example of a funeral from a New Kingdom private tomb is in Theban Tomb 100, which belongs to the vizier Rekhmire.[143] It contains more funerary scenes than any other tomb and some of the episodes have no parallel elsewhere. Since there is a Sacred District in this tomb, it has been a major source for research on the *Mww*. This tomb, however, is only representative of the period in which it was constructed, which is around the time of Thutmose III and Amenhotep II. During the eighteenth dynasty it was common for funerary scenes to be organized into three or more registers and to have larger illustrations of funerary deities, such as Osiris, Anubis, and the Goddess of the West, poised at the western end of each register.

Theban Tomb 100 seems to have been decorated right when changes begin to appear in the way a funeral is depicted on the tomb walls. During the latter part of the eighteenth dynasty, from Amenhotep II onward, less attention is given to the funeral procession in the tomb decoration. It is also at this time that the display of the Sacred District decreases dramatically. The tomb of Nebamun (TT 17) is one example that dates to this period and still retains many elements of the earlier decorative program, including an abbreviated Sacred District.[144] Other traditional elements that are still preserved include the *tekenu*, the procession of burial goods, and the mourning women. By the Ramesside Period, the procession has been truncated further and more attention is given to a series of booths that were erected along the processional route and at the tomb.[145] Following Altenmüller, Seyfried postulates that these bower scenes replace the scenes that depict the journey to Sais, Buto, and Heliopolis and the reception by the *Mww*. He claims that these bower scenes were used instead of the Sacred District scene in the nineteenth and twentieth dynasties.[146] This is an area that needs further study and is outside the limits of this work.

The Sacred District is always displayed in association with the funeral procession. Although comprehensive funeral scenes have been discovered from the fourth dynasty onward, the Sacred District appears only at the very end of the seventeenth dynasty. Possible precursors to the Sacred District can be detected as early as the Old Kingdom in the form of the *Mww*. The funeral provides the context for the Sacred District, at least on an artistic level. The illustrations in the tomb of Rekhmire provide the most complex example of a New Kingdom funeral and Sacred District. However, by this time the micro-scenes have been placed on several registers and no longer appear as an inclusive unit as they do in their earliest rendition (for example, Reneny's scene at Elkab, TC 7).

Voyages to the Sacred Localities

When Egyptologists discuss ritual voyages, they refer to specific boat scenes depicted in tomb art where the deceased is ferried to religiously significant sites to participate in festivals that honor the gods, either while the deceased individual was still alive or during the proceedings of their funeral. These scenes are regularly placed among the funeral scenes in tomb decoration. Since the Sacred District scene is presumed to have Butic overtones and scholars have consistently suspected that it alludes to very early funerary rituals, the site of Buto in the western Delta is inevitably part of this discussion. Ancient Buto, or modern Tell el-Fara'in, was originally made up of two cities: Pe and Dep. At some point in its early history Pe and Dep merged into one city and was named after the cobra goddess Wadjet, who was the patron deity of Lower Egypt and protectress of the king. Archaeologists believe that Buto had been a thriving religious center and that its culture was eventually absorbed by an Upper Egyptian culture when Egypt was unified, beginning *c.*3350 BCE.[147] In later centuries Buto was considered to be the home of the "souls" of Pe (royal ancestral spirits). To employ the word "Butic Burial" when describing something, means that its quality is characteristic of this site and its early culture.

Throughout the dynastic period Buto and Sais are represented by stylized depictions of their religious structures. In essence, these depictions served as symbols of these sacred precincts in the context of ritual journeys illustrated in tomb decoration. Buto was identified by a row (or rows) of alternating vaulted shrines and palm trees, and Sais by a rectangular shrine (or *temenos*), flanked by flagstaffs with triangular pennants. However, the shrine from Sais changed shape over time. In its earliest representations it is depicted as a sanctuary with a flat roof and two divine standards in front. Karl-J Seyfried suggests that

[143] N. Davies 1973. Davies divides the episodes that appear within the eleven sub-registers into sixty-eight scenes.

[144] Säve-Söderbergh 1957: 22–32, pl. XXV.

[145] Muhammed 1966: 165; Seyfried 2003: 64–65.

[146] Seyfried 2003: 63. Following Altenmüller (1972).

[147] Kemp 2018: 83–84.

this architectural design was misinterpreted by later artists who linked the two pennant-like standards and produced a gabled-roof instead.[148] It is understood that since predynastic times, ceremonial visits to major religious sites in the Delta have been part of the funerary customs of rulers.

Beginning with the ancient city of Buto, sacred journeys involved travel from Buto to Sais and Heliopolis (Lower Egyptian ritual sites). Other important cult centers were also sometimes included in the funerary voyages, for example the cities of Mendes and Hutweru. The earliest depictions of sacred localities date to the Early Dynastic Period. There is a wood tag from the reign of Aha that was found in his tomb complex at Abydos and it shows Aha's visit to the shrine at Sais, which most likely originated from the area of Memphis.[149] The tag is only a couple of centimeters high and was probably attached to his burial goods. Another ivory tag, probably from Naqada, shows Aha visiting a different shrine, one that cannot be identified.[150] On a plaque from Abydos and dating to the reign of King Djer, there is an illustration of the ancient city of Buto,[151] which can be identified as such because of its similarity to a later scene from Memphis that is accompanied by the label "*ḏbʿw.t*," an early version of that city's name.[152] In the upper right corner of two of these plaques there are two registers of shrines, each coupled with a palm tree and separated vertically by a water canal (Figure 3). There are no accompanying captions in these early examples.

From the Old Kingdom, the third dynasty panels of King Djoser from beneath the Step Pyramid complex at Saqqara also invoke imaginings of the sacred Delta localities (Figure 4). There are six limestone relief panels in the substructure of the funerary complex that show the king running between territorial markers and performing other ritual functions. The northern panel shows Djoser standing with one foot forward and carrying a staff in one hand and a mace in the other.[153] He wears the White Crown of Upper Egypt and the serekh of the king is situated in front of him. Further in front, there are two standards, one topped with a Chons emblem/king's placenta/

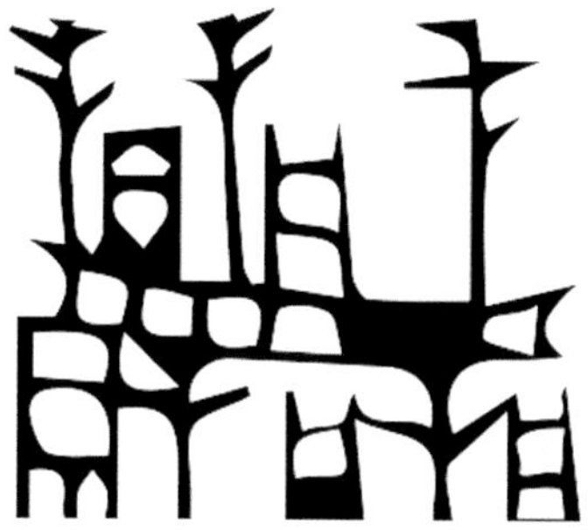

Figure 3: An ivory plaque from Abydos that dates to the reign of King Djer. Adaptation by Roman Reed.

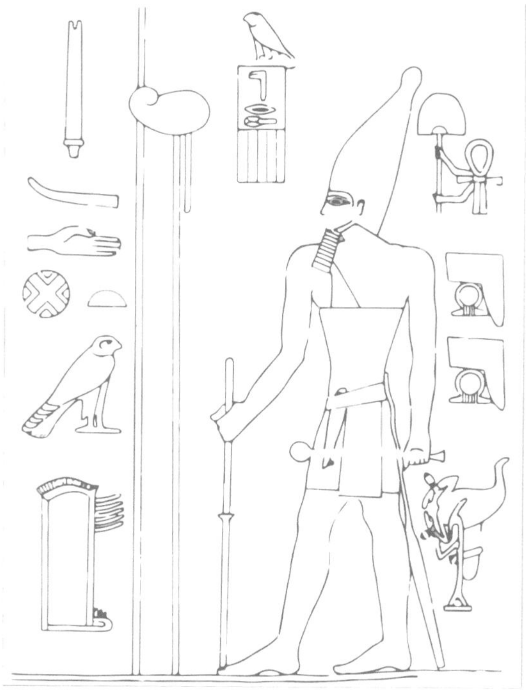

Figure 4: "The preserved part of the northern panel under Djoser's step pyramid at Saqqara. Adaptation by Roman Reed after F. Friedman 1995: figure 12.

throne cushion and one topped with a jackal (Sed, later known as Wepwawet, the Opener of Ways)—a standard that has typically accompanied the king since the first dynasty.[154] Djoser's panel reads, "Standing in the Upper Egyptian shrine of *ḥr Bḥdt.*"[155] This is relevant, because, in the later version of this scene from Apries' palace, one finds the designation for Buto: *ḏb`w,t*. The other significant difference between these two scenes is that the original rendition belonging to Djoser does not include the two rows

[148] Seyfried 2003: note 45. See also Junker 1940: Abb. 6.
[149] Baines 2020: 181. University of Pennsylvania, Archaeology and Anthropology Museum E9396. T. Wilkinson 1999: 318–320.
[150] Baines 2020: 182. Cairo, Egyptian Museum CG 14142.
[151] Bietak 1994: 10 ff; Scharff 1929: *Abb*. 92; T. Wilkinson 1999: 319–320.
[152] Junker 1940: 17.
[153] F. Friedman 1995: fig. 10a.
[154] See F. Friedman 1995: 4, for various interpretations.
[155] F. Friedman 1995: 18.

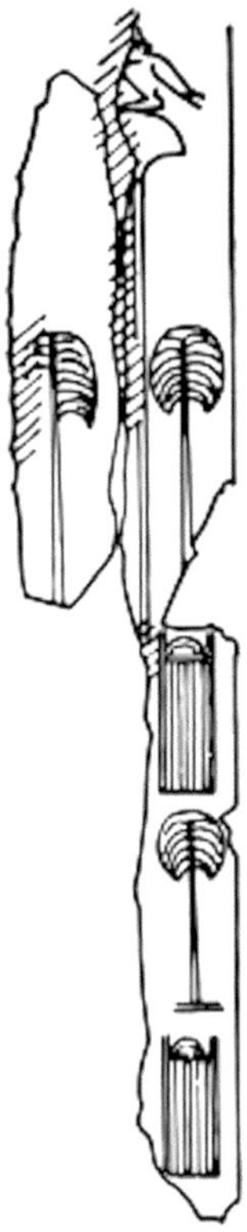

Figure 5: Scene from Snefru's valley temple. Adaptation by Roman Reed after Settgast 1963: *Abb*. 8.

of shrines and palms separated by a waterway. For Djoser, these representations immortalize his Sed-Festival, which he celebrated while he was alive.[156] Other Old Kingdom prototypes of the Sacred District come from Snefru's fourth dynasty valley temple at Dahshur and Niuserre's fifth dynasty valley temple at Abusir (Figure 5).[157]

Vestiges of these pilgrimages also appear in several private tombs from the Old Kingdom, such as the tomb of Nebkauhor at Saqqara, where several men stand with their fists together on their chest before a lector priest. These men are clearly identified as the *Mww*, both by the headdresses they wear and by the caption above them. Behind the lector priest are the remains of three *ḥm*-chapels with vaulted roofs.[158] In the register below, the barge carrying the coffin is pulled toward two lector priests, who are accompanied by two men, each holding a staff and a scepter. These men stand in front of the Saite shrine—other than the caption labeling the shrine as "Sais" there are no other captions. The fifth dynasty tombs of Ptahhotep I (mastaba D62) and II (mastaba D64) at North Saqqara also depict these sacred journeys (Figure 6).[159] In the latter tomb, the lector priest, two *Mww,* and two other men stand in front of the Saite shrine while greeting

Figure 6:Scene from the fifth dynasty tomb of Ptahhotep II at Saqqara (mastaba D64). Adaptation by Roman Reed.

the arrival of the funerary cortege.[160] In the early sixth dynasty tomb of Seshseshet Idwt at Saqqara the various decorative fragments depict the funeral cortege meeting the lector priest, again accompanied by a man carrying a staff and a scepter. In the register above, there are at least six *pr-nw* shrines in a row, each one coupled with a stylized palm tree.[161]

Evidence for pilgrimages to the Delta continue into the Middle Kingdom, but it is images of the *Mww* that most clearly connect these tomb scenes with those of the Old Kingdom, as opposed to the Delta shrines. There are examples of the *Mww* appearing in the tomb of Senet (TT 60),[162] on Louvre stela C 15, in

[156] F. Friedman 1995: 8.

[157] Fakhry 1961: 60, fig. 35; Borchardt 1907: *Abb*. 17.

[158] See Junker 1940: *Abb*. I for a line drawing of the scene.

[159] See Junker 1940: 4, *Abb*. 5 and *Abb*. 3, respectively.

[160] Junker 1940: 5, *Abb*. 3; Reeder 1995: 72.

[161] Macramallah 1935: pl. VIII; Junker 1940: 6–7, *Abb*. 4. The name of these shrines is questionable. See Appendix Two for more information.

[162] In a twelfth dynasty variant of the traditional dragging scene, the tomb of Senet shows six people, three men and three women, who walk in her funeral procession with their arms in a pose resembling Gardiner's A 28 sign (1957: 445). These people precede the dragging of the bier on the sledge after the ceremonial rites on the water (Davies, Davies, and Gardiner 1920: pl. XIX). N. Davies suggests that the front group of six provides for a change of teams (1920: 20). Evidently the cortege is sailing downstream to Abydos. Davies asserts that there is no sequence of acts depicted in these scenes (1920: 21). Likewise, he states that the group shouts, "The god comes. Prostrate (yourselves)," but this phrase does not appear in the figure. The six individuals walking in the A 28 pose represent the populations of five centers of worship: Sais, Dep, Pe, Unu (for Hermopolis Parva, see Hannig 1997: 1325), and Hutweru. Gardiner translates the first group of signs as "Siut," but perhaps it should be "Sais" (see Faulkner 1991: 209) and Hutweru is still unidentified (Hodel-Hoenes 2000: 54). The latter designation may refer to a town in the Western Delta, according to Griffiths, who notes that in PT 189a, in a series of cultic allusions, it appears after Dep. Similar designations

Figure 7: Scene of the funeral procession with the *Mww* from the sixteenth dynasty tomb of Sobeknakht II at Elkab. From Tylor 1896: plate III.

a scene from the twelfth dynasty tomb of Sehetepibre at Thebes, and in the sixteenth dynasty tomb of Sobeknakht II at Elkab (TC 10) (Figure 7).[163]

As noted above, reminiscent of the Old Kingdom examples is a Saite illustration from the palace of Apries at Memphis, where two rows of *pr-nw* shrines are interposed with palms (Figure 8). Between the two registers there is a winding water way just as in the first dynasty plaques found at Abydos.[164] In the upper right corner of the depiction the caption reads "*ḏb3w.t*." According to Donald Redford, the presence of a traditional motif on the gateway of the palace of Apries at Memphis was possibly due to the influence of Amasis and the revival of the mortuary cults of the third dynasty kings.[165] This particular example is reminiscent of the third dynasty panels of King Djoser, mentioned above, and like its prototype, the king here too stands with one foot forward and carrying a staff in one hand with a mace in the other. While Djoser wears the White Crown of Upper Egypt, Apries wears the Red Crown of Lower Egypt. In both depictions, a bird soars above the king carrying a symbol in its talons. Above Djoser, flies a falcon carrying a *shen*-sign, and above Apries flies a vulture carrying an *ankh* sign. In each case the *serekh* of the king is situated in front of his face. In the case of Apries, one finds the designation for Buto, *Ḏb3w.t*, adjacent.[166] When Apries' gateway was first encountered, the excavator thought it was from the twelfth dynasty because of its

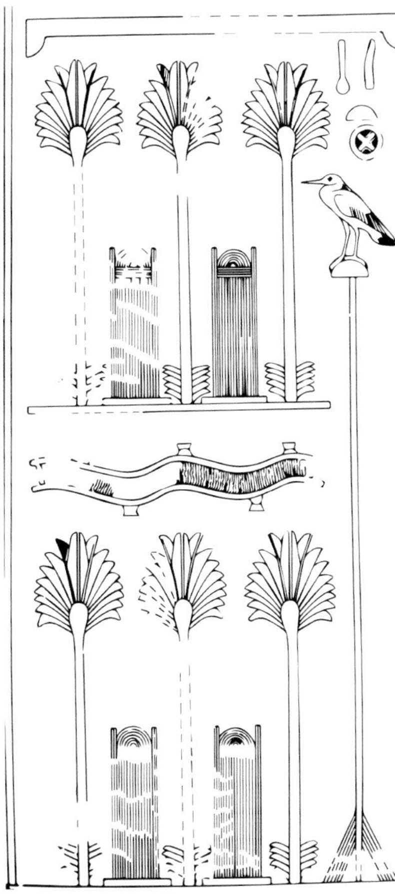

Figure 8: Scene from Apries palace gateway in Memphis. Adaptation by Roman Reed after Petrie 1909: plate VI.

occur in TT 17 and TT 24 (Griffiths 1958: 118). Davies notes that participation by the laity in the cult ritual is rare (1920: 20, pl. XIX). However, the people, or Souls of Pe and/or Dep regularly appear as participants in the funerary procession. There are many contrasting opinions as to the identity of these people. Men with similar captions also occur in the eighteenth dynasty tomb of Ramose (TT 55), where they represent the localities of Pe and Dep, Hermopolis Parva, Sais, and Hutweru (Hannig 1997: 1364). In the tomb of Senet, the inhabitants of Pe, Dep, Busiris, Unu, and Hutweru say, "'Come in peace to the west… For thou hast not come dead. Thou hast come alive. Seat thyself on the throne of the living and control the charges which thou hast laid on the living'" (Davies, Davies, and Gardiner 1920: 21. Cf. PT §§134 and 833). This scene represents an early example of what will develop into a common New Kingdom scene appearing in numerous private tombs on the west bank of Thebes and at Elkab (Settgast 1963: *Taf.* 2).

163 The tomb numbers at Elkab have been revised by the Belgium Mission and TC 10 is now known by no. 66 (W. V. Davies 2016: note 2). I have decided to retain TC 10 as it is the better-known designation.

164 Petrie 1909: fig. 6; Junker 1940: 19, *Abb.* 9; Kaiser 1987: *Abb.* 4 and 9; Robins 2008: 212.

165 Redford 1986: 331.

166 F. Friedman 1995: 18.

Figure 9: Scene of west wall of the tomb of Khnumhotep II at Beni Hasan. Photo by author.

good quality; however, later it was assigned to the third dynasty based on its similarity to the later discovered panels of Djoser. It is now dated to the twenty-sixth dynasty. The relief is, however, only comparable, not identical. The Saite artists were looking to revive and reinterpret, not copy.[167] Hence, Lower Egyptian ritual places were symbolized by illustrating the emblematic shrine that identified that particular locale.[168] Whether or not actual pilgrimages to these distant sites took place during the Old Kingdom, these localities remained significant as evidenced by their persistent inclusion in tomb scenes. And, in any event, the deceased had the desire to travel to these ancient sites so that he might take part in the ancient traditions.[169]
Beginning in the Middle Kingdom, if not earlier, the nature of these pilgrimages changed. Osiris "foremost of the westerners" who was revered at Abydos, would eventually become significant throughout Egypt and be the central point of the visit.[170] Abydos is an agriculturally rich area in Upper Egypt, which today is located several kilometers west of the Nile and comprises about 720 hectares.[171] Throughout the Middle Kingdom and into the New Kingdom, building activity at Abydos was state sponsored and rivaled other major cultural and religious centers, such as Memphis and Thebes.[172] Abydos was continuously used as a conceptual landscape for over five thousand years. After 2000 BCE the site of Abydos became a focal point of pilgrimage for followers of Osiris, when the tomb of the first dynasty King Djer became known as the tomb of the god. Osiris became popular because of his dramatic death: he was murdered by his brother Seth, his body was dismembered, and its parts were dispersed throughout Egypt. It was thanks to his sister-wife Isis and his other sister Nephthys that his limbs were eventually collected and put back together again. This process led to the revivification of the deceased Osiris. With that, Osiris set an example that all Egyptians wished to duplicate, namely having life after death. In addition to his miraculous reincarnation, Osiris became the king of the Underworld and was imagined occupying and ruling over this area.

One of the most significant events that took place at Abydos was the annual processional festival, which reenacted the death and rebirth of Osiris. Archaeological evidence from the site of Abydos seems to suggest that people from all over Egypt participated in his cult. Stelae and cenotaphs were set up to commemorate the pilgrimages made to the site.[173] This religious pilgrimage was the inspiration

[167] Robins 2008: 212. See also Petrie 1909: 5–6; Mogensen 1930: 95 (pl. 102); Porter and Moss 1981: 830.
[168] Kemp 2018: 68–69; 145–151.
[169] Junker 1940; Settgast 1963; Altenmüller 1972 and 1975a; Seyfried 2003.
[170] O'Connor 2009: 31–42.
[171] Richards 1999: 91.
[172] O'Connor 2009: 33.
[173] See Simpson 1974.

for the Abydos journey that is depicted in private tombs of the Middle and New Kingdoms. Middle Kingdom examples of the Abydos voyage appear in the private officials' tombs at Beni Hasan, while images from the New Kingdom abound in the private tombs at Thebes.[174]

In her study of the decoration in Khnumhotep II's Beni Hasan tomb, Janice Kamrin discusses the riverine voyages of this Middle Kingdom official. Here she remarks that the voyages occur within a sequence of scenes on the west wall of the tomb. The journey south to Abydos appears on the right, or north side of the west wall, while the return trip from Abydos is on the left, or south part of the west wall. These images flank either side of the tomb entrance (Figure 9).[175] Kamrin also notes that the arrangement shows the boats sailing south with the prevailing wind and rowing north with the river's current. She describes three of these boats as being typically Middle Egyptian, consisting of high prow and stern. The fourth boat Kamrin categorizes as a cult barque.[176] On the right side of the entrance the first boat, with its sail up, tows the second boat, which is the cult barque. The accompanying caption reads: "Sailing upstream in order to learn the requirements of Abydos, by the Hereditary Prince, Count, Overseer of the Eastern Desert, Neheri's son Khnumhotep."[177] The cult barque is a papyrus skiff with an upturned prow and stern, which identifies it as the funeral boat used since Old Kingdom times, according to Kamrin. The occupant lying on the lion bier in this boat is labeled as Khnumhotep. The voyage scene to the left of the entrance shows two boats traveling downstream and is labeled, "Coming and bringing the requirements of Abydos by the count, Neheri's son, Khnumhotep, possessor of reverence."[178] On the return voyage, Khnumhotep now wears a cloak and sits under a shrine at the front of the boat. Kamrin rightly points out that this scene illustrates the pilgrimage to Abydos; however, she does not remark on whether this journey was actually undertaken as part of Khnumhotep's funeral.[179]

The orientation of these two scenes within the tomb confirms the identification of this journey to and from Abydos as taking place on the Nile. Yet, if in fact the journey was only symbolic, the ritual would be carried out locally on the river or within the necropolis. If the voyage was done symbolically at least during part of the deceased's funeral, then part of the cemetery at Beni Hasan could have been designated as Abydos. This would have functioned as a "magical surrogate" for the real pilgrimage, an idea put forth by several scholars, including Edward Brovarski, James Hoffmeier, and Jan Assmann.[180] Yet, Kamrin suggests a third possibility, one that presents a solar journey and evokes the symbolic waters of Nun.[181] In this case, the west wall of the tomb of Khnumhotep II would magically ensure the transfiguration of the deceased into a resurrected being. Depicted in the decoration of this wall are desert, floodplain, the Nile, marshes, and canals, and Kamrin points out that if the depiction were laid flat the geography of Egypt would emerge. It shows the river in the middle flanked by the floodplain, which in turn is bordered by the desert and the marshes and canals below.[182] Kamrin interprets the desert as the location of the tomb itself, making the juxtaposition of the marshes and canals to this area a bit curious. She argues convincingly that the cycle of seasons (*shemu*, *peret*, *akhet*, *shemu,* and *peret*) is represented on the north wall to ensure the perpetual maintenance of the deceased through the harvest. Thus, the evidence here is not conclusive, but the tomb of Khnumhotep II demonstrates that a ritual voyage to Abydos was significant for the resurrection of the deceased.

Although Buto and Sais remained significant in tomb art, the site of Abydos as the cult center for the god Osiris surpassed the others in importance. According to Assmann, this "cultural reorientation" occurred sometime after the First Intermediate Period when people began to hark back to earlier times before the Old Kingdom.[183] At that point Abydos had been the most sacred necropolis and so it came to be again that Abydos was interpreted as the "ideal necropolis and center of mortuary belief."[184] Not only was Abydos thought to be the location of Osiris' grave, but also a place where the realm of the living and the

174 Kamrin 1999: 76-82; Assmann 2005: 305.
175 Kamrin 1999: 76.
176 Kamrin 1999: 77.
177 Kamrin 1999: 77.
178 Kamrin 1999: 78–79.
179 Kamrin 1999: 78.

180 Kamrin 1999: 78; Brovarski 1977: 107–115; Hoffmeier 1981: 167–177; Assmann 2005: 229. The question that arises from this assertion is: Could the superimposition of Abydos occur at any place in Egypt during the course of an individual funeral ceremony concerning the riverine voyages and the traversing of the Sacred District (which does not occur in the scenes at Beni Hasan)? See also Smith (2017: 231–235) and Kemp (2018: 151).
181 Kamrin 1999: 80.
182 Kamrin 1999: fig. IV.20.
183 Assmann 2005: 229.
184 Assmann 2005: 229.

realm of the dead could communicate. Abydos and the Mysteries of Osiris replaced Memphis and the pyramid rituals, and the Great God Osiris (coupled with the archaic kings) took the role of the king and provided divine presence for all buried in the Abydos cemetery.[185]

Pictorial evidence from the New Kingdom suggests that not only were ritual voyages popular, but that a journey to Abydos had surpassed others. Participation in festivals had also grown in importance by the New Kingdom. At Thebes, the officials who were buried on the west bank illustrated the sacred voyage to Abydos and back in their tomb decoration. This journey the deceased took to Abydos in the tomb scenes mirrored the religious pilgrimage made by some Egyptians during their lifetime. The purpose of participating in the journey to Abydos was to take part in the Mysteries of Osiris that were celebrated there. There is a difference of opinion as to whether the deceased actually partook in these ritual voyages, as is the case for the earlier voyages as well. Some scholars suggest the depictions were purely symbolic. Assmann postulates that when the voyages to the sacred Delta localities were depicted in the New Kingdom private tombs, they were purely figurative representations, while the Abydos journey was represented as an actual journey by boat.[186] The association between the deceased and the god Osiris created by this pilgrimage helped the deceased transition to the afterlife. Abydos was the one place on earth that was closest to the Netherworld because of its long history as a holy site and because it was home to Osiris. Accordingly, Abydos seemingly opened into the Netherworld and as such, Assmann suggests this was where the Judgment of the Dead took place.[187]

The journey to Abydos, whether real or symbolic, is relevant to this study for two reasons. First, the Sacred District scene has often been characterized as "Butic" and encouraging an association with the sacred Delta localities to the north. However, the journeys northwards are actually depicted outside of the Sacred District scene and are not an integral part of it. Second, the journey to Abydos is also shown adjacent to the Sacred District scene, and this coupled with the appearance of Osiris inside and to the end of the Sacred District, suggests that the nature of the Sacred District is more closely associated with Abydos. A significant aspect of the journey to Abydos is that it is depicted as heading toward the focal point of the tomb, generally along the passage, while the return journey is shown emerging from the interior of the tomb.[188] This placement is intriguing as it reinforces the association between the symbolic "west," or the focal point of the tomb chapel, and Abydos, as the final destination of the deceased. As the deceased longs to be associated with Osiris and to live forever in the hereafter, Osiris himself, as "foremost of the westerners," resides in the land of the dead in the west, and not coincidentally at the end of the Sacred District scene.[189] Nevertheless, it is true that this western region could simply refer to the cemetery itself or could be a distinct sphere of the cosmos or underworld. Going back as far as the Old Kingdom, the sources do not state clearly what the "west" designates specifically or exclusively.[190] Therefore, we are confronted with two possible locations, which may or may not be mutually exclusive: the land of the dead in the west and the site of Abydos to the north (based on the location where the illustrations are found). Yet, the artists managed to unite both concepts and create one single picture.[191]

Therefore, although the shrines symbolizing the sacred Delta localities appear in many of the same tombs as the Sacred District, they should be considered distinct scenes. The ritual voyages to the Delta connect with the Abydos journey as both represent excursions to locations where the deceased desired to visit. The Sacred District displays more direct parallels with the sacred journey to *Abydos*—the Sacred District scene appears adjacent to the journey to Abydos, Osiris is present within the Sacred District, and the focal point of the tomb (the west) is oriented to coincide with the illustration of Osiris standing in his shrine or seated on his throne.

Osiris and the Passage to the Afterlife

The greatest single change to conceptions of the afterlife happened mid-fifth dynasty when Osiris became the focus of belief and aspiration.[192] The god Osiris was the most important afterlife deity in ancient Egypt, as it was in connection to this god that one of the first beliefs in life after death is attested in the historical period.[193] Osiris' name first appears on

[185] Assmann 2005: 229.

[186] Assmann 2005: 305.

[187] Assmann 2005: 306.

[188] Engelmann-von Carnap 2014: 339–340.

[189] The concept of the west as a land of the dead was in existence at least as early as the first dynasty (Smith 2017: 55–56; Köhler 2012: 292–297).

[190] Smith 2017: 56–57; Bestock 2009: 31, 36.

[191] Robinson 1996: 42–44.

[192] Smith 2017: 191.

[193] Griffiths 1980: 64–65.

a relief fragment from the pyramid temple of the fifth dynasty king Djedkare Izezi at Saqqara.[194] Thereafter, Osiris' name is found in written records from the end of the fifth dynasty when he is mentioned in the *Pyramid Texts* of Unas and in the offering formulae of private mastabas.[195] From this time, he was the quintessential god of the hereafter and was associated with immortality. Most of the contemporary references to Osiris are only allusions to his character or actions, which presupposes a familiarity with his story, so there was no need to recount it in its entirety. It was not until the time of Plutarch (46-119 CE) that a full-length narrative of the Osirian legend is preserved. Osiris had many cult places throughout Egypt, and it was imagined that a body part of his had washed up at each one of them after his body was dismembered at the hands of Seth. The most important cult sites were Busiris in Lower Egypt and Abydos in Upper Egypt, and probably not coincidentally, these are two of the sites where much of the action in the Myth of Osiris takes place.[196]

Although often seen as a newcomer to the Egyptian pantheon, some scholars have suggested that Osiris had a much longer history, especially in the northern portion of Egypt.[197] However, there are no Egyptian sources that record how, or under what circumstances, belief in Osiris emerged.[198] For example, Baines suggests that Osiris could have had a cult located in the Delta before he had one at Abydos.[199] The Delta site Busiris is first associated with Osiris in an offering formula from the late fourth dynasty tomb of Queen Meresankh. Here, Busiris is named as a cult place in the Delta, ahead of Abydos, Osiris's other cult center in the south. This notion corresponds with James Henry Breasted's theory that the prehistoric "Osiris faith" was probably local to the Delta.[200] He posited that "in the beginning" (before unification) Osiris had been a local deity, his home being in Dedu, a site that was later called Busiris by the Greeks. Further, Breasted contends that his popularity eventually spread southward, where Osiris possibly found a home at Siut, but ended up in the area of Abydos as successor to Wepwawet, the "foremost of the westerners."[201] Osiris is identified by this epithet in the *Pyramid Texts*, but he becomes better known as "Lord of Abydos." These Abydene epithets became more popular than any connection he had previously with Busiris.[202] Therefore, Osiris is eventually associated with the south, despite any ancient northern origins. The first known attestation of Osiris at Abydos is from the eleventh dynasty, despite the connection made earlier by court officials in the late Old Kingdom.[203] A more recent theory has been put forth by B. Mathieu, where according to him, it was the state that was responsible for the diffusion of the Osirian cult throughout Egypt.[204] He posits that Osiris was created by the Heliopolitan priests to promote political stability and support for the royal family. In some ways, this is a retelling of Breasted's century-old theory that there was a gradual Osirianization of Egyptian religion in terms of the afterlife. Specifically, Breasted suggests that the Heliopolitan theologians merged purposely the Horus legend and the Osirian phenomenon during the Old Kingdom.[205] The growing prestige of Osiris and his mortuary realm put him in competition with the solar and celestial hereafter, and he sees this as a struggle between the state form of religion (court and state priesthoods) and the popular faith of the masses.[206] Nonetheless, Mathieu uses select passages from the *Pyramid Texts* to demonstrate how the state invented the god, decreed the establishment of his cult and sent emissaries to spread the new gospel. Other scholars, such as Mark Smith, find flaw with Mathieu's theory because he fails to prove that the dogma was consciously formulated and imposed by the state.[207] Unfortunately, there are no Egyptian sources that record how or under what circumstances belief in Osiris emerged, so as of now, we must be satisfied with not having all the answers.

The *Pyramid Texts* have been a major source for scholars who attempt to uncover the nature of Osiris and what he meant to adherents who wished to partake in an Osirian afterlife. The deceased sought to be associated with Osiris, but he remained distinct and subordinate.[208] This identification was ritually

[194] Smith 2017: 114–115.

[195] Griffiths 1980: 41; Smith 2017: 114–123.

[196] Faulkner and Goelet 1994: 149.

[197] Griffiths 1980: 41–44; Faulkner and Goelet 1994: 149. For a summary and references to additional material, see Smith 2017: 107–108, 127, note 129.

[198] Smith 2017: 127.

[199] Baines 2020: 187–188.

[200] Breasted 1959: 143.

[201] Breasted 1959: 38. From the Middle Kingdom onward, this name becomes an epithet of Osiris (Kemp 2018: 141; Smith 2017: 55, 65–69).

[202] Breasted 1959: 39.

[203] Kemp 2018: 141.

[204] Mathieu 2010: 77–107; Smith 2017: 130–133.

[205] Breasted 1959: 40–41; Griffiths 1980: 18–19.

[206] Breasted 1959: 141.

[207] Smith 2017: 130–133.

[208] Smith 2017: 191.

contingent and allowed the deceased to come to Osiris, enter before him, and be at his side.[209] What is perhaps most intriguing is that the dead could interact with Osiris in the Underworld *and* the land of the living. This is a significant departure from what we see earlier. Later sources envisage a specific festival celebrated for Osiris at Abydos, but the earlier ones do not. This means that the deceased could go to Abydos and participate with the living.[210] According to Mary-Ann Pouls-Wegner, Abydos received more support after it was annexed by the Thebans in the eleventh dynasty.[211] In the Middle Kingdom Abydos was the interface between this world and the next, and the mysteries were a time when distinction between realms was abolished and the living and the dead could join to worship Osiris together. It is not known if other sites had festivities of this nature in the First Intermediate Period or the Middle Kingdom, but in Ptolemaic times they did.[212]

As far back as the *Pyramid Texts* there is an abundance of references to both an Osirian afterlife and a solar afterlife. Most scholars agree that these two types of "passage to the next world" should be distinguished from one another, and not only by their chthonic or solar overtones. On one level this interweaving creates great confusion in the Old Kingdom doctrine for modern scholars. J. Gwyn Griffiths has suggested that the Osirian religion was very different than the solar theology because it was concerned with the preservation of the body itself. He calls it a "corporeal conception."[213] Throughout the early *Pyramid Texts*, the celestial and solar aspects trump the subterranean kingdom of Osiris, which remains in the background.[214] The sun god travels through the sky during the day and enters the underworld in the western horizon each evening. A significant connection between the celestial/solar and the Osirian doctrine had to do with the fact that the sun god dies every day in the west, at which point he passes through the underworld during the night.[215] This worked well with Osiris' new identification as "foremost of the westerners," whose kingdom was imagined to exist in the west below the horizon. Here Re encounters and temporarily unites with Osiris. In the *Pyramid Texts*, Osiris is called "Lord of the Duat" and acted as king of the realm of the dead. The texts that associate the king with Osiris imply that the king does not die at all, but simply passes to the next realm and continues to live there. The critical significance of Osiris for the Egyptians lay in what he personally had experienced—his life, death, and resurrection. His fate was tied to theirs, and therefore he figures more prominently in the textual and material record than other divinities.

Re was also significant for the aspirations of the dead. In the fifth dynasty the dead want to be an *imakhu* in the presence of Re, and in the *Pyramid Texts* and contemporary non-royal sources the dead want to travel to the sky, become an intimate of the sun god, and join his following. The *Coffin Texts* and contemporary offering formula corroborate and continue this idea. The dead want to ascend to the sky, be close to Re, become a follower, and travel in his bark.[216] It is, however, rare for sources to imagine the dead interacting with two gods simultaneously, because Re and Osiris belong to different realms– one to the sky and one to the underworld. The dead's interaction with Re and Osiris together is rarely attested, but there are some exceptions, for example *Coffin Text* 1130 suggests the dead will be like Re in the eastern horizon and like Osiris in the Netherworld. There are also some texts that note the dead's participation in the sun god's nocturnal journey through the underworld, and in Spell 1068 the dead greets Re and asks him to make Osiris gracious to him.[217]

There is more to Osiris than just being a deity who lives in the earth. Griffiths rejects the claim that Osiris was strictly chthonic.[218] Beginning in the Old Kingdom, Osiris is repeatedly associated with water—he is both the source of water and the water itself. *Pyramid Text* §589 tells us, "Horus comes, he recognizes his father in thee, youthful in thy name of 'Fresh Water.'" This sentiment continues into the Ramesside Period as evidenced by an inscription by Ramesses IV from Abydos, "Thou art indeed the Nile, great on the fields at the beginning of the seasons; gods and men live by the moisture that is in thee."[219] Here, Osiris is associated with the inundation that floods Egypt annually and with the flood water that gets deposited onto the surrounding fields and into basins. So, in his capacity as a water source—the river, the Mediterranean Sea, the water of the earth, and the water of the sky—he was identified as a source

[209] Smith 2017: 195.
[210] Smith 2017: 231.
[211] Wegner 2002: 66–67.
[212] Smith 2017: 234–5.
[213] Griffiths 1980: 66.
[214] Breasted 1959: 160.
[215] Breasted 1959: 159.
[216] Smith 2017: 247–250.
[217] Smith 2017: 251.
[218] Griffiths 1980: 65–66.
[219] Breasted 1959: 18 who cites Mariette 1880: 54, 1.7.

of fertility and a life-giving agent.[220] He was the water that brought life to the soil. The *Pyramid Texts* also express a connection with vegetation, specifically with the palm and the sycamore. An excerpt from *PT* §699 reads, "...O thou opener of the *ukhikh*-flower who is on his sycamore; O thou lord of brightener of regions who is on his palm; O thou lord of green fields."[221] Considering these associations, it does not seem unusual for palms, sycamore trees, garden plots, and water basins to appear as aspects of the Sacred District landscape, an area presided over by Osiris. It is evident from these earlier sources that Osiris was identified with waters, soil, and vegetation, and as such, Breasted calls him "the imperishable principle of life."[222]

Since the Sacred District is primarily a late seventeenth dynasty to early eighteenth dynasty creation, it is also necessary to consider the roles that Osiris and Re play in the *Book of the Dead*, as this was a contemporary funeral text. Osiris is prominent in New Kingdom funerary literature and no god appears more than he does in the *Book of the Dead*.[223] Not only is Osiris referenced through myriad epithets, but he is also mentioned by name. In his work on the *Book of the Dead*, Raymond Faulkner states that the other deities who appear in this compendium of funerary chapters emerge either as a cohort to Osiris or as his enemy via allusions to his legend.[224] It may seem counter-intuitive that one of the major works where Osiris appears was called "The Book of Going Forth by Day," when Osiris never went forth by day, but was relegated to the Duat. It follows that there must have been another aspect of the deceased that would go forth by day. Life beyond the tomb consisted of both an Osirian afterlife and a solar one in the New Kingdom as well. Therefore, the combination of Osirian and solar symbolism that was seen earlier persisted in a dual idea of the afterlife.[225] Re's influence on Egyptian culture throughout ancient history can best be seen in the creation of Osiris-Re, a syncretism of the two gods who first appears in a royal context in the New Kingdom.[226]

For a long time, it was thought that a belief in a solar afterlife for private individuals became popular during the New Kingdom.[227] However, it is now accepted that this phenomenon took place at least as early as the First Intermediate Period.[228] It was also in this context that Re's sphere of influence changed; he was now able to traverse areas of the Underworld with such gods as Osiris, Sokar, and Anubis. Just like Osiris, Re had to combat the forces of chaos in the Underworld as he made his way to rebirth in the morning in the form of Khepri. Faulkner points out that the *Papyrus of Ani* begins with the hymn to the god Re before the hymn to Osiris, indicating that both deities were of utmost importance at this time. Considering the prominence of both Re and Osiris in the quest for immortality, it is not surprising that imagery pertaining to both gods appears in the Sacred District. It was, therefore, not problematic that the pair of obelisks, symbolic of the sun, stood in juxtaposition to the shrines of Anubis and Osiris. It is for this reason that scholars such as Alix Wilkinson, who follows Hartwig Altenmüller, have interpreted the Sacred

---

[220] Smith 2017: 3.

[221] Breasted 1959: 22.

[222] Breasted 1959: 23.

[223] Faulkner and Goelet 1994: 149. It is generally thought that the *Book of the Dead* was reproduced *en mass* so that the funerary chapters would be readily available. It must be noted, however, that only a small percentage of Egyptians were literate, and there is some evidence in the *Book of the Dead* that at least some of the chapters were considered restricted knowledge. For example, *BD* chapter 137a states in its epilogue, "Beware greatly lest you do this before anyone except yourself, with your father or your son, because it is a great secret of the West, a secret image of the Duat, since the gods, spirits, and dead see it as the shape of the Foremost of the westerners" (Faulkner and Goelet 1994: 119). This particular chapter is intriguing because it is the same chapter that speaks of rituals being performed in conjunction with four basins, a common micro-scene found in the Sacred District. One of the standard micro-scenes of the Sacred District scene shows two women kneeling and making offerings of *nw*-jars in front of four basins of water (see Appendix I, §10). The Sacred District was illustrated in the tomb chapel, which was accessible to family and friends of the deceased. It is possible that these visitors would not have understood these illustrations, in that they were not privy to the secret knowledge necessary for understanding their meaning. Faulkner theorizes that there may have been a hidden meaning behind some scenes, and that only a few initiates knew this secret knowledge. Passage to the next world was one of those areas that required special knowledge, as the next world was a mystery. Knowledge was the key to power in the afterlife, a concept that is visible in the readings of the *BD* chapters when the deceased had to "know the names" of particular guardians in order to continue. He suggests that one had to be initiated into the world of the dead in a similar manner as if one were becoming a member of a secret society.

[224] Faulkner and Goelet 1994: 149.

[225] This concept dates to the *Pyramid Texts* where both the solar and Osirian notions of an afterlife are expressed (Griffiths 1980: 65).

[226] Faulkner and Goelet 1994: 149; Smith 2017: 306–308.

[227] Faulkner and Goelet 1994: 150.

[228] Smith 2017: 245–251.

District as representing both the eastern and western horizons of heaven, with the pool with the palm trees as the place on the eastern horizon where the sun god purified himself before he went of his daily journey across the sky.[229] This may be one possible way to explain this scene. Alternatively, because Osiris had been connected previously with the north, specifically with the town of Dedu in the Delta, he may have been part of the religion of the kings of Lower Egypt (i.e., the Butic kings). Thus, another way to interpret the Sacred District scene is as containing elements of a Butic burial (because it is Osirian).[230]

Descriptions of the afterlife and allusions to arriving there permeate mortuary literature beginning in the *Pyramid Texts*. The West was a land distinct from the land of the living and could only be reached by a journey. The Sacred District scene illustrates a version of this transition whereby the deceased ritually engages with divine beings on his way to the hereafter. The necropolis, as the domain of the gods, is presented as a landscape overflowing with fertility through which the deceased may proceed to Osiris and enjoy the status of *imakhu*. This scene exists so that the deceased may enter to Osiris in the west, be in the god's following, and be given life everyday like him. One of the most prominent micro-scenes in the Sacred District is that of the shrine of Osiris, which typically stands at the district's end. These wishes are attested clearly in the *Coffin Texts*, offering formulas, and hymns to Osiris into the thirteenth dynasty, just prior to the emergence of the Sacred District scene.[231] Osiris is the most important and most frequently depicted god in the Sacred District scenes. There are two associations that seem to underlie his significance: his role as a deity who acts in the hereafter to the benefit of the deceased and his role as a water source and lord of green fields. These latter correlations also act in the service of the deceased's eternal revivification. This was possibly the biggest attraction to the Osirian faith and one of the reasons the Sacred District was displayed in tombs—it was the gateway to the realm of Osiris.

Summary

Thus, the history of Osiris and his associations is significant for understanding the meaning and function of the Sacred District as it appears in the private tombs on the west bank of Thebes, Elkab, and Hierakonpolis. There is little doubt that both celestial and Osirian symbols of the afterlife appear within this district, but what exactly this meant to the owner of the tomb is unknown. This combination occurs as early as the Old Kingdom for royalty, where celestial and solar aspects trump the Osirian afterlife, evidenced by the *Pyramid Texts*, but rarely are both gods found interacting with the deceased in the same context. More clearly, the Sacred District scene eternalized the ritual activity involving the engagement of the deceased with Osiris. It is a record of it, a performance of it, and it will be repeated without any additional human intervention. The "monumentalizing" of this idea perpetuated its effects. These images are to make things happen and are a means to an end. It confirms the deceased's status as a follower of Osiris, attests to his power to achieve this goal, and confirms any associated attributes. Osiris is the deity most frequently identified with the deceased because of his powers and aspects, which are the most useful for the deceased in transitioning from this life to the next. The Sacred District scene illustrates the deceased as proceeding to Osiris' domain and in the following of this god. Those who illustrated this scene imagined a posthumous existence where the dead interact with Osiris. This was possibly the biggest attraction to the Osirian faith and one of the reasons the Sacred District was displayed in tombs—it was the gateway to the realm of Osiris and was an effective method of showing ritual engagement with the Osirian afterlife.

[229] A. Wilkinson 1994a: 391; Altenmüller 1975a: 745–765.
[230] However, the shrines that were symbolic of the sacred Delta localities to which the Butic kings journeyed during the predynastic period appear adjacent to the Sacred District, not within it.
[231] Smith 2017: 202–204.

CHAPTER FOUR: THE SACRED DISTRICT SCENE

The Sacred District has intrigued scholars for decades with its enigmatic *Mww*, ancient edifices, and beautiful gardens. In many cases, it was the *Mww*, with their unusual conical headdresses, who attracted the attention of modern scholars to these tomb paintings because of their bizarre headdresses and dancing postures, which resulted in the Sacred District being by the tomb owners, their families, visitors, and the artists who created them. By describing what the artists have left for us, and attempting to find patterns in their work, we might get closer to understanding certain basic components of the scene, such as the reasoning behind the choice of geographical location for the construction of the tombs, or perhaps when the tombs that contain the Sacred District were built. Many scholars have studied the connections between the positioning of artistic images and the architecture of a tomb, so the types of tombs that feature this scene may be reflective of its meaning.[233] The potency of this scene must have been felt by the people who had

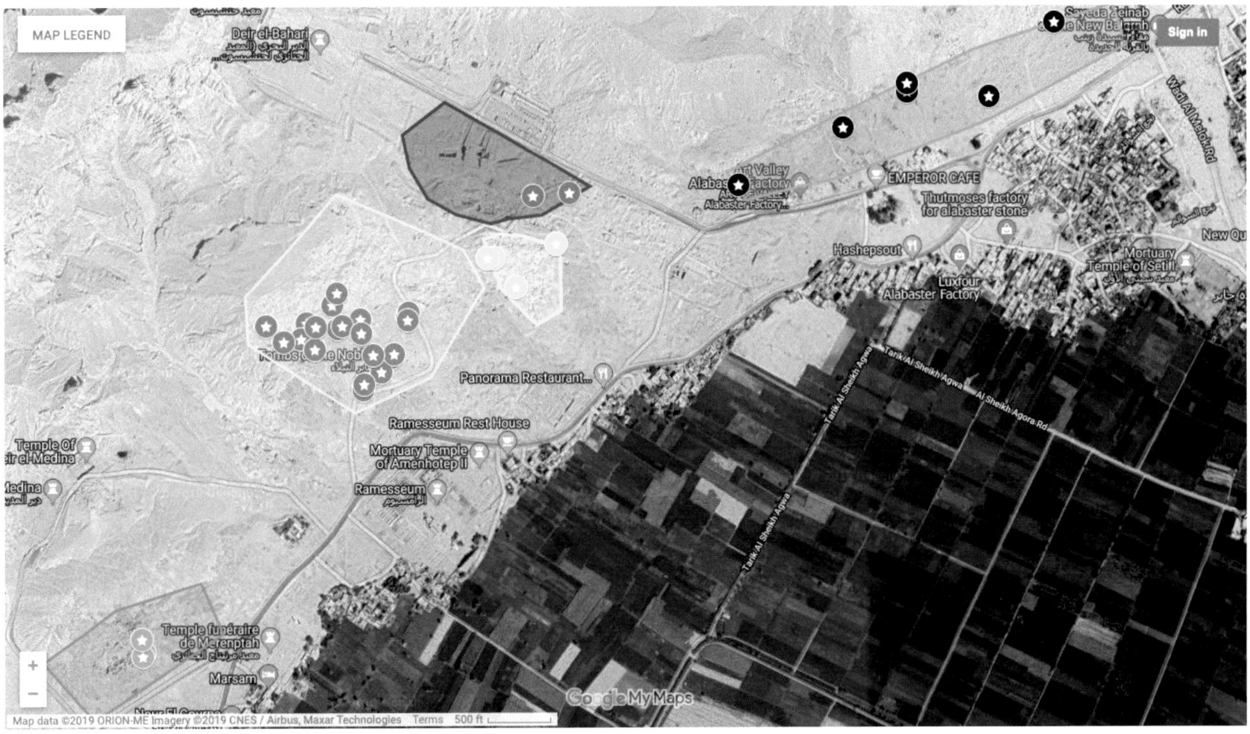

Figure 10: Map of the Theban necropolis showing the locations of tombs that depict a Sacred District scene. Green = Qurnet Murai; Blue = Sheikh Abd el-Gurna; Yellow = Khôkha; Red = Asasif; Black = Dra Abu el-Naga.

defined in relation to them. However, there is much more to this ritual landscape than just the *Mww*, and the ubiquity of this scene raises exciting questions about how ideas about life and death were expressed. These tomb scenes communicate perceptions of the landscape that in a sense were acts of remembrance. Yet, landscapes are experienced, and their meanings are inconsistent through space and time.[232]

What we really want to know is how people experienced and understood this landscape because that could tell us why it is so ubiquitous in the first part of the eighteenth dynasty and what sort of interactions might have taken place with it in the chapels. I want to try to describe this scene as it was experienced it included in their decorative programs, so again the relationships that existed between the different owners who copied the Sacred District scene into their tomb has relevance. If it is possible to discern the style of art or the identity of the artists whose work we are analyzing, can we also see patterns in the professions whose members utilized this scene more frequently? Was this scene passed down from predecessor to successor? Or can patterns of usage be seen within the network of blood relations? Thirty-nine tomb scenes have been considered for this study, including the Middle Kingdom tomb of Senet and the Second Intermediate tomb of Sobeknakht II at Elkab.

[232] Ingold 1993: 153.

[233] Assmann 2003; Hartwig 2004: 15–19.

Spatial Context and Chronology

The tombs that contain this scene are on the west bank of Thebes and farther south at Elkab on the east bank and Hierakonpolis on the west bank of the Nile. Within the Theban necropolis, the tombs that contain the Sacred District scene are found in five of its subdivisions: Sheikh Abd el-Qurna, Dra Abu el-Naga, Khôkha, Qurnet Murai, and the Asasif (Figure 10).

Twenty of the tombs that display the Sacred District scene are from Sheikh Abd el-Qurna, the main cemetery at the center of the Theban necropolis. These represent, by and large, the highest number of tombs with this scene to be found in a single area. Hatshepsut's officials developed this hill, and her high-ranking contemporaries built their tombs here. This was a place that had not seen much construction since the Middle Kingdom. Sheikh Abd el-Qurna was probably inaugurated by Aametju/Ahmose, the owner of TT 83, who was the vizier under Thutmose II. Hatshepsut's men had their tombs located at the northern edge, oriented toward Hatshepsut's temple at Deir el-Bahri, but some of her officials were buried closer to the Asasif, for example, the Second Prophet of Amun, Puiemre (TT 39).[234] By far the earliest tomb at Sheikh Abd el-Qurna to include any kernel of the Sacred District scene is Theban Tomb 60, a Middle Kingdom tomb belonging to the Lady Senet.[235] She was the wife/mother of Antefoker, the vizier to King Senwosret I (*c*.1971-1926 BCE) of the twelfth dynasty. Although this tomb does not display a typical New Kingdom version of the Sacred District, it does feature the *Mww* and offers the name of the location—the *t3 ḏsr*. Theban Tomb 60 is unique for two reasons. First, it is a tomb that was built for a woman, although patronized by her husband/son Antefoker, and second, it represents one of the very few decorated Middle Kingdom tombs on the west bank of Thebes. Other tombs of this date were either destroyed or reused, so TT 60 is an anomaly. It is therefore possible that, were more Middle Kingdom tombs to come to light, we might find additional precursors to the New Kingdom Sacred District scene. Due to these circumstances, Senet's tomb marks the very beginning of the inclusion of the Sacred District scene in private elite tombs on the west bank of Thebes.

Six tombs with this scene are found in the sub-division of Dra Abu el-Naga, located north of the Asasif close to the bay of Deir el-Bahri. These tombs belong to the mayor of Thebes, Tetiky (TT 15), the scribe of accounts of grain and scribe of the southern city, Wensu (A4), the scribe and physician of the king, Nebamun (TT 17), the overseer of the granary of the king's wife and the king's mother Aahotep, Hery (TT 12), the bearer of the floral offerings of Amun, Nakht (161), and the scribe, the weigher of Amun and overseer of the plough lands of Amun, User (TT 260).

The building of these six tombs spans the reigns of Ahmose/Amenhotep I to Amenhotep III. Dra Abu el-Naga was the royal necropolis of the seventeenth dynasty kings, so perhaps it is no surprise that this site features two of the earliest examples of the Sacred District scene, those of Hery (TT 12) and Tetiky (TT 15). However, it is at the neighboring site of Sheikh Abd el-Qurna that this scene rises in prominence during the reigns of Hatshepsut and Thutmose III, two to three generations later.

Four tombs with the Sacred District scene were built in the sub-division of Khôkha. Khôkha is located southeast of the Asasif and borders on the lower enclosure of Sheikh Abd el-Qurna. The tombs here belong to the scribe and counter of grain in the granary of divine offerings of Amun, Nebamun (TT 179), the second prophet of Amun, Puiemre (TT 39), and the royal butler and child of the nursery, Mentiywiy (TT 172). There is also a Saite tomb that was constructed in Khôkha for an unknown official (TT 392) that includes a Sacred District scene. This tomb is one of the few Late Period tombs included in this study in what appears to be part of an archaizing trend.

There are only three tombs with the Sacred District scene at Qurnet Murai, a small hill at the most southern part of the private Theban necropolis. These tombs are all relatively late examples, with two of them dating to the Ramesside period. In fact, the majority of the tombs at this site date to the reigns of Amenhotep III, Ay, and Tutankhamun. These three tombs belong to the overseer of the treasury of gold and silver, the judge, and overseer of the cabinet, Amenemopet (TT 276), the head *wab*-priest and Divine Father in the temples of Amenhotep III and Sokar, Sobekmose (TT 275), and the first prophet of Montu, Hekmaatrenak (TT 222). All these tombs post-date the climax of the appearance of the Sacred District in tomb decoration and, therefore, the use of this scene here may be considered a holdover from its earlier glory days during the reigns of Hatshepsut and Thutmose III, especially those of Sobekmose and Hekmaatrenakht.

[234] Engelmann-von Carnap 2014: 338–339.

[235] Davies, Davies, and Gardiner 1920.

Table 1: Tombs with Sacred District Scene at Sheikh Abd el-Qurna

No.	Name of Tomb Owner	Reign/Period
TT 60	Senet	Senwosret I[236] (only *Mww*)
TT 100	Rekhmire	Thutmose III-Amenhotep II
TT 81	Ineni	Amenhotep I-Thutmose III (?)
TT 21	User	Thutmose I
TT 125	Duauneheh	Hatshepsut
TT 71	Senenmut	Hatshepsut
TT 224	Ahmose, called Humay	Hatshepsut/Thutmose III
TT 110	Djehuty	Hatshepsut/Thutmose III
TT 127	Senemiah	Thutmose III
TT 112	Menkheperreseneb[237]	Thutmose III
TT 122	Amenhotep (with Amenemhet)	Thutmose III
TT 123	Amenemhet	Thutmose III
TT 82	Amenemhet	Thutmose III
TT 53	Amenemhet	Thutmose III
TT 84	Amunedjeh	Thutmose III
TT 96B	Sennefer	Amenhotep II-Thutmose IV
TT 69	Menna	Thutmose IV
TT 120	Anen	Amenhotep III
TT 41	Amenemope, called Ipy	Ramesses I-Sety I
TT 342	Djehutymose	Thutmose III
TT 92	Suemniwet[238]	Amenhotep II

Table 2: Tombs with Sacred District Scene at Dra Abu el-Naga

No.	Name of Tomb Owner	Reign/Period
TT 15	Tetiky	Ahmose-Amenhotep I
TT A4	Wensu	Thutmose III-Amenhotep II
TT 17	Nebamun	Amenhotep II
TT 12	Hery	Amenhotep I
TT 161	Nakht	Amenhotep III
TT 260	User	Thutmose III

Table 3: Tombs with Sacred District Scene at Khôkha

No.	Name of Tomb Owner	Reign/Period
TT 179	Nebamun	Hatshepsut
TT 39	Puiemre	Hatshepsut-Thutmose III
TT 172	Mentiywiy	Thutmose III-Amenhotep II
TT 392	Unknown official	Saite

Table 4: Tombs with Sacred District Scene at Qurnet Murai

No.	Name of Tomb Owner	Reign/Period
TT 276	Amenemopet	Thutmose IV
TT 275	Sobekmose	Ramesside
TT 222	Hekmaatrenakht, called Turo	Ramesses III-IV

---

236 The tomb of Senet dates to the Middle Kingdom and therefore is related to this study only in terms of its scenes acting as prototypes for those of the New Kingdom.
237 This tomb was usurped in the Ramesside Period by the prophet of Amun, "Great of Majesty," Aashefytemwaset.
238 TT 92 does not include a proper Sacred District scene. It includes only the *ḫbt*-dancers micro-scene, which has been determined to be outside of the district itself.

In the Asasif, the area south of Dra Abu el-Naga and inside the bay at Deir el-Bahri, there are two tombs with the Sacred District scene in their decoration programs: the tomb of the *sm3ti*-priest, chamberlain of Min, *ḥsk*-priest, and mayor of the southern city Basa (TT 389) and the tomb of the chief steward of the Divine Adoratrice Ibi (TT 36). These tombs, as well as Theban Tomb 392 from Khôkha (noted above), represent an archaizing trend that was prevalent during the Saite Period.[239] Artists of the Saite period tended to ignore the more recent artistic developments from the New Kingdom and Third Interediate Period and instead harked back to Old Kingdom models for inspiration. Although certain micro-scenes within the Sacred District do date back to the Old Kingdom, the comprehensive Sacred District scene is a New Kingdom phenomenon, and it is this rendition that is imitated in these tombs. Donald Redford suggests that this renaissance originated in the Western Delta toward the end of the Third Intermediate Period, and was then adopted by the Kushite rulers who spread the trend throughout Egypt in both the royal and private spheres.[240] This dissemination was due to the importation of northern craftsmen "under Sudanese sponsorship."[241] So, the so-called "Renaissance" dates back to before the Kushites, who simply adopted a fad already in style.[242] Theban Tombs 392 (see above), 389, and 36 represent private examples of tomb decoration in which artists drew off of the New Kingdom models that surrounded them.

Table 5: Tombs with Sacred District Scene from the Asasif

No.	Name of Tomb Owner	Reign/Period
TT 389	Basa	Saite
TT 36	Ibi	Psameticus I

Moving up the Nile to the site of Elkab, one finds three tombs with the Sacred District scene and one tomb with only the *Mww*. This is the only other site that has multiple known tombs that contain the Sacred District scene. The earliest example is the sixteenth dynasty tomb of Sobeknakht II that features the *Mww*. His scene shows two oxen in a procession following behind two *Mww* who wear the typical conical headdress, white kilt, and collar. They appear to be walking forward with their legs positioned in a stepping motion. Both have their arms spread out to either side of their body with their palms facing upward. The *Mww* is the only micro-scene to appear here.[243] The other three rock-cut tombs are located close together on a small rocky cliff side. These include the tomb of Reneny (TC 7), that of Paheri (TC 3), and a tomb belonging to Setau (TC 4). The tomb of Reneny is the earliest one of these three and is more or less contemporary with such tombs as Tetiky (TT 15), Ineni (TT 81), and Hery (TT 12) from Thebes. Paheri's illustration epitomizes a typical example from the reign of Thutmose III, the time period to which most examples of this scene date. That of Setau is a noteworthy example as it is of a relatively late date and appears to represent an exact duplicate (albeit fragmentary) of the scene preserved in the tomb of Paheri. Although many Sacred District scenes are similar, this is the only example where there is a potential replica.

Table 6: Tombs with Sacred District Scene at Elkab

No.	Name of Tomb Owner	Reign/Period
TC 10	Sobeknakht II	Sixteenth Dynasty[244] (only *Mww*)
TC 7	Reneny	Amenhotep I
TC 3	Paheri	Thutmose III-Amenhotep II
TC 4	Setau	Ramesses III-IX

There is only one known example of the Sacred District scene at Hierakonpolis, and that appears in the tomb of Djehuty. Djehuty was the overseer of stone masons during the reign of Thutmose I.

The tombs of Tetiky (TT 15) and Hery (TT 12) are most likely the earliest New Kingdom examples of the Sacred District scene at Thebes, not including the tomb of Senet (TT 60), who just has the *Mww*. They are both located at Dra Abu el-Naga, the site of the tombs of the seventeenth dynasty kings. It might have been at this juncture that the images were transferred farther south to the site of Elkab. We know that the family who governed Elkab had ties to the royal family at Thebes (see chapter six). The latest New Kingdom tombs date to the Ramesside Period, with

[239] Robins 2008: 210–211.
[240] Redford 1986: 328–330.
[241] Redford 1986: 330.
[242] Redford 1986: 328.
[243] Tylor 1896.
[244] The tomb of Sobeknakht II dates to the sixteenth dynasty (the reign of Nebiryrau I), and therefore relates to this study only in terms of its scenes acting as prototypes for those of the New Kingdom (W. V. Davies 2010: 223).

Figure 11: Map of the Theban necropolis showing locations of Saite tombs that depict a Sacred District scene. Yellow = Khôkha; Red = Asasif.

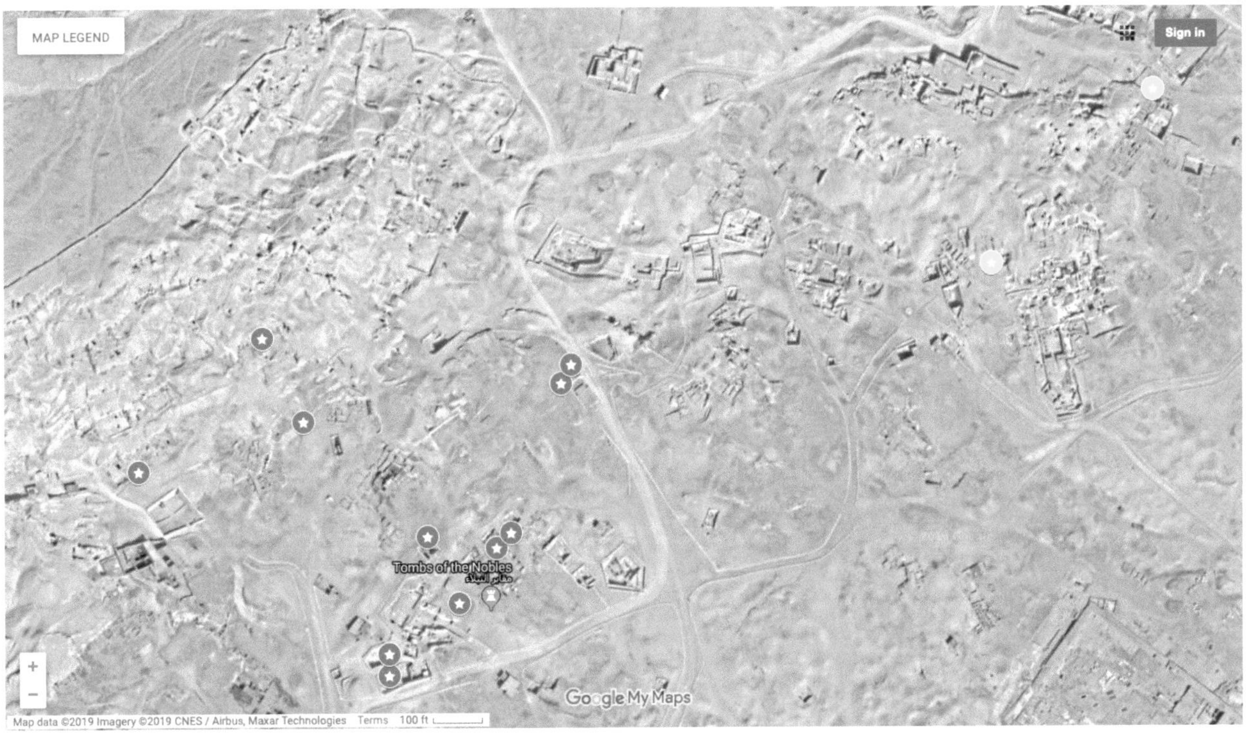

Figure 12: Map of the Theban necropolis showing locations of tombs from the reigns of Hatshepsut and Thutmose III that display a Sacred District scene. Blue = Sheikh Abd el-Qurna; Yellow = Khökha.

two examples from Qurnet Murai, one each at Sheikh Abd el-Qurna and Elkab. The three Saite examples are from tombs in the Asasif and Khôkha, which are relatively close to each other (Figure 11).[245]

Most of the tombs that have the Sacred District scene date to the early part of the eighteenth dynasty, with thirteen of them dating to the reigns of Hatshepsut and Thutmose III alone (Figure 12). The reigns of these two kings (their joint reign followed by the sole reign of Thutmose III) mark the pinnacle of the appearance of this scene in terms of its frequency. Leading up to this, of the thirty-nine tombs included in this study, six date to the very beginning of the eighteenth dynasty: TT 12, TT 15, TT 21, TT 81, TC 7 at Elkab, and Djehuty's tomb at Hierakonpolis. Study of the chronological and geographical distribution of the Sacred District scene has revealed patterns in its usage. Since there are early prototypes of this scene at both Thebes and Elkab, TT 60 and TC 10 respectively, the site of Dra Abu el-Naga appears to be a good starting point for understanding the spread of this scene in tomb art. It might be argued that both of the pre-eighteenth dynasty examples have more in common with the Old Kingdom illustrations of the *Mww*, but since they appear at two of the sites that have the later Sacred District scene, they provide a clue to its distribution. The Sacred District scene appears only sporadically during the remainder of the New Kingdom, with some isolated examples in the Saite Period.

Tomb Type

The architectural categories this work employs are those of Friederike Kampp-Seyfried, as presented in her 1996 study on the architectural developments of the private rock-cut tombs in the Theban necropolis. Her study was based on the examination of over 600 private tombs, both decorated and undecorated.

It is known that particular areas of the Theban necropolis were preferred for tomb building at certain times and that there was a relationship between the orientation of an official's tomb and the Temple of Millions of Years of the king under whom that official worked.[246] It is this relationship that contributes to the apparent pattern between *when* the Sacred District scene was employed and *where* the tombs that employ the scene are situated. Furthermore, this association suggests that the architecture of the tombs that include the Sacred District scene may be consistent with other patterns over space and time.

Kampp-Seyfried's classifications are not a typology, but a catalogue. The goal in using her categories is to acknowledge methodically the architecture of the tombs in which the Sacred District scene appears using a well-known and popular system within Egyptology. This is a relevant endeavor in as much as it has been argued that tomb decoration is intimately connected to the architecture of the tomb in which it is produced.[247] Kampp-Seyfried's tomb shapes are organized I through X with subcategories added for most shapes. For example, shape V includes Va through Ve, with each letter designation indicating a variant on the original design.[248] The most common kind of tomb found at the Theban necropolis during the New Kingdom is the classic T-shaped tomb, shapes V-VIII according to Kampp-Seyfried. Since the Sacred District scene appears most frequently during the reigns of Hatshepsut and Thutmose III, it was illustrated mostly in tombs of certain shapes. Of the thirty-nine examples of the Sacred District scene included in this study, nineteen fall into category V. Category V represents one version of the classic T-shaped tomb, and in its most basic form it consists of an entrance, a broad or transverse hall, and a passage or longitudinal hall. Its variants include the addition of a small shrine or niche at the end of the passage, the addition of a second broad hall, the addition of a rear broad hall, or the inclusion of side chambers coming off the front broad hall. This tomb category represents almost half of the tombs that employ the Sacred District scene.

In the Theban necropolis, tombs of the following types contain the Sacred District scene: IIb, IVa, IVb, Vb, Vd, Ve, VIa, and VIIa.[249] Types I-V are

[245] Diamond, "Mapping the Sacred District Scene in the Theban Necropolis and at Elkab."

[246] Kampp-Seyfried 2003: 2.

[247] Kampp-Seyfried 2003; Hartwig 2004; Kamrin 1999.

[248] Kampp-Seyfried 2003: fig. 2.

[249] Type III tombs belong specifically in the Middle Kingdom. While the first tomb type noted above belongs to the one-room tomb chapel category, Type III tombs have more architectural elements, for example, additional space close to the chapel-like core area of the tomb. Theban Tomb 60, the tomb of Senet, from Sheikh Abd el-Qurna, is the only example of a Type IIIa tomb that is relevant to this study. Type IIIa can be defined as a tomb form that consists of a square chapel (with or without a recess at the back) located at the end of longitudinal corridor. The entrance to this type of tomb usually consists of an abrupt opening in the façade, in contrast to a transition from the corridor to the chapel space carved out of the rock passage (Kampp-Seyfried 1996: 18). There has been a lot of confusion surrounding the women shown in this tomb. According to Wolfram Grajetzki, there are two women depicted in TT 60, one is the priestess of Hathor, Zatzasobek, and the other is Senet,

tomb plans without weight-bearing elements, such as columns or pillars, and Types VI-X have weight-bearing elements. By far the most common tomb types to depict the Sacred District are Vb and Vd.

Type IIb
The tombs in the Type II category belong to the group of one-room tomb chapels, but in contrast to Type I these tombs have a niche in the wall opposite the entrance. With the Type IIb variant, the tombs have a longitudinal space and niche as opposed to a transverse hall.[250] Theban Tomb 179 at Khôkha and TT 161 at Dra Abu el-Naga are the only tombs included in this category.[251]

Type IVa
The tombs of Type IV differ in a small, but significant way from those of Type III. The main subcategory of interest for this study is variant IVa (like the similar type IIIa), which consists of an entrance corridor and subsequent sanctuary. However, Type IVa does not have a square chapel, but rather a rectangular one that creates a transverse space. In most cases, the carving of the frame of the chamber door emphasizes the entrance to the tomb. The same long corridor appears in Type IVa tombs as in Type IIIa tombs.[252] There are three tombs of this type that depict the Sacred District scene (TT 12, TT 122, and TT 224). TT 122 and TT 224 were built at Sheikh Abd el-Qurna, but TT 12 is situated at Dra Abu el-Naga.

Type IVb
TT 81 is the only tomb from this category. It seems to have been originally an eleventh dynasty *saff* tomb with a shallow court that backs onto a row of pillars. It was altered by the tomb owner, Ineni.[253]

Type Vb
The last type of tomb, without columns or pillars in the inner rooms, is Type V. Type Vb differs from the basic form by expanding the rear wall in the longitudinal hall into a cult destination in the form of a niche or a chapel with a niche. There are twelve examples of this variant form that include the Sacred District scene (Theban Tombs 17, 21, 53, 69, 82, 100, 172, 222, 275, 276, 392, and A4). This is by far the most common tomb type to illustrate the Sacred District.

Type Vd, another variant, has two additional side galleries, at the end of the longitudinal corridor. This creates two transverse rooms, but not directly behind one another as in Type Vc. Instead, they are separated by a longitudinal hall. The rear transverse space can be individually extended with a niche or chapel.[254] According to Kampp-Seyfried, the chronological distribution for the variant Type Vd shows a clear time limit of the eighteenth dynasty and within this period a striking accumulation in the reign of Hatshepsut and Thutmose III.[255] Kampp-Seyfried's conclusion is echoed in the numerous examples of the Sacred District scene that appear at this same time (however, there are not as many Type Vd examples as there are Vb examples). There are five examples of tomb Type Vd that depict the Sacred District scene (Theban Tombs 112, 123, 125, 127, and 342). All five tombs were built in the subdivision of Sheikh Abd el-Qurna.

The last subtype of the "T-shaped" tomb is Ve. These tombs possess side chapel-like niches in the "western wall" of the original transverse hall on either side of the longitudinal corridor. Theban Tombs 39 and 84 fall into this subcategory.

Looking at the Type V tombs and their chronological distribution in conjunction with the regional distribution, the following conclusions can be drawn. While the two conventional Theban forms are Va and Vb, they provide a relatively balanced view from the beginning of the eighteenth dynasty until the end of the Ramesside Period, both chronologically and regionally. The highest number of Type Vb tombs occurs at Sheikh Abd-el Qurna. With this being one of the most common tomb types to display the Sacred District scene, it stands to reason that the majority of the examples appear in this area of the necropolis. Of those thirty-five tombs, twelve include the Sacred District scene. Types Vc-Ve suggest more significant results; they date primarily to the eighteenth dynasty

begotten of Dui, the tomb owner. Both women bear the title "his beloved wife," presumably referring to the vizier Antefoker. The vizier himself is described as "born of Senet." The fact that one of the more important figures in the tomb decoration has been erased several times does not help the situation (Grajetzki 2009: 162–163).

250 Kampp-Seyfried 1996: 17–18. See fig. 10 in Kampp-Seyfried.

251 TT 260 from Dra Abu el-Naga during the time of Thutmose III may be of Type IIa. It is an unpublished tomb but looking at the drawing in Porter and Moss (1970: 334) it appears to be a one room rectangular tomb with a niche opposite the entrance. Kampp-Seyfried suggests the tomb has been altered.

252 Kampp-Seyfried 1996: 21. See fig. 19 in Kampp-Seyfried 1996: 21.

253 Baines 2013: 77–79.

254 Kampp-Seyfried 1996: 25.

255 Kampp-Seyfried 1996: 26.

with a clear focus on the reign of Thutmose III. It is also noteworthy that there is a total absence of Types Vd and Ve at Qurnet Murai and Type Vd in the Asasif. Type Vd is distributed in proportion to the size of each part of the necropolis, spread evenly over Dra Abu el-Naga, Shiekh Abd el-Qurna, and Khôkha, but the tombs with the Sacred District scene appear only at Sheikh Abd el-Qurna. The variant Ve appears in individual examples at Shiekh Abd el-Qurna and is concentrated there, but TT 39—a Ve tomb with the Sacred District scene—was built in Khôkha near the Asasif.[256]

Type VIa

The following tomb type exhibits supporting elements in its inner rooms in the form of pillars or columns. Subtype VI tombs can be grouped together. Their front transverse halls do not have pillars or columns, unlike the subsequent rooms within the tombs. The variant VIa consists of a transverse hall and a subsequent longitudinal hall, followed by a pillared room. There is only one tomb of this type that illustrates the Sacred District scene, which is Theban Tomb 110, belonging to Djehuty and located in Sheikh Abd el-Qurna.

Type VIIa

Four of the tombs that feature the Sacred District scene belong to Type VIIa (Theban Tombs 41, 71, 120, and 92). Type VIIa represents the simplest form of this type and consists of a transverse hall with pillars, a longitudinal hall, with a chapel or niche at the rear of the tomb as a subsidiary feature. A striking aspect of the chronological distribution of Type VII is not only that about three-fourths of the tombs date to before the beginning of the Amarna period, but also the fact that this type does not appear before the reign of Hatshepsut.[257] Of the four tombs noted above, only TT 71 falls into the time frame when the Sacred District scene is most popular. TT 41, TT 92, and TT 120 were decorated when the Sacred District scene was on the decline. It is feasible that the decorative programs in these tombs were influenced by the art found in the surrounding tombs. Sheikh Abd el-Qurna is the location where most Sacred District scenes appear, so it is not unreasonable that this subject might remain fashionable here longer than in the other subdivisions of the necropolis.

The following Table 7 illustrates the different tomb types that display the Sacred District scene on the west bank of Thebes. It provides the Theban Tomb numbers and gives the total number of tombs for each type according to Kampp-Seyfried's categorizations. The four tombs from Elkab, the one tomb from Hierakonpolis, and TT 60 are excluded from Table 7, as is TT 96B since it is a burial chamber. Likewise, TT 15 is of a special shape and not categorizable by Kampp-Seyfried's styles. The two Saite tombs (TT 36 and TT 389) from the Asasif are also not included.

Table 7: Types of Tombs that Illustrate the Sacred District

Tomb Type	Theban Tomb Numbers	Total Number of Tombs
IIb	161, 179, 260	3
Iva	12, 122, 224	3
IVb	81	1
Vb	17, 21, 53, 69, 82, 100, 172, 222, 275, 276, 392, A4	12
Vd	112, 123, 125, 127, 342	5
Ve	39, 84	2
Via	110	1
VIIa	41, 71, 92, 120	4

The tombs constructed on the west bank of Thebes that utilize the Sacred District scene in their decorative programs are primarily of the following types: Type IV = seventeenth dynasty and early eighteenth dynasty; Type V (b, d, e) and Type VIa = middle of the eighteenth dynasty. Predictably, this pattern indicates that the type of artwork within the tomb reflects the type of tomb in which it was created, and that both of these aspects, in turn, relate to the time period in which they were produced.

The Sacred District Scene within the Decorative Program

Of the almost forty tombs included in this study, the register(s) in which the Sacred District occurs can be confirmed for only twenty-five.[258] Of these twenty-five tombs, only the tombs of Rekhmire (TT 100) and Amenemope (TT 41) have the Sacred District

[256] Kampp-Seyfried 1996: 27.

[257] Kampp-Seyfried 1996: 30.

[258] The number thirty-nine includes thirty-five Theban Tombs, three tombs at Elkab and one tomb at Hierakonpolis. The two earliest tombs mentioned in this work, TT 60 and TC 10 at Elkab, are not included in the total number of tombs with a Sacred District scene as it was known at the outset of this study that they do not display a full Sacred District, only the *Mww*.

Figure 13: The scenes shown in the register above are placed slightly to the right of the scenes in the register below. Illustration by author."

displayed in the upper registers. In Rekhmire's tomb, register nine illustrates the pool and palms, sycamore trees, slaughtering area, *Mww* in their hall, garden plots, and braziers—the quintessential markers of the Sacred District. However, this tomb is somewhat of an outlier, in that it contains the most complete version of a Sacred District, in addition to the most elaborate funerary scenes. In most other examples, the Sacred District appears among the images in the lower registers. It is commonly depicted in the lowest register (Theban Tombs 12, 21, 39, 53, 82, 112, 123, 125, 342, and TC 3 and TC 4). In several of these latter examples, the district also covers the second register from the bottom, but it is still the lowest tableau (or compendium of related episodes) on the wall (Figure 13). It is common for the Sacred District to appear in more than one register of the wall, especially in the examples that contain many micro-scenes. The number of registers can vary in the different tombs, but usually ranges between three and five. The pattern that emerges is that the Sacred District scene is typically illustrated on the lower half of the left wall of the passage of a T-shaped tomb, or on the left wall of a rectangular chapel.

As noted above, Rekhmire has a very large Sacred District scene that takes up multiple registers beginning at the top of the left wall of the passage. This is a significant tomb of this study because it acts as a comparative to all other examples of the Sacred District. We might look at this tomb as a fuller version of what all other tombs might have looked like had their owners been as high status as Rekhmire. Harold Hayes, in his article on rites of passage and Egyptian syntax, uses the funerary scenes in the tomb of Rekhmire to demonstrate how Egyptian ritual structures defy narrative's demand for a beginning, middle, and end.[259] This study is useful here because Hayes helps elucidate a broader context for the individual micro-scenes that appear in several other tombs. He reads the scenes from top to bottom beginning with the south (or left) wall, and then he continues on the north wall from bottom to top. Hayes assembles the events in the nine registers into a number of processions and identifies the different destinations. Accordingly, these processions ultimately lead to the tomb.[260] The five destinations are as follows: the necropolis, the embalming place, Sais, Abydos, and the tomb.[261] The first procession to the necropolis is laid out before the hieroglyphs representing the necropolis and Osiris. The second procession heads to the place of embalming and is laid out before the god Anubis. Below is the procession to the sacred Delta localities, followed by the procession to the site of Abydos. Lastly, the final procession leads to the Goddess of the West and the actual tomb. This schema demonstrates that the core area of the Sacred District lies in or near the necropolis with Osiris flaking these registers (Figure 14).

Following this analysis, the micro-scenes that commonly appear associated with the Sacred District in other more abbreviated tombs are scattered in processions one and two, those leading to the necropolis and to the place of embalming. What is also made clear is that the journeys to the sacred Delta localities are separate from the Sacred District, they are not one and the same event. This is significant because several scholars describe the Sacred District as located between the embalming workshop and the tomb, but it is the procession to the sacred Delta localities that appears in this position in the tomb of Rekhmire. This tomb also reiterates that the journey to Abydos is separate—although this has not been up for debate. The Sacred District appears located more generally in the necropolis, and in this case, several micro-scenes (guardians of the great gate, the three pools, and several open gods' shrines) are placed in the procession to the embalming place, which

[259] H. Hayes 2013: 170.

[260] H. Hayes 2013: 173.

[261] H. Hayes 2013: fig. 5.

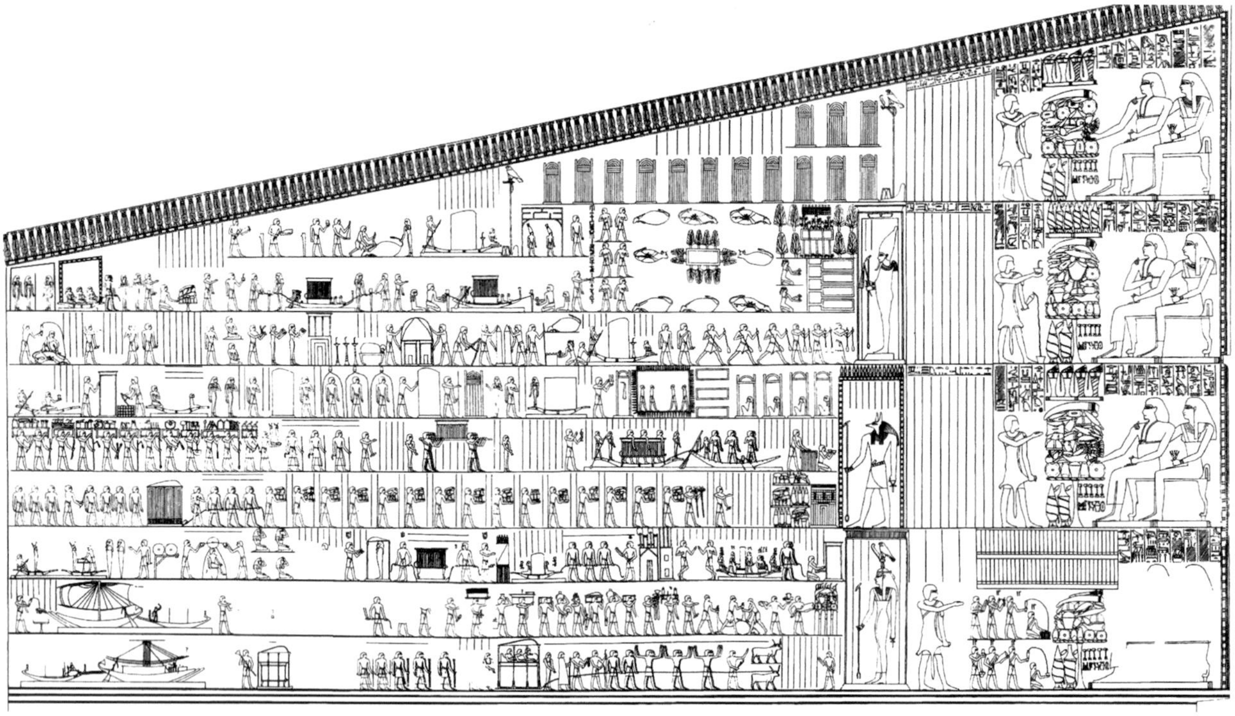

Figure 14: Line drawing of the south wall of the passage from the tomb of Rekhmire (TT 100). Adapted from N. Davies 1973: plate XXIV.

happens to have been situated in the necropolis. Thus, the comprehensive scenes in the tomb of Rekhmire clarify two important details about the Sacred District: its status as a separate entity from anything that takes place at the Delta shrines and its nature as a divine place superimposed on the necropolis in general.

There are some exceptions to this scene's regular placement on the left wall of the passage of a T-shape tomb. For example, Reneny's tomb at Elkab (TC 7) shows the Sacred District depicted on the *right* wall of his rectangular tomb, instead of the left wall (see chapter nine). Yet, three of the most unusual placements of the Sacred District occur in TT 39, TT 41, and TT 122.

Oriented toward Hatshepsut's temple at Deir el-Bahri, the tomb of Puiemre (TT 39) is situated at the site of Khôkha, to the north of Sheikh Abd el-Qurna. Most of the tombs of Hatsheput's officials are located on the north slope of Sheikh Abd el-Qurna and grouped around the Asasif as a whole, in and around the causeway leading to her temple. In her study of TT 39, Barbara Engelmann-von Carnap describes the artists' work in the tombs of Hatshepsut's high officials as, "unusual, original, and also cleverly thought-out and varied...." This was true for influential high officials and for other administrators as well (ex. TT 110 and TT 127).[262] These novel ideas are prominent in the tomb of Puiemre (TT 39). His tomb is not as close as Senenmut's tomb, but it is still nearby to Hatshepsut's valley temple.[263] The plan of TT 39 is also unusual in that it resembles a traditional T-shaped tomb but has two additional rooms that open off the transverse hall and flank the passage in a parallel fashion. The passage is also extremely short, and the tomb's entrance does not face east, but opens onto the processional route. This means that the rear of the tomb faces south, and not west. The question thus arise, is the transverse hall functioning as a passage would in a traditional T-shaped tomb? The largest of the three chambers sits on the right side of the tomb, or on its west end. On the back wall of this chamber is a false door, and Puiemre's burial chamber lies behind it.[264] It is in this chamber that the Sacred District scene is illustrated. The destination of the funeral procession is configured as the Goddess of the West (the actual tomb?) who stands on the right wall of the chapel (the west wall of the west chapel). So, the positioning of the Sacred District scene in this instance responds to the architecture of the tomb. On the north side of the west wall three Sacred District micro-scenes are shown in the bottom register: the pool with palms (two sycamore also line the bottom of the pool), the women's tent, and the guardians of the great gate (Figure 15).

Theban Tomb 122, although fragmentary, is another

[262] Engelmann-von Carnap 2014: 359.

[263] Engelmann-von Carnap 2014: 343.

[264] Engelmann-von Carnap 2014: 350.

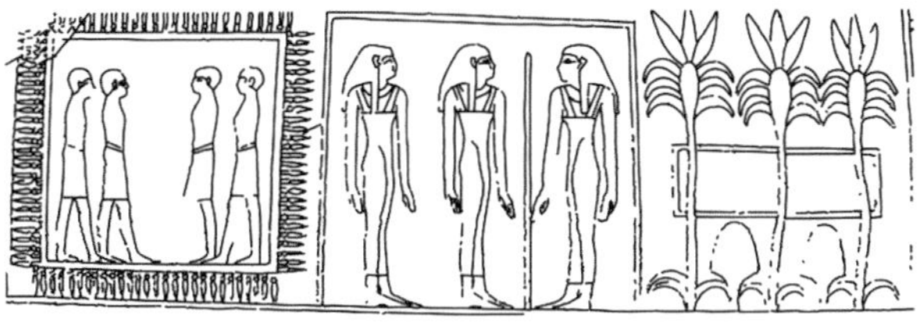

Figure 15: Line drawing of the Sacred District as it appears on the north wall of the north chapel in the tomb of Puiemre, TT 39. Adaptation by Roman Reed after N. Davies 1923: plate XLVII.

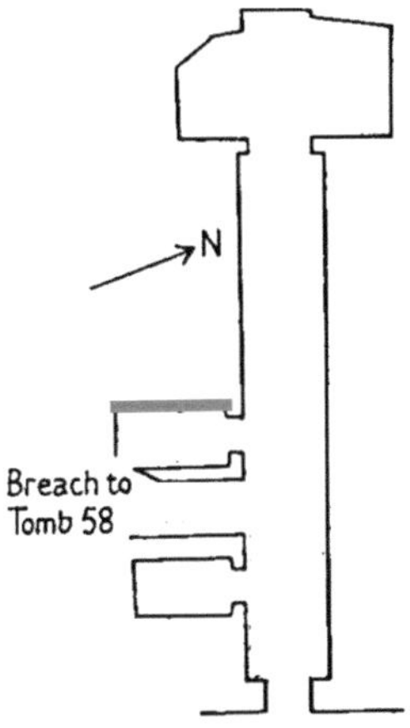

Figure 16: Plan of TT 122 noting the placement of the Sacred District scene. Adapted from Porter and Moss 1970: 232.

example of a tomb with an unorthodox positioning of the Sacred District scene (Figure 16). Located on the northern slope of Sheikh Abd el-Qurna, TT 122 has a distinctive architectural plan, with a long corridor and unfinished rear chamber with a niche. There are three side chapels that open off of the south wall of the corridor, and there is an intrusive small chamber jutting off the northwest corner.[265] Side chambers are not a normal feature of eighteenth dynasty tombs, but when they do appear in a traditional T-shaped tomb, they are usually constructed symmetrically.[266] This tomb was used by two contemporary individuals: Amenhotep and Amenemhet (with the side chapels belonging to the latter). According to JJ Shirley, the kinship terminology found in the inscriptions in this tomb indicate that the owner of the side chambers was part of a younger generation than the owner of the corridor, and that the rear chamber and side chambers date to the latter part of the reign of Thutmose III.[267] She suggests that we might be looking at a case of father and son taking part in a tomb-sharing endeavor, but this cannot be confirmed.[268]

The Sacred District scene appears on the west wall of the Third Chapel (Chapel B in Porter and Moss). There are four registers showing the funerary procession but there are no extant inscriptions. What is curious is the decorative flow of the wall. In the bottom two registers, the scenes are oriented from south to north (or left to right), while the top two registers move from right to left, or in the opposite direction. This Sacred District is in the third, or middle register, with the rites to the mooring-post on the second to bottom register (Figure 17). On the opposite wall of the chapel, among the rites performed in front of the deceased's mummy, there is a slaughtering scene. Slaughtering areas are also illustrated within the Sacred District in Theban Tombs 100, 21, 81, 179, 127, 112, 82, A4, 69, and 36.

Figure 17: Photo of the Sacred District scene and the rites to the mooring-post as they appear in the tomb of Amenhotep and Amanemhet (TT 122). Photo by author.

The tomb of Amenemope (TT 41) is also different from the majority of the tombs that illustrate the Sacred District. This tomb is one of the latest New Kingdom tombs to include this scene, and so it is an anomaly in that respect. Likewise, the placement of the Sacred District in the top two registers and the manner in which it turns the corner, continuing from one wall to the other, are also unusual features (Figure

265 Shirley 2010: fig. 1.
266 Shirley 2010: 272.
267 Shirley 2010: 280.
268 Shirley 2010: 291.

Figure 18: Photo of the Sacred District scene on the west wall of the transverse hall of the tomb of Amenemope (TT 41). Photo by author.

18). Additionally, the Sacred District does not appear in its usual place on the left wall of the passage but instead begins on the left wall, or south wall of the pillared transverse hall and then turns the corner onto the west wall running toward the opening of the passage. On the left or south wall of the court there is a less elaborate funeral scene that includes the rites to the mooring-post. So, the rendition of the Sacred District here is quite unconventional, perhaps because of the later date of this tomb. TT 41 was constructed beside that of Djehuty (TT 110), who has a Sacred District scene in his tomb, so it is possible that the idea to include this scene was passed to Amenemope in this manner.

Theban Tomb 41 provides an interesting case for studying the Sacred District scene because it dates to a later period. It differs from most scenes in a variety of ways, and for this reason it may tell us more about the function or purpose of the scene. Assmann has discussed the increasing "sacralisation" of New Kingdom tombs and he sees a transition from the tomb as a "house of the dead" to becoming a "private mortuary temple."[269] For example, one major architectural change that takes place after the Amarna Period is in the layout of the courtyard in front of the tomb. Previously, they served the cult of the deceased and his communication with his family. However, later they acted as a private temple court where the tomb owner could worship the gods.[270] Assmann notes that a similar change took place in the interior tomb decoration as well.[271] It is probably for this reason that the Sacred District scene has been reorganized and repositioned higher up on the wall in the tomb of Amenemope, a late eighteenth dynasty tomb.

Summary

The evidence shows that most examples of the Sacred District scene have been discovered at the Sheikh Abd el-Qurna subdivision of the Theban necropolis. Their location and date are connected because this hill was developed during the reign of Hatshepsut, when the production of the Sacred District scene peaks. However, some of the earliest New Kingdom examples come from Dra Abu el-Naga, the royal necropolis of the seventeenth dynasty. It may have been at this time that the Sacred District scene was copied into the tombs at the more southern site of Elkab since the family who governed that city at the time had royal ties. Or the transfer may have occurred in the other direction. There are even earlier depictions of only the *Mww* in tombs at both Thebes (TT 60) and Elkab (TC 10). With earlier examples of the *Mww* appearing in various parts of Egypt it is challenging to trace the spread of this imagery which eventually produced the Sacred District scene in the early eighteenth dynasty. Kampp-Seyfried's tomb category V is the most common type to illustrate the Sacred District, most likely because this is the style of tomb that was built during the reign of Hatshepsut when the scene's popularity increased. Typically, it appears on the left wall of the passage on one of the lower registers. However, the tomb of Rekhmire (TT 100), which places the Sacred District in several of the upper registers, demonstrates that this scene echoes an area associated with the necropolis, and is separate from the voyages to the sacred Delta localities and Abydos. In Theban Tomb 41, where the decorative program has dictated that the religiously important scenes appear in the upper registers, the Sacred District scene is placed there as well. It is difficult to judge what this change in positioning signifies.

[269] Assmann 2003: 46–49.

[270] Kampp-Seyfried 2003: 10.

[271] Assmann 2003: 46–52.

CHAPTER FIVE: GARDENS IN ANCIENT EGYPT

Since natural elements feature prominently in the Sacred District scene it is only fitting that a discussion on gardens is included in this work. The Sacred District scene offers a unique example of an ancient Egyptian garden landscape that is highly recognizable by its standard features. The combination of micro-scenes that isolate the Sacred District from the funerary scenes, and distinguish it from other garden scenes, not only create a backdrop for ritual activity, but also imbue this liminal space with magic to guide the deceased to Osiris and to sustain him in the afterlife. These micro-scenes characterize this space as lush, watery, fertile, and rejuvenating—all qualities symbolic of the god Osiris. As a landscape for funerary ritual, the Sacred District offers a setting for interaction with the divine. It was these objectives that controlled the scene's design.

Sacred District as a Landscape

To use the word "landscape" to describe the Sacred District is quite imprecise. Landscape can mean many things—various concepts, countless definitions, several aesthetic visions—and the different ways that people interact with landscapes are almost unending. Wendy Ashmore and A. Bernard Knapp, in their work *Archaeologies of Landscape: Contemporary Perspectives*, reveal that there is a plurality of coda by which landscape may be interpreted.[272] This means that in the ancient Near East certain landscapes have remained important because of sacred events having taken place there, such as cosmologically or mythically significant events and that these were dynamic places that gathered things together, such as associations, experiences, histories, and memories.[273] Landscapes are both natural and cultural as they are places that are often experienced through activities and performances that express a group's identity in relation to others.[274] Paul Coones, in his article "One landscape or many? A geographical perspective" expresses the idea that it is the "complex, interrelated and unified material product of the geographical environment," in which nature and human activities interpenetrate.[275] To fully understand the Sacred District, both the cultural and physical landscape must be studied in tandem, as this scene expresses the connections between the Egyptians and their environment.

The cultural and physical connection is something that has often been overlooked in landscape analysis in preference to political or economic motivation.[276] Landscapes can also do many things: map memory, declare identity, and help interpret society.[277] Possibly most important for this study, landscape can become a key reference point for the expression of individual or group identity. As a landscape, therefore, the Sacred District can be interpreted from many perspectives: political, religious, historical, and mythical, to name only the more obvious avenues. Because of this, no amount of analytical thought will allow us to fully understand this scene and what it meant to every individual or group. The micro-scenes in the Sacred District mean more than this one depiction shows. Each one is more significant than its spatial background. In a way, the Sacred District scene, therefore, cannot be pinned down or interpreted singularly, and it maintains its ambiguity for its plurality of interpretations.

This work is in some ways the study of a historic cultural landscape, a landscape scene produced by the artists of the New Kingdom that reflects a cultural memory infused with their surroundings, whether that be Thebes or Abydos, that embodied one perspective of the Sacred District. This scene shows a piece of land that has been altered from a space to a place through human activity, such as the planting of trees, the construction of garden plots, and the digging of basins. These artists were literally constructing the Theban landscape through tomb production, while reproducing another landscape on the tomb walls. This work is an attempt to classify and evaluate the sets of artifacts in this landscape. The Sacred District is in itself a "quasi artifact," part nature and part culture, in that it was culturally fashioned but represents non-human elements.[278]

It may be useful to think of the Sacred District as "ideational." Even though a landscape is always an objective physical space, it is also a subjective cognized image of that place.[279] This means that we might consider the scene to be an external object

[272] Ashmore and Knapp 1999: 19.

[273] Richards 1999: 83.

[274] Tilley 2006: 14; Ashmore and Knapp 1999: 14. I understand that these are not universal terms, but I think they are useful in discussing the Sacred District.

[275] Coones 1985: 5.

[276] Richards 1999: 84.

[277] Ashmore and Knapp 1999: 16.

[278] Tilley 2006: 19.

[279] Tilley 2006: 20.

that was corelative with an idea. It is a landscape of the mind that is imaginative, emotional, and inside a particular point of view.[280] It is imaginative because it is a mental image. It is emotional because it elicits some spiritual value or an ideal. And it shows an insider's perspective. Ironically, I am imposing ideational notions from the outside, as an Egyptologist. According to Ashmore and Knapp, ideational landscapes can provide a moral message, recount mythic histories, and record genealogies, but in general they do not suggest a unified doctrine or ideology. This means the Sacred District was produced by the artists, desired by the tomb owners, and understood by the chapel's viewers, which represent a tripartite appreciation. These images were mediated by their ideas about their world and their social identities. The artists presumably knew what memories or ideas were associated with this imagery, so they did not spell it out. Or perhaps, they did not fully understand it either, at least in its original intent. However, the Sacred District is a conceptual landscape, and only a constructed landscape in the sense that a picture of it was reproduced by artists.

Certain micro-scenes within the Sacred District developed in art over a long period of time (ex. the *Mww*), while others appear for the first time in the New Kingdom. So, to the modern viewer aspects of the Sacred District seem old, such as the *Mww* or the Delta shrines, when it is quite possible that their use in this landscape was really more recent in origin, and possibly (re-)invented. In fact, establishing an "identity" for a place can be tricky because its meaning can vary. The physical landscape inevitably influenced society, and what people did in and around the Theban necropolis affected how they reproduced this environment. In this sense, both landscapes and reproduction of landscapes had agency and affect.

Landscape and History

One function of a landscape is its ability to identify with specific histories. It can do this because a landscape can embody time. Multiple times and multiple places simultaneously materialize, which exhibit both continuity and sequence, and change and transformation.[281] The presence of these shrines arrests time and change and provides something traditionally authentic to the Sacred District illustrations. They might also be symbolic of historical beginnings or memories of a glorious past and be useful as tools of legitimation.

The Sacred District is a cultural landscape that has been maintained collectively in symbolic and ceremonial terms through its artistic reproduction. By adding historical elements into the illustration, the artists, or society at large demonstrate the social and sacred significance of this place. Special markers within the Sacred District single out past events. For example, Osiris as legendary king who rose from the dead to live in the hereafter is evidenced by his presence. Any markers that could even be loosely associated with the Delta have historical significance. The Hall of the *Mww* and the Delta shrines (even if the latter scene is adjacent to the Sacred District scene) have some political, mythic, or historical importance. These decorated tomb chapels are aids to remember the past and they help to preserve memories, but in a selective manner.

A symbolic return to the past often acts as a retreat from an uncertain present.[282] If this can apply to the Sacred District, then maybe there was a societal need to root and maintain one identity in response to some sort of political change. Perhaps a new family from the south seizing power? The Sacred District scene emerges at the end of the seventeenth dynasty during a politically tumultuous time. Another way to think about this is if things are required to be preserved it must be because they have already been forgotten (and this scene appears only in Upper Egypt). So, what is it about this landscape that might need to be remembered? When the Theban artists illustrated the sacred Delta localities, they transformed them locally so that these shrines become reconfigured from the outside. Power can also be attributed to certain landscapes, like the Sacred District, or elements within the Sacred District like the pools of water. These natural features have power or qualities that are desirable and might be considered sacred or holy, but not necessarily. Or it could be through mental superimposition that a sacredness is attributed to these pools of water, perhaps because of the qualities they possess. In this case, to hydrate the deceased in the arid desert. The various sources of water and the vegetation might be special markers that symbolize fertility.

It is a popular idea to think of a landscape as a "palimpsest" in that archaic forces form a powerful deposit of cultural significance. And, according to Ashmore and Knapp, what creates this palimpsest is "the repetitive use and structured modification of an ideational landscape."[283] Particular practices and

280 Ashmore and Knapp 1999: 12.

281 Ashmore and Knapp 1999: 18.

282 Tilley 2006: 14.

283 Ashmore and Knapp 1999: 18.

meaning melt away and new ones emerge in the same space.[284] The Sacred District is a landscape that appears to have been worked and re-worked by people over time, at least in its artistic rendition, and interpreted and understood from different agendas, throughout the ancient past (and in the modern era). It was both the past and the present when it was reproduced in the New Kingdom private tombs. For example, the shrines of the Delta restore architecturally the past *in* the present, and project possibilities for the future.

Landscape and Myth

Mythical, cosmological concepts and folk memories of burial grounds were embedded in the collective memory of the Theban community and in the individual memories of its members. The ancient Egyptians have left behind an abundant mortuary record that allows us some insight into how they perceived death. These memories and ideas were used as ways to exist in their landscape and utilize the Theban necropolis. It was through memory that the repetition of this cultural landscape in the tomb decoration (or its continuity in general) was accomplished. These illustrations cannot be interpreted in a vacuum but as products of human creativity. By re-using the Sacred District scene and reinterpreting its micro-scenes over time, the artists re-inscribed past meaning onto their contemporary landscape, and reinterpreted part of the Theban necropolis in terms of Abydos (mythical and political) and the Delta (mythical and historical). Ancient Egyptian myths assimilate historical events and processes into a local understanding of the world, and this is what makes the world seem self-evident and obvious to people. In this way, the afterlife could be understood in terms of the familiar features of Thebes or Abydos. The relationship is not arbitrary. This concept is succinctly stated by Christopher Tilley in his 2006 article "Introduction: Identity, Place, Landscape and Heritage": "[t]he 'inside' of the myth embedded in the local, in place, incorporates knowledge of the world beyond."[285] These myths can also manipulate time so that past and present can exist side by side and help produce the desired future.

Names

Names are of vital significance because they transform a physical space into something historically and socially experienced.[286] In essence, names create landscapes. Landscape is connected with the understanding and describing of things as they are experienced, and in a sense, it is the objectification of that process.[287] Human experiences, feelings and thoughts help shape how the ancient Egyptians knew their places. And, of course, places are more than locations because they have meaning and value for people. The Sacred District scene is not generally accompanied by narrative inscriptions, but what they do include are names. Labels, such as "guardians of the great gate," "shrine of Osiris," "pool of Sokar," etc. proliferate this landscape. These captions transform a rather generic space into something that is historically, socially, and mythically experienced. By giving these micro-scenes names, the artists have created places of human import. In fact, a description of this setting is accomplished only through these place names. The names are used as contextualizing devices for people to locate a narrative event within the landscape.[288]

Mapping

The illustrations of the Sacred District could also be interpreted as a form of a map. The purpose of all maps is to clearly depict a geographical space. It is common among all people to have a need for an image of the environment in which they live. This is a map of sorts that stands on its own without much context or narrative about the micro-scenes, except for the surrounding funerary scenes and its placement in a tomb. The "map" is supplemented with images (the micro-scenes themselves) but is otherwise static and without scale. This "map" provides a semi-linear progression but is interrupted by the breakdown into multiple registers. This can allow for the emergence of a non-linear narrative for the modern viewer, which may or may not have been intended by the ancient artists. The modern "reader," however, may make connections that the ancient artists did not intend.

Peter Robinson's work on applying cognitive geography to ancient Egypt provides a useful viewpoint for interpreting this image as a map.[289] He states that cognitive maps tend to be selective in their portrayal of environs in that the information is filtered before being illustrated. Areas that are familiar to the map creators tend to be exaggerated in size, while areas less familiar, or farther away, tend to be smaller and distorted.[290] This misinterpretation of faraway places

[284] Heynickx, *et al.* 2012: 8.
[285] Tilley 2006: 25.
[286] Tilley 1994: 18.
[287] Tilley 1994: 12.
[288] Tilley 1994: 19.
[289] Robinson 1996: 6–44; Robinson 2005.
[290] Robinson 1996: 8.

lends itself to cognitive stereotypes.[291] It is necessary to take into consideration that the Sacred District was an unfamiliar place that no one had visited and come back to tell of it. Therefore, renditions are not based on the first-hand experiences of the creators actually seeing a physical place.

There is no doubt that artists from the New Kingdom were experienced draftsmen and fully capable of rendering a particular geographical area, albeit in a stylized form. The ancient Egyptians perceived their world from the Delta lands of the north looking south toward the Nile valley and were keenly aware of the rising and setting of the sun. Hence, their word for "east" was related to their word for "left" and their word for "west" was related to their word for "right."[292] The visualization of the Sacred District by the artist, at least in the beginning, was an amalgamation of several ideas and physical spaces. As time progressed, new images of the Sacred District were based on images with which the artist was familiar. So, the Sacred District scene that is portrayed in the private tombs is an example of art performing the function of a map.

Attempts to describe the Otherworld date back to the Old Kingdom, when in the *Pyramid Texts* the routes to arrive there were explained. This phenomenon continued into the Middle Kingdom through the descriptions of the hereafter in the *Coffin Texts* and the *Book of Two Ways*. Both the *Pyramid Texts* and the *Coffin Texts* mention an area called the "Field of Reeds," a type of paradise to spend the rest of one's life. This area is only marginally related to the Sacred District scene, but it is a parallel example of an ancient location that no one had ever visited, yet it appears as if a real location is depicted. The afterlife books of the New Kingdom are interpreted as showing the deceased passing through various dangerous realms and uttering special incantations to allow for safe passage. In essence, these illustrations were meant as a comprehensive guide through these regions, supplying views of the landscape at the same time. When writing about the New Kingdom books of the afterlife, Robinson rightly states that it is not unreasonable to view these vignettes as maps, or route-planners, through the afterlife.[293] This could also apply to the Sacred District scene.[294]

Artistic Conventions

The ancient Egyptians did not have a word that corresponds to our idea of "art," which has an aesthetically pleasing aspect, and for this reason it is often said that ancient Egyptian art always had a function associated with it.[295] According to Gay Robins, "to represent was…to create," so there is a need to understand why a particular depiction was produced and why it took its particular form.[296] Ancient Egyptian art has often been criticized for being static and unchanging, and for the lack of skill evident in some pieces; however, none of this was relevant to the ancient Egyptians because it had little to do with a work's purpose.[297] It was the most recognizable version of something that was always shown. In this respect, being creative was not what was important to the artist or the viewer. It was making the entity known through its most characteristic aspect. For example, offering bearers carrying just boxes was not sufficient for the ancient Egyptians; they needed to also have shown what was inside the boxes, and they did so by illustrating the contents on top of them.

For two-dimensional art, designs were ordered by a system of registers whereby the lower border acted as the ground line on which the figures stood. Items could not be randomly placed in a composition, as this would exude chaos—there were a series of conventions geared to combat chaos. Stacked items meant that what was on top should be interpreted as behind what was on the bottom. In overlapping items, the Egyptians demonstrated that what was behind was further from the viewer than what was in front. Size was an indicator of importance, and the relative height of a person mirrored his or her social position. The king was always taller than his subjects, but only slightly shorter than, or the same size as, the gods. It is not unusual to find hieroglyphs intermingled with illustrations, and short texts could act as captions or labels for the participants. Sometimes these texts balanced out a scene, or the image itself acted as a determinative for the caption.

When depicting plants and trees in the Sacred District, the artists made a compromise between the

[291] Robinson 1996: 9.

[292] Robinson 1996: 11.

[293] Robinson 1996: 33.

[294] It was possibly the *Mww* who were thought to navigate the waterways of the Sacred District for the deceased (Reeder 1995). This may account for the "rites to the mooring-post" regularly performed in the vicinity of the Sacred District (see Appendix I, §18). It was not unusual for travel to be by boat in the various afterlife books of the New Kingdom and the *Book of the Dead* (Robinson 1996: 34).

[295] Stevenson Smith 1998: 1–6; Robins 2008: 12ff.

[296] Robins 2008: 12.

[297] Robins 2008: 19.

ideal and the actual.[298] To some extent, these plants were symbolic, but often the plants were true botanical illustrations that provide enough detail to confirm the identification of the plant. These illustrations, especially in a mortuary context, were imagined to come alive in the next world and exist for the benefit of the deceased. There were fixed conventions for representing gardens and little leeway to change or disregard them, so the ancient Egyptians employed simultaneously aerial views, plans, profiles, and frontal views of their subjects. Egyptian art has been considered "a-spective" because objects were shown "as known" not "as-seen."[299] Sometimes details are portrayed that would otherwise have been hidden; an example is the offering bearers, mentioned above. Because the Sacred District scene shows a timeless reality, as opposed to one specific moment in time, individual details are not necessary. Convention outranked individuality. That being said, the Sacred District scene appears in multiple versions within the various tombs. For example, two sycamore trees are represented in some tombs, but not in others. Some Sacred Districts have garden plots, and some do not. But although the *combination* of micro-scenes (or episodes) differs dramatically from one tomb to another, there are only small difference in the details of an individual micro-scene. Again, using the sycamore tree as an example, sometimes the artist created this tree in a rather leafy manner. Other times, he drew only the outline which resembled more a triangle on a stick. Primarily, the plants and trees needed to be recognizable, while style and creativity were not as important. It is possible that some of the variance seen in examples like the sycamore tree might be due more to the artistic ability of the artist than anything else.

Plants and flowers were usually shown from their most representative viewpoint. Sometimes characteristics like fruiting or flowering were shown in order to make a tree more recognizable. However, two different trees could be shown side by side in their best recognizable forms even if in reality those forms did not occur simultaneously according to season. They could be shown from above, in profile, and sometimes from below. Sometimes the tree illustrations correspond to their image as signs in the hieroglyphic script, which makes identification easier. However, the sign for sycamore tree often functioned as a determinative for any number of tree names, which makes recognition more challenging because it is sometimes difficult to associate an ancient Egyptian tree name with an actual tree.

Enclosed spaces within the Sacred District, such as the Hall of the *Mww*, were usually shown in aerial view (bird's eye view), but the people inside were shown in profile. Conversely, the gods' shrines in the Sacred District are depicted in frontal view, and when they are open the deities inside are shown in profile. This systematization reiterates the timeless reality of the Sacred District.

Ancient Egyptian Gardens

At first glance, the Sacred District appears as a garden scene. Evidence of gardens in ancient Egypt can be seen in archaeological remains, documents written on stone or papyrus, illustrations, and models.[300] The most extensive garden scenes date to the New Kingdom, and in most cases, the construction of a garden was inspired by the need to create a concrete reality for a mythical place, as described in religious literature.[301] Connected to this idea is the notion that tomb garden representations were intended to instigate the regeneration of the deceased. There are plenty of regenerative symbols present in garden scenes, and for this reason the ancient Egyptians deemed the garden a blessed place in and of itself.[302] There is also a general consensus among scholars that when a garden is present in a tomb scene the deceased would benefit from its produce in that the garden would actualize for him in the afterlife, and everything in the scene would remain available to sustain the deceased eternally.[303] Therefore, a garden protected the deceased against hunger and thirst, and provided him with an agreeable future. The pictures of plants and trees were understood, not as strict representations, but as the actual plant itself that would soon be brought to life by magical means.[304] Plants could also be used in tomb illustrations as a background, or context, for human activities when performed in their ideal condition. Although the Sacred District scene appears in tomb decoration and is part of the funerary scenes, it is distinct from an ordinary tomb garden for the deceased for several reasons.

---

[298] Weeks 1979: 69; A. Wilkinson 1998: 16.

[299] A. Wilkinson 1998: 17.

[300] A. Wilkinson 1998: 2. See Daines (2008: 15) and Loeben and Kappel (2009) for a summary of past research on gardens not included here.

[301] A. Wilkinson 1994b: 2.

[302] Robins 2008: 12ff.

[303] Bolshakov 1997: 210–213, 264–266; A. Wilkinson 1998: 15–16; Hartwig 2004: 37–40.

[304] A. Wilkinson 1998: 15.

Figure 19: Photo of area in front of Hatshepsut's Temple of Millions of Years at Deir el-Bahri. Photo by author.

Before we can understand why the Sacred District is a distinct garden, we have to recognize normal patterns of garden construction. The seasonally inundated alluvial plain was most suitable for creating an ancient Egyptian garden, and more specifically, the ridges and hillocks along the fertile area offered a place where the ponds could access the underground water but where the plants, trees, and flowers could not be damaged by the inundation. There is also sufficient archaeological evidence for the maintenance of gardens in infertile soil in the desert, for example, the recently discovered garden plots near TT 11 and TT 12 at Dra Abu el-Naga by José Galán's Spanish Mission and the now well-known garden plots from Tell el-Amarna.[305] There is also evidence at Hatshepsut's Temple of Millions of Years at Deir el-Bahri, among other places, for trees having been planted in the courtyard and for the installation of pools (Figure 19).[306] Likewise, the excavations conducted by the Austrian mission at Avaris under Manfred Bietak have revealed trees and tombs in combination, but the terrain may not have been as arid as in Upper Egypt.[307]

A good inundation was important for agriculture in ancient Egypt. The Nile had a very predictable cycle that dictated farming activities. In fact, the ancient Egyptian calendar named its seasons after the three agricultural stages: inundation (*akhet*), coming forth (*peret*), and dry season (*shemu*). Every June and July the Blue Nile flooded in the highlands of Ethiopia when the summer monsoon rains fell. This would bring the inundation into Upper Egypt in late July and early August, with the more northern parts of Egypt flooding slightly later. The ancient Egyptians directed and controlled the water in the natural flood basins of the Nile Valley in order to maximize its effectiveness. This type of agricultural system is called "basin irrigation."[308] Levees were built, and cross-cutting dikes were created to manipulate the flow of the water. Beginning in the New Kingdom, the *shaduf* was used to move water from one place to another. The s*haduf* consisted of a bucket connected by rope to a long, weighted lever. It could not move large amounts of water, but it would have been ideal for watering small garden plots. The water wheel was a more effective way to lift water to higher elevations, but it was not introduced into Egypt until Graeco-Roman times. There was little rain in ancient Egypt, which made the Nile's water essential.[309] If the Nile's inundation was low for several years in a row, the food supply would be reduced, and it could have meant famine. However, when the flooding was too high, villages could be destroyed, and the excess water could wreak havoc on the villagers. Since the inundation water arrived in Egypt late in the month of July, in conjunction with the heliacal rising of the star Sirius, it was July 19th that served as the first day of the New Year. The fact that the inundation marked the ancient Egyptian New Year signifies its importance for the ancient Egyptians.

The layout of any garden reflected its purpose. Most plants were chosen for tomb art because of their symbolic significance. This meaning dictated where they would be "planted" or situated within any given composition. Orchards, vegetable gardens, and flower gardens were planted and grown in ancient Egypt. Avenues of trees were also quite common and could provide a cool tunnel through a garden or create a protective wall. Orchards of fruit trees were planted in rows, often around a pool, and vegetables were grown in rectangular plots, just like in modern Egypt today (Figure 20).

In addition to vegetation, Egyptian gardens also included hard landscaping. Often, natural elements were flanked by buildings, which offered structure for the gardens. Buildings and structures could furnish a background for plants and provide texture for the composition. A garden house was a common element in the necropolis garden scenes found in the Theban tombs and were typically located in close proximity to the garden pond. However, no garden houses are

305 Galán, "4,000 Year Old Funerary Garden"; Galán 2020: 40–47; Galán and Garcia 2019: 4–8; Moens 1984: 36.

306 A. Wilkinson 1994b: 12.

307 Bietak 1994 and 1996.

308 Butzer 1976.

309 Baines and Málek 1980: 14.

Figure 20: Photo of garden plots in the modern village of Garagos in Upper Egypt. Photo by author.

Figure 21: Date palm. Luxor, Egypt. Photo by author.

found in the Sacred District scenes. The structures that do appear are two obelisks, the Hall of the *Mww*, the gods' shrines, a gate, and a tent. Most frequently, a pool or rows of shrines acted as the focal point for the arrangement of micro-scenes that comprised the Sacred District. Yet, there is an example in the tomb of Rekhmire (TT 100) where a slaughterhouse is positioned centrally.

The Egyptians appreciated symmetry in their landscaping with twin trees and pools frequently found in garden illustrations, and the Sacred District scenes are no exception.[310] Likewise, twin obelisks appear in some examples of the Sacred District, and when people are present, they too appear in pairs. Actors, such as the *Mww* and the *ḏr(y)ty* were often depicted in such a manner; however, there are usually three women inside the "women's tent." Geometrical arrangements also feature prominently in the Sacred District. The natural elements featured in this scene were highly structured, reflecting the general tendency to depict gardens as symmetrical units with geometry and pattern in their design.[311] Sculptures and statues could also appear in garden scenes, and in tomb gardens these represented the tomb owner. Yet, statues such as these do not occur in the Sacred District. Other standard garden items that do not appear in the Sacred District include terraces, walls, loggias, quays, and menageries.[312] In artistic depictions, fish and birds are often shown in and around smaller bodies of water, but this type of interaction is also conspicuously absent from the Sacred District scenes.

The Sacred District scene offers a series of features unique to its constitution. The chosen micro-scenes characterize this locale as generative, verdant, and revivifying, which also reflects many attributes of the god Osiris. Not only was this district a landscape for funerary ritual, but it was a setting where the deceased could interact with the divine on his way to the hereafter.

Trees and Plants

In an ancient Egyptian landscape, trees function as the focal point of most compositions. It was common for lines of trees to appear in the central part of a garden, and for trees to be planted in rows, forming parallel lines or rectangles. To create an equal distance between the planted trees was also common, and usually trees of the same species were planted in one row, but sometimes one can find two or more alternating species.[313] When gardens were created in the dry, infertile soil, pits were filled with Nile mud to provide fertile soil for the plants. These pits, with their brick or stone borders, do not appear in the

[310] A. Wilkinson 1998: 6.

[311] A. Wilkinson 1998: 7.

[312] For more information on these elements see A. Wilkinson 1998: 9–11.

[313] Moens 1984: 39.

Figure 22: Doum palm. Luxor, Egypt. Photo by author.

Sacred District scene. This might indicate that we are not seeing a desert garden or, at least not a garden that was a garden susceptible to the desert climate. Alternatively, the water sources that are illustrated close to the trees were intended to be sufficient. Trees appear in garden compositions as early as the first dynasty and they remain a standard feature in tomb scenes throughout the Pharaonic period. Date palms, doum palms, and sycamore-figs are the most common trees that were illustrated, and these are precisely the varieties that appear in the Sacred District scenes.

The date palm (*Phoenix dactylifera*) is an evergreen tree that can grow to a height of forty meters, is native to northern Africa, southwest Asia, and India, and grew all over Egypt (Figure 21).[314] Today, this is the most commonly cultivated tree in Egypt.[315] This tree has an undivided stem and often has off-shoots with pinnate leaves and small white flowers on a branched spadix surrounded by a solitary, large spathe.[316] The date palm can grow in a variety of soils as long as it is sufficiently irrigated for its shallow roots, which can withstand both drought and partial inundation.[317] The fruit is cylindrical, reddish-brown and has a pit inside. The fruits could be eaten dried, in fruitcakes, as a sweetener, or as extra ferment in beer.[318] As for their produce, date wine and date syrup come from this fruit and the Egyptians used the tree sap for palm wine. Dates are very rich in carbohydrates and proteins, and because of their high sugar content they were used in prescriptions as vehiculum.[319] Similarly, dates were found in treatments of ulcers and as vermifuge because of the tannins of the green date.[320] The wood of the date palm is light and fibrous, but also durable. It was used as building material and for making furniture. The leaves and the fibers surrounding the base were used for matting, basketwork, and funerary garlands, among other items, and as such, both the leaves and the dates are found in Egyptian decorations and crafts. The imitation of the leaves is also found in the palmiform columns that begin to appear in the fifth dynasty.[321] The Egyptian word for date palm is *benret*, of which the earliest writing occurs in the first dynasty at Abydos.[322]

Doum palms (*Hyphaene thebaica*) are also an evergreen tree, but differ from the date palm in that the trunk divides low on the tree so that the palm appears to have two stems (Figure 22).[323] They have a light chocolate-brown trunk with black stripes, and the leaves are palmate-cleft with a terminal crown on each branch, which resembles a large fan.[324] This tree features small, yellow flowers that bloom from February to April, and a spongy, sugary fruit with a pit, which can be eaten after being soaked in water. This is a slow-growing plant, and it produces fruit only for five to six years. The doum palm has long roots, which can easily reach the underground water and can thus grow on very arid soil. It can grow in the southern Nile Valley in silt and in the western oases in sandy soil.[325] The doum can tolerate high heat and even fire.[326] Today doum palms grow in Upper Egypt but are uncommon elsewhere. It was first identified in Thebes, hence the epithet *thebaica*.[327] The fact that doum palms were illustrated regularly in garden scenes in New Kingdom private tombs at Thebes, indicates that this tree must have been quite common in this area in ancient times, as well. Conversely, the palms that appear in the Sacred District do not have Y-forked stems, so this is not one of the species that appears within the Sacred District.

Like the date palm, the doum palm is also a useful tree. The water that gathers in the kernels of the doum

[314] Moens 1984: 30; A. Wilkinson 1998: 42.
[315] Springuel 2006: 115.
[316] This technical description comes from Moens 1984: 30.
[317] Springuel 2006: 115.
[318] Moens 1984: 31.
[319] Moens 1984: 31.
[320] Moens 1984: 31.
[321] Moens 1984: 31.
[322] Bircher 1995; Faulkner 1991: 83.
[323] A. Wilkinson 1998: 42.
[324] Moens 1984: 31.
[325] Springuel 2006: 110.
[326] Springuel 2006: 110.
[327] Springuel 2006: 110.

Figure 23: Sycamore-fig tree. Karnak Temple, Egypt. Photo by author.

palm nut could alleviate the thirst of the deceased.[328] It has also been suggested that the leaves of the doum palm blowing in the wind symbolized fresh air for the deceased.[329] The Egyptian word for doum palm is *mama*. The wood could be employed as building material and for making furniture as it is compact and hard, and its leaves were used for basketry and ropemaking. Likewise, its fruits are edible and could also be crushed to make a drink—one that is still popular in modern Egypt.

The argun palm is another species of palm tree that is now rarely found in modern Egypt.[330] It is difficult to know how common this tree was in antiquity, although it did grow in the gardens of Thebes during the New Kingdom.[331] Remains of the fruits of this tree were found in the tomb of Tutankhamun, and the tree is also known to have been included in gardens in the eighteenth dynasty.[332] Today it grows mostly in northern Sudan but in the 1950s it was rediscovered in the western oases.[333] It is possible that the argun palm was depicted in the Sacred District, and that the bottom layer of foliage in the depiction of the palms in the tomb of Puiemre (TT 39), for example, represents the old dry leaves drooping from the trunk.

Both the date palm and the doum palm were considered to be sacred trees in ancient Egypt and were associated with several gods and goddesses. The date palm was connected to Thoth, Min, and Re, and was also home to a tree-goddess. Thoth, the god of wisdom and writing, in his baboon form, was associated with the doum palm because baboons often fed on the fruit of this tree; in fact, several Pharaonic illustrations show the baboon on the doum-palm.[334]

The sycamore-fig (*Ficus Sycomorus* L.) is another tree that is illustrated in pairs in the Sacred District scene. The sycamore is a large evergreen tree that grows in warm climates and can reach a height of twenty meters (Figure 23).[335] This tree is not indigenous to Egypt but has been cultivated there for a long time. It is native to the southern Arabia peninsula and extends from north to tropical east Africa.[336] Currently, the sycamore fig grows in Upper Egypt, the western oases, and the Sinai, but not north of Cairo in the Delta region.[337] This tree can only grow

[328] Moens 1984: 45.

[329] Moens 1984: 45 after Bruyère-Kuentz (see note 217). See Theban Tomb 3 at Deir el-Medina (Porter and Moss 1970: 9–10).

[330] See figure 1 in Ali for a photograph of a single-stem argun palm with fan-shaped leaves (2016: 146).

[331] Springuel 2006: 113–114; Ali 2016: 145.

[332] Springuel 2006: 113; Ali 2016: 145.

[333] Ali 2016: 145.

[334] See Springuel 2006: 111 for a hand-drawing of a limestone *ostracon* from Thebes showing two baboons climbing a doum-palm, now in the Agricultural Museum. See Houlihan 1996: 210 for a monkey/baboon in a doum palm sketched in black and red ink on a limestone ostracon now in the Fitzwilliam Museum, University of Cambridge.

[335] Moens 1984: 29.

[336] Springuel 2006: 91.

[337] Springuel 2006: 91. This detail may be significant in the on-going debate about which real-life locale is illustrated in the Sacred District. The Egyptians were aware of their natural environment and probably would not have depicted a

in places where there is water close to the surface; the Nile Valley being an ideal location. The sycamore tree has deep roots and can be found in the bottom of dry washes at the edge of the desert.[338] The leaves are coarse and thick, and its foliage is dense; thus, it can provide a good amount of shade. It has a short, knotted trunk and provided durable wood for the Egyptians. The sycamore-fig belongs to the same family as the common fig tree and is a good source of both shade and fruit.[339] This tree produces fruit all year round and the figs grow on short thin stalks. The sycamore-fig is a plump receptacle holding a large bunch of small flowers on its inner surface.[340] When the sycamore fruit is represented in offerings, it is recognizable by the gash in each fruit.[341] This is also how they can be distinguished from the common fig. The sycamore-fig was a significant foodstuff in ancient Egypt, and the sap of the tree was used for medicinal purposes because of the pepsine it contained.[342] Its latex was also used to cure scorpion and snake bites and skin diseases.[343]

In Egyptian, the name of this tree is *nehet*.[344] The sycamore was a sacred tree to the ancient Egyptians and was imagined to be inhabited by the goddess Hathor, the goddess of love (among her many other attributes). The tree's symbolism today is similar to what it was in ancient Egypt. It was associated with lovers because it offered an isolated place where they could meet. The Love Songs of the New Kingdom attest to its qualities.[345] In the Sacred District this tree is stylized in various ways—compare the pear-shaped trees in TT 39 with the leafy-branched trees in TT 15. An actual sycamore tree growing in Egypt today resembles more closely the latter style; however, the former style is more commonly depicted in tomb decoration. This tree would certainly have made a good addition to any desert garden with the addition of good soil and frequent watering.

It is well known that the ancient Egyptians imported cedar from Lebanon to build large items, such as boats, but they also used local trees extensively. The trunks of palms could be used as ceiling rafters in homes, and the hard wood of the doum palm was perfect for furniture. Palm leaves were used for basketry, and palm ribs for boxes and furniture. Other local trees whose wood was used in crafts were the persea tree, sidder, tamarisk, acacia, and willow.

In addition to trees, there are several plants and flowers that appear regularly in garden scenes; however, they are conspicuously absent in all of the Sacred District scenes. One of the flowers that would be most expected in a tomb garden would be the lotus flower (blue water lily). It closes its petals at night and reopens them again with the rising sun in the morning. Due to this, the lotus is associated with fertility and rebirth, the key ingredients to any tomb's decorative program. The dead often identify themselves with the lotus because of this cycle of death to new life. The papyrus and the mandrake are plants that are regularly shown in tomb gardens, but curiously they do not appear in the Sacred District scene either. As all three plants function as symbols of fertility, rebirth, and resurrection, it is puzzling as to why they are not included, especially since it would have been beneficial to reproduce these qualities for the deceased. Similarly, there are no offerings shown in the Sacred District scenes, only empty braziers (which is a less common episode at that). One might expect to see illustrations of such resources in the tomb scenes so that the deceased could have access to them in the hereafter. However, the trees that are depicted, the date palm, the argun palm, and the sycamore-fig, do provide fruit and may have been perceived as encompassing this attribute. Or perhaps these gardens were intended to display only the bare necessities of shade (trees), food (garden plots) and water (pools and basins), whereas flowers were not essential.

Water Sources

As noted above, the pond is often shown as the focal point of the Sacred District scene, an item common in garden scenes in general because of its ability to offer a cool respite from the arid desert. A pool or pond would have been dependent on the underground water for its water supply, with the level of the inundation water in the nearby channels determining the height of the underground water. The Egyptians worked very hard to control the river water and divert it to where it was needed, and basin irrigation has been the norm in the Nile Valley.[346] Irina Springuel, in her book *The Desert Garden: A Practical Guide,* suggests that a subsurface irrigation system would have worked

tree from a foreign environment. This detail might suggest an Upper Egyptian location for the Sacred District.

338 Harlan 1986: 12.

339 Wilkinson 1998: 42.

340 Moens 1984: 29.

341 Harlan 1986: 12.

342 Moens 1984: 29.

343 Springuel 2006: 92.

344 Faulkner 1991: 135.

345 Fox 1985: 46–51, 78. Scamuzzi 1965: Turin Cat. 1966. Early twentieth dynasty.

346 Springuel 2006: 56; Butzer 1976.

well for desert plants, as the advantages of this type of system are that water could be brought directly to the roots so there would be no increase in the salinization of the soil, animals would not damage it, and water would not evaporate on the surface.[347] Specifically, "buried clay pot irrigation" is the traditional and most effective way to water desert plants. In this case, a clay pot is buried in the soil and filled with water. Water could seep through the porous clay into the soil. Tubes could also be used for plants with long roots.[348]

Pools were generally drawn in two shapes: rectangular and T-shaped. Only rectangular pools are found in the Sacred District. The Sacred District scene in the tomb of Amenemhet (TT 53) demonstrates that a border could be constructed around the pool to protect the trees and the vegetation planted there. If the border around the pool was painted green, this may have indicated surrounding vegetation.[349] Theban Tomb 53 offers a second example of a garden, but this time the trees appear to be planted around a basin. Considering the topography of the necropolis on the west bank of Thebes it seems unrealistic to suggest that natural ponds existed in the rocky, mountainous terrain where many of the tombs are located. Garden plots have been discovered in the less rocky landscape of Dra Abu el-Naga outside of TT 11 and TT 12, but family members probably watered these gardens manually or they might have used basins.[350] It would have been possible for water to be transferred to such basins from ponds located lower down. Since the pond assured a continuous irrigation of the garden, its central position in the Sacred District scene was an efficient one. Pools and ponds are not specific to just religious and mortuary settings—smaller pools have also been found in private dwellings.[351]

The subsoil of the flood plain west of the present Nile at Thebes has recently been used to prove the former existence of a minor branch of the Nile. It is thought that this branch emerged by a regional partial river avulsion and was then silted up at the end of the New Kingdom. A flood basin divided the New Kingdom channel from the main channel of the Nile in the central axis of the valley. This appears to have been a natural branch that was not manipulated by humans.[352] This is significant for understanding the cultural activity on the west bank because this channel would have facilitated transportation to the various ritual places and supplied a closer water source. This channel's existence may also help us to better understand the configuration of this area in terms of ritual activity. It may also explain the artistic renditions of this landscape found in the Theban Tombs and the availability of water to the Theban necropolis.

The Plan

Most gardens are depicted as being rectangular or square in plan and typically have a main entrance. The pool, surrounded by trees, commonly marked the center of the Sacred District and was the most eye-catching component because of the bright blue paint. In the case of the Sacred District, it appears as though the Hall of the *Mww* functioned as the entrance point. Usually, the main entrance to a garden and a pond are shown in the same longitudinal axis, which is attested to in the Sacred District scene in the tomb of Reneny at Elkab (TC 7). Here the *Mww* stand in their hall on the right side of the area and face left toward the pool, which is surrounded by seven palms. This same symmetry appears in Theban Tomb 53 where two *Mww* stand in their hall and face left toward the pool (or basin), four palm trees, and four sycamore trees. Garden scenes are also usually formal, symmetrical, and functional, in that the geometric planning also facilitated irrigation. Many garden scenes include an enclosure wall, however, this feature in not present in the Sacred District scenes.

The manner in which the different micro-scenes within the larger composition of the Sacred District are arranged suggests some sort of fixed planning, and sometimes gives the impression of a proscribed area, even though the illustrations do not detail any sort of enclosure. It is easy to imagine an enclosed, or delineated area, considering the register lines that provide order for the illustrations, and also form the ground lines. The register lines are employed to separate vertically scenes of different content. In her article "Narration in Egyptian Art," Helene Kantor explains that items in a specific frieze are unified by their common ground line and thus separated from items in other friezes.[353] Even though having privacy and protection in this liminal space would probably have been important, a physical enclosure was not necessary or desirable around the Sacred District. The vertical registers functioning as ground lines, the episodic nature of the micro-scenes, the architectural features of the tomb, and the deities who bracket the

347 Springuel 2006: 58.
348 Springuel 2006: 59, fig. 19.
349 Moens 1984: 38.
350 Galán, "4,000 Year Old Funerary Garden.
351 A. Wilkinson 1998: 10–11.
352 Toonen *et al.* 2018.

353 Kantor 1957: 44–45.

end of the registers, all help to encapsulate the Sacred District, making the addition of a physical wall repetitive.

Alternatively, horizontal ground lines could evoke a false connection when they are related to a figure taller than the individual registers.[354] In the case of the Sacred District scene, it is Osiris, Anubis, or the Goddess of the West, who bracket the registers and function as the destination of the funeral procession and journey of the deceased. One example is the scene in the tomb of Paheri at Elkab (TC 3) where the viewer sees the deceased kneeling before Osiris at the end of the left wall, closest to the focal point of the chapel. Here Osiris sits on his throne in his shrine and faces the deceased. His image brackets the two registers to the left of his shrine. The larger figure of Osiris at the end of the register is connected to both of the shorter registers to the left, as opposed to just the bottom register with which it shares a ground line.

The placement of the Sacred District scene among the funerary scenes suggests narration; a type of narration that begins in the Old Kingdom funerary scenes. This category of tomb scene represents the precursor to the Sacred District scene, where a number of episodes of the funeral ritual are presented together, but actually occurred on different days. The sequence of events is expressed in composition form. The standard presentation is to have the episodes eased together in registers that were read from one end to the other, proceeding in the direction of the figures.[355] Kantor points out that the episodes are juxtaposed without any gestures to connect them, but instead, a building or a glance in a particular direction could keep the continuity of the scene.[356] As part of the narration of these scenes, the functionaries were labeled, and written captions were added. In the New Kingdom, this style of composition was improved by the enhancement of the Sacred District scene to mark the point where the deceased passed from this world to the next.

Summary

The Sacred District is a landscape invested with mythological understandings and ritual knowledge intimately linked to bodily routines and practices. It was also formed by social memory; a memory that was reproduced throughout the early part of the New Kingdom. The artists reconstructed pasts and they imagined the foreseeable future, in the sense that the landscape would facilitate the deceased reaching Osiris in the west. Therefore, the Sacred District embodies social continuity in terms of monuments to mortuary rituals and ancestor veneration, if that is how we identify the *Mww*. Yet, what we see is the "afterlife" of these monuments. Were these shrines still in use in the early New Kingdom? Most scholars agree that voyages to the sacred Delta localities were no longer taking place. Instead, artists were using these vestiges of the past to recreate it. Consequently, this is a landscape of the mind, or this is a landscape of the mind (or a mental landscape). Because the Sacred District scene was created at the end of the seventeenth dynasty or beginning of the eighteenth dynasty in Upper Egypt it may be a southern variation on an ancient cultural memory. And this idea had a shelf-life in that it underwent a swift decline by the mid-eighteenth dynasty. So, this scene's emergence and subsequent decline may signal a fundamental change in the social perceptions of this landscape or its past, or the people from the past. If these renditions of a sacred landscape represent a symbolic return to the past, what sort of social or political uncertainties were present at this time? This scene has been challenging to analyze because we cannot detect the meaning or significance of this landscape over time, at least not by just looking at it. Irrespective of any attempt to semiotically decode its significance, we may never truly understand its importance or the effect it had on the artists, the tomb owner, his family and friends, or the viewer in general. Could these artistic elements symbolize a secure, stable resource to forge a new social identity?[357] What did this landscape produce for the tomb owners? What did it imply about their identities? How do we know which memories were important? Or what was actually associated with the imagery? These are not questions this work can address fully, but instead it can suggest potential avenues of research that should be explored in the future.

---

354 Kantor 1957: 45.

355 Kantor 1957: 47.

356 See also Angenot 2014.

357 Tilley 2006: 14.

CHAPTER SIX: PATRONS AND ARTISTS

The people who chose the Sacred District scene for their tomb's decorative program belonged to the highest ranks of the administration, most notably the vizier and mayor of the southern city, but it is also common in the tombs of regional governors. It is possibly through these latter offices that the scene spread farther south to Elkab and Hierakonpolis. Some lower administrators who had small tombs also managed to include at least one quintessential micro-scene into their decorative programs in order to symbolize the entire Sacred District by synecdoche. As well as professional groups, it also appears that members of certain families employed the Sacred District scene more than others. This scene appears in tombs of officials who had either a religious post in the temple or a civil administration position (Table 1); however, there is much overlap in the categories of titles these men held. Employment of the Sacred District scene was not limited to specific professional or familial groups but was also connected to the construction of tombs in a particular portion of the Theban necropolis—the area that was intrinsically linked to the reigning king. In this respect, the popularity of the Sacred District scene during the reigns of Hatshepsut and Thutmose III dictated that the majority of the Sacred District scenes would appear at Sheikh Abd el-Qurna, the location where the elite private tombs were erected in that era, and among those officials who worked for these two kings. During the reigns of Hatshepsut and Thutmose III, a new class of officials emerged to support the burgeoning bureaucracy, and these men had personal value to the king: they were his friends, they were considered to be loyal warriors, and they had been part of the king's military while abroad. Once these men returned to Egypt, they were given important posts in the royal house because they were trusted. Another practice relevant to perpetuation and distribution of the Sacred District scene is that there are explicit examples of artists borrowing and recopying it in adjacent tombs, a topic that is explored below.

The earliest officials known to have the Sacred District depicted in their Theban tombs are Hery (TT12) and Tetiky (TT 15), who are closely followed by Reneny (TC 7) at Elkab. However, there are earlier examples of the *Mww* in tomb decoration, most notably in the tombs of Senet (TT 60) at Thebes and Sobeknakht II (TC 10) at Elkab.[358] Senet was the wife or mother of the vizier Antefoker and Sobeknakht II was also probably a vizier.[359] These latter scenes do not yet include a full Sacred District, but because of their locations and their date, they act as the most immediate prototypes for the Sacred District scene which emerged at the very beginning of the eighteenth dynasty.

It can be problematic to create distinct categories of professions for the early eighteenth dynasty, but this work follows the classifications presented by Betsy Bryan in her work on the administration of Thutmose III.[360] Bryan acknowledges two initial categories, temple posts and the civil service; however, she notes that distinguishing between the holdings of the king and the holdings of the state is difficult and that the relationship between these two entities was fluid. In the state bureaucracy there were three tiers of officials. The first and highest tier included the vizier, the overseer of the seal, and the overseer of the granaries. Among the second-tier posts, one finds the overseer of the gold and silver houses, the royal herald, and the royal messenger. These latter three posts connected the king's domain to the state. The royal household (*pr nsw*) equates with the state on many levels, and therefore positions can be seen as belonging to one of four groups: state, *pr nsw*, temple, and military.[361] One complication is that officials held several titles at the same time, some being subordinate to others and some being honorific. Third-tier posts consist of the chief royal steward, royal butler, child of the *kap*, the royal nurse, and the regional administrators (mayors and king's son of Kush). There were also military posts, such as overseer of the army. The officials who included the Sacred District in their decoration held various positions within the administrative hierarchy. Temple posts are also ubiquitous in the titles presented in the tombs that have the Sacred District scene. In

---

[358] See Reeder (1995: 72) for a drawing of a scene from the twelfth dynasty tomb of Sehetepibre at Thebes where a pair of *Mww* appear.

[359] There is a third vizier mentioned on the "stèle juridique" whose name is Sobeknakht. There were also several mayors of Elkab who had this same name. In the Second Intermediate Period officials first become governor and then after that vizier (Grajetzki 2009: 41, 112). This Sobeknakht was clearly an important person, but he is difficult to date within the Second Intermediate Period. He was a member of a powerful family which ruled Elkab over several generations (Grajetzki 2009: 120–121).

[360] Bryan 2006.

[361] Bryan 2006: 69–70.

the early eighteenth dynasty, especially during the reigns of Hatshepsut and Thutmose III the popularity of the cult of Amun grew exponentially.[362]

The most important office within the bureaucracy was the vizier. The vizier was the highest juridical authority and had great power. Rekhmire (TT 100) was one of the celebrated viziers during the reign of Thutmose III. He controlled everything within the *pr nsw*. Most of his jobs were juridical in some way, and he had to supervise the police, act as the king's agent, be his military escort, provide security to the king, and be the chief executive officer for the royal household.[363] The next most important official was the overseer of the seal, which was a royal appointment. The chief treasurer and the overseer of the gold and silver houses reported directly to the overseer of the seal. He was responsible for grain, food, produce, stone, metal, and various other resources, and together with this task he also commanded royal expeditions. His duties were associated with the *pr nsw* but they overflowed into other areas as well. Senenmut (TT 71) held the titles overseer of the seal and overseer of the gold and silver houses. In the case of Senenmut, he was also the steward of Amun, a title that outranked both of his previous titles.

The overseer of the granary of Upper and Lower Egypt was another important post. This man was responsible for the collection and distribution of grain. He would have to record everything, report to the king, and supervise the storage facilities. There were two overseers of the dual granary and each of them would have had a scribal staff. They were the administrators of a national institution, as opposed to the *pr nsw*, but Bryan states, "the operations of the *per nesu* are frequently impossible to differentiate from those of other administrative entities," so the intricacies of the positions are sometimes obscure.[364] Duauneheh (TT 125) and Amunedjeh (TT 84) were both overseers of the granaries, and Senemiah (TT 127) and Amenemhet (TT 123) were scribes of counting bread for Upper and Lower Egypt, a title that associates them with the two former officials. Likewise, Senemiah (TT 127) was overseer of the gold and silver houses (like Senenmut, TT 71) and counter of grain for Upper and Lower Egypt. Amenemhet (TT 123) was also overseer of the granaries of bread. Therefore, there are six men who ranked among the highest officials, whose titles associated them with granaries (or in the case of Senenmut, other resources), who included the Sacred District scene in their tomb decoration: Senenmut (TT 71), Amunedjeh (TT 84), Amenemhet (TT 123), Duauneheh (TT 125), Senemiah (TT 127) and Amenemopet (TT 276).[365] Some of these men were part of the same administration. Amunedjeh was versatile and involved himself in many aspects of the bureaucracy holding the titles: overseer of works under Hatshepsut, overseer of the *ruyt*, royal scribe, and first royal herald. Since each official held several titles, it is difficult to determine which titles linked one official to another. Usually, it was the last title before the official's name that signified his main title.

The post of vizier ties together another group of officials at Thebes who have the Sacred District in their tomb decoration. Through the progenitor of the powerful Theban family of Aametju (TT 83), we can connect Rekhmire (TT 100), his grandson and successor in the vizierate, Amenemhet (TT 82), a lower-level official and Steward to Rekhmire's predecessor, and his contemporary Amenhotep (TT 122).[366] It is also possible that Aametju's wife was the sister of Ineni (TT 81), who also has a Sacred District scene in his tomb. Amenemhet (TT 82) controlled work for the vizier, and he also held the title scribe of counting grain of Amun; he may have worked under the leadership of Senenmut (TT 71), who was the steward of Amun at this time. This title might have further linked him in an official capacity to his relatives mentioned above in relation to the control of grain, but Amenemhet's titles suggest he worked for the temple of Amun, and therefore ranked in a parallel hierarchy headed by the priest of Amun. His is an intriguing case in that he was a contemporary of Senenmut (TT 71), who is known to have usurped many responsibilities associated with the vizierate during the time of Useramun, for whom Amenemhet was steward.[367] The titles of Amenemhet show that one person could work for two separate bureaucracies: the *pr nsw* and the temple.

Among the second-tier offices, the overseer of the silver and gold houses supervised materials used from the treasuries. This official would open these coffers with the vizier, who had control over all the wealth of the *pr nsw*. The overseer of the silver and gold houses was a subordinate of the overseer of the seal.

[362] Bryan 2006: 107.

[363] Bryan 2006: 71.

[364] Bryan 2006: 83.

[365] Although this tomb is discussed in reference to the Sacred District elsewhere, it will be shown that TT 276 does not have a Sacred District scene.

[366] Dorman 2003: 37.

[367] Bryan 2006: 95. Bryan remarks that the position of chief steward was diminished by the time of Amenhotep III, perhaps because of the liberties taken by Senenmut earlier in the dynasty.

This position was also connected to the royal steward in the time of Thutmose III.[368] As noted above, Senenmut (TT 71) was the overseer of the seal and the overseer of the silver and gold houses. Puiemre (TT 39) had the same responsibilities as an overseer of silver and gold houses, but he bore the title second priest of Amun. Not only did both men include a Sacred District in their tomb decoration, but this is another example of the fluidity between the different branches of the administration. Senemiah (TT 127) held the title of overseer of silver and gold houses for Hatshepsut, but he does not mention having access to precious materials like others do. Bryan suggests that Senemiah may have been more of an accountant.[369] Another overseer of the treasury of gold and silver was Amenemopet (TT 276), who probably worked under Thutmose IV. It appears that having an affiliation to the houses of gold and silver may have generated examples of the Sacred District scene: Senenmut (TT 71), Senemiah (TT 127), and Puiemre (TT 39).

Another second-tier position was overseer of the *Ruyt*, who had to answer to the vizier. The *Ruyt* was an area managed by the vizier that was a portico or gate area at the main entrance of the palace. One of the best-known overseers of the *Ruyt* was Amunedjeh (TT 84), who also held the titles overseer of the granaries and first royal herald. He began his career as overseeing the construction of monuments in Thebes and Heliopolis until he entered the military, after which he was promoted to first royal herald. Senenmut (TT 71) held this position, as well.

Royal herald was another second-tier post that involved speaking on behalf of the king. A royal herald functioned in the *ˁryt* (waiting rooms of the palace) and places outside Egypt where the king campaigned; therefore, this position could be part of the *pr nsw* or part of the state bureaucracy. Furthermore, a royal herald worked for the king himself organizing matters and announcing people. Amunedjeh (TT 84), Djehuty (TT 110), Duauneheh (TT 125)[370] and Djehutymose (TT 342) all held this title, and each had the Sacred District scene illustrated in his tomb.

The most important job within the palace administration was the office of chief steward (*mr pr wr n nsw*). This is a post that was held by Senenmut (TT 71), who administered the royal household and thus was close to the king. Another important official was the royal butler. He was a highly trusted member of the royal circle who provided provisions for the palace. He could also accompany the king on foreign missions and represent the king in foreign countries. Mentiywiy (TT 172) was royal butler under Thutmose III and Amenhotep II, and it is known that he accompanied Thutmose III on his campaign in the Levant and crossed the Euphrates with him.[371] Suemniwet (TT 92) was also a royal butler under Amenhotep II. Both men included the Sacred District among their tomb scenes.

Other officials associated with the palace administration were the royal nurse and child of the *kap*. The *kap* refers to an enclosure within the protected area of the palace, and this designation was for people who were raised in the court from a young age. Due to this, these men did not hold the highest-ranking titles, but their palace positions reflected their close relationship with the king. Mentiywiy (TT 172) is the only one in this group who was a child of the *kap,* and it was probably through this association that he was a trusted military companion and then a royal butler.

Paheri from Elkab has previously been attributed the title royal nurse to Prince Wadjmose, the son of Thutmose I; however, current scholarship recognizes this title to belong to his father Itireri.[372] Paheri was a painter, a scribe accountant of grain, a confidant of the treasurer, and later the governor of Elkab and Esna, and the chief of Nekhbet's priests.[373] There is another royal nurse, Ahmose-Pennekhbet, who is also buried at Elkab, but he does not have a Sacred District depicted in his tomb. However, Senenmut was also a royal nurse to Hatshepsut's daughter Neferrure, as was Ahmose Humay (TT 224). Royal nurses tended to be close to the king and were often educated alongside the royal children. Because Reneny (TC 7), a predecessor to Paheri's mayoral position at Elkab, does have a Sacred District in his tomb, it is most likely that this professional connection generated the Sacred District in Paheri's tomb. Moreover, in her article "The Artistic Copying Network Around the Tomb of Pahery in Elkab (EK3): a New Kingdom case study," Alisee Devillers makes the argument that Paheri's tomb at Elkab can be connected with the tomb of Wensu (a.k.a. Siuser, TT A4) at Thebes through Paheri's job as "painter of Amun." At an earlier stage in Paheri's career he may have personally

[368] Bryan 2006: 85–86.

[369] Bryan 2006: 86.

[370] According to Bryan, Duauneheh was a first herald and dealt with the *gs-pr* at Karnak. She does not consider him to be part of the *pr nsw* administration (2006: 92).

[371] Bryan suggests that his tomb was probably decorated early in the reign of Amenhotep II (2006: 95–96).

[372] Devillers 2018: 34.

[373] Devillers 2018: 34; W. V. Davies 2009: 142.

decorated TT A4 because it belonged to one of his colleagues in the administration of grain accounting. Then, he might have re-used part of this iconographic program in his own tomb.[374] This chronology of tomb decoration may be feasible; however, I disagree that Paheri necessarily would have created this decorative program himself. It is more likely that he was copying from a common source. As Dimitri Laboury points out, copying was integral to the phenomenon of iconographic creation in ancient Egypt and should not be used as a means to track individual creators.[375]

The Sacred District scene also appears in the tombs of several members of the regional administration. The mayors, or *ḥ3tyw-ʿ*, were responsible for the economies of the nomes. They had to answer to the vizier, but were in charge of cultivation, harvest, taxes, collection and transportation of said taxes, and the deliveries of grain. They may also have had to support local temples and state institutions.[376] Some of the mayors have combination titles that include agricultural duties, but it seems that mayors were involved with monumental building as well. Paheri is a good example of someone who had this combination of titles later in life. It can be seen in the decoration of Rekhmire's tomb (TT 100) that grain is being delivered from Elkab and Esna to Thebes. Unfortunately, the current mayor is not named, but it is possible that it could have been Paheri. What is remarkable is that none of the known tombs of mayors of the Thinis nome contain a Sacred District scene.[377] Similarly, the official Min, who was an Overseer of the Priests of Osiris at Abydos, does not have a Sacred District scene in his tomb.[378]

In general, tombs of provincial mayors and mayors of the Southern City do not include a Sacred District, but exceptions include Sobeknakht II (who has only the *Mww*), Reneny (TC 7) and Paheri (TC 4) of Elkab and Tetiky (TT15), Sennefer (TT 96B), Wensu (TT A4), Rekhmire (TT 100), and Basa (TT 389) of the Thebaid.[379] This suggests that this scene was more meaningful for people living and working in the Theban area or for provincial officials whose families were somehow connected to the Thebaid, than it was for anyone else. It is noteworthy that the Sacred District scene is conspicuously absent from the tombs of men who held military titles. However, it is present in the tombs of Amunedjeh (TT 84), Mentiywiy (TT 172), and Suemniwet (TT 92), men who returned home after the military campaigns of Thutmose III and were given great positions within the palace. It may be in the capacity of these later posts that they decided to have the Sacred District scene included in their tomb decoration, as there is nothing to suggests that it was a popular scene among men engaged in the military.

The cult of Amun grew immensely during the reigns of Hatshepsut and Thutmose III, which created a parallel hierarchy with the high priest of Amun at the top. Hapuseneb, an official completely involved with the Temple of Amun during the reign of Hatshepsut, does not have a Sacred District scene in his tomb, but two men, both named Menkheperreseneb (TT 86 and TT 112) succeeded Hapuseneb in office, and one of them does have a Sacred District scene in his tomb (TT 112).[380] It was originally thought that these two men were one and the same and that he had two tombs prepared for himself. Peter Dorman has concluded that these two men should be considered as two separate high priests of Amun, with the owner of TT 112 being the later priest and the nephew of the owner of TT 86.[381] Bryan agrees that there were indeed two Menkheperresenebs, but she believes that the owner of TT 112 is probably the earlier of the two based on the tomb's decoration.[382] It is clearly the owner of Theban Tomb 112 that is of interest for this study because he has a Sacred District displayed in his tomb, and he has a curious connection to Puiemre (TT 39). Puiemre, the second priest of Amun during the reigns of Hatshepsut and Thutmose III, was another member of the Amun Temple staff who had the Sacred District displayed in his tomb. He was also overseer of the cattle of the fields of Amun. In this capacity, he received goods from the oases and Nubia and was involved in royal constructions at Karnak Temple. He married the daughter of the abovementioned High Priest of Amun, Hapuseneb, and it was probably through this connection that he earned his temple post. Hapuseneb's successor Menkheperreseneb and his son-in-law Puiemre are connected through his

374 Devillers 2018: 38.
375 Laboury 2012: 204.
376 Bryan 2006: 99.
377 Three mayors of the Thinis nome, whose tombs are known, are Satepihu, Intef, and Min (Bryan 2006: 99–100).
378 This is one of the key pieces of evidence to suggest that although the scene has been Osirianized it is not specifically illustrating the wadi that leads to Poker at Abydos, but instead illustrates a Theban version of this journey to the afterlife across the valley on the west bank—one perhaps modeled on the former.
379 Rekhmire also held the title of mayor of the Southern City in addition to that of vizier.

380 Dorman 1995: 148–154.
381 Dorman 1995: 148–154.
382 Bryan 2006: 108.

Table 8: Occupations of Officials with the Sacred District Scene Displayed in their Tomb

Bureaucratic Posts		
TT 12	Hery	Overseer of the Granary of King's Wife and Mother
TT 15	Tetiky	Mayor of the Southern City
TT 21	User	Scribe, Steward
TT 69	Menna	Scribe of the Fields
TT 96B	Sennefer	Mayor of the Southern City
TT 100	Rekhmire	Governor of the Town, Vizier
TT 123	Amenemhet	Scribe, Overseer of the Granary, Counter of Bread
TT 127	Senemiah	Royal Scribe, Overseer of all that grows
TT 276	Amenemopet	Overseer of the Treasury of Gold and Silver, Judge and Overseer of the Cabinet
Palace Posts		
TT 17	Nebamun	Scribe and Physician
TT 84	Amunedjeh	First Royal Herald, Overseer of the Gate
TT 92	Suemniwet	Royal Butler, clean of hands
TT 110	Djehuty	Royal Butler, Royal Herald
TT 172	Mentiywiy	Royal Butler, Child of the Nursery
Temple Posts		
TT 36	Ibi	Chief Steward of Divine Adoratrice
TT 39	Puiemre	Second Prophet of Amun
TT 41	Amenemope	Chief Steward of Amun
TT 53	Amenemhet	Agent of Amun
TT 112	Menkheper-reseneb	First Prophet of Amun
TT 120	Anen	Second Prophet of Amun
TT 122	Amenhotep (with Amen-emhet)	Overseer of the Magazine of Amun
TT 161	Nakht	Bearer of the Floral Offerings of Amun
TT 179	Nebamun	Scribe and Counter of Grain in the Granary of Divine Offerings of Amun
TT 222	Hek-maatrenakht	First Prophet of Montu
TT 224	Ahmose	Overseer of the Estate of the God's Wife, Overseer of the Two Granaries of the God's Wife Ahmose Nefertari[383]
TT 260	User	Scribe, Weigher of Amun, Overseer of the Ploughed Lands of Amun
TT 275	Sobekmose	Head *w3b* priest, Divine Father in the Temples of Amenhotep III and Sokar
Dual Posts		
TT 71	Senenmut	Chief Steward, Steward of Amun
TT 81	Ineni	Overseer of the Granary of Amun[384]
TT 82	Amenemhet	Scribe, Counter of the Grain of Amun, Steward of the Vizier
TT 125	Duauneheh	First Herald, Overseer of the Estate of Amun
TT 389	Basa	*sm3ti*-priest, Chamberlain of Min, *ḥsk* -priest, Mayor of the Southern City

[383] Porter and Moss 1970: 325.
[384] Porter and Moss 1970: 159.

person in his capacity as the high priest of Amun. Albeit a tenuous one, this link may account for the Sacred District scene in the tombs of both Menkheperreseneb (TT 112) and Puiemre (TT 39).

Other officials that held posts in the temple of Amun are the well-known Senenmut (TT 71), who has been mentioned previously, the overseer of the workshop of Amun Duauneheh (TT 125), and the temple functionary, god's father, and pure priest Amenemhet (TT 53). It is curious that Amenemhet (TT 53) mentions the god as his source of support, not the king, which begs the question, how did this affect his ability to construct and decorate his tomb?

At Sheikh Abd el-Qurna several tombs that date to the reign of Amenhotep II (TT 96B, TT 92, and TT 84[385]) include an abbreviated version of the Sacred District scene.[386] With many Sacred District scenes dating to the reign of Thutmose III, the predecessor of Amenhotep II, and Sheikh Abd el-Qurna being the prime location for tombs with this scene, this pattern explicitly shows the tapering off of the scene, or its decrease in importance. Sennefer (TT 96B) was the mayor of the Southern City, Suemniwet (TT 92) was a royal butler, and Amunedjeh (TT 84) was the first royal herald. All three men reported to the vizier, held high-ranking positions, and had predecessors who also employed the Sacred District scene in their tombs.

Ibi (TT 36) and Basa (TT 389) were two Saite officials who opted to include the Sacred District scene in their tomb decoration. Ibi was the Chief Steward of the Divine Adoratrice Nitocris, and Basa was a *smꜣti*-priest, a Chamberlain of Min, a *ḥsk*-priest, and the mayor of the Southern City. Ibi's tomb can be firmly dated to the reign of Psammeticus I, while that of Basa can be dated only to the Saite Period in general. Theban Tomb 392 may also date to the Saite Period but there is no name or title preserved to us today to clarify the situation.[387] So, why did these men decide to include the Sacred District scene in their tomb decoration hundreds of years later? It is noteworthy that Basa (TT 389), as mayor of the Southern City, included a Sacred District in his tomb's decoration, possibly modeling it on earlier New Kingdom mayors' tombs such as Tetiky (TT 15) or Rekhmire (TT 100). Many antecedents of Ibi who worked for the Temple of Amun also shared an interest in the Sacred District scene, so this may have been his inspiration as well. It is less likely that earlier tombs in the area of the Asasif acted as prototypes for the decoration of these Saite tombs, since there were not many prototypes of the Sacred District in the immediate vicinity of either tomb, at least based on our current state of knowledge. The closest, or most accessible tomb, would have been that of Puiemre (TT 39) located at the edge of Khôkha in the Asasif.[388]

Provincial Cemeteries and Regional Associations

Thebes is not the only necropolis with tombs that illustrate the Sacred District scene. There were also several men buried at Elkab and Hierakonpolis who employed the Sacred District as part of their decorative programs. It has already been recognized that the *Mww* displayed in the tomb of Sobeknakht II (TC 10) at the regional capital of Elkab appear to be the prototype for these southern examples of the Sacred District, even though the *Mww* alone do not constitute a Sacred District.[389] Sobeknakht II's tomb is the largest and best preserved of the Second Intermediate Period.[390] It is the western-most tomb with interior decoration at Elkab, and it was hewn into the upper layer of the good stone. It was probably the earliest tomb to be constructed here and has been given a thirteenth dynasty date by some, but William Vivian Davies dates Sobeknakht II's tomb to the sixteenth dynasty.[391] There are two *Mww* who face to the right and wear the typical conical headdress, white kilt, and blue collar.[392] They hold their arms out to their sides, elbows bent with palms facing upward, unlike other examples of the *Mww*, and the left arm is slightly higher than the right arm. They are similar to other *Mww* in that they appear to be walking or stepping, and unlike the figures in front of them, their feet are not flat on the ground-line (the ground-line on which they stand is slightly higher than the ground-line on which the procession approaches). As for their

[385] The relevant part in this tomb was usurped by Mery during the reign of Amenhotep II, although the original owner of the tomb dates to the reign of Thutmose III (Porter and Moss 1970: 167–169).

[386] These would not be complete Sacred District scenes. Sennefer (TT 96B) includes only related scenes that have been connected to the Sacred District by previous scholars. TT 92 does not include a proper Sacred scene. It includes only the ḫbt-dancers micro-scene, which has been determined to be outside of the district itself..

[387] Porter and Moss 1970: 442.

[388] Engelmann-von Carnap 2014: 342–344.

[389] Tylor 1896: pl. III.

[390] Also called Tomb 66 in recent publications (W. V. Davies 2001: 120).

[391] W. V. Davies 2010: 223.

[392] The original plates published by J. J. Tylor (1896) show a greyish flap at the front of the kilts.

positioning, they are placed next to the oxen that drag the coffin; however, they face in the same direction and therefore look as though they are leading them, rather than greeting them. The procession is much abbreviated, and the oxen pull a wheeled cart carrying a cult barque (see Figure 7). This example at Elkab is followed chronologically by the tomb of Reneny, which dates to the beginning of the eighteenth dynasty (reigns of Ahmose/Amenhotep I) and the tomb of Djehuty at Hierakonpolis, which dates to the reign of Thutmose I.

Reneny was the governor of Elkab, as was his father Sobekhotep, and he was buried in the vicinity of the tombs of other men who held similar titles to him. A hieratic visitor inscription in the tomb of Sobeknakht II dated to year 22 of king Nebpehtyra Ahmose identifies the writer as "the scribe Reneny, son of the governor of Elkab Sobekhotep, born to the hereditary princess(?)... Ahmose." This is probably the same Reneny who is buried in TC 7. This indicates that Sobekhotep was still governor in year 22 of king Ahmose and that Reneny must have become governor in the reign of Amenhotep I.[393] It also demonstrates that Reneny visited the tomb of Sobeknakht II and must have viewed the scene of the *Mww*, possibly getting the idea to include this scene in his own tomb.

Djehuty, the overseer of the stone masons, also has one of the earlier Sacred District scenes. The south wall of his tomb features three registers of decoration illustrating the funeral scenes. The Sacred District is in the top register and shows multiple episodes from the compendium of micro-scenes. From what is known, the closest parallel seems to be that of Reneny at Elkab, but it also bears resemblance to the scenes in the tombs of User (TT 21) and Ineni (TT 81) farther north at Thebes. Later, the tombs of Paheri and Setau at Elkab also include the Sacred District scene (see chapter nine).

It is impossible to confirm which tomb offers the earliest example of the Sacred District scene. The contenders are Reneny at Elkab (TC 7), Hery (TT 12), and Tetiky (TT 15). To achieve a better understanding of how the tombs at Thebes and Elkab might relate, it is perhaps important to look at the genealogies of the men buried in these early tombs. At Elkab, the story begins with Aya, the governor and later vizier, from whom two men later descended. Renseneb (TC 9) and Sobeknakht II (TC 10).[394] Aya was the governor of Elkab, who later became a vizier under Merhetepra Ini of the late thirteenth dynasty.[395] He married two different princesses: Khonsu, the daughter of Queen Nubkhas, the wife of a late thirteenth dynasty king, and Reditenes, possibly the daughter of Meneferra Ay. Renseneb (TC 9) married the granddaughter of Aya and Khonsu, and Sobeknakht II was Aya and Reditenes' great grandson. W. V. Davies, following C. J. Bennett, suggests that Sobeknakht II probably became governor of Elkab sometime during the reign of king Nebiryrau I or during the reign of one of his three successors.[396] He succeeded his father Sobeknakht I as governor of Elkab and preceded his son Sobeknakht III. Sobeknakht II had two wives: the royal ornament Ta-inty and the hereditary princess Reditenes (Table 9).[397] The family of viziers is mainly known from the "*stèle juridique*" discovered at Karnak, as provincial courts were very much connected to the king's court at Thebes, probably due to the insecurity in the country.[398] This document tracks the transfer of the Elkab governorship to Sobeknakht's father, also named Sobeknakht (I). At this time, Egypt was divided into several territories and Thebes was the capital of Upper Egypt. It was common for the king to incorporate influential men from the provinces into his court at the capital, as it was in the king's best interest to find new loyal servants who were not related to the older officials.[399] This trend seems to have begun with the abovementioned Aya. Aya's son, Iymeru, was also a mayor of Elkab and he eventually became vizier as well.[400] So, the Elkab governorship was retained by one family from the reign of Merhotepre Ini of the late thirteenth dynasty into the seventeenth dynasty, and members of the family of Aya filled the post of mayor of Elkab for five generations (seven members of his family) during the Second Intermediate Period, possibly managing to place three viziers next to the king.[401] Unfortunately, his family was displaced under Ahmose, when a new household superseded them. The replacement's name was Sobekhotep and he was appointed governor of

393 W. V. Davies 2010: 237.

394 Aya is also known as Iy.

395 W. V. Davies 2010: 224.

396 W. V. Davies 2010: 225.

397 Grajetzki 2009: 162; W. V. Davies 2010: 230.

398 Grajetzki 2009: 40; W. V. Davies 2010: note 8.

399 Grajetzki 2009: 41.

400 Grajetzki 2009: 41. Aya's son, Neferhotep, also married a princess. Aya, Sobeknakht, and Renseneb all held the title "Overseer of *gs-pr*."

401 According to Shirley, this process began with Aya who was related to the vizier at the time. Aya had married two princesses providing evidence that the kings of the time were seeking support in the provinces (2013: 551–552). See also Grajetzki 2009: 41.

Elkab. In the reign of Amenhotep I, Sobekhotep's son Reneny succeeded him.[402] Reneny was the last of his family to hold this post, in spite of the fact that he may have had up to thirteen sons.[403] According to Sheila Whale, Reneny's mother was named Ahmose (a name that did not become popular until the late seventeenth or early eighteenth dynasty).[404]

Little is known about the family of Reneny, and the people who are preserved in his tomb's decoration have caused confusion for modern scholars.[405] There have been several suggestions as to how the individuals are related to each other, but recently W. V. Davies has made a convincing argument showing that it is Reneny himself and his senior wife Idy who are seated at the far end of the left wall in the principal offering scene. Previously, this man was thought to be a governor named Sobekhotep whose mother and wife were named Ahmose and Idy, respectively. Opposite, on the far end of the right wall, Reneny's parents, Sobekhotep and Ahmose receive offerings. Until recently it has been thought that the wife of Reneny, Nehi, played a rather insignificant role in his tomb decoration, appearing only once in the funeral procession. Now, it appears that Reneny's chief wife was Idy, who does appear with him where she is supposed to. The fact that his mother Ahmose appears in some important scenes may signify that Idy predeceased her and that she lived to ripe old age.[406]

Further information about Reneny's family has come to light at the site of Deir el-Bahri. Here, Reneny's son Neferhotep, who appears twice in his father's tomb at Elkab making the *hnw*-gesture with his brothers, left a hieratic graffito in the form of a stela inscription in black ink on the east wall of a grotto in the cliff north of the upper terrace of Hatshepsut's temple.[407] This inscription confirms that Neferhotep was the son of Reneny and Nehi. He served as an accounting scribe who kept records on the progress of the work in the construction of Hatshepsut's mortuary temple, a fact that is relevant for establishing a connection between the capital at Thebes and this distinguished family from Elkab. Moreover, William C. Hayes published an ostracon found at Deir el-Bahri that confirms that twenty-three men from Elkab were employed as laborers in the construction of Hatshepsut's Deir el-Bahri temple.[408] Edward Wente has suggested that the Elkab magnates played a significant role in government during the thirteenth through seventeenth dynasties and that this inscription indicates their continued importance.[409] Additional evidence includes one of the tombs discovered by the Spanish mission (Djehuty Project) at Dra Abu el-Naga that belongs to the high-level official Ahhotep, who was called "spokesman of Nekhen."[410] Another rare find is an inscription on a pyramidion found in the complex of Mentuhotep II at Deir el-Bahri. On it, Djehuty's name, "Commissioner of Hierakonpolis" is inscribed. In the eighteenth dynasty, this title became an appellative of the vizier and was relatively scarce. This has led José Miguel Serrano to suggest that this inscription might refer to the Djehuty buried in TT 11, about fifty years after Hery.[411] These finds further corroborate the connection between Thebes and the region in and around Elkab and between the families buried in these two areas. If members of the royal family intermarried with the provincial family at Elkab in the seventeenth dynasty (or earlier), this would also account for their close ties to the king.[412] Political connections like these created tangible relationships between the owners of the tombs at Elkab and those at Thebes at the beginning of the eighteenth dynasty.

This brief summary suggests that one's professional and familial ties may dictate tomb scene selection and that an on-going relationship existed between members of the gubernatorial family at Elkab and the royal family at Thebes. Evidence for this comes from a pattern of royal appointments, royal policies to incorporate influential men into provincial

[402] Shirley 2013: 558. According to records in his tomb, Reneny's father Sobekhotep had twelve sons, who appear making offerings to their father and maternal grandmother Ahmose.

[403] Whale 1989: 17.

[404] Whale 1989: 18.

[405] Tylor and Griffith 1894: 3; Bennett 2002: 123–155; W. V. Davies 2010: 236, note 73. Whale suggests that Reneny decorated TC 7 as his own and represented his father and brother and their families because he inherited his title from them. She notes that it is unclear why Reneny's wife is not represented seated with him in the tomb in the same way as the wives of his father and brother are positioned. Whale does not believe that Nehi predeceased Reneny, as other scholars have thought, since she is one of the mourners at his funeral; although she is hard pressed to justify why Reneny's mother Ahmose has such a prominent position in his tomb. Whale does suggest that Ahmose may have had a connection to the royal house, thus accounting for Reneny's inheritance of the position of mayor of Elkab (1989: 18–20).

[406] W. V. Davies 2010: 236–237.

[407] Wente 1984: 47–54.

[408] W. Hayes 1960: 34.

[409] Wente 1984: 50–51.

[410] EurekaAlert, "Djehuty Project discovers significant evidence of the 17th Dynasty of Ancient Egypt."

[411] Serrano, "Djehuty, 'Commissioner of Hierakompolis.'"

[412] Grajetzki 2009: 162.

Table 9: Chronological Overview and Familial Associations of the Governors/Viziers at Elkab

Kings	Date if known	Governor of Elkab/ Vizier	Familial Information
Meneferra Ay	*c.*1700 BCE. He was last attested king for both north and south		
Menhetepra Ini		Aya Mayor and Vizier (promoted in yr. 1 of Merhetepra Ini)	• Married Khonsu, daughter of Queen Nubkhas and Reditenes, daughter of Meneferra Ay
		Iymeru Mayor and Vizier	• Son of Aya
		Renseneb (TC 9)[413]	• Married granddaughter of Aya and princess Khonsu
		Sobeknakht I	• Father of Sobeknakht II
Nebiryrau I	16th dynasty (?)	Sobeknakht II (TC 10)	• Great grandson of Aya and Reditenes • Son of Sobeknakht I • Father of Sobeknakht III • Married two royal women including hereditary princess Reditenes
Nebiryrau II		Sobeknakht III	• Son of Sobeknakht II
Semenra	*c.*1600 BCE dynasty 16-17??		
Bebiankh Sewoserenre			
		New Family	
Ahmose	*c.*1550 18th dynasty	Sobekhotep	
Amenhotep		Reneny (TC 7)	• Son of Sobekhotep

government, and opportunities for social mobility (from mayor to vizier in at least three cases).

At Thebes, the situation is similar to that of Elkab, in that the early twelfth dynasty tomb of Senet (TT 60) offers a prototype for the Sacred District parallel to that of Sobeknakht II. Her tomb also features only the *Mww* and not a complete Sacred District, yet it is the closest analogue to the New Kingdom Sacred District in this area. Senet's tomb was commissioned by the vizier Antefoker, who in fact appears in her tomb so frequently that it was initially published as his tomb. It is most likely not a coincidence that both Antefoker and Sobeknakht II, the men who contracted these tombs, held the position of vizier.[414]

It is difficult to create a secure chronology for the earliest tombs that depict a Sacred District at Thebes, that but they include the tombs of Hery (TT 12), Tetiky (TT 15), Ineni (TT 81), and User (TT 21). Hery was overseer of the granary for Ahmose's wife and mother, Tetiky was mayor, Ineni was overseer of the granary of Amun probably beginning in the reign of Amenhotep I, and User was a scribe and the steward to Thutmose I. All four officials worked between the reigns of Ahmose and Thutmose I, a time period that lasted not quite sixty years. It is during this era that the Sacred District scene begins to generate status, as these early tomb owners were high ranking, prestigious individuals. The construction of the tombs of Ineni and User most likely post-dates those of the former two officials and was probably contemporary with Djehuty's tomb at Hierakonpolis.

Hery (TT 12) appears to be a pivotal character

[413] See W. V. Davies for the genealogy and related materials for Renseneb at Elkab (2010: fig. 4).
[414] For earlier examples, see Junker 1940.

in terms of connecting Thebes and Elkab during the reign of Ahmose. At the beginning of the eighteenth dynasty Hery was scribe and supervisor of the granaries to the royal wife and mother of the king, Ahhotep. He was probably born during the reign of Ahmose, or possibly earlier, and lived through the reign of Amenhotep I. The name of Hery's mother, Ahmose, is known from his tomb, but there is no reference to his father. His mother Ahmose bears the title *ḫrw-nswt,* which suggests she may have belonged to the royal family.[415] Hery's tomb is much nicer than other contemporary tombs, and for this reason it has drawn the attention of scholars. This part of the necropolis, Dra Abu el-Naga, was used by the royal family and the courtiers of the seventeenth dynasty.[416] As noted, the continuous associations between the gubernatorial family at Elkab and the royal family at Thebes may have contributed to the transference of the Sacred District scene between these sites, and it may have been Hery in particular that started this trend. Most scholars agree that Reneny's tomb dates to the reign of Amenhotep I, implying that the tombs of Hery (TT 12) and Tetiky (TT 15) predate it. If this is the case, then perhaps Reneny modeled his tomb decoration on that of Hery or Tetiky. Likewise, there may have been a strong desire to emulate the tombs of influential and powerful contemporaries at Thebes as opposed to copying an image from the tomb of a rival family—that is, if Sobekhotep's appointment to governor of Elkab caused friction.

Evidence suggests that what perhaps began as an elite Theban decorative motif emerged as a pseudo-national trend sometime during the latter part of the reign of king Ahmose. Considering the prominence of Elkab at the beginning of the eighteenth dynasty, it is not surprising that this provincial cemetery exhibits an elite trend that would later permeate the Theban necropolis during the reigns of Hatshepsut and Thutmose III. It is also not surprising that the decorative motifs in some of the tombs of Ahmose's high officials exhibit Osirian overtones in the form of the Sacred District scene, taking into account his building activity at the site of Abydos (see chapter eight).[417] It has also been suggested that once the area of Abydos was incorporated into the Theban kingdom, the cult center received state support (Table 10).[418] It was Reneny's profession as mayor of Nekheb and the overseer of prophets that gave him access to this fashionable scene and could link him professionally to Hery and Tetiky. Reneny, as a provincial mayor, would have been interested in the tomb decoration of his high-ranking contemporaries to the north.[419] It is, therefore, not a coincidence that Reneny's more or less contemporary in Thebes, Tetiky, was also a mayor and that his tomb is one of the earliest Theban examples to depict the Sacred District.

Beginning in the seventeenth dynasty hereditary positions and close ties to the king became more important in terms of hierarchy.[420] Within the four categories of officials: *pr nsw*/civil administration, regional administrators, religious offices, and the military, patterns emerge with regard to their display of the Sacred District scene. Officials who worked for the *pr nsw*/civil administration and for religious offices present the Sacred District scene in their tombs more often than officials who worked in the provinces, and there are no examples in the tombs of men strictly connected to the military. It is clear that the mayor of Elkab was a powerful position at this time and that whoever held this position was influential at court. The man in this position was governor of his region, the high priest of the local temple, and the local judge.[421] In general, local governors helped to support the king, and loyal men were rewarded with promotions. The provincial town of Elkab was no exception and several men were promoted from mayor to vizier, titles that were not held simultaneously during this period.[422] The vizier was the head of the provincial administration and promoted the relationship between the court and the provinces.[423] Possibly because of this connection, members of this same family worked

[415] Galán and Jiménez-Higueras 2015: 101.

[416] Galán 2020: 42.

[417] By the time of the twelfth dynasty the royal tombs had become identified as the burial place of Osiris. At this same time an area at the edge of the Northern Cemetery was dedicated to the erection of votive stelae, now referred to as the "terrace" of the Great God. Janet Richards suggests that "[i]t is tempting to see this diversification of organization and function of the North Abydos conceptual landscape as reflecting the reorganization of social groups in the political and religious realms" (1999: 94). Ahmose was engaged in building activity at South Abydos, where he constructed a monumental cult complex (Harvey 1998). It is evident that Abydos went through a transition in and around this time and that Ahmose and his administration was instrumental in this evolution.

[418] Smith 2017: 229–230; Wegner 2002: 66–67.

[419] Based on a scene in the tomb of Reneny that shows him worshipping the cartouche of Amenhotep I, his tomb is slightly later than those of Tetiky and Hery at Thebes (Devillers 2018: 42).

[420] Shirley 2013: 548.

[421] Grajetzki 2009: 111.

[422] Grajetzki 2009: 112.

[423] Grajetzki 2009: 109.

Table 10: Cyclical Relationship between Thebes, Elkab, and Abydos

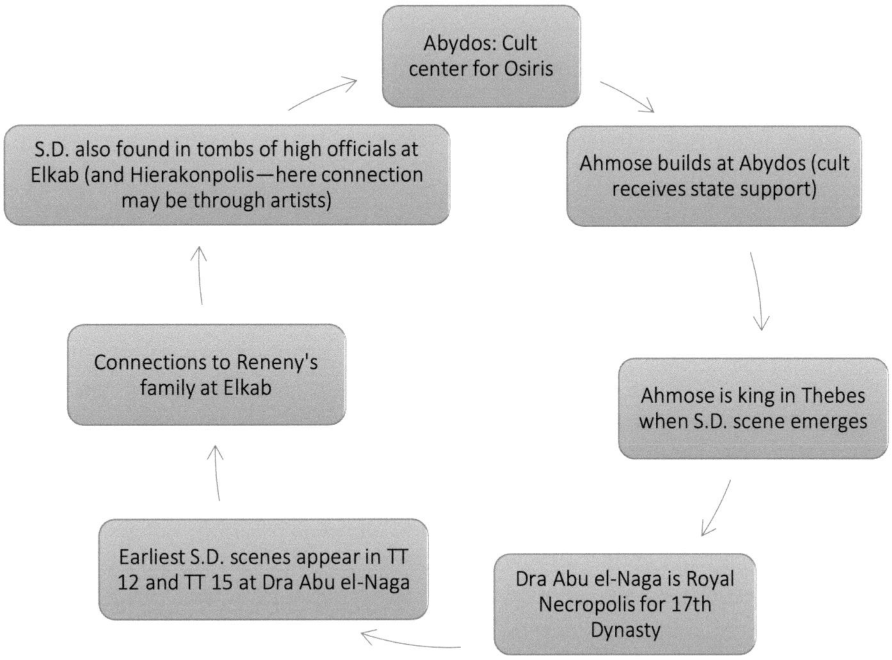

at both Thebes and Elkab. Elkab was also the burial place of the vizier's family at the end of the seventeenth dynasty, further augmenting the prominence of this town.[424] It is, therefore, not surprising that (almost–) contemporary high-ranking officials shared the same taste in tomb art.[425]

Artists and the Diffusion of Artistic Motifs

Private tomb chapels served as memorial monuments for the owners of the tombs and as places where their relatives could perform burial rituals and funerary cult ceremonies. It is logical to assume that the images that appear in these chapels were chosen by the tomb owners to transmit particular notions about their lives.[426] Due to this, artists would have had to adapt to the particularities of their patrons' wishes while still following the iconographic traditions and creating an effective decorative program for the tomb. So, another way to examine the connections that exist among the tombs at Thebes and between those at Thebes and Elkab (and Hierakonpolis) during the transition from the seventeenth to the eighteenth dynasties is through the artists and their work.

There are three areas in Upper Egypt—Thebes, Elkab, and Hierakonpolis—where private elite tombs have been decorated with the same scene, or variations thereof. The Sacred District is recognizable for its uniqueness and its specific usage in space and time. It is apparent that there are professional connections between the men who chose to have this scene illustrated in their tombs, but the artists may also have played a role in the transference of this scene. Several scholars, such as Betsy Bryan, Dimitri Laboury, and Inmaculada Vivas Sáinz, have studied the working processes, the mobility, and the ingenuity of the ancient Egyptian artist.[427]

It is the collection of private Theban tombs that provides the main source of data about the manners in which painters and sculptors worked.[428] At first glance it might seem impossible to learn about the producers of the work that has been left to us as most of it was not signed by its maker. Yet, the artwork preserved in these private tombs should not be considered anonymous because we have the name of the commissioning patron who has "self-thematized" himself through the art.[429] When there is evidence of an artist's signature, they are of two types according to Laboury: signatures of scribes of forms and graffiti. What is curious here is that the latter category indicates that many painters visited the monuments made by

[424] Shirley 2013: 551.
[425] See Den Doncker 2017.
[426] Hartwig 2004: 5–15.

[427] Bryan 2001 and 2010; Laboury 2012 and 2017; Viva Sáinz 2016.
[428] Vivas Sáinz 2016: 208.
[429] Laboury 2012: 199.

their colleagues decades and centuries later.[430]

These tombs were most likely decorated by artists from across Egypt, as suggested by Bryan, as there were most likely insufficient numbers of trained artists to complete the abundance of tombs constructed during the eighteenth dynasty.[431] The study of these private tombs also exposes that artists did not limit themselves to just copying extant scenes, but instead they used their creativity to produce new scenes and themes.[432] Several recent studies have demonstrated that the decoration of a private Theban tomb chapel was a group project whereby several types of "scribes" were responsible for performing different jobs within a tomb.[433] Using the unfinished tomb of Suemniwet (TT 92), Bryan has suggested that up to twenty-five artists worked simultaneously on a tomb. If this was the case, identifying individual artists and tracking their movement within Egypt would be complicated by the idea of workshop-crews. Based on the number of tombs decorated during the eighteenth dynasty, it can be assumed that the amount of people who worked in the Theban necropolis was high. Due to this, many artists might have come from outside the Theban area to fill the demand for workers.[434] There are no written sources to confirm any transfer of artists from one region to another, but perhaps the location of the royal court and its affiliations would have some bearing on the situation. In fact, this seems to have been the case at the end of the seventeenth dynasty and beginning of the eighteenth dynasty when members of the royal family (Theban court of Ahmose) had connections to officials in the provincial government at Elkab. The funerary art produced at this time suggests that artists from the palace workshops had some mobility and that this mobility was a factor in the transmission of iconography and innovations in art.[435] The diffusion of ideas or copying methods, can mean several things: the circulation of iconographic motifs; the copying of a register or wall; a recurring detail that was situated in a new context.[436] Additionally, artists would have possessed varying levels of experience, they would have come from different backgrounds, and they would be able to express different degrees of originality or creativity in their work. When it comes to the latter point, private tombs probably exhibited more originality in their artwork than any piece of state art or anything produced under royal patronage.[437]

According to Melinda Hartwig, it is possible to distinguish two types of styles in the funerary paintings in the Theban necropolis: those tombs belonging to the "state class" and those connected to the religious administration of the temples. She uses the term "state class" to refer to officials associated with the military, palace, and civil and regional administration, and suggests that these men's tombs would have been decorated by painters from the palace workshops. Painters linked to Karnak temple would have decorated the tomb chapels of religious officiants.[438] Hartwig asserts that a tomb would have exhibited the deceased's professional and societal identity through the style of decoration and its placement within the cemetery among tombs of similarly titled officials. She also notes that it is difficult to prove intentionality on the part of the patron because there is no evidence for contracts or work orders.[439] When it comes to the men who had the Sacred District illustrated in their tombs, there are a number of officials who had dual posts, or multiple titles, belonging to both of the abovementioned groups. Therefore, other factors may have come into play, such as the point in an official's career when his tomb was decorated, the post he associated himself with most, or his highest-ranking affiliation. It is also possible that artists from any workshop could be hired privately by the owner of a tomb to do work. We also know that successors to some posts wanted to emulate their predecessor's tomb. For example, Vivas Sáinz has demonstrated that the vizier Amenemope (TT 29), who succeeded the vizier Rekhmire, ordered the construction of a tomb that emulated in some respects that of his predecessor, TT 100. The pattern of the appearance of the Sacred District scene also appears to corroborate this point (although not in the case of TT 29—he does not have a Sacred District scene).

Another noteworthy example is the relationship between the tomb of Senet (TT 60), which was commissioned by Antefoker, vizier to Senwosret I of the twelfth dynasty, and that of Amenemhet (TT 82), steward of the vizier Useramun. Alexis Den Doncker has suggested that during the performance of his task of supervising the work for the tomb of

430 Laboury 2012: 200.
431 Bryan 2001: 70.
432 Vivas Sáinz 2016: 212; Laboury 2017.
433 Bryan 2001: 63–72; Bryan 2010: 1006; Vivas Sáinz 2016: 206.
434 Bryan 2001: 70.
435 Vivas Sáinz 2017: 107. Evidence for the transmission of iconographic patterns in artistic copies can be traced back to the Middle Kingdom (Devillers 2018: 31).
436 Merzeban 2014: 341.
437 Vivas Sáinz 2017: 108.
438 Hartwig 2004: 122. See also Vivas Sáinz 2016: 213.
439 Hartwig 2004: 122.

Useramun (TT 61), Amenemhet visited TT 60, which was only ten meters away. The illustrations inside TT 60 inspired the decoration of his own tomb, TT 82, especially the "old-fashioned" scene of the pilgrimage to Abydos and the *Mww*.[440] Laboury points out that it is the extreme rareness of particular scenes that helps to identify the imitation process, in that the less usual the imitated image, the easier to expose the copying process. In Laboury's writing, he refers to the scene of a dancer who leaps into the air and appears in both tombs, not the Sacred District scene; but, the antiquity of some of the elements included in the latter scene does make it unique.[441] Amenemhet also left a graffito on the wall of TT 60, proving that he undoubtedly visited the tomb chapel that was commissioned by his boss's predecessor (for his mother Senet).[442] The copied version of the Sacred District in TT 82 is not an exact replica of what appears in TT 60. Part of the reason for this is that TT 60 is an example of Middle Kingdom funerary art and the Sacred District as a composition does not appear until the very end of the seventeenth dynasty. In fact, until the Second Intermediate Period, the *Mww* is the most prominent micro-scene (of those that would eventually constitute the Sacred District) to appear in tomb art. It was not until the very end of the seventeenth dynasty that the *Mww* developed into the Sacred District. So, in this case, I would suggest that Amenemhet did not blindly reproduce a visual scene, but instead interpreted the meaning behind the scene, and had it repurposed in his own tomb in line with contemporary artistic trends.

At Elkab there are three examples of the Sacred District scene, one in the tomb of Reneny (TC 7) that dates to the beginning of the eighteenth dynasty, one in the tomb of Paheri (TC 3) that may date to the reign of Thutmose III, and a later Ramesside example in the tomb of Setau (TC 4).[443] Several scholars have worked on the artistic network surrounding the tomb of Paheri, because Paheri himself was a painter. His titles from his tomb describe him as *sš-ḳd n ỉmn,* a painter of Amun. Paheri started his career as an artist and a scribe accountant of grain, and then became governor of Elkab and Esna near the beginning of the eighteenth dynasty.[444] We know that Paheri's father, Itireri, was the tutor of prince Wadjmose, a son of Thutmose I, and that his grandfather was Ahmose, son of Ibana (TC 5), who was buried nearby.[445] There are four tombs that can be discussed in reference to that of Paheri: Wensu (TT A4), Setau (TC 4), Reneny (TC 7), and Djehuty (Hierakonpolis).

Using fragments now in the Louvre, Lise Manniche identified various scenes belonging to the "lost" tomb chapel of the official Wensu, a contemporary and colleague of Paheri from Thebes. Wensu was a scribe accountant of grain whose T-shaped tomb (now known as TT A4) was most likely constructed at the site of Dra Abu el-Naga.[446] There are many similarities in the scenes of Paheri's tomb and Wensu's, including the presence of a Sacred District.[447] The funerary scenes, although now completely lost, have been reconstructed by Manniche using the sketches made by Robert Hay, and although several of the same micro-scenes appear in both tombs, the overall compositions are quite distinct.[448] According to Devillers and Laboury, TT A4 predates the copying of TC 3 and should be considered the inspiration for the latter production. As Paheri had been a painter of Amun at an early stage in his career, it has been suggested that he may have personally decorated TT A4 and then re-used this decorative program when designing his own tomb.[449] Even if this is the case, by this time there were already several examples of the Sacred District in the tomb chapels at Thebes from which the artist of TT A4 could have copied. Because there is also an earlier example of the Sacred District scene in the tomb of Reneny at Elkab and one across the river in the tomb of Djehuty at Hierakonpolis that predate both Wensu's and Paheri's examples, Paheri should have been familiar with the Sacred District before he created it in Wensu's tomb at Thebes.[450]

The situation with Setau's tomb is a little different. His tomb is located adjacent to Paheri's tomb and was decorated by the artist Meryre of Esna. Jean Marie Kruchten and Luc Delvaux date his tomb to sometime between 1175 and 1122 BCE.[451] The similarities between Setau's tomb and Paheri's tomb are textual

[440] Den Doncker 2012: 30–31.
[441] Laboury 2012: 235.
[442] Den Doncker 2012: 30; Laboury 2012: 235.
[443] The earliest example of the *Mww* at Elkab appears in the sixteenth dynasty tomb of Sobeknakht II.
[444] Paheri began his career during the first years of the reign of Thutmose III (Devillers 2018: 34).

[445] The tomb of Ahmose, son of Ibana, was made "by the son of his daughter, the one who directed all the works in this tomb as the one who causes the name of the father of his mother to live, the scribe-of-forms of Amun, Pahery, the justified one" (Laboury 2012: 201).
[446] Manniche 1988: 62–87.
[447] Manniche 1988: 62–87; Laboury 2017: 242–247; Devillers 2018: 34–38.
[448] Devillers 2018: 38.
[449] Devillers 2018: 38; Laboury 2017: 242.
[450] R. Friedman 2001: 107–110.
[451] Kruchten and Delvaux 2010: 184–185. This corresponds to the reigns of Ramesses III–Ramesses IX.

and iconographic, but the funerary scenes appear to be exact copies. In this case, it was probably the proximity of the two tombs that facilitated the copying of Paheri's scenes into Setau's tomb, because we know that Meryre of Esna was the hired artist. However, we cannot discount the possibility that Meryre acted more purposefully and copied the iconography of Paheri's tomb because he was also an artist. Setau was the first prophet of Nekhbet and Paheri was an artist and later mayor, so there are no obvious professional connections. However, Reneny (TC 7), who also has a Sacred District scene, was an overseer of prophets, so perhaps there was some professional affiliation between those two men.

Reneny's tomb is situated on the same terrace as the tombs of Paheri and Setau, so it is likely that Paheri was aware of the scenes preserved inside his chapel when he first began working at the site or planning his own tomb. In fact, F. Ll. Griffith noticed the similarities between these two tombs in his 1900 publication.[452] Although Devillers states that "there is no general similarity with regard to the funerary scenes. At the most, there is the reuse of the coffin pullers, the '*mww*' dancers, the shrine bringers, the t*ekenu* and the garden patterns," I disagree that there is no connection. This is one of the earliest examples of the Sacred District scene that potentially perpetuates this network of copying. As is noted above, Reneny was the governor of Elkab at the beginning of the eighteenth dynasty, after his father Sobekhotep.[453] Reneny left a *graffito* in the nearby tomb of Sobeknakht II, who was also a governor of Elkab several generations earlier. What is remarkable is that the tomb of Sobeknakht II is the earliest tomb at Elkab to have even a kernel of the Sacred District included—in the form of the *Mww*. So, both Reneny and Paheri took inspiration from earlier tombs at the same site in order to connect themselves with the earlier high ranking officials of Elkab.

The tomb of Djehuty, located across the river from Elkab at Hierakonpolis, also has an example of the Sacred District scene in its chapel. This tomb was decorated during the reign of Thutmose I, so it post-dates slightly that of Reneny. Although we cannot say with certainty that the same artist decorated both tombs, W. V. Davies has shown that artists did travel between these two sites around this time. The tomb of the governor Sobeknakht II (TC 10) at Elkab was apparently decorated by the painter Sedjemnetjeru, who identified himself in his tomb. This same artist also decorated the tomb of Horemkhauef at Hierakonpolis.[454]

Summary

To summarize, many different professionals were able to include the Sacred District scene in their tomb's decoration over the course of the New Kingdom. The earliest officials were connected to the royal household and the state bureaucracy in their professional capacity. Over time, some of these men held the highest positions in the land, such as Tetiky (TT 15), Sennefer (TT 96B), and Basa (TT 389), who were each mayor of the Southern City. Several of these officials held the title overseer of the granary (TT 12, TT 81, TT 224, TT 123), which was an extremely important position within the ranks of the administration. Additionally, Rekhmire (TT 100) was vizier during the reigns of Thutmose III and Amenhotep II. It is also noteworthy that Tetiky (TT 15) was a mayor in the Southern City who bore the title "King's Son." Tetiky was clearly high profile, and his tomb was one of the earliest to include a Sacred District scene in the Theban necropolis. Likewise, Mentiywiy (TT 172), who bore the title "child of the nursery," grew up in the palace along with the royal children. Djehutymose (TT 342), a hereditary prince, also included the Sacred District in his tomb.

Although artists are generally anonymous, and the tomb owner as patron was usually the one connected to the production of an art piece, looking at the flexibility and mobility of artists is another avenue for exploring the transference of the Sacred District scene. Artists were most likely responsible for the details of compositions and the ways of rendering particular illustrations despite the tomb owner choosing the main themes for his monument. It is likely that the artists who worked in Thebes at the end of the seventeenth dynasty and the beginning of the eighteenth dynasty were the same artists who worked on the contemporary tombs at Elkab and Hierakonpolis. Perhaps they were palace artists who were lent out to high officials, in this case to the vizier and his family, who were buried at Elkab. The earliest tombs decorated with the Sacred District scene all have owners connected to the royal family in one way or another.

[452] Tylor and Griffith 1900: 1.

[453] W. V. Davies 2010: 237.

[454] W. V. Davies 2001: 113–125; Laboury 2012: 201.

CHAPTER SEVEN: COMPOSITION OF THE SACRED DISTRICT WITHIN THE TOMB

The ancient Egyptian artists situated their depictions of the Sacred District scene among the funerary scenes within each tomb. This scene was illustrated most frequently in the passage of a T-shaped tomb, and it functioned artistically as a transitional region, or buffer zone, between the scenes of the world of the living and the scenes of the world of the dead. The Sacred District is composed of a sequence of micro-scenes (or episodes) that could be placed on one or more registers, with the different micro-scenes occurring adjacent to one another. The established pattern of illustration acknowledges that the ancient Egyptians interpreted the nature of this scene as transitional, liminal, and transformative.

The most common type of tomb at Thebes in which the Sacred District is found is the T-shaped tomb. The Sacred District scene is habitually depicted on the west wall of the passage of this type of tomb. The passage, which leads from the transverse hall to the focal point of the tomb in the symbolic west, was considered to be a place of transition for the deceased within his tomb. For this reason, it made sense to have all things funerary displayed here, as the architecture could direct the deceased toward the focal point of the tomb—the land of the dead. However, the Sacred District does appear in tombs that are not T-shaped, and these examples are particularly informative because they represent attempts to make this scene effective without the complimentary architecture.

The Sacred District Scene in Non-T-Shaped Tombs

The typical positioning of the Sacred District scene is on the left wall of the passage of a T-shaped tomb, yet artists made use of this scene and included it in other styles of tombs as well. The artists were able to adapt to other architectural settings, and their choices reinforce the liminal nature of the Sacred District. Even when a passage is not present in the architecture of a tomb, the artists have still considered the symbolic meaning of the Sacred District and placed it in an appropriate position. This chapter discusses Theban Tombs 41, 122, and 39, and demonstrates how the Sacred District in these tombs fulfills its purpose without the existence

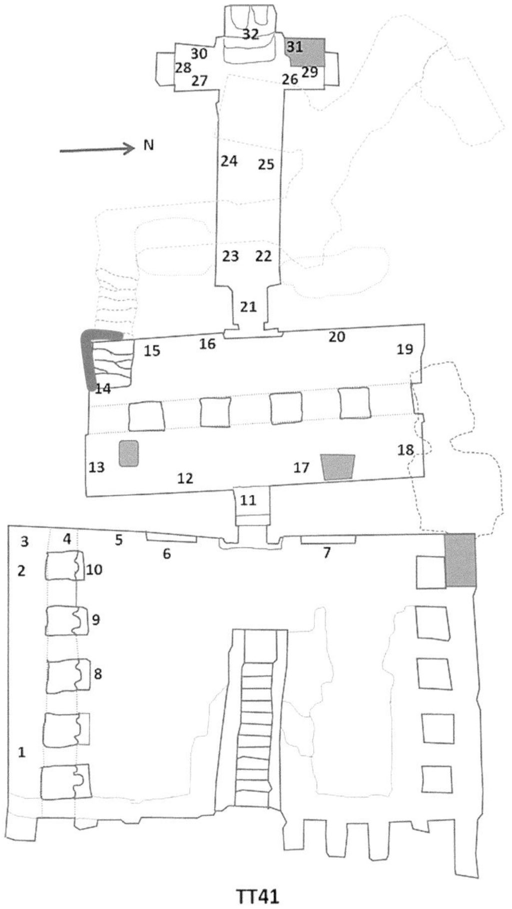

Figure 24: Plan of the tomb of Amenemope (TT 41) showing the location of the Sacred District scene in red. Adapted from www.osirisnet.net

of the passage found in the T-shaped tomb, thus corroborating the liminal nature and transformative power of this scene.

Theban Tomb 41, the tomb of Amenemope, illustrates a late example of the Sacred District in what is essentially an elaborate T-shaped tomb with a sunken courtyard before a transverse hall. This tomb is anomalous because it includes not one, but three funerary scenes in different locations throughout the tomb (Figure 24).[455] Although the rites to the mooring-post, the voyage to Sais, and the Goddess of the West occur on the left wall (south wall) of the front courtyard behind the southern colonnade, the acred District scene can be found in the top two registers of the left wall of the second court (Figure 25). This scene runs along the registers and turns the corner at the end of the wall to continue onto the adjoining west wall (see Figure 18). The walls have deteriorated quite a bit so some of the images are difficult to discern, but we are concerned with the west part of the south wall and the west wall. On the west part of the south wall in

[455] Assmann 1991.

Figure 25: Photo of Sacred District scene on the south wall of the transverse hall of the tomb of Amenemope (TT 41). Photo by author.

the top register the artists have illustrated, from left to right, two men erecting two obelisks, two *ḫbt*-dancers facing each other, two *ḥm*-chapels stacked, and the two kneeling women holding *nw*-pots. Below, and moving from left to right, there are two *Mww* facing to the right and wearing their conical headdresses, two *ḥm*-chapels stacked, and the four guardians of the gate. At this point the scene moves from the south wall onto the west wall. In the top register and continuing from the two kneeling women, is the remainder of this micro-scene in the form of four water basins. This micro-scene typically consists of two women kneeling in front of four basins of water. In this case, the four channels of water lead from each basin to a common trough that is clearly visible and painted blue. This is followed by a pool with five palm trees, but then there is a short interlude where general funerary scenes appear—scenes that are not part of the Sacred District. The final episode is three open shrines with gods inside. Below this register, moving from left to right, are general funeral scenes strictly unrelated to the Sacred District. These scenes end with three open shrines with gods inside, which is a typical component of the Sacred District. At this point, the deceased is shown in front of a table of offerings and there is a break in the wall for the opening that leads into the tomb. So, even though the plan of this tomb is more elaborate than a typical T-shaped tomb, the artists were able to situate the Sacred District in a comparable position that still expressed the symbolic nature of the scene's content: liminality and transformation.

What is striking about TT 41 is that the shaft to Amenemope's burial chamber is situated in the southwest corner of the transverse hall, directly under the Sacred District scene. Here, there is an opening with a staircase of ten steps leading down and to the west. I argue that the juxtaposition of the Sacred District scene and the opening for the burial chamber was purposeful. This combination can also be seen in the rectangular tomb of Reneny at Elkab, where the last experience of the deceased (according to the decorative program of the tomb) was to traverse the Sacred District before entering the next life.

A second example where the Sacred District scene appears in an unusual location is in Theban Tomb 122. As discussed in chapter four, the scene appears on the west wall of the Third Chapel (Chapel B in Porter and Moss), where four registers exhibit the funerary procession. There are no extant inscriptions. JJ Shirley has elaborated on the complexities of this tomb and the various building phases that might have accounted for its curious design.[456] TT 122 was used by two men who were contemporaries: Amenemhet and Amenhotep (Neferhotep).[457] Both men were overseers of the granary of Amun and at least one of them was a member of the family of Rekhmire (owner of TT 100).[458] Since two men of the same profession were sharing the tomb, it has been categorized as a double burial structure,

[456] Shirley 2010.
[457] Amenemhet seems to be the owner of the side chapels.
[458] Shirley 2010: 271–272. See chapter six of this work for networks of relatives who include this tomb scene in their decorative programs.

Figure 26: Photo of Sacred District scene in TT 122. Photo by author.

a special version of Kampp-Seyfried's Type IVa.[459]

The funerary scenes in TT 122 occupy the four registers on the west wall of Chapel B, but the Sacred District appears only in the second register from the bottom. In the upper two registers the figures are oriented to the left and in the bottom two register they are oriented to the right. This means that we should interpret the episodes of the Sacred District as progressing from left to right (or moving from the exterior of the tomb to the interior of the tomb). The second register with the Sacred District is at some points divided into two sub-registers; this allowed the artist(s) more leeway in presenting the different micro-scenes. Beginning on the left there is a fragmentary patch in the upper sub-register and below it two individuals remain. Next, two sycamore trees are stacked one above the other and are followed by five palm trees positioned above a garden plot topped with a line of braziers. All of these are standard episodes of a Sacred District scene. The next portion of this register is quite damaged, but it is possible that the remains of someone's legs are preserved. If this is the case, then this would be an unexpected interruption to the Sacred District. Yet, both to the right and below this damaged part are lines of closed *ḥm*-chapels. The upper sub-register displays six or seven shrines, and the lower sub-register has possibly ten. Above the last couple of shrines on the lower sub-register are the guardians of the great gate and to the right of the last shrine on the bottom sub-register are the three pools (Figure 26). At this point, the sub-registers disappear, and the shrine of Osiris occupies the height of the full register. He also faces to the right, in-line with the orientation of the figures; however, he should be facing in the other direction. After all, he exists in the world of the dead, not in the world of the living (Figure 27). It is difficult to surmise if this is a product of the unusual placement of the Sacred District or an error. Most illustrations of the Sacred District follow the rules of compositional decorum; nevertheless, the tomb of Paheri at Elkab (TC 3) also exhibits the shrine of Osiris where his orientation is not what is expected (Figure 28). The last episode of Amenemhet's Sacred District is the two women who carry *nw*-pots and kneel before the four basins of water. At this point the wall ends. This micro-scene, as the terminating scene of the Sacred District, has parallels in Theban Tombs 81, 179, 82, 21, and 100. Another typical way to present the conclusion of the Sacred District was with the (small) shrine of Osiris, as seen in the tomb of Paheri.

When considering the architecture of TT 122 there are three side chapels that protrude from the left wall as one travels to the west along the corridor. Therefore, there are three potential "west walls" to record the funerary scenes. The artist(s) of this tomb chose the last chamber on the left and the one closest

[459] Shirley 2010: 272; Kampp-Seyfried 1996: 412; Polz 1990: 318, 334.

Figure 27: Osiris standing in his shrine and facing toward the symbolic west. Scene from TT 122. Photo by author.

Figure 28: Osiris standing in his shrine and facing toward the "west" and also sitting in his shrine facing toward the "east." Scene from Paheri's tomb at Elkab (TC 3). Photo by author.

to the west and focal point of the tomb.[460] So, again the architecture of this tomb and the placement of the Sacred District suggest that this scene was the buffer zone between the world of the living and the world of dead. Furthermore, Shirley has suggested that the chapels were part of the original plan of the tomb, and thus TT 122 is an example of planned tomb-sharing.[461] This means the placement of the Sacred District scene was intentional and part of the original decoration of the tomb. The artist(s) chose the closest location to the west and created this transformative scene so that the scenes on the walls would reflect the deceased's traversing from this world to the next. The scenes physically walk the viewer from east to west, from dead to alive, and from the exterior of the tomb to the focal point of the cult within.

The third atypical tomb is that of the Second Prophet

[460] Shirley 2010: 291.
[461] Shirley 2010: 291.

of Amun Puiemre (TT 39), which has been excellently preserved. He worked under Hatshepsut and retained his position under Thutmose III. His tomb's entrance does not face east, but instead is oriented toward the processional route of Hatshepsut's Temple of Millions of Years. Most other tombs from this period were built at Sheikh Abd el-Qurna. The plan of his tomb is unusual in that it resembles a traditional T-shaped tomb but has two additional side chambers of unequal size that open off of the transverse hall and parallel the short central passage. This means that the rear of the tomb faces south, and not west. The largest of the three chambers sits to the right side of the tomb, or on its west side. On the back wall of this chamber is a false door, and Puiemre's burial chamber lies behind it.[462] It is in this chamber that the Sacred District scene is illustrated among the funeral scenes that appear on either side of the doorway and continue on the wall to the north. So, although the construction of the tomb is atypical, the artists responded to the architecture of the tomb and managed to depict the Sacred District in its traditional liminal location. In this case, the destination of the funeral procession is the Goddess of the West who stands in the center of the right wall of the chapel—the western wall of the western chapel. It is also noteworthy that Puiemre's tomb is another example where the Sacred District scene has been depicted in conjunction with the location of the burial chamber.

Most decorative programs have the Sacred District depicted in one of the lower registers of the wall, while in the later examples (when evidence is available) the scene has been moved higher up on the wall. Since the majority of the Sacred District scenes date to the early part of the eighteenth dynasty and are concentrated in the reigns of Hatshepsut and Thutmose III, they appear in the lowest registers. This practice, then, should be considered typical or conventional. For illustrations that post-date the Amarna Period, the Sacred District appears higher up—Theban Tomb 41 being a good example. This trend may reflect Jan Assmann's supposition that in the Post-Amarna Period the decoration of the tomb is split into two spheres, an upper and a lower sphere.[463] Assmann interprets this new division as evolving from stela decoration and as an effort to create sacred space within the tomb chapel. He suggests that by this time the court has become the place of transition. This notion corroborates my argument that the Sacred District was transformative and liminal in nature because it appears in the upper registers of the court in TT 41. With this new division the upper areas of the tomb walls are decorated with sacred scenes, such as gods and goddesses, and the lower areas of the walls are decorated with the funeral cult.[464] This would mean that the Sacred District, at least during the period when TT 41 was decorated, was considered not only a sacred scene but one showing divine elements.

Compositional Rules

There were certain rules of composition that governed the way artists positioned figures in the registers on the chapel walls. This positioning aids in the "reading" of the tomb scenes in that it helps the viewer understand which way a person is traveling or directing his or her attention. Plainly put, figures of the deceased face out of the tomb, looking from the realm of the dead toward the realm of the living.[465] This could be the owner of the tomb, his wife, deceased family members and any deities that occupy the west. In turn, figures of the living (family members, offering bearers, priests, etc.) face into the tomb toward the symbolic west. These figures would have paralleled the actual officiants as they performed the funeral rites on the day of burial. The owner of a tomb was the most important person in the decorative program, and to show this dominance the Egyptians considered placement on the right the primary position and orientation to the right as establishing lateral dominance. Gay Robins, in her work *The Art of Ancient Egypt*, has pointed out that on some tomb walls the figure of the deceased is right facing, as is expected, but that on the opposite wall he must be reversed in order to face toward the tomb entrance.[466]

Through the illustration of the Sacred District in the tomb of Tetiky, these compositional rules become evident. In his 1925 work "The Tomb of Tetiky at Thebes (No. 15)," Norman de Garis Davies describes the scenes of the burial ceremonies as being on the left wall when entering from the east door. He calls TT 15 a "strange vault" probably intended to act as a passage leading to a burial chamber.[467] Moving from left to right, or from this world to the next, the funeral procession approaches three *Mww* who greet the cortege in the upper register of the south wall. This part marks the beginning of the micro-scenes that comprise the Sacred District. The procession moves toward the right and the *Mww* stand facing to the left. However, in this example there is one intervening

[462] Engelmann-von Carnap 2014: 350.

[463] Assmann 2003: 49.

[464] Assmann 2003: 49–51.

[465] Robins 2008: 74.

[466] Robins 2008: 74; *idem*. 1994: 35–36.

[467] N. Davies 1925: 16.

scene before we get to the main district area, where a priest performs a ritual on the mummy of Tetiky. The priest faces to the right and the coffin of Tetiky stands upright under a canopy and faces to the left. The Sacred District proper is broken into two sub-registers that are bracketed by the Hall of the *Mww* on the left and the shrine of Osiris on the right. Inside the Hall of the *Mww,* the two male figures face to the right and wear the typical conical headdress. The structure they occupy is shown in plan from above with the arched doorway drawn in profile (two different perspectives are combined). It is unclear if these are intended to be the same *Mww* who greet the procession earlier in the register, or if they are distinct. According to de Garis Davies' drawings, their headdresses are the same, but the original *Mww* wear broad collars and more elaborate kilts.[468] The ones inside the hall appear to be watching over the Sacred District as they are turned toward it. The orientation of the *Mww* is dependent on whether they are greeting the funeral cortege or standing in their hall. In the former case, they face toward the land of the living, but in the latter case they survey the Sacred District and face toward it. At this point, the scene divides into two sub-registers. On the upper register, there are two obelisks attached at their base, followed by two sycamore trees, and four open shrines—the first three have standing anthropomorphic deities inside. In the last shrine, there are the four guardians of the great gate. They are not typically shown inside a shrine, but instead in a structure called the great gate. However, their placement immediately in front of Osiris in his shrine is standard. This shrine is a quadrangular hut with four corner posts, vertical sides, and is covered with a barrel vault, probably of wattle-work. It resembles the national sanctuary of Lower Egypt, but with an additional *ẖkr*-frieze on top.[469] The *ẖkr*-frieze represents the ornamental tufts at the upper end of a papyrus stalk wall that are tied together in bundles. This type of ornamentation is regularly found at the top of wall decoration and was used since the predynastic period.[470] In the sub-register below, starting on the left, there are three date palms, a garden pool, and four additional shrines of the same type as noted above. The first one contains three pools—which do not ordinarily appear in a shrine—and the last three each contain a standing deity, the first two anthropomorphic and the third one composite (anthropomorphic with a canine's head). This third deity is probably Anubis who appears in a larger shrine in the Sacred District in the almost contemporary tomb of Reneny at Elkab. All of the deities in these shrines face to the left, or toward the entrance of the tomb in the east. The only exception to this is the guardians of the great gate who appear in their usual style in pairs facing each other (see Appendix I). At the very end of the scene, Osiris stands in his shrine facing to the left, as he occupies the land of the dead. It appears that the Hall of the *Mww* and the shrine of Osiris encapsulate the other elements, essentially demarcating the beginning and the end of the Sacred District, respectively.

There are relatively few figures that appear in Sacred District scenes, except when there is a series of open shrines, as in the case of Tetiky (TT 15). In many tombs the deceased appears at the end of the scene, either standing or kneeling before Osiris, and facing toward the realm of the dead. At this point, the deceased has traversed the Sacred District and has reached Osiris. The deceased can also appear sitting in front of an offering table and facing to the left as one of the blessed dead, having finished his journey through the Sacred District.

Reading the Scenes in Context

Reading the funerary scenes is not an easy endeavor; in fact, some maintain that it is just not possible. Many scholars assume that these scenes are only excerpts of a typical funeral and that the relationships between the scenes are ill-defined.[471] However, according to Janice Kamrin who has worked on the tomb of Khnumhotep II at Beni Hasan, groups of scenes, and even entire walls, can be read in sequence.[472]

Due to the relative homogeneity of the placement of the Sacred District scene, I contend that reading the scenes can be accomplished in most cases. In the majority of examples, this scene is the last scene that appears before the realm of the gods and is illustrated regularly before Osiris. This is visible in such examples as Theban Tombs 15, 100, 81, 122, 224, and in the tombs of Reneny and Paheri at Elkab. In addition to Osiris, there are two other deities who can appear in this position: Anubis and the Goddess of the West. Sometimes two or more of these deities appear terminating the registers that depict the funerary scenes (ex. TT 100). There are also a few cases where two gods stand adjacent to each other and conclude the Sacred District scene specifically (ex. TC 7). Osiris can appear in two different manners: standing in his shrine (ex. TC 7) or sitting on his throne (ex. TC

468 N. Davies 1925: pl. V.

469 Badawy 1990: 64.

470 Badawy 1990: 86.

471 Muhammed 1966: 161–175.

472 Kamrin 1999: 42–44, 47.

3). In both scenarios he should face toward the living, however in a minority of scenes he faces toward the west (ex. TT 122) (see Figures 27 and 28). Osiris can appear larger than the other figures in the scene and bracket the register, or he can appear small, usually standing in his shrine, and function as a micro scene within the larger tableau of the Sacred District. In the tomb of Paheri at Elkab we see both versions (see Figure 28). In the tomb of Reneny at Elkab, Anubis appears standing in his shrine beside Osiris and within the Sacred District, but the registers are larger than what is typical, so this example is an outlier. Since this is one of the earliest examples of the Sacred District it may be a precursor to two traditions in that both Osiris and Anubis end the Sacred District but appear larger and inside their individual shrines. A similar version appears in the tomb of Tetiky (TT 15), also an early version of the Sacred District. Later examples of Osiris show him either smaller and in his shrine as a micro-scene of the Sacred District composition or as a large figure situated at the end of the registers he brackets (as do Anubis and the Goddess of the West).

There are several distinguishable patterns in the order of the micro-scenes, for example, the guardians of the great gate often appear immediately before Osiris (or the realm of the dead). This can be observed in the tomb of Paheri at Elkab and in Theban Tombs 15, 39, 81, 122, and 21. The two women who kneel before the four basins of water are also regularly juxtaposed with the shrine of Osiris. For instance, Paheri's tomb illustrates the guardians, Osiris in his shrine, and the two kneeling women, moving from left to right, before a larger seated Osiris, who strictly speaking, is outside of the Sacred District in this case. TT 122 displays the guardians, Osiris in his shrine, and the kneeling women as the last micro-scenes of the register, while TT 17 depicts the guardians and the kneeling women before a large Goddess of the West. In TT 81 the artists have placed a small Osiris next to the kneeling women but without a large bracketing deity standing nearby.

Another common sequence of scenes combines the journey to Abydos and the Sacred District. Barbara Engelmann-von Carnap, in her work *Unconventional Versions: The Theban Tomb of Puiemra, Second Prophet of Amun under Hatshepsut*, states that in a standard T-shaped tomb from this time period the voyage to Abydos is combined with the funeral scenes and precedes them. However, she does not separate the Sacred District from the rest of the funeral ceremonies. So, when brought together on the same wall, the journey to Abydos typically precedes the Sacred District.[473] Many of the tombs that have a Sacred District scene also include the voyage to Abydos (ex. Theban Tombs 39, 125, 81, 21, 71, 127, 123, 112, 53, 82, and 100). According to Engelmann-von Carnap, the Abydos journey is chronologically sensitive and extremely useful for dating a tomb correctly.[474] She has organized the scenes at Sheikh Abd el-Qurna from the early eighteenth dynasty into three types.

Type 1 predates Hatshepsut/Thutmose III (ex. TT 81 and TT 21). In these examples, the departure for Abydos begins in the symbolic west and travels toward the symbolic east, while the return trip is directed back to the west. In the tomb of Ineni (TT 81) the two ships are visible in the top left corner of the wall, above the Sacred District. The lower of the two ships represents the departure north, presumably to Abydos. The ship above heads south, as the sails are visible in the illustration, presumably heading back to Thebes. In this case, the symbolic west would represent the Theban necropolis, the physical location of the burial of Ineni, and where the Sacred District was imagined to be. Following this logic, the Sacred District may depict the environs of Thebes. This point argues that there are indeed other sites than Abydos during the New Kingdom that may have functioned as an interface between this world and that of Osiris.[475]

Type 2 represents the main phase of these depictions and dates to the co-regency of Hatshepsut and Thutmose III and into the latter's sole reign (ex. Theban Tombs 71, 39, 17, 125, 127, 123, 112, 53, and 82). In examples of Type 2, the boat travels toward the west and returns from the west. In the tomb of Amenemhet (TT 82), the voyage to Abydos is in the upper register and directed west toward the focal point of the tomb. The return trip is shown above and reversed.[476] This pattern implies that the symbolic west should be interpreted as Abydos. When Amenemhet sails "west" the sails are down, meaning that the trip is imagined to be traveling north with the current of the Nile. In his return to the symbolic "east" the sails are up. This means Amenemhet is traveling south with the wind, and back to Thebes. Since the Sacred District in Amenemhet's tomb is extremely fragmentary, and because the micros-scenes are not depicted in a tight group as is common in earlier tombs, the reading of these scenes is more complex and does not lead to firm conclusions (Figure 29).

Type 3 dates to the final phase of Thutmose III's

[473] Engelmann-von Carnap 2014: 352.
[474] Engelmann-von Carnap 2014: 339.
[475] Smith 2017: 195.
[476] N. M. Davies and Gardiner 1915: pl. 12.

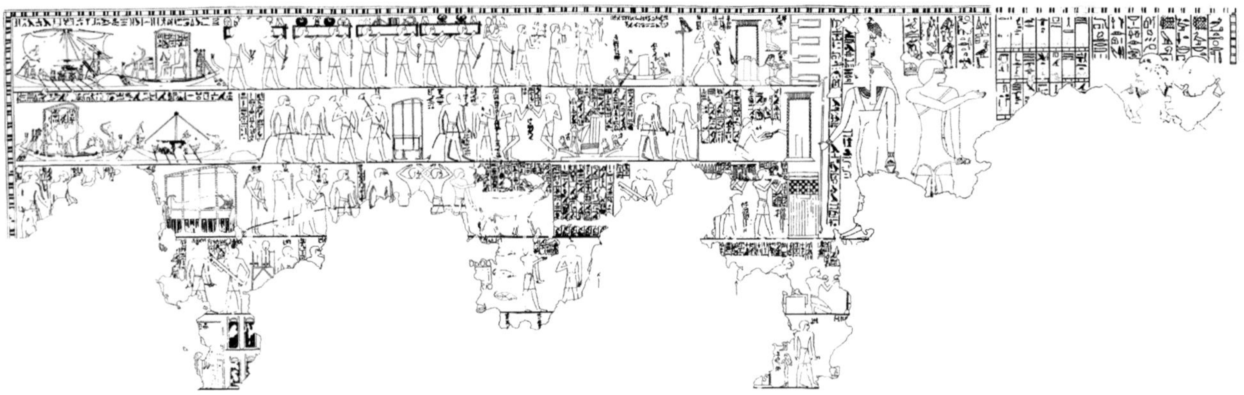

Figure 29: Line-drawing of the funerary scenes and Sacred District in the tomb of Amenemhet (TT 82). Courtesy of www.osirisnet.net.

sole reign during Hatshepsut's proscription. There are no clear examples of this type of voyage in tombs that contain the Sacred District. No change appears at the beginning of Thutmose III's sole reign, and any new developments seem to be connected with the reign of Amenhotep II.[477]

Engelmann von-Carnap's study implies that the voyage to and from Abydos was intimately connected to the Sacred District in terms of its frequency over time, the date of its employment, and where it was placed within the artistic scheme. Her work also emphasizes that the artists painstakingly produced these images in consideration of the cardinal directions. Therefore, Abydos and symbolic "west" are synonymous for Type 2 illustrations, but Type 1 illustrations show the deceased sailing to Abydos and returning to Thebes—the symbolic west.

Summary

The Sacred District scene serves as a buffer zone between the scenes that represent events taking place during the actual funeral in the cemetery, in this world, such as the dragging of the coffin and the deposition of burial goods, and those scenes depicting the hereafter, such as Osiris and the deceased accepting offerings. Its consistent placement in the passage of a T-shaped tomb (or the equivalent thereof) furthers this supposition. Since the passage itself functioned architecturally as a transitional zone connecting the transverse hall to the statue chapel it effectively guides the deceased toward the world of the gods. As Assmann has aptly noted, it is the passage that symbolizes the transition from this life to the next in the T-shaped tomb, as does what is depicted on the walls, "[t]ransition led the deceased into the mystery of Osiris."[478] And Osiris, poised in his shrine or sitting on his throne, is the last scene before the mortuary service done in the tomb's holy of holies, the west end of the passage.

[477] Engelmann-von Carnap 2014: 339.
[478] Assmann 2005: 147–163.

CHAPTER EIGHT: THE TERM *T3 D̲SR* AND ITS ASSOCIATION WITH THE SACRED DISTRICT

One of the major difficulties to emerge with this study is in assessing how this depiction may or may not represent a real location. The Sacred District scene seems to represent a space captured by the mind's eye, and based on its constituent components, it is a place where divinities reside and where the deceased can come into contact with them on his day of burial. It appears that this space facilitates communication between the spiritual and physical realms and acts as an interface accessible to the funeral cortege on the day of burial so that the deceased might continue his afterlife journey. Since it is the presence of divinity that makes a space sacred, this area was most likely created as a "sacred" space to symbolize the meanings and accommodate Egyptian rituals.[479] By and large, a sacred space is a place worthy of spiritual respect that inspires awe, but it must be set apart. A space as such stands out in relation to the profane, is usually considered to belong to the same dimension, and is an integral part of "religion."[480] However, at the same time these spaces are autonomous and outside the normal time and space continuum—they are eternal.[481] Sacred spaces have the power to focus on events, conduct, relationships, and people that a society finds important. They also must have an explicit purpose in that particular objects or actions that carry religious meaning are connected to the site.[482] A sacred space must be understood in three important ways: It encompasses a ritual space that offers a location for formalized, repeatable, symbolic performances; it must be interpreted as a significant place that raises questions about life; and it must emphasize the significance of being human. Each illustration of the Sacred District implies that this space was understood in these three significant ways. Since it is depicted on tomb walls, it represent an eternal and perpetual location for ritual. The scene appears in abundance, especially during the early part of the eighteenth dynasty, and it was an integral part of the Egyptians' conception of the journey to the afterlife.

[479] Barrie 1996: 1.

[480] There is no word in ancient Egyptian for "religion" (Manassa 2019: 159).

[481] Heynickx, *et al.*, 2012: 7.

482 Heynickx, *et al.*, 2012: 8.

Modern Egyptologists sometimes employ the English word "holy" to describe this area, but there is a difference between "sacred" and "holy." Rajesh Heynickx, *et al.*, in their introductory chapter to *Loci Sacri: Understanding Sacred Places*, suggests that sacred places deal with memories and cannot be obliterated, while something holy relies on experience.[483] Holiness can be associated with certain rituals, but holy actions do not necessarily render a place holy. With the Sacred District there are indeed glimpses of ritual activity, but the full nature remains wholly unknown. David Bell remarks that holiness can be attributed to a site for religious, political, national, or economic reasons.[484] This brings up a significant point, namely that the Sacred District scene offers evidence for its national significance. For example, one could argue that the Lower Egyptian shrines of Buto and Sais have national significance (even though they appear adjacent to the Sacred District), or alternatively that the rows of *ḫm*-chapels (if interpreted as *pr-nw* shrines) represent the national sanctuary of Lower Egypt, which resonated with people Egypt-wide. It is fascinating to contemplate the residual sanctity the memory of these buildings might have had fifteen-hundred years later, or how these antiquated structures were perceived by inhabitants of Upper Egypt. Yet, sacred space does not have to be only architectural, in fact, in this case the Egyptians depict a landscape with both natural and architectural elements. Being so far removed from the ancient world it is difficult, if not impossible, to truly comprehend how the Egyptians understood the concept of "sacred" (the word *d̲sr*) in reference to our own experiences in the modern world. Consequently, the material culture left to us implies that these illustrations represent a space in this world *and* in the next world—a space that is both mythical and legendary.

To continue, two points must be established. First, this area is segregated artistically in the early tomb depictions. The registers give the immediate appearance of a demarcated area, and as sub-registers are also employed, one is left with the notion of a tightly organized space. The Hall of the *Mww* often acts as a "guard house" or entrance point to the Sacred District and marks the beginning of the scene. This hall denotes security and segregation, and because it extends to the top of the register it might imply a physical structure blocked entry. Second, the quality of this area is sacred because of the divine presence. This point is verified by the open gods' shrines and

[483] Heynickx, *et al.*, 2012: 11.

[484] Bell 2012: 14.

the shrines of Osiris and Anubis. Most frequently, the shrine of Osiris stands at the end of the district and marks the terminal point of the scene. Sometimes Osiris is substituted with Anubis or the Goddess of the West. The Hall of the *Mww* and the shrine of Osiris function as two constructed entities controlling entry and exit, encapsulating the Sacred District (physically). This chapter explores the etymology of the term *tꜣ ḏsr* and investigates supplementary textual sources for a better understanding of this space. Additionally, I present evidence to confirm the importance of Abydos in relation to the *tꜣ ḏsr* and its connection with the necropolis.

Etymology

The ancient Egyptian term *tꜣ ḏsr* has been found in two private tombs to refer to the area that I term the Sacred District. According to Siegfried Morenz, who follows other scholars such as Francis Llewellyn Griffith and Sir Alan Henderson Gardiner, in its original sense *ḏsr* means to "set apart" or "segregate."[485] It has also been recognized that *ḏsr* can mean "holy" or "sacred" when used in a religious context. When the determinative of a hand holding a stick was employed this signified the warding off of evil or unclean forces, thus making an area sacred. With *ḏsr* having an original meaning of "segregated," it was by proxy that *ḏsr* came to have the meaning "sacred."[486] This makes sense because areas or objects were segregated because they were sacred.

It is the application of the term *tꜣ ḏsr* to the scene in question that allows the area to be labeled. Although this label is not ubiquitous in the examples of the Sacred District scene, it does appear in the tomb of Senet (TT 60) and the tomb of Tetiky (TT 15). In the tomb of Senet, the caption is found on the south wall of the passage above images of the funeral procession. It reads as follows: *drỉ r sḥ n Mww r rwy tꜣ ḏsr* "Putting down at the Hall of the *Mww* at the entrance to the *tꜣ ḏsr*."[487] Here, four *Mww* come out to greet the cortege. The second attestation is from the upper scene on the south wall of the early eighteenth dynasty tomb of Tetiky. The inscription reads: *ḥtp dỉ nsw (n) Wsỉr ḫnty ỉmntyw Inpw ḫnty sḥ nṯr tpy ḏw.f ỉmy-wt nb tꜣ ḏsr* "An offering which the king gives (to) Osiris, foremost of westerners, and Anubis, foremost of the god's shrine, he who is upon his mountain, he who is in the place of embalming, lord of the sacred/segregated land" (Figure 30). This caption appears above the oxen dragging the coffin. They stop behind the lector priest who extends his right hand out to the *Mww*. The three *Mww* each have one foot raised as if stepping forward and their index fingers on both hands point down to the ground in front of them. These inscriptions in TT 60 and TT 15 describe the point in the tomb decoration where Senet and Tetiky (respectively) encounter the *Mww,* and in the case of Tetiky, the Sacred District. The tomb of Senet is too early to have a complete Sacred District recorded. The majority of Sacred District scenes does not have captions, or at least they are not preserved to us today. This is what makes Theban Tombs 60 and 15 so valuable. These labels inform us that the *Mww* mark the beginning of the *tꜣ ḏsr,* and Tetiky's tomb decoration shows us that the shrine of Osiris ends it. This pattern holds true for most of the Sacred District scenes.

The name given to this area by the ancient Egyptians reveals that they considered this land as segregated—that is, sacred land. The reason a cemetery is called *tꜣ ḏsr* is because necropolises were located away from inhabited places, in areas cut off from the living. So, the phrase *tꜣ ḏsr* emerged from the understanding of this space as a separate area that was home to the transfigured spirits and blessed dead. The artistic renditions of the Sacred District bear out this point. The members of the funeral procession do not cross into this area, nor is there any tangible human action inside the proscribed place, except in isolated examples. This substantiates the point that the space illustrated in these New Kingdom scenes was pure and that it was desirable to preserve the sanctity of the space by warding off evil and any unclean elements. The *Mww* stand at the entrance to the Sacred District as greeters and overseers of the district and were responsible for maintaining the sanctity of the land.

Sources

The appellation *tꜣ ḏsr* establishes the fact that this space was a segregated area that was sacred to the Egyptians. In past scholarship, the Sacred District has been considered to be a mythical setting, an afterlife landscape, a ritual precinct, and a cemetery proper. The procession scene in Theban Tomb 60 depicts the coffin being dragged to the tomb in the necropolis, and therefore illustrates a rendition of an authentic funeral taking place in this world, in the sense that it follows the paradigm for a real-life procession. There are three sources that provide additional information on the *tꜣ ḏsr*: *The Story of Sinuhe* from the Middle Kingdom, the Abydos steal of Khutuwyre Ugaf from the Second Intermediate

[485] Morenz 1973: 100.
[486] Hoffmeier 1985: 1.
[487] Davies, Davies, and Gardiner 1920: pls. XXI, XXII; see also Settgast 1963: 30, 48.

Figure 30: Reconstruction of the Sacred District in the tomb of Tetiky (TT 15). Adapted from N. Davies 1925: plate V by Roman Reed.

Period, and several Middle Kingdom stelae from the Theban area.

The Story of Sinuhe

The Story of Sinuhe provides textual evidence for the *Mww* in the context of a real-world setting, albeit in a work of literature. There is no reference to the *tꜣ ḏsr* in this text but presuming that the *Mww* exist in the *tꜣ ḏsr,* some observations can be made. Widely considered to be the greatest literary piece to come out of ancient Egypt, *The Story of Sinuhe* is preserved on five Middle Kingdom papyri, two New Kingdom papyri, and twenty-five New Kingdom ostraca.[488] The story is set in the reign of Senwosret I (*c.*1961–1917 BCE) and the plot opens with the death of his father and co-regent Amenemhet I. Historically, Amenemhet I died in his thirtieth year on the throne, which probably corresponds to his son tenth regnal year.[489] In the story, Sinuhe hears of the death of the king and flees Egypt, landing himself in Syria. Here, he becomes a prominent tribal leader, marries, and has children—but he is not happy. Sinuhe longs for Egypt and begins to contemplate his funeral and his afterlife. King Senwosret hears about Sinuhe's adventures abroad and writes to him pressing him to come home. Yet, instead of being admonished, Sinuhe is granted wealth and given a spot in the royal necropolis for his tomb. The copy of the royal decree bought to Sinuhe reads:

> A procession will be made for you on the day of interment, the anthropoid sarcophagus (overlaid) with gold [leaf], the head with lapis lazuli, and the sky above you as you are placed in the outer coffin and dragged by teams of oxen preceded by singers. The dance of the Muu will be performed at your tomb, and the necessary offerings will be invoked for you. They will slaughter at the entrance of your tomb chapel, your pillars to be set up in limestone as is done for the royal children.[490]

James P. Allen describes this procession as taking place between the embalming house and the tomb, where the dance of the *Mww* was performed.[491] This passage demonstrates that during the Middle and New Kingdoms the *Mww* performed a ritual dance in front of the funeral procession on the day of entombment. Oxen drag the bier that holds the coffin and singers walk in front. The procession encounters the *Mww* at the entrance to the tomb, where the offering-list is recited, and animals are slaughtered. Since this literary tale was meant for entertainment and describes a real-world funeral, the mythologized aspects of the *Mww* are not present. So, when Greg Reeder discusses two versions of the *Mww* in his study "The Mysterious Muu and the Dance They Do," this example represents those performers, or ritualists, who attend the funeral on the day of burial (see Appendix I). Therefore, *The Story of Sinuhe* potentially corroborates the real-life performance of the *Mww* at the funeral on the day of burial.

The Abydos Stela of Khutawyre Ugaf

An intriguing example of the term *tꜣ ḏsr* occurs on a thirteenth dynasty stela from Abydos (Cairo JE 35256).[492] The red granite stela of Khutawyre Ugaf, usurped by Neferhotep I, was found in the North cemetery at Abydos and provides evidence for a *tꜣ ḏsr* existing at this site.[493] This text is a monumental royal decree that was inscribed on a stela set up to protect

---

[488] J. Allen 2015: 55.

[489] J. Allen 2015: 56.

[490] Simpson 2003: 62. See also Lichtheim 1975: 229 and J. Allen 2015: 119–120. Allen transliterates and translates text B, which equates to pBerlin 3022 and pAmherst n-q. The line I am concerned with is B 194: *ỉr.tw ḫbb nnyw r r ỉs.k*. Allen notes that *ḫbb nnyw* means literally, "dance of the inert ones" and refers to a ritual in which performers representing the ancestors of the deceased welcomed the arrival of the procession at the tomb. He reinterprets *Mww* and instead reads the signs as *nnyw,* noting that this word is of unknown meaning but is perhaps a plural nisbe of *mw* "water," or *mwỉw* "watery ones" (after Altenmüller 1975b).

[491] J. Allen 2015: 120–122.

[492] Leahy 1989: fig. 1 and pl. VI.

[493] The original titulary on the stela has been recut with the names of Neferhotep I.

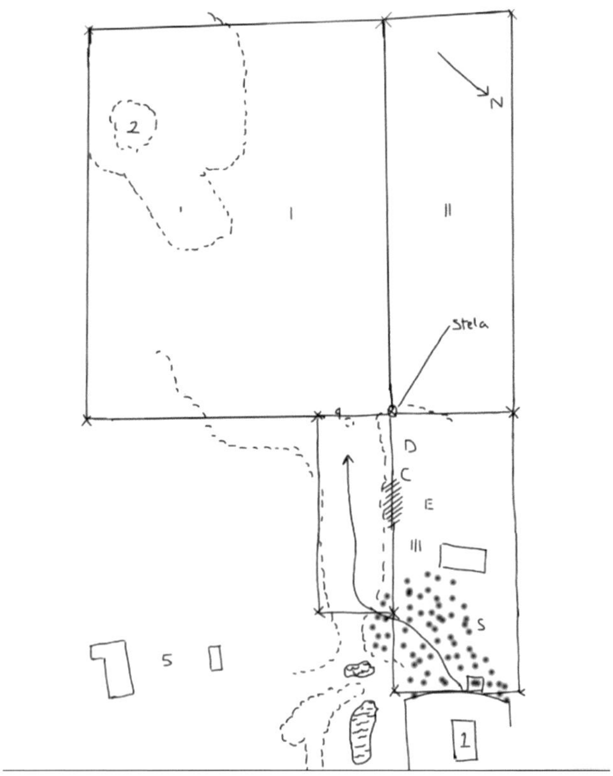

Figure 31: Diagram of processional route from the Osiris temple to Umm el-Qa'ab at Abydos. Adaptation by Roman Reed after Leahy 1989: figure 2.

a sacred area dedicated to Wepwawet.[494] It has four purposes: to protect the area sacred to Wepwawet, to order the establishment of four stela as boundary markers, to establish penalties for intruders, and to remind people that they can construct tombs outside the Sacred District. The reason the area is dedicated to Wepwawet is because he is the "Opener of Ways" who leads the procession. It also emphasizes that anyone who is caught in the *tꜣ ḏsr*, except for the priests, will be burnt. According to John Gee, this was one of a set of four stelae that would have acted as boundary markers and would have been placed around the wadi leading from Kom el-Sultan to Umm el-Qa'ab, thus marking the processional way.[495] It is not known if the extant stela is one from the north or south pair, or if it was erected in the east or the west. The measurements of this area are also unknown because of a history of poor recording at Abydos.[496] The text recounts that this is a sacred area where no tombs or chapels are allowed to be built. It reads:

> It is for his father Wepwawet, lord of the necropolis (*tꜣ ḏsr*), that he has made as his monument: Year four, My Majesty, l.p.h., decrees the protection of the holy land (*tꜣ ḏsr)* south of Abydos for his father Wepwawet, lord of the necropolis (*tꜣ ḏsr)*, like that which Horus did for his father Osiris Wennefer, forbidding anyone to trespass upon this holy land (*pꜣ tꜣ ḏsr*).[497] Two stelae are to be set up on the south and two on its north, carved with the great name of My Majesty, l.p.h. The south of the holy land (*tꜣ ḏsr*) is to be defined by those stelae which shall be set up on the south side, and the north by those stelae which shall be set up on the north side. As for anyone who shall be found within these stelae, except for a priest about his duties, he shall be burnt. Moreover, as for any official who shall cause a tomb to be made for himself within this holy place (*tꜣ st ḏsr)*, he shall be reported and this law applied to him and to the necropolis-guard as (is the case) today. But as for everywhere outside this holy place (*ꜣ st ḏsr)*, (it is) an area where people may make tombs for themselves and where one may be buried.[498]

Anthony Leahy, in his article "A Protective Measure at Abydos in the Thirteenth Dynasty," suggests that the *tꜣ ḏsr* is the wadi at Abydos where the Festival of Osiris takes place. Perhaps the wadi was threatened by the dense building of funerary monuments in the north cemetery. It had to be kept clear because it was the processional route from the Osiris temple to the Umm el-Qa'ab. Processions were likely to have run from the south-west gate of the temple enclosure, through the memorial chapel area, and across the north cemetery (Figure 31).[499] This inscription explicitly states that no one could use this low-lying area for burial, but that there were other areas nearby that were open. This suggests that *tꜣ ḏsr* does not refer to a necropolis in the conventional manner. The description of the four stelae used to demarcate the holy area is reminiscent of the boundary stelae used to define the area of

[494] Leahy 1989: 41–61, esp. 54. For Wepwawet, see Spiegel 1973: 54–59.

[495] Gee 1998: 48–50, following Leahy 1989; Kemp 1975: 35–36; James 1982: 78–79.

[496] Leahy 1989: 51–52.

[497] Here *pꜣ* acts as a specifier according to Leahy (1989: 44). This sense is continued later by the feminine *tꜣ ḏsr* See also Hoffmeier 1985: 138.

[498] This stela was discovered by A. Mace at Abydos (1902). For a more recent reconstruction see Leahy 1989, fig. 1. It is currently in the Cairo Museum (JE 35256) (Leahy 1989: 43). For translation see Richards 2005: 79-80 (transliteration added by author). The last line of this text, not reproduced here, suggests a possible name for this area: "Provider of Breath" (Leahy 1989: 43, 46).

[499] Leahy 1989: 50–54.

Akhetaten, but is otherwise not widely attested. Leahy reconstructs the *tȝ ḏsr* as a rectangular space using the known stela as an anchor for the rectangle in the extreme south-western end of the North Cemetery on the north-western side of the wadi.[500] He supposes that the stela was found *in situ* since it is made of heavy red granite and suggests that this must have been the preferred method of delineating a particular piece of land, as opposed to the building of walls.[501] Stelae would definitely have been less costly. However, there are no stelae illustrated in the Sacred District in the private New Kingdom tomb scenes, nor are there any walls present other than those of the buildings situated therein: the Hall of the *Mww*, the great gate, gods' shrines, etc. However, the main reason the stelae were constructed was to prevent burial or trespass to an area that had originally been protected by custom.

The *tȝ ḏsr*, as described on the Abydos stela of Khutawyre Ugaf, is a sacred area adjacent to an already existing cemetery, located in a wadi slightly south of the Terrace of the Great God. Barry Kemp suggests that this wadi divided the Abydos necropolis into two parts while acting as the processional way for the Osiris Festival, a theory supported by Leahy and Janet Richards.[502] This processional route was for the annual festival when the cult statue was brought from the temple and transferred to the area of Umm el-Qa'ab. This annual procession began at the southwestern gate of the temple to Osiris-Khentyimentu and continued west through the memorial-chapel area, across the North Cemetery and then down toward the area called Poker.[503] During the Middle Kingdom the first dynasty tomb of King Djer was reconditioned to be the tomb of the god Osiris, at which time erecting a memorial chapel/stela or tomb as close as possible to the processional route was part of the pilgrimage experience. This way cult devotees could experience the annual procession eternally. The processional route must have been in danger of encroachment from the tomb building in the North Cemetery, so the purpose of this decree was to prevent further construction in a specific area at the site of Abydos—the area referred to as the *tȝ ḏsr*.[504]

Leahy highlights the fact that if an area with tombs had restricted access, families would not be able to visit the graves of their ancestors, and this would have been impious. Moreover, there is no mention in the decree of existing tombs in this space. This inscription is intriguing because it reveals that tombs were not permitted in the *tȝ ḏsr*, therefore, the term *tȝ ḏsr* in this context is not specifically referring to the necropolis *per se*, but to a holy area within the larger Abydene funerary landscape.[505]

There are discrepancies as to exactly how the site of Abydos should be reconstructed, so it cannot be fully understood. The site was occupied for a long period of time, the excavations have not been exhaustive, and we can never truly understand what Abydos meant to the ancient Egyptians.[506] Abydos was a provincial center in the eighth southern Egyptian nome and was historically significant because of its symbolic value and emotional power.[507] It was not a national center or a royal city, nor did it have any strategic, military, or economic value. The Osiris temple that stood on the site probably had the same status as any other provincial temple, but David O'Connor suggests that through the preserved mortuary texts a much richer understanding of Abydos comes to light. The texts reveal that in the national landscape Abydos had a higher symbolic value than most centers. Osiris was actually linked to many sites, such as Heliopolis, Letopolis, Rosetau, Herakleopolis, and Nareref, but Abydos was special because it was the access point to both subterranean and celestial versions of the afterlife.[508] The mortuary landscape stretches across the low desert between the fertile land and the cliffs in the west, and according to Richards, a natural depression was used as a processional way for almost three millennia.[509] This observation is significant for the identification of the Sacred District scene as being reminiscent of the processional way that linked the Osiris temple in the North Abydos town with the tomb of Osiris in the west—the destination of the procession. The Sacred District scene consistently shows Osiris as the destination in the deceased's journey to the hereafter or as one of the last micro-scenes within the district.[510] This royal decree also reveals that burial in this area was monitored, or that

[500] Leahy recognizes that space may not be rectilinear (1989: 52). See fig. 2 in Leahy 1989: 51.

[501] Richards 2005: 80.

[502] Kemp 1975: 35–36; Leahy 1984: 199, note 5; Leahy 1989: 54; Richards 2005: 79.

[503] Collier and Manley 2002: 54–55.

[504] Leahy 1989: 52–54.

[505] Leahy 1989: 50. See also Richards who reports that this stela is recording the prohibiting of access to the wadi (2005: 136).

[506] O'Connor 2009: 71.

[507] O'Connor 2009: 72.

[508] O'Connor 2009: 73.

[509] Richards 2005: 130.

[510] A typical order may represent the Goddess of the West as the necropolis, then Anubis as guardian of the cemetery and the one who leads the dead to Osiris, followed by Osiris himself (Muhammed 1966: 162).

in the past someone had breached its perimeter and new regulations had been established.[511] The peaceful, quiet atmosphere described on the stela is reminiscent of the drawings of the Sacred District in the private tombs and evocative of the descriptions of Osiris as the Lord of Silence. It is unknown if this sacred space was specific to Abydos and the Mysteries of Osiris. It may have been the case that such areas were commonly located adjacent to active cemeteries. Or the process could be reversed in that locations for tomb-building were selected for their proximity to sacred areas. In any case, the decree on Khutawyre Ugaf's stela was successful because the areas on either side of the processional way were used and reused for tomb building for centuries, but the wadi itself was not used for burials until the Roman Period.[512] Another facet of the Abydos landscape worth noting is an area to the southeast of the Osiris enclosure where a sacred lake of the temple lay. Beatrix Gessler-Löhr, following Émile Chassinat, suggests Poker should be located in this area instead of at Umm el-Qa'ab. This lake may have played a role in the Osiris Mysteries and may account for the watery landscapes depicted in the private New Kingdom tombs at Thebes.[513] Khutawyre Ugaf is attested generally in the south: Semna, Mirgissa, Elephantine, Medamud, and Karnak. This demonstrates a southern interest in the religious cult at Abydos.[514]

Perhaps it was Abydos that the artists adapted for the decoration of high officials' tombs at Thebes, Elkab, and Hierakonpolis, similar to the employment of the river voyage to Abydos scene. Or maybe it was an imagined version of this sacred space that melded with the Theban landscape, with the divine realm superimposed on the physical landscape. Yet, none of this explains the presence of the shrines of the Sacred Delta localities and thus this is more reason to exclude them from the Sacred District proper.

The combined evidence from the inscriptions and scenes in Theban Tombs 60 and 15, the *Story of Sinuhe,* and the stela of Khutawyre Ugaf from Abydos indicate that the *tꜣ ḏsr* was an area near the burial ground, but only in the vicinity of the tombs, not the burial ground proper. These texts also support the location of the *tꜣ ḏsr* being on the west bank of the Nile and possibly embodying a ritual district, imagined between the embalming place and the tomb, or mimicking the area between the Osiris Temple and Umm el-Qa'ab. It appears that access to the Sacred District was achieved via the necropolis on the day of burial.

[511] Richards 2005: 79.

[512] Leahy 1989: 53–54.

[513] Gessler-Löhr 1983: 425–437; Chassinat 1966: 254–260.

[514] Leahy 1989: 48, note 13.

Private Funerary Stelae

Already in the Middle Kingdom Abydos was a cult center for Osiris, especially the Umm el-Qa'ab area and the tomb of Djer, and there are several stelae from the Theban area that illustrate the Osirian nature of the afterlife during the Middle Kingdom.[515] They also evidence the national character of the Osirian cult and provide a more nuanced view as to how adherents who lived in Thebes hoped to access Osiris at Abydos. The Middle Kingdom offering formula wish the dead be given offerings with the followers of Osiris during the festivals of the necropolis together with the ancestors who existed in the past. Likewise, they travel with the great god during his voyages to Poker.[516]

Among the significant developments that took place within the cult of Osiris during the Eleventh Dynasty, is the so-called early "Abydos formula" that is first seen on round-topped stelae from Abydos. This formula eventually made its way onto Theban stelae, four of which belong to Tjetji,[517] Henenu,[518] Qemnen,[519] and Intef.[520] According to Miriam Lichtheim, these private tomb stelae of the eleventh dynasty exhibit examples of Osirian afterlife wishes on the part of their owners.[521] Although the Abydos formula begins in the eleventh dynasty, it is fully solidified in the twelfth dynasty on stelae from both Abydos and Thebes.[522]

The stelae of Qemnen and Intef have no provenance, but Tjetji's stela was discovered in his Theban tomb, and it is assumed that Henenu's stela was set up in his Theban tomb (TT 313) as well.[523] These latter two stelae are significant because they demonstrate that Osirian rituals were practiced at Thebes as early as the eleventh dynasty. Furthermore, they evidence the progress of Osirian symbolism in that Henenu's stela includes wishes that are both identical to those of Tjetji's and newer ones. Both of these inscriptions begin with an Old Kingdom core derived from the

[515] Leahy 1989: 55.

[516] Smith 2017: 203.

[517] BM 614.

[518] Moscow 4071.

[519] Turin 1517.

[520] Ny Carlsberg Glyptothek inv. 963.

[521] Lichtheim 1988: 57.

[522] Smith 2017: 204.

[523] This stela was acquired in Luxor by Golenishev and is probably one of four stela that once stood in the deceased's tomb. This stela does not have a titulary (Lichtheim 1988: 59).

sixth dynasty (but reinterpreted) and continue with the addition of Osirian wishes. These Osirian nuances suggest that the deceased will be received at Abydos and that he wishes to reach the celestial regions where Re and Osiris reside.[524] Mark Smith, in his work *Following Osiris: Perspectives on the Osirian Afterlife from Four Millenia*, adds that collectively these wishes in the formulae show that the dead want to be allowed to participate in the cult, especially the festival at Abydos during the inundation season.[525] Perhaps the watery landscape in the Sacred District scene references this fertile potential the flooding brings. In fact, Henenu's stela exhibits Osirian overtones within the original core which stems from the Old Kingdom. Both of these eleventh dynasty stelae allude to a council of gods and the judgment of the dead. The following is an excerpt from Henenu's stela:

> May he cross the firmament, traverse the sky,
> Ascent to the great god,
> Land in peace in the good west, as one honored by Osiris.
> May he travel to the western lightland, to where Osiris is,
> May the desert open him her arms,
> May the west give her hands to him.
> May he open the ways he wishes in peace, in peace,
> May he tread the paths of the necropolis with the followers of Osiris.
> May the west open him her door,
> May Hapy bring him his offerings.
> … May hand be given him in the *neshmet*-bark on the ways of the west,
> May "welcome in peace" be said to him by the great of Abydos.
> May he ply the oars in the night-bark,
> May he land in the day-bark,
> May the great ones tell him "travel in peace to Re in the sky."[526]

The stelae of Qemnen and Intef do not include the Old Kingdom core but are entirely Osirian in character with specific mention of Abydos. Based on the style of Qemnen's stela, it probably dates to the end of the eleventh dynasty, as does that of Intef. The wishes on Intef's stela make explicit mention to the divine judgment:

> May his *ka* be with him, his offerings before him, his voice be found true at the reckoning of the surplus: 'Tell your fault and it shall be removed for you from all you have told,' for the
> honored Royal Seal-bearer, the truly beloved of his lord, his praised one whom he favors, the
> Troop commander Intef, justified.[527]

Lichtheim notes that both of these stelae demonstrate additions and variations in the Osirian wishes, if one uses Tjeti's stela as a basis.[528] But, unlike the stela of Tjeti, which first notes the celestial component of the afterlife, the Theban stela of Meru is more focused on the site of Abydos and the rituals that take place at that site.[529] The stela of Meru was found in his Theban Tomb (TT 240) and dates to year 46 of the reign of Mentuhotep II. The relevant passage follows:

> Year 46. O priests, priestesses, songsters, songstresses, musicians male and female, 'servant and master' of Thinite Abydos! It is a good name that you recall on the monthly feast, the
> half-monthly feast, on the *Wag*-feast, and on every feast of Abydos, since there occurred the
> good beginning when Montu gave the Two Lands to King Nebhepetre, ever living!...
> Honored before the great god, lord of Abydos, the Overseer of the treasury Meru.
> The Overseer of the Treasury, his lord's favorite Meru, justified, as he gives praise to Osiris,
> kisses the ground to Khentamenthes and Wepwawet, the honored Meru.[530]

During the eleventh dynasty these Osirian afterlife wishes were still developing, and according to Lichtheim, should not be considered formulaic until the early twelfth dynasty when the worship of Osiris climaxes on Abydene private stela in a standard twenty-one wish sequence.[531] What is intriguing for the sake of this work is that some of the earliest examples of this new theology are evidenced at Thebes.

It is also at this time that the journey to Abydos appears as a motif in the tomb decoration of private tombs, with the earliest example occurring in the

[524] This celestial component is not recognized in the sixth dynasty private examples but instead is part of the so-called "democratization of religion" that occurs at this time. The origin of the celestial ascent lies in the *Pyramid Texts* that are attested for royalty alone (Lichtheim 1988: 58).
[525] Smith 2017: 204.
[526] This translation is from Lichtheim 1988: 60.
[527] Lichtheim 1988: 58, 62–63.
[528] Lichtheim 1988: 62, note 4.
[529] Turin 1447.
[530] Lichtheim 1988: 63–64.
[531] Lichtheim 1988: 58, 129.

tomb of Dagi (TT 103) from the late eleventh dynasty.[532] Furthermore, the epithet *m3ʿ-ḫrw* appears after personal names at this time, as evidenced by inscriptions on stelae from Thebes (see the stelae of Intef and Meru above). Lichtheim also records a graffito left in TT 60 by the scribe, Ramose-nefer, "...a scribe righteous from his mother's womb, the scribe Ramose-nefer, justified...".[533] Therefore, there are several proofs supporting the popularity of Abydos and the cult of Osiris within a Theban context.

Leahy attributes this spread of Osirian influence to state encouragement of the cult and suggests that by the reign of Senwosret I the Mysteries of Osiris were being celebrated and Abydos had become a pilgrimage site.[534] As noted earlier, this interest in the cult of Osiris may correspond to Abydos' absorption into the Theban state. The fact that the Osiris cult was appealing to both the royal and private spheres made this cult unique in the history of ancient Egypt. The decorative programs in the early eighteenth dynasty tombs farther south at Elkab and Hierakonpolis further indicate the extent of the spread of the Osirian cult at this time and in the succeeding period.

Royal Interest in Abydos

There was intense royal interest in the area from the reign of Senwosret III to the late thirteenth dynasty, at which time more personal involvement on the king's part took place.[535] In the seventeenth dynasty there was a strong interest in the site of Abydos by the kings who resided in Thebes.[536] This is the site of the last known royal pyramid and the place where Ahmose built an elaborate mortuary complex about a kilometer southeast of that of Senwosret III. Within this complex Ahmose constructed smaller pyramids for his grandmother Queen Tetisheri and his sister-queen Ahmose-Nefertari, and Abydos expanded greatly at the beginning of the New Kingdom.[537]

This complex was Abydene in character and here Ahmose was identified with the god Osiris. Some of the reliefs in the temple's court were executed in Ahmose's reign, but other parts were completed during the reign of his son Amenhotep I.[538] Both Ahmose and Amenhotep I were recipients of the cult. Queens Tetisheri and Ahmose-Nefertari also had cult chapels in this complex, which has suggested to some that it was seemingly designed as a royal family mortuary center.[539] Indeed, Ahmose's mortuary complex was the first monument to be located outside of the original core landscape at Abydos, marking a change in the use of the site. As concerns Queen Tetisheri's mortuary structures, fortuitously we do not need to rely solely on the archaeological record to reconstruct them, because they are described on a stela erected by king Ahmose for his grandmother:

> Your grave and your cenotaph are now on ground belonging to the Theban and Thinite nomes respectively. I tell you this because My Majesty desires to have a pyramid and a chapel built for you on holy land near the monuments of My Majesty, so that its pool can be dug out, its trees planted and the amount of its sacrificial bread fixed, colonized with people, furnished with arable land, endowed with herds and tended by *ka*-priests and priests of the dead bound (to its service).[540]

Like Hatshepsut's later Temple of Millions of Years, the site of Abydos during the late seventeenth and early eighteenth dynasties must also have furnished funerary gardens within some of the structures.[541] This text also connects the sites of Abydos with Thebes through the erection of complementary funerary monuments. Also from the early eighteenth dynasty is a stela from the Osiris temple that records a direction by Thutmose I to the priesthood to provide for his pyramid at Abydos.[542] Subsequently, Thutmose III established a chapel adjacent to that of Ahmose and Amenhotep I, as did Amenhotep III just to the northeast. Bricks stamped with Hatshepsut's name have also been found in the ruins of Ramesses II's temple, so she may have had a temple constructed at Abydos.

The expansion of and interest in Abydos as a religious site during the early eighteenth dynasty is further evidenced by texts from the Osiris temple recording royal gifts from the time of Thutmose I. There were also increased endowments and offerings during the reigns of Thutmose III and IV, with dedications of both royal and elite statuary continuing throughout these reigns.[543] Votive offerings left by pilgrims at Umm el-Qa'ab indicate that the processional festival that took

[532] Leahy 1989: 56. See also Altenmüller 1972: 42.
[533] Lichtheim 1992: 40.
[534] Leahy 1989: 56. He references the stela of the vizier Mentuhotep as evidence (Cairo CG 20539).
[535] Leahy 1989: 59; Kemp 1975: 38.
[536] Wegner 2002: 66–67.
[537] O'Connor 2009: 105.
[538] O'Connor 2009: 108.
[539] O'Connor 2009: 108.
[540] Translation from Kees 1961: 243–244.
[541] A. Wilkinson 1998: 84–87.
[542] O'Connor 2009: 105; Breasted 2001: 39, line 15.
[543] O'Connor 2009: 113.

Figure 32: View of the west bank at ancient Thebes (modern Luxor). Photo by author.

place between the Osiris temple and Umm el-Qa'ab continued in the New Kingdom. At this time, most of the offerings were left on a low hill at the processional approach about three hundred meters from Umm el-Qa'ab proper. According to O'Connor, most pilgrims would have stopped at this area called "Hekreshu Hill," with only a few elite participants continuing onto the more restricted area.[544] Hence, excavations at Abydos have revealed that early New Kingdom rulers were concerned with and fascinated by Abydos and the cult of Osiris. This attentiveness parallels roughly the appearance of the Sacred District in the decoration of elite private tombs farther south at Thebes, Elkab, and Hierakonpolis.

The Nature of the Sacred District

The textual evidence provided by the tombs of Senet (TT 60) and Tetiky (TT 15) in the Theban necropolis, in addition to the Abydos stela of Khutawyre Ugaf, indicate specifically that the term *tꜣ ḏsr* refers to a location in a necropolis. Yet here the sources diverge. The former two, which are each accompanied by an illustration, pinpoint the location of the Sacred District at the tomb of the deceased. However, Tetiky's tomb shows the entire district, while Senet's tomb illustrates only the *Mww*. It has already been established by Reeder that there are two versions of the *Mww*, one that takes part in the funeral on the day of burial, and one that is mythological and appears in the spiritual realm. Tetiky's tomb presents both, while Senet's presents only the former. The Abydos stela corroborates the district's location at a cemetery but refers specifically to the necropolis region at Abydos, and not to the area in and around the tombs. In fact, it dictates that no tombs be constructed in the Sacred District. So, in other words, this stela describes a space, or sub-section, of the necropolis at Abydos and a location in this world. There is also abundant evidence to support the contrary claim that the *tꜣ ḏsr* designates a space in the world of the gods. Osiris, Anubis, or the Goddess of the West frequently appear in the Sacred District, in addition to the many unnamed deities who sit in open shrines. Additionally, the guardians of the great gate help to establish this area as a mythical space.

Supplementary textual references to the *tꜣ ḏsr* also imply the Sacred District is in the realm of the gods. The first example is the compendium of spells in the *Coffin Texts*, where the term *tꜣ ḏsr* appears regularly. Special attention should be paid to *Coffin Texts* 38 through 40. These spells contain a unique variant of the term *tꜣ ḏsr,* which both Raymond Faulkner and James Hoffmeier discuss in their respective studies.[545] Faulkner describes these passages as presenting a dialogue between a recently deceased man and his father.[546] The father has already reached *tꜣ pw ḏsr nty.f* "this sacred land in which he is" but the son has not. In this case, the *tꜣ ḏsr* is not the necropolis,

[544] O'Connor 2009: 114.

[545] Faulkner 2004: 30; Hoffmeier 1985: 1–58.

[546] Faulkner 1962: 36–44.

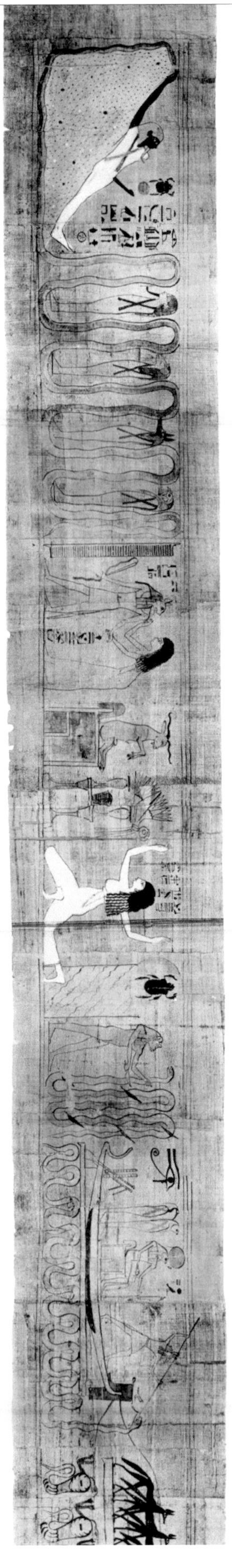

Figure 33: Vignette from the papyrus of Herweben. Adapted from Piankoff and Rambova 1957: plate 2.

but the place where transfigured spirits reside. The terms are the same in both cases, the only difference is that in the longer version the precise location within the sacred area needs to be distinguished. So, there are two people who are in the other world, but in different regions, and it is the area where the father resides that needs to be specified, hence *tꜣ pw ḏsr nty.f*. Hoffmeier also distinguishes between two variants of the phrase "sacred land," namely, *tꜣ ḏsr* and *tꜣ pw/pf ḏsr*.[547] The latter could be a variant writing of *tꜣ ḏsr*, but Hoffmeier contrasts the former, casually meaning "the necropolis," with the latter, meaning "a special area reserved for those who have retained eternal life."[548] Therefore, *Coffin Texts* 38–40, in which the latter variant occurs, illustrate the other worldliness of this area.

Hoffmeier also states that *ḏsr* can mean "sacred place." He cites CT IV, 366 k–m, "I pass by the Valley, I cross the Sacred Place, I pass through the double doors of the judgement-hall(?)... ."[549] This passage expresses the rebirth of the deceased and his traveling westward toward the next life. Here the deceased must cross the Nile, pass through the Valley, and cross the "Sacred Place." This passage describes the journey from the east bank to the western desert (Figure 32). Hoffmeier rightly suggests that this "Sacred Place" is the sphere of Osiris.[550] Furthermore, CT V, 52 explicitly states that the sacrificial bulls are located *m-ẖnw ḏsrw*. Sacrificial bulls feature as one of the micro-scenes within the larger Sacred District scene and appear in ten of the tombs included in this study. Slaughtered bulls are also mentioned in conjunction with the *Mww* in the *Story of Sinuhe*.[551]

A later example where *tꜣ ḏsr* denotes the divine realm is in the twenty-first dynasty papyrus of Herweben in Cairo.[552] According to Alexandre Piankoff and Natacha Rambova in their work *Mythological Papyri*, the term *tꜣ ḏsr* is joined with the *Duat* and the mound of Khepri in a synonymous fashion. It is a place in the Field of Reeds that the deceased must cross. It is closed off by a door and looked after by a guardian (Figure 33).

Discussion

Paradoxically, the label *tꜣ ḏsr* describes both the place where the deceased is physically interred in the ground and the place where the gods reside: the place the deceased is heading toward. Hence, the obstacle that one faces when attempting to identify the location presented in the New Kingdom private tomb illustrations is the same as the challenge that one encounters when looking at the meaning of the word *tꜣ ḏsr* in the textual material. Both the artistic evidence and the textual evidence suggest the dual nature of this region and further corroborate the supposition that the Sacred District scene is indeed a transitional zone. It is possible that the ancient Egyptians perceived the superimposition of the divine realm onto the activities performed in the earthly realm on the day of burial. Both Hoffmeier and Edward Brovarski suggest that parts of the funeral could be considered to be taking place in the heavenly realm.[553] More specifically, it was the tent of purification, which according to Brovarski, stood at the water's edge marking the beginning of this other worldliness and indicating the beginning of the funerary complex. Brovarski states that the entrance to the next world, that is the doors of heaven, allowed access for the deceased to enter the celestial counterpart of this world.[554] Although by the New Kingdom these tomb scenes may be depicting something slightly different, the general concept is the same. One might also consider the site of Abydos as the subject of the Sacred District and the interface where the living and dead can jointly participate in Osirian rituals. Since most of the tombs that have this scene are located at Thebes, perhaps these depictions offer evidence that Thebes, too, could function as an interface between the world of the living and the world of the dead.[555]

Working independently, Hoffmeier, in his work on the *ibw* and the *sḥ nṯr*, remarks that the places most connected to the king's purification in the *Pyramid Texts* are the Field of Reeds (*sḫt iꜣrw*) and the Lake of Reeds (*š iꜣr*).[556] He reiterates that purification and solar theology are connected and states that not only is the deceased king purified in the Field of Reeds but so are Re, Horus, and Osiris.[557] A caption in the tomb of Paheri at Elkab mentions the "the Field of Reeds" and appears above his funeral procession. The inscription reads as follows, "Making a beautiful

[547] For list of references to the *tꜣ ḏsr* in the *Coffin Texts* see Rami Van der Molen 2000: 703.
[548] Hoffmeier 1985: 85.
[549] Hoffmeier 1985: 98; Faulkner 2004: 279.
[550] Hoffmeier 1985: 98.
[551] J. Allen 2015: 120; Lichtheim 1975: 229.
[552] Piankoff and Rambova 1957: 76. This was brought to my attention by the late Lanny Bell.

[553] Brovarski 1977; Hoffmeier 1981.
[554] Brovarski 1977.
[555] Smith 2017: 195.
[556] Hoffmeier 1981: 174.
[557] Hoffmeier 1981: 175.

Figure 34: Paheri's funeral scenes with the deceased kneeling before the shrine of Anubis (TC 3). Photo by author.

funeral for the nomarch Paheri; bringing the nomarch Paheri justified, toward his tomb in the necropolis, in peace, in peace, before the great god. Going in peace towards the horizon, towards the Field of Reeds, towards the Duat." The Field of Reeds is a paradise reserved for the righteous and appears very much like the environment of Egypt. The deceased would farm in this agricultural dreamland and have food for eternity. As no daily life activities are depicted in the Sacred District scene it is more likely that the *tꜣ ḏsr* provides only access to the Field of Reeds and is not to be thought of as synonymous with this area. Nevertheless, one should consider the fact that Egyptian art lacks perspective and instead portrays permanence and immortality.[558] What is perhaps more significant in Paheri's tomb is an inscription two registers below, in the middle register of the funerary scenes, where Paheri kneels before Anubis in a shrine. Here the caption reads, "Approaching Anubis, lord of (?), of the god. The landing in Abydos by the nomarch Paheri" (Figure 34). This episode culminates in the Sacred District scene followed by Paheri kneeling before Osiris sitting on his throne. Paheri appears in a worshipping position and is presenting the pile of offerings that sits before him. The inscription above him reads in part, "The nomarch of Nekheb, Paheri, justified, he says: Greetings to you, noble god, lord of the land, great in the nome of This, mighty in Abydos! I am come toward you, my lord, in peace! Give me peace!" These inscriptions are compatible with the Sacred District as an enduring and immortal sphere that the deceased must traverse, not only in order to reach Osiris, but to be purified in the process, so that he is accepted by Osiris. This inscription also implies that the environment depicted may be imagined as Abydos (not Elkab or Thebes). The sacred landscape that appears primarily in early New Kingdom private tombs depicts what may have been *originally* conceived of as a celestial realm but has now been Osirianized and superimposed on the cemetery during the funeral of the deceased.

Reeder's work on the *Mww* also corroborates the superimposition of the divine realm on to the human realm, and argues that there were two sets of *Mww*, one for the earthly realm and one for the world of the gods:

> What is depicted in the tomb scenes is either actually transpiring in the Next World, or the real-life participants in the funeral rites symbolically represent the people of Pe [who he associates with the *Mww*], their actions in this world magically ensuring that those same actions will take place in the Hereafter.[559]

As noted, the *Mww* have a long history in Egyptian tomb decoration dating back to the Old Kingdom. In the Middle Kingdom, examples of the *Mww* come from the twelfth dynasty tombs of Sehetepibre and Senet (TT 60) from Thebes, and Djehuty-nakht from

[558] Bakir 1967: 161.

[559] Reeder 1995: 77.

El-Bersha, the stela of Abkaou from Abydos (Louvre stela C 15), and the coffin of Heqaib from Aswan, among others.[560] However, many examples of the *Mww* come from the Sacred District scenes in the New Kingdom beginning in the reign of Ahmose. There are thirteen examples where the Hall of the *Mww* marks the beginning of the Sacred District, and hence the beginning of this holy area the deceased must cross in order to reach the realm of Osiris. Since the *Mww* typically face toward the Sacred District, this shows they are part of the divine realm. The *ḫbt*-dancers (the dancers who presumably do the dance of the *Mww* at the funeral on the day of burial) appear in sixteen tombs, with seven of these tombs also containing the Hall of the *Mww*. In these cases, the artists illustrate both sets of *Mww*—those of this realm and those of the next. There are no early examples of the *ḫbt*-dancers as they tend to appear in the later tombs, beginning in the reign of Hatshepsut. Perhaps the imitation of the *Mww* at the funeral on the day of burial was a later invention. The *ḫbt*-dancers occur only twice in conjunction with the *Mww* welcoming the deceased *outside* of their Hall (TT 17 and TT 41). This pattern may imply that the *ḫbt*-dancers could act as a substitute for the *Mww* as greeters. Furthermore, there are nine examples of the *Mww* wearing their conical headdress and welcoming the funeral cortege to the Sacred District outside of their Hall. It is intriguing to note that this is a common scene in the earliest illustrations of the Sacred District: Hery (TT 12), Tetiky (TT 15), Reneny (TC 7), and Ineni (TT 81). It is most likely the result of its continuing popularity from the Middle Kingdom. There is an example of the *Mww* welcoming the funeral cortege in the tomb of Sobeknakht II at Elkab (sixteenth dynasty), which may have been responsible for the appearance of the *Mww* in Reneny's tomb.[561] It remained a popular micro-scene into the reigns of Thutmose III, Amenhotep II, and Amenhotep III. The Hall of the *Mww* and the *Mww* wearing their conical headdresses who welcome the deceased occur in only four tombs, three of which are included in the previous category: Tetiky (TT 15), Reneny (TC 7), Ineni (TT 81), and Amenemope (TT 41). The first three tombs listed are the earliest New Kingdom tombs to display the Sacred District scene, while TT 41 is a post-Amarna tomb and an outlier in many ways. After the emergence of the Sacred District scene, and thus after the experimental phase, one set of *Mww* becomes the norm. It may be accurate to state that in the later tombs the *ḫbt*-dancers replace the *Mww* greeting the deceased, as only TT 17 (reign of Amenhotep II) and TT 41 (post-Amarna tomb) display both examples.

As Osiris sits at the end of the Sacred District ready to receive the deceased after his journey, there is no doubt that this micro-scene reveals the divine nature of the space. The presence of Osiris and his placement at the end of the Sacred District, which is between the funeral cortege and the arrival of the deceased in the west, corroborates this area's liminal nature. The deceased crosses the valley toward the west and moves into the Sacred District, which is situated in *dešret,* just east of the cliffs and the realm of Osiris. Perhaps it is not a coincidence that the twenty-first dynasty papyrus of Herweben is reminiscent of the earlier New Kingdom Sacred District scenes in that it describes the *tꜣ ḏsr* as closed off by a door and looked after by a guardian (the guardians of the great gate and the *Mww*).

There are many contradicting images of the afterlife in ancient Egypt, but in general, the ancient Egyptians regarded their afterlife as parallel to their everyday world. This world and elements of the next world were imagined in combination with each other. In the case of the Sacred District scenes, a kernel of tangible geography does exist, but the scene is not meant to be a real three-dimension place. There is a warping of space and time in these depictions, which may seem quite different from our modern perception.[562]

Summary

The Sacred District functions as a buffer zone, both in its artistic placement among the funeral scenes but also conceptually between this world and the next. More appropriately, one should see this space as a transitional zone, a notion which the appellation *tꜣ ḏsr* reinforces. The *tꜣ ḏsr* is a mysterious and inaccessible region for the living—hidden and secret, segregated from the profane world. Yet, it is both this world and the next. The *Mww* guard the gate and watch over it from the entrance, and Osiris and the guardians of the great gate patrol the other end. This space reflects the superimposition of the divine world onto this world, or as Peter Robinson states, it is "a transparent overlay over the temporal living world."[563] The physical entrance to the *tꜣ ḏsr* is the necropolis, from which point the deceased is transported magically to the other

[560] For a line drawing of the *Mww* in the twelfth dynasty tomb of Sehetepibre at Thebes, see Reeder 1995: 72. For Louvre stela C 15, see Gayet 1889: 12, pl. LIV and Louvre Museum, "Abkaou stele."

[561] Tylor 1896: pl. III.

[562] Robinson 1996: 44.

[563] Robinson 1996: 44.

realm through his crossing of the Sacred District. All the private stelae cited above suggest a familiarity with Abydos by Thebans, and Ahmose and his immediate successors confirm this connection. So, Abydos was patronized by both the private and royal spheres of society during the New Kingdom. It is not surprising then, that Theban tombs feature this imagined sacred space that brings a piece of Abydos to the Theban necropolis (and Elkab and Hierakonpolis). This scene gives viewers a glimpse into an otherwise inaccessible realm—at least for the living—that leads the deceased to rest with Osiris.

The meaning of the Sacred District and its constituent parts changed over time. As certain ritual practices melted away and others emerged, the Sacred District responded to the evolving circumstances. It was flexible. A sacred site always means more than the location of an event, structure, or object and the way the ancient Egyptians interacted with their surroundings was multifaceted. As modern scholars, it may never be possible to understand fully the thoughts and memories associated with this scene, especially since people do not always engage with places in only practical ways. Sacredness is always diverse and complex, and its implications are difficult to assess.

CHAPTER NINE: THE SACRED DISTRICT SCENE AT ELKAB[564]

This study of the Sacred District scene has concentrated on the T-shaped tombs located on the west bank of Thebes in the areas of Qurnet Murai, Sheikh Abd el-Qurna, Khôkha, and Dra Abu el-Naga. By far the majority of tombs that contain this scene occur in these areas; however, there are three examples of the Sacred District scene that occur in a different type of tomb located farther south at Elkab.[565] This chapter concentrates on how the Sacred District scene was incorporated into the decorative program of the rectangular chapel at Elkab.

Figure 35: View of the private New Kingdom rock-cut chapels at Elkab. Photo by author.

The three examples from Elkab occur in the rock-cut tombs of Reneny (TC 7), the mayor and overseer of prophets, Paheri (TC 3), the mayor of Nekheb (Elkab) and of Inyt (Esna), and Setau (TC 4), the first prophet of Nekhbet. The tombs themselves are located along the eastern part of the rock necropolis on the east bank of the Nile, north of the town enclosure (Figure 35). They are oriented on a north-south axis with the chapels of Paheri and Setau aligning slightly more with a northwest-southeast axis. All of the chapels are roughly rectangular with a varying number of side chambers and auxiliary rooms. Reneny's rectangular chapel is the largest, and like the other two, there is an extra room that extends to the east from the northeast corner of the chapel. Unlike Paheri's and Setau's tombs, it becomes narrower as one proceeds north. The tomb of Paheri has three additional rooms that extend from the main chapel to the east. The chapel of Setau is slightly smaller than the other two with one auxiliary room carved farther into the cliff toward the north and two rooms extending out from the east wall.[566] The only parts of the structures that are of concern for this study are the decorated portions of the rock-cut chapels that are immediately visible upon entry.

It is informative to examine the Elkab tombs in terms of how the artists have positioned the Sacred District within the decorative program because they offer an alternative model for this space as a liminal zone. This area, as depicted in the tomb decoration at Elkab, maintains its transitional nature and is situated artistically between the world of the living and the world of the dead.[567]

The Tomb of Reneny (TC 7)

The tomb of Reneny dates to the time of Amenhotep I and is the earliest of the three tombs under discussion here. It is located on the same terrace as the tombs of Paheri and Setau, all the way to the far left or west

[564] A version of the material presented in this chapter has been previous published in *JARCE* 48 (2012): 97–110.

[565] Only the decoration of the open tombs has been considered for this study. The sixteenth dynasty tomb of Sobeknakht II (TC 10) is also located at Elkab, but it does not include a complete Sacred District scene, only the *Mww*.

[566] The eastern rooms are not present in the plan from Porter and Moss (1962: 178). See Kruchten and Delvaux 2010: 322, pl. 2.

[567] Diamond 2010b: 41; *idem.* 2011: 42.

Figure 36: The interior of the tomb chapel of Reneny (TC 7) at Elkab. Photo by author.

side. Its shape is also generally similar to the tombs of Paheri and Setau in that the main part of the chapel is rectangular with a vaulted ceiling (Figure 36). The primary difference between the chapel of Reneny and the other two, described below, is that the artist placed the funerary scenes on the right, or east wall of the chapel instead of on the left, or west wall as in the others. Likewise, the funerary scenes are not at the end of the rectangular chamber, but rather immediately on the right upon entering the tomb. They occupy a rather large portion of the right wall, indicating the importance of these scenes.[568] By and large, the funerary scenes are placed on the left wall of the tomb chapel, as in the Theban T-shaped tombs that feature the Sacred District scene.

One can "read" these scenes best if one thinks of a parade. The entities are constantly moving, and they all travel in the same direction. Those illustrated closest to the end of the "parade route" (in the case of the upper register one could think of the Goddess of the West as the end of the route) are the ones that began the procession. In the tomb of Reneny the procession travels from right to left because of the placement of the funerary scenes on the right wall. The orientation of the figures shows that those who inhabit the world of the living face left and proceed to the "west," the world of the dead. Those who inhabit the other world, like the Goddess of the West, Anubis, and Osiris face right, toward the living. The viewer is seeing the procession in its entirety—everything is displayed at the same time. If one were sitting along a parade route one would view each individual entity as it passed. In order to understand the order of appearances one must start on the left and move toward the right, despite the fact that the movement of the scene is traveling from right to left.[569]

What has been restored in the tomb chapel of Reneny consists of three large registers. Immediately on the right, upon entering the tomb, from top down one finds the funerary scenes (Figure 1). The top register illustrates the dragging of the coffin to the tomb and the entourage. The Goddess of the West waits at the far end of the register for the deceased to arrive. The sequence of participants consists of the following: two men, a man dragging the *tekenu* on a sledge, and two men carrying a lion bier surmounted by the canopic chest with a *ḏryt* standing underneath. Placed in the middle of the procession are three *Mww* who receive the funeral cortege as it approaches. They mark the beginning of the *tꜣ ḏsr*.[570] The *Mww* wear their typical conical headdress and short white kilt, and each one holds his left leg forward in the air. Immediately in front of the *Mww* is the sledge with the coffin. This part of the scene is very fragmentary. There are the remains of a *ḏryt* flanking the foot end of the coffin and a priest donning an animal-skin garment standing on the sledge. In front of the sledge a man pours water to lubricate the way. There are at least four men who hold the rope and pull it. Between these men and the two oxen that bear the brunt of the work walk three men alternating with three women with their arms upraised in an unusual version of Gardiner's A 28

[568] At the ARCE Annual Meeting in Oakland in 2010 Dr. Gay Robins presented a paper, entitled "The Decorative Program in Single-Roomed Pre-Amarna 18th Dynasty Tomb Chapels at Thebes" discussing the limited wall space for decoration and the importance of the scenes that were selected for the tomb chapels. She demonstrated that when wall space is at a premium the Sacred District scene still appears in the repertoire of scenes (examples are TT 161 and TT 179) (2010: 78–79). See also fig. 41 of this work.

[569] This description is particular to Reneny's tomb at Elkab as the funeral scenes are on the right wall. It would be the opposite for most tombs since the funerary scenes are usually on the left wall.

[570] Seyfried 2003: 62.

Figure 37: The Sacred District scene in the tomb of Reneny (TC 7) at Elkab. Photo by author.

pose.[571] This gesture can be contrasted with a similar one expressed by men participating in the dragging scene in the tombs of both Paheri (TC 3) and Setau (TC 4).

It is in the middle register that the Sacred District is found (Figure 37). As noted above, these scenes narrate the funeral proceedings beginning from the top and moving down to the lowest register. However, between the funeral procession reaching the Goddess of the West and the Sacred District there are a series of scenes illustrated that are not included in the decorative programs of Paheri nor Setau. From right to left, the following scenes are depicted: the journey to Abydos and back, the deceased sitting on a vessel being purified by two priests, a group of female mourners, the censing of the mummy in its coffin on a bier, and the Opening of the Mouth ceremony. Most of these scenes depict rituals that would have taken place in the various workshops at the tomb before the interment. It is at this point in the proceedings that the Sacred District scene is placed. In many other examples of funerary scenes where the Sacred District occurs one finds the procession ending at said location (see Paheri). It is also rather common on the west bank of Thebes to find the above-mentioned scenes placed to the left of the Sacred District scene on the left wall of the passage of a T-shaped tomb.[572] Likewise at Thebes, the voyage to Abydos is commonly placed beside the Sacred District.[573]

The first micro-scene within the Sacred District of Reneny is the Hall of the *Mww*, with two *Mww* dancers standing inside facing to the left and watching over the area. The tomb of Reneny features two variations of the *Mww*: the greeters and the guardians. The *Mww* mark an important position in the deceased's transference into the afterlife. It is clear in the tomb of Reneny that the first appearance of the *Mww* as greeters occurs in this world on the day of burial.[574] The second time the *Mww* appear, they are in the Sacred District in the world of the gods. As noted in the previous chapter, Greg Reeder proposes that what is illustrated in the tomb scenes could actually have taken place in the next world, or the people participating in the funeral rituals were symbolically representing the People of Pe (whom he associates with the *Mww*). The ritual would thus ensure that the same would take place in the hereafter.[575] The tomb of Reneny appears to represent both of these *Mww* as the Sacred District represents the superimposition of the mythical realm on the necropolis, and in this sense the illustration of Reneny is in the minority.[576] As noted in the previous chapter Edward Brovarski and James Hoffmeier have suggested that parts of the funeral could be considered to be taking place in the heavenly realm.[577] More

[571] Diamond 2010a: 62–67.

[572] TT 21, TT 123, TT 224.

[573] TT 17, TT 39.

[574] Reeder 1995: 69–83.

[575] Reeder 1995: 77.

[576] Diamond 2010b: 41; *idem*. 2011: 42.

[577] Brovarski 1977: 107–115; Hoffmeier 1981: 177.

specifically, it was the tent of purification which, according to Brovarski, stood at the water's edge and marked the beginning of this other worldliness, which also indicates the beginning of the funerary complex. He suggests that the entrance to this next world, that is, the doors of heaven, allowed access for the deceased to enter the celestial counterpart in this world.[578] This general supposition by both Brovarski and Hoffmeier is corroborated by the placement of the Sacred District scene in the tomb of Reneny among others. After the Hall of the *Mww*, the register splits into two sub-registers. In the upper section there are two obelisks and two sycamore trees, and in the bottom register there is a long, rectangular pool bordered by seven palm trees and followed by garden plots. The trees in the tomb of Reneny are stylistically different from those appearing in the tomb of Paheri.[579]

In the bottom register, and outside of the Sacred District, going from right to left, there is a line of priests facing to the left followed by a large gap, another group of mourning women, two men carrying a chest accompanied by two mourning women, one walking beside them and the other in front. It appears that they are walking toward a slaughtering area where two men work. Below the Sacred District is a banquet scene with members of the deceased's family each sitting in front of a table of offerings facing to the left with vessels on the ground.

Following the funerary scenes and closer to the focal point of the chapel, one finds Sobekhotep and his wife Ahmose (the father and mother of Reneny) sitting before a table of offerings and facing to the right toward the world of the living.[580] There has been much controversy over the identification of the family members portrayed in Reneny's tomb and the relationships that exist between the tomb owners at Elkab in general.[581] According to J. J. Tylor, the Sobekhotep that sits in front of this offering scene is Sobekhotep II, the son of Sobekhotep I and the father of Reneny. Sheila Whale has a different theory—she believes that Sobekhotep I was actually Reneny's eldest brother, possibly Sobekhotep-wer, and that he succeeded his father as governor of Elkab.[582] This would make Sobekhotep I the son of Sobekhotep II, a theory which accounts for the fact that both Sobekhotep I and Reneny have a mother named Ahmose. Whale maintains that Reneny wanted to honor both his eldest brother and his father since he had inherited his post from them—a position he would not have otherwise held. However, it would be unusual for Reneny not to depict himself in his own tomb sitting with his wife, in the same manner as the wives of his brother and father. Recently, W. V. Davies has made a convincing argument showing that it is Reneny himself and his senior wife Idy who are seated at the far end of the *left* wall in the principal offering scene. As noted, this man was thought previously to be a governor named Sobekhotep whose mother and wife were named Ahmose and Idy, respectively. Opposite, on the far end of the right wall, Reneny's parents, Sobekhotep and Ahmose receive offerings. It has been thought that the wife of Reneny, Nehi, played a rather insignificant role in his tomb decoration, appearing only once in the funeral procession. Now, it appears that Reneny's chief wife was Idy, who does appear with him where she is supposed to. Reneny also appears with his mother Ahmose who plays a prominent role in the tomb decoration. Whale suggests that his mother may have provided a connection to the royal house, thus accounting for her prominence in the tomb, or that Reneny gained his post because he and Sobekhotep shared a mother.[583]

This offering scene to Reneny's parents is the last scene on the right wall, as there is a doorway cut into the wall immediately following the pair. It is this room that contained the burial, and it is as though the artists were leading the viewer toward the place where Reneny was actually buried, as opposed to the symbolic west.[584] This phenomenon does not occur in the later tombs at Elkab or at Thebes. In the later Theban tombs the burial shaft is often located in the courtyard or at one end of the transverse hall of a T-shaped tomb, demonstrating that there was no relationship between the Sacred District scene and the actual burial spot of the deceased (except in the case of TT 41). As the eighteenth dynasty progressed the funerary scenes became standardized and protocol prescribed that these scenes appear on the left wall and that the burial was to be placed elsewhere, a convention seen at Thebes. The tombs of Paheri and Setau at Elkab follow this Theban tradition where the Sacred District scene is situated close to the focal point or

578 Brovarski 1977: 107–110.

579 The part of the scene from the tomb of Setau is no longer intact.

580 Whale 1989: 18. This is a correction to a previous article I published in *JARCE* 48 (2012), where I mistakenly identified the seated couple as Reneny and his wife.

581 Whale 1989; Bennett 2002; Ryholt 1997.

582 Whale 1989: 18–19.

583 Whale 1989: 20.

584 Through discussion with Lanny Bell, it was realized that in the case of Reneny the artwork is strategically placed so as to channel the viewer's focus directly to the place of burial.

Figure 38: The Sacred District scene in the tomb of Paheri (TC 3) at Elkab. Photo by author.

shrine in the chapel—the symbolic west. They have their funerary scenes on the left wall of the chapel, yet the place of burial was still to the east.[585]

As the tomb of Reneny contains one of the earliest examples of the Sacred District scene, its placement with regard to the burial spot is significant. Not only does the Sacred District lead to the place of burial, which is cut into an auxiliary chamber to the east of the main chapel, but the fact that the burial chamber is to the *east* of the main chapel is intriguing. Perhaps the burial practices of the time dictated burial in the east, or on the right in the case of Reneny, and thus one also finds the funerary scenes placed on the right. Most likely this case represents an earlier tradition that is not continued at Thebes or Elkab. It is possible that this scene recognizes the deceased's aspiration to have both a solar and Osirian afterlife (see chapter three).[586]

The Tomb of Paheri (TC 3)

The second tomb under discussion is that of Paheri (TC 3) which dates to the early eighteenth dynasty, possibly to the reign of Thutmose III.[587] It is by far the best preserved of the three chapels at Elkab. In this tomb the Sacred District scene appears at the north end of the left side, or west wall of the rectangular chapel. The funerary scenes occupy all five registers of the northernmost portion of the west wall. The Sacred District scene has been placed in the bottom two registers with a large scene of the deceased kneeling before Osiris enthroned in his shrine (Figure 38). The logical progression of the funerary scenes involves the participants traveling from left to right, from the top down. Consequently, those who lead the procession are to be found down in the fourth register approaching the Sacred District. The upper three registers show the funeral procession of Paheri, including the coffin being dragged, the visit to the sacred Delta localities and Abydos, the dragging of the *tekenu*, and the bearing of papyrus stems. The beginning of the fourth register shows the funeral procession arriving at the Sacred District. The first thing the cortege encounters is a series of garden plots surmounted by a row of braziers and a pool surrounded by three palm trees. This sequence of events is uncommon in that the most usual element encountered by the funeral procession is the *Mww*, who sometimes greet the entourage or stand in their hall and observe the district. In the case of Paheri the Hall of the *Mww* is situated at the end of the

[585] Kruchten and Delvaux 2010: 322.

[586] This possibility was suggested to me by Lanny Bell.

[587] Porter and Moss 1962: 177 places this tomb in the eighteenth dynasty. Tylor and Griffith classify this tomb as mid-eighteenth dynasty in their 1894 study of the tomb (1894: v). Lise Manniche suggests that the Sacred District scene from the tomb of Paheri resembles the decoration from TT 100 and from TT A4, noting that they must all be of a similar date. Manniche dates TT A4 (that of Wensu) to the reign of Thutmose III (1988: 62–87). See also Lichtheim 1976: 15; Devillers 2018: 34; Laboury 2012: 201; Benderitter, "Pahery."

district, as the last episode before we find the deceased kneeling before Osiris. And in this case, the *Mww* face toward Osiris. After the garden plots, braziers, pool, and palms, there are two sycamore trees placed one above the other and two rows with five shrines each. The last three shrines in the bottom row have gods sitting inside them, whereas all of the other shrines are closed. The first two have human-headed gods that resemble very closely the hieroglyphic determinative for god. The third shrine contains a canine-headed deity.

Continuing in the fifth and final register one finds the guardians of the great gate. Although unlabeled in the tomb of Paheri, this scene is so captioned in the tomb of Rekhmire at Thebes (TT 100). Following the great gate there is the shrine of Osiris containing the label *Wsỉr nṯr ˁ3*. Osiris stands in his typical tight-fitted garment with his arms crossed holding the crook and flail. Faint green paint remains on his skin, and his garment and headdress are white. In many other examples of this scene Osiris is situated as though he inhabits the land of the dead, the west, and is looking out toward the living who are approaching him. In other words, figures residing in the world of the gods face left, out from the tomb, while those who are approaching the tomb from the land of the living face right. So, like the *Mww*, Osiris too unexpectedly faces to the right. This is the final scene in the tomb of Paheri, so the first shrine is redundant. In the earlier tomb of Reneny the shrine of Osiris is the last micro-scene of the Sacred District and functions as the destination of the procession. The artists may have used that tomb as a prototype and then added the larger seated figure of Osiris with the deceased kneeling before him, an image commonly found in later tombs from the Theban area, although he is typically standing.

Just following the first shrine of Osiris are two women facing to the right toward the "west" who kneel before four basins of water. The caption above their heads identifies them as *ḏryt nḏst* and *ḏryt wrt*. Variants in the caption for these two women appear in Theban Tombs 82 and 100; instead of *ḏryt nḏst* and *ḏryt wrt* the two appellations used to identify the women are *dmḏyt* and *mnknwt/knwt*.[588] Both of these are archaic titles, with the former having the meaning of "bone or limb collector."[589]

The last scene of the Sacred District is the Hall of the *Mww*. In the case of Paheri, the *Mww* stand inside their hall and face toward the West. It is more common in the compendium of Sacred District scenes to have the *Mww* watching over the district, not turned away from it. If the hall was positioned earlier in the scene then the direction the *Mww* face would be typical. Since they are situated at the end of the Sacred District and face to the right, they are unable to monitor it as per their usual circumstance. This micro-scene concludes the Sacred District in the tomb of Paheri. As with other examples the episodes are placed in registers, which has led some scholars to identify the area as a *temenos*.[590] This designation thus corroborates the interpretation that this is a sacred area that has been segregated for its sanctity. This characterization is also born out in the label ascribed to this district as a whole in other tomb scenes, that is *t3 ḏsr*, or sacred/segregated land.[591]

The Tomb of Setau (TC 4)

The third example of the Sacred District scene from Elkab is in the tomb chapel of Setau (TC 4) which dates to the time of Ramesses III-IX.[592] This tomb is located to the west of the tomb of Paheri (TC 3). Unfortunately, the Sacred District scene in this tomb is badly damaged and it has been possible to restore only a couple of fragments to the wall (Figure 39).[593] The shape of the tomb chapel is reminiscent of that of Paheri with one auxiliary room protruding out from the northwest end and two extending out from the east wall.[594] The main chapel is rectangular just like that of Paheri, and indeed that of Reneny, as well. Because of this there are many similarities between the tombs of Paheri and Setau with regard to the placement and composition of the Sacred District scene.

Despite the fact that almost the entire left wall of the chapel of Setau is now devoid of decoration, it is still possible to see the remains of the Sacred District scene there. The Sacred District scene was placed at the very end of the left wall among the funerary

[588] Diamond 2008; *idem*. 2015a; *idem*. 2017.

[589] Diamond 2017. The appellation *(mn)knwt* is more enigmatic (Diamond, *In progress*). First recorded on what is now known as Ramesseum Papyrus E, found in a re-used Middle Kingdom tomb, a *knwt* appears as a prescribed ritualist in a template for a funerary liturgy. It is difficult to ascertain precisely what her role is in these proceedings, but what is known is that she acted in conjunction with the *dmḏyt* (another cult performer), she may have performed role-playing and dialogue, and she most likely walked in procession during the ceremony.

[590] Assmann 2005: 305.

[591] Davies, Davies, and Gardiner 1920: pls. XXI, XXII; N. Davies 1925: 10–18, pl. V; Hoffmeier 1985: 85–87.

[592] Porter and Moss 1962: 181. See also Limme 2008: 26; Kruchten and Delvaux 2010.

[593] Kruchten and Delvaux 2010: 352–353.

[594] Kruchten and Delvaux 2010: 322.

Figure 39: Remaining fragments of the Sacred District scene in the tomb of Setau (TC 4) at Elkab. Far end of the left wall. Photo by author

scenes, just as in the tomb of Paheri. As concerns its composition, in the upper register the remains of the dragging scene appear where the men hold their arms in the A 28 pose. The second register is extremely fragmentary, but at the far right one can see the carrying of the canopic chest. The third register is almost entirely absent except for a man oriented to the right and bearing a papyrus stem in procession at the far right of the register. All of these scenes are identical to those in the tomb of Paheri. The funerary scenes extant in the tomb of Setau appear to be exact replicas of those preserved in the tomb of Paheri next door. It is therefore logical to assume that what once appeared in the lower registers in the tomb of Setau is the same as what is currently preserved in the tomb of Paheri.

There are several factors that indicate the existence of the Sacred District scene in the lower two registers. First and foremost, one can see the figure of Osiris enthroned in his shrine with his back to the symbolic west (actually the northwest) and facing out toward the world of the living. His figure equals the height of two registers. In front of him there is a pile of offerings and the deceased Setau is visible kneeling before him. Again, this is exactly what one sees in the tomb of Paheri. Additionally, the legs of the *Mww* who stand inside their Hall can faintly be detected. Unfortunately, the rest of the Sacred District scene is lost. As noted above, a couple of fragments have been restored, such as the remains of a shrine with a man kneeling in front of it, facing to the right. However, this fragment seems to have been placed arbitrarily within the space allotted to the Sacred District. It is possible that this fragment should have been placed higher up in the third register in line with the man bearing the papyrus stem in the procession to the "west." The second fragment may depict a squatting falcon-headed god in his shrine. The way he has been replaced on the wall has him facing in the opposite direction than the enshrined gods in the tomb of Paheri. However, his placement may be questionable, as well.

It is clear that the artists who decorated the tomb of Setau were using the decoration in the tomb of Paheri as an archetype for the funerary scenes.[595] In light of the available evidence from the Theban necropolis, this is a rather late example of the Sacred District. There are no other *confirmed* Ramesside tombs that include this scene in their decorative program.[596] As

[595] Many scholars have noted that tomb decoration changes around the time of Amenhotep II–Thutmose IV, then again during the reign of Amenhotep III, with further stylistic changes emerging in the Ramesside Period (Muhammed 1966: 170–172; Assmann 2003). The Elkab artists were not copying the contemporary styles used in the Theban necropolis.

[596] There are tombs, such as TT 127 and TT 222, that were reused in Ramesside times, but the inclusion of the Sacred

it stands now, Elkab and Hierakonpolis are the only other New Kingdom sites with tombs that include the Sacred District scene in their decorative programs.

Discussion

The Sacred District scene as presented in the New Kingdom tombs at Elkab fits in well with those examples preserved in the Theban necropolis farther north. At Elkab, the scene is included among the depictions of the funeral just as at Thebes, and its placement in the tombs of Paheri and Setau can be compared to its position on the left wall of the passage of a Theban T-shaped tomb. The location of the scene on the right wall in the tomb of Reneny is unusual, but there are several tombs at Thebes that display the scene some place other than the left wall of the passage (see chapter seven).[597] The rectangular shape of the Elkab tombs is reminiscent of the passage leading to the focal point in a T-shaped tomb. Likewise, there are rectangular shaped tombs at Thebes that also contain the Sacred District scene; however, they are in the minority.[598]

According to Jan Assmann, one function of the Egyptian tomb was to provide a passage or an interface for the dead between this world and the next.[599] Assmann also suggests that the tomb needs to give form to this passage which the deceased must transverse in the course of the funerary ritual, and that it is the *passage* that links the transverse hall to the shrine that fulfills this function.[600] This is why the funerary scenes usually appear in the passage of a T-shaped tomb. It is clear when looking at the placement of the Sacred District scene in the T-shaped tomb that the Sacred District is the last area the deceased passes through before he meets Osiris and appears in the world of the gods.[601] Yet, does the transitional nature of this scene that is evident in the T-shaped tombs at Thebes also hold true for the rectangular tombs farther south at Elkab?

In the tomb of Reneny, despite the placement of the Sacred District scene on the *right* wall, one can see that immediately to the left of it, closer to the focal point of the tomb chapel, Reneny's deceased mother and father appear accepting offerings.[602] Reneny appears in an equivalent scene on the opposite wall (west wall) with his wife Idy and their small son. Here, they too receive offerings.[603] On the right wall, immediately after the image of Reneny's parents, an opening to the auxiliary room extends to the east. There is no more decoration before the shrine. This same general positioning of the Sacred District scene can be seen in the later tombs of Paheri and Setau at Elkab, but in these latter two tombs the Sacred District scene is the last scene on the *left* wall before the deceased appears kneeling before Osiris. Yet, it is clear from the Sacred District's placement in all three tombs that, artistically speaking, it is the scene that terminates the compendium of funerary scenes. Before the cortege reaches the Sacred District, the figures are oriented toward it; on the other side of it the deceased either looks back toward the district, or he appears with Osiris in the other world. Reneny is an outlier as he appears offering a haunch to his deceased parents just to the left of the Sacred District on the east wall of his tomb (Figure 40). Yet, he appears in the latter position on the *left* wall. Clearly Reneny wanted to honor his parents in his tomb, as well as create a home for himself for eternity with scenes and inscriptions that would help sustain him in the afterlife. The Sacred District

District scene dates to the original decorative programs from the early eighteenth dynasty (Polz 1990: 312). Another late example is TT 41, which Assmann dates as early as the reign of Horemheb, but Kampp-Seyfried dates to sometime between Horemheb and Sety I (Assmann 1991; *idem*. 2003: 46–52; Kampp-Seyfried 1996: 235). Assmann also points to this tomb as the last one to display "Butic elements." This later date is supported in Porter and Moss (1970: 78) which dates TT 41 to the time of Ramesses I–Sety I. Another later tomb that also contains the Sacred District is TT 222, which is dated to the reigns of Ramesses III–IV (Porter and Moss 1970: 323; Kampp-Seyfried 1996: 496). Settgast includes this tomb in his study on *Der Heilige Bezirk* (1963: 48–74; N. M. Davies 1946: 70, pl. 13). With the available information it is difficult to decide if TT 222 should be excluded from this study. TT 275 is another late tomb that includes the Sacred District; however, there is some debate regarding its date. It may date as early as the reign of Amenhotep III according to Gabolde (1995: 159, note 27), to the time of Tutankhamun or Horemheb according to Kampp-Seyfried (1996: 546–547), or as late as the Ramesside Period (Porter and Moss 1970: 352).

597 For example, TT 161 has an abbreviated version of the Sacred District on the right wall of the hall (Figure 41). See also TT 39, TT 41, TT 122.

598 Two Theban tombs compare to the rectangular tombs at Elkab, in that they are not typical T-shaped tombs: TT 161 and TT 179. TT 161consists of rectangular hall with a small shrine at the back (Porter and Moss 1970: 272) and TT 179 is rectangular and gives access to TT 180 from its east wall (Porter and Moss 1970: 282).

599 Assmann 2003: 46.

600 Assmann 2003: 47–48.

601 Diamond 2010b: 41 and 2011: 42.

602 This is a correction to a previous publication in *JARCE* 48 (2012): 109. There has been much debate over the identification of these people. See W. V. Davies 2010: 237.

603 W. V. Davies 2010: 236–237.

Figure 40: North end of east wall in tomb of Reneny (TC 7) at Elkab. Photo by author.

scene functions as a transitional zone between the two worlds. It is a liminal space, a threshold, where the boundaries dissolve and the deceased passes into the hereafter.

Furthering this supposition is the door leading to the burial chamber that is located immediately after Reneny makes an offering to his parents in the realm of the dead. As noted above, the funerary scenes on the right wall illustrate the deceased passing from life to death through the Sacred District—a visual journey that ends in the *burial chamber*. Additionally, the art and the architecture of the tomb channel the deceased (all of them) toward the rising of the sun, possibly reflecting the Osirian and solar afterlife aspirations of Reneny.

Although Reneny's tomb has not been confirmed as a family tomb, this area of Elkab should be considered as constituting a family complex. It is a complex of related tombs of governors of Elkab, their extended families, officials, and associates.[604] In a graffito left in the tomb of Sobeknakht II (TC 10), the scribe Reneny describes himself as "the son of the Governor of Elkab, Sobekhotep and born to ... Ahmose."[605] It is believed that this is the same Reneny who is buried in TC 7 at Elkab.[606] Thus, Reneny was aware of his connection to these earlier men, even if that connection was only through a shared profession (see chapter six).

As concerns the micro-scenes included in the Sacred District in the Elkab tombs, there are no unique architectural or natural elements that occur here, all of the episodes have parallels in the Theban necropolis. No two Sacred District scenes are identical, yet many are similar.[607] There must have been a compendium of episodes, or micro-scenes, for the artist to choose from, any of which would have been considered acceptable for inclusion in such a liminal space.[608]

[604] W. V. Davies 2016: 75–76.

[605] W. V. Davies 2001: 120.

[606] Whale 1989: 16–20; W. V. Davies 2001: 120.

[607] The decoration in the tomb of Setau is one possible exception to this rule.

[608] If the Sacred District scenes in the tombs of Paheri and Setau are identical it may have been that by the time of the mid-twentieth dynasty the artists at Elkab were no longer

A noteworthy anomaly found at Elkab, in comparison with the Theban tombs, appears in the tomb of Setau. Not only is the presence of the Sacred District scene in a post-Amarna tomb rare, but the tomb of Setau, dated to the twentieth dynasty, may make it the latest New Kingdom example to contain a Sacred District scene. This Ramesside tomb preserves the decorative scheme of an early eighteen dynasty tomb in its wall-filling tableau scheme and the architectural plan of a typical Elkab tomb, with burial in the east.[609] The tomb dated most closely to the tomb of Setau is Theban Tomb 41, which Assmann has studied in detail.[610] The tomb of Hekmaatrenakht (TT 222) is also included in this study and has remains of some Sacred District episodes that date to the early eighteenth dynasty, before this tomb was usurped by this official.

Summary

It is evident from the decorative programs presented in the tombs of Reneny, Paheri, and Setau that the Sacred District scene was vital and fulfilled the same function as it did in the Theban Necropolis, namely, artistically acting as a transitional zone for the deceased to pass through to the hereafter. Despite the difference in tomb architecture, this scene's placement remained the same—it was the last scene before the shrine, the focal point of the chapel. Or in the case of Reneny, it was the last scene before the actual burial spot of the deceased. The rectangular shape of the Elkab tombs mimicked the function of the "passage" of the T-shaped tomb farther north and served as an actual passage for the deceased to be channeled into the afterlife. Additionally, the evidence from Elkab demonstrates the importance of the Sacred District scene, in that when space is at a premium this scene is still included in the decorative program at the expense of other less useful scenes.

---

functioning off a compendium of scenes for inclusion, but had to copy what was available to them, i.e., Paheri's scene. By this time, the Sacred District was no longer included in the decorative programs of officials' tombs, neither here nor at Thebes.

[609] This term was used by Assmann to describe this principle of wall decoration in the pre-Amarna Period (2003: 49).

[610] Assmann 1991. Theban Tomb 41 dates to the transitional period between the eighteenth and nineteenth dynasties. Assmann notes that in TT 41 the Sacred District scene turns a corner. The corner acts as the boundary between events occurring in this world and those occurring in the next. The corner marks the borderline between what happens in the tomb and what happens beyond the tomb (Assmann 2003: 49). We agree that this scene is a transitional zone; however, I am not convinced that the corner reflects this boundary because the two kneeling women occupy one side, and then the four pools they kneel in front of, the other. These two elements are clearly part of the same micro-scene. Assmann does suggest that vertical superimposition is attempted in this tomb, but he does not categorize it as a later tomb that expresses the parallelism of the upper and lower. As maintained by Assmann, in post-Amarna tombs a new vertical axis has been created within the space of the tomb. Accordingly, the sacred scenes involving depictions of gods are illustrated in the upper sections, as opposed to scenes of the world of the cult illustrated in the lower sections. Evidence for the "sacredness" of this scene may be seen in Theban Tomb 41 where it has been categorized by the artists as a "sacred scene" and placed in the upper register. However, this categorization to the "sacred" area does not occur in the tomb of Setau at Elkab (see chapter seven), or his tomb does not evidence this new vertical axis.

CONCLUSION

With the collection and description of numerous Sacred District scenes spanning both the New Kingdom and Saite Period, this book has explored this mythologized realm seemingly located on the west bank of Thebes. It is a scene that conjures up images of a holy landscape, possibly reminiscent of how this area appeared during the late seventeenth and early eighteenth dynasties. It was an image of a mythical area that was thought to materialize at the edge of the desert upon entering the cemetery during the funeral procession. There were no tombs constructed here as it was a segregated land that should remain restricted and pure. The landscape was perceived as sitting between the place of embalming near the edge of the fertile land and the tomb itself. The Sacred District was an expanse to be traversed by the deceased for the pursuit of immortality, via entrance into the west, the realm of Osiris. Thus, having evolved from an Early Dynastic pseudo-historical context it was eventually Osirianized by later Egyptians, at which time its reproduction in tomb art no longer emphasized a Lower Egyptian setting but instead featured an amalgamation of Theban and Abydene influences, although remnants of the Delta shrines still lingered on the side lines.

Since this is a scene that was illustrated only in tombs, it unmistakably has a funereal quality in the sense that its meaning was relevant to the deceased's passing. In fact, accouterments for funerary rites are prepared in this landscape scene, yet no ritual performance actually takes place—this is what has led scholars to interpret this area vaguely as a "space for ritual," and, although the pools and palms have been mistaken for a scene of daily life or a daily life wished for in the hereafter, the Sacred District scene is absolutely one with funereal significance for the *passing* of the deceased.

While the priests, officials, ritualists, and family members performed the traditional burial rites for their loved one, another drama ensued on a different plane. The burial goods were deposited into the tomb and the Opening of the Mouth ritual was performed at the real burial site and the deceased's spirit navigated the pools, palms, and sycamore trees of the Sacred District, passing by the garden plots and braziers. The deceased experienced the gods in their shrines and gently made his way to Osiris, the essence of immortality, who sat on his throne or stood in his shrine in the west. As ritualists did the dance of the *Mww* in the funeral proceedings, the real *Mww*, the divine ferrymen, magically welcomed the funeral cortege to this mythical, or liminal realm, i.e., the Sacred District. So, although this space was deific, it was also a liminal place. The deceased interacted with this landscape only temporarily as he spiritually crossed it on his journey to the hereafter.

With the closer and more familiar aspects of the Theban environment amplified in the artwork, this sacred area began at the far edge of the fertile valley on the west bank, as one left *kemet* and entered *dešret* as part of the funeral procession. Still today you can see what the ancient artists were visualizing in their artistic work if you stand in the east and look across the river toward the west—the route to the land of the dead is clear. One crosses the river Nile and passes through the fertile land before reaching the desert's edge and the necropolis in the hills. The sycamore trees underscore the familiar elements of the lush Theban landscape with which the artists were acquainted. These images span settings across the Nile valley and low desert. The Sacred District scene maps this westward journey in a rudimentary manner that is unlike our current maps. Since the ancient Egyptians did not have mapping conventions that were commensurate with actual ancient space, it was through representational aspects that a correspondence was created between a map and absolute physical space. These spaces were not presented in terms of miles, or cost, or time, so the measurement (or production) of the Sacred District scene was non-linear according to these terms.[611] Another feature of this Egyptian "map" is that the individual pictorial episodes represent both what took place and what was imagined taking place, especially in terms of the symbolic features of the setting (not necessarily the actors). The aim of the artists was to create a memorable garden environment for the blessed dead to pass through, employing imagery derived from their own surroundings—images that invoked sustenance, hydration, and rest—places where Egyptians enjoyed spending their time.

I believe this journey was conceptualized to some extent as occurring at Thebes because this was the landscape with which most artists were familiar and where the majority of the Sacred District scenes were created. However, Abydos, the cult center for the god Osiris was also paramount in this imagery. The image of Osiris summons ideas of both the land of the dead,

[611] Baines 2013: 45.

the west, and his cult center at Abydos. The prominence of Osiris, the "foremost of the Westerners," is clearly significant, but it is uncertain to what degree the geography of Abydos should be incorporated into this model. The peaceful, quiet atmosphere described in the thirteenth dynasty stela of Khutawyre Ugaf, later usurped by Neferhotep I, from the North Cemetery at Abydos seems reminiscent of the drawings in the New Kingdom private tombs, and tomb building was prohibited in this segregated area. There may be about a hundred and sixty-year time span between when this stela was erected and the first illustrated example of the Sacred District appearing at the end of the seventeenth dynasty/beginning of the eighteenth dynasty. Even more convincing evidence for a connection may be found in the tombs of Nebamun (TT 17) and Puiemre (TT 39) where the journey to Abydos is juxtaposed with the Sacred District. In fact, the sacred voyage to Abydos ends where the Sacred District begins. Therefore, it is likely that the Sacred District scene illustrates the imagined landscape—the destination—of this mythical journey the deceased takes to Abydos.

Therefore, the physical journey took place at Thebes (the funeral), but the mythical destination was a version of Abydos, but more importantly, the location of the god Osiris. Perhaps Thebes functioned as an Osirian interface like Abydos in the early New Kingdom. It is no coincidence that the wadi at Abydos linking the fertile area with the revered tomb of the god was called the *tꜣ ḏsr*—the same name given to this location in some tomb depictions. The Sacred District is an amalgamation of two thousand years of death rituals and quests for immortality, in which elements of the predynastic Lower Egyptian royal rituals persist to a small degree, that is projected in the images of the Sacred District scenes in the private New Kingdom tombs. Imagery from the *Pyramid Texts* is layered with notions that emerged from the Osirian cult and with the physical characteristics of the local Theban environment. By the end of the seventeenth dynasty religious thought had culminated in the creation of the Sacred District scene for use by elite private individuals in Upper Egypt as an expression of their pursuit of eternal life through association with the god Osiris.

From here scholarship can move forward and work toward a better understanding of the varying ancient Egyptian concepts of the afterlife, how these ideas evolved over time, and how they were expressed by the ancient Egyptians. This work contributes specifically to understanding contemporary practices of landscape design, the relationship between nature and culture, and patterns in landscape architecture and garden design, and more generally to studies on peer-polity relations in terms of craft specialization, the movement of artists, and cultural influence.

APPENDIX ONE: INDEX OF EPISODES THAT COMPRISE THE SACRED DISTRICT SCENES

Each Sacred District scene is made up of a sequence of episodes, or micro-scenes, that combine in particular ways. Although certain patterns of micro-scenes are evident, there is no standard order or lay-out to them. No two Sacred Districts are alike, so each one should be considered unique and reflective of its own place and time.[612] The following section names and describes each of the micro-scenes that were chosen for inclusion in the Sacred District scenes illustrated in the tombs. Theban Tomb 100, that of Rekhmire, is by far the most extensive in its detailing of the various micro-scenes and it includes all of the episodes.

1. Hall of the Mww and Mww with conical headdress welcoming deceased

The *Mww* appear in two variants within the Sacred District: standing in their hall and welcoming the deceased to the necropolis. There has been considerable debate within past scholarship as to who these men are, what they are doing, and whether or not the same men are depicted in all examples. There is also a possible third version of the *Mww*. These men have been described as doing the dance of the *Mww* but are not *Mww* themselves. I will refer to them as the *ḫbt*-dancers moving forward, and they are included in this list as a separate entity.[613] The *Mww* wearing the conical headdresses and welcoming the deceased have the longest history in tomb art, but the *Mww* who stand in their hall are pervasive in the Sacred District from the eighteenth dynasty onward.

Traditionally, the *Mww* have brought scholarly attention to the Sacred District scene and have elicited diverse theories. According to Emma Brunner-Traut in her work *Der Tanz im Alten Ägypten nach bildlichen und inschriftlichen Zeugnissen*, there are three kinds of *Mww* dancers.[614] The first type greets the funeral procession at the entrance to the necropolis. These *Mww* wear the tall conical wickerwork crowns and use their hands to gesture to the leader of the procession. The second kind stands guard in their hall watching over the Sacred District. The third kind of *Mww* is connected with the People of Pe and is usually depicted as dancing the *ḫnw*-dance. The *ḫnw*-dancers have bare heads and consist of two males opposite one another. Greg Reeder calls this the "ferryman's dance."[615] This third group corresponds to the pair of men who do the dance of the *Mww* but are not the *Mww* themselves. They are sometimes labelled as *ḫbt mww* (the *ḫbt*-dancers).[616]

Hartwig Altenmüller saw the *Mww* as appearing in four different contexts within the Sacred District. He rejects the *ḫnw*-dancers as a sub-division of the *Mww*, recognizing only those men wearing the traditional *Mww* costumes, and notes that the Hall of the *Mww* appears in fourteen New Kingdom tomb illustrations.[617] Reeder reviews the past work of Brunner-Traut, Junker, and Altenmüller and modifies the categories by fusing them into two distinct groups: those who are the *Mww* and those who do their dance.[618] Alix Wilkinson calls the *Mww* "ancestors" and points out that Altenmüller, whose work she regularly cites, regards them as guardians at the frontier and as guides in the otherworld.[619] Writing in 2003, Seyfried notes that there are two sets of *Mww*, those who are impersonators, or ritualists, and the actual ancestors, this explaining why there are two different ways to depict the *Mww*. Accordingly, the dancing *Mww* who greet the deceased at the cemetery are the ritualists, and the *Mww* who stand in their hall are the actual ancestors. I agree that there are two categories of *Mww*, those in this world and those in the next; however, there are two distinct ways that the *Mww* in the next world are illustrated: standing in their hall and greeting the deceased, both in their conventional attire. I like the term "*ḫbt*-dancers" for the ritualists who impersonate the *Mww* on the day of burial at the cemetery, as they do not wear the traditional outfit.

The conical headdress of the *Mww* has been

612 The one exception to this is the Sacred District scene from the Ramesside tomb of Setau's at Elkab. It appears to have been identical to that in the neighboring eighteenth dynasty tomb of Paheri.

613 Past scholarship has also included a third variety of the *Mww*. This pair of men do the dance of the *Mww* but are not themselves the *Mww*. They are labelled as *ḫbt mww* and henceforth will be called the *ḫbt*-dancers.

614 Brunner-Traut 1938: 4.

615 Reeder 1995: 69.

616 Brunner-Traut was of the opinion that the Sacred District, where the *Mww* appear, represented the ideal landscape for a tomb (1938: 43).

617 Reeder 1995: 74. This work uses *ḫbt*-dancers instead of *ḫnw*-dancers.

618 Reeder 1995.

619 A. Wilkinson 1994a: 391, 396, note 12.

responsible for several controversial theories concerning their function. This headdress led early scholars to suggest that they were jesters who entertained the deceased. Reeder, following the work of Altenmüller, elaborates on the materials used to construct these conical headdresses, noting that they were made of papyrus stalks and were not modeled on the Upper Egyptian White crown or the *Atef* crown, as others have suggested.[620] He calls them wickerwork crowns and theorizes that they were meant to resemble the papyrus skiffs used by people in the Delta. He uses this connection to further the assumption of the *Mww* as ferrymen. The *Mww* can also wear a floral headdress reminiscent of the papyrus stalk, although this headgear is much less common and should be considered an early version of the headdress. Reeder suggests this floral headdress is connected to the celestial ferrymen and theorizes that the two headdresses distinguish two types of *Mww* (especially in the Old Kingdom illustrations)— "His-face-in-front-His-face-behind."[621]

In many examples, the *Mww* make an odd sign with their fingers. This has been interpreted as a gesture of protection.[622] In these cases, the *Mww* reach out with one arm and hold their hand vertically with the thumb shown on top and one or two fingers extended. Richard Wilkinson discusses this gesture in relation to the Old Kingdom tomb scenes that show hunters with hippopotami or crocodile.[623] He connects this gesture with similar amulets that were used for protection. Robert Ritner agrees that this may be a magical gesture and he draws attention to several scenes involving cattle fording, one example being a scene in the Old Kingdom mastaba of Ti.[624] Reeder's interpretation of this gesture as appropriate for the *Mww* is two-fold, not only are they protectors of the dead during the passage from this life to the next but they are also the divine ferrymen who would be familiar with such water spells.[625] In addition to this two-fingered gesture, other examples of the *Mww* show their arm raised out in front of them with the palm facing outward, a gesture suggestive of support, protection, praise, or salutation.[626]

Within the collection of Sacred District scenes dating to the eighteenth dynasty or later, there are thirteen examples of the Hall of the *Mww*. This structure often marks the beginning of the Sacred District and hence the beginning of the segregated area the deceased must cross in order to reach the realm of Osiris. According to Jürgen Settgast, the Hall of the *Mww* and the four basins indicate the beginning and the end of the Sacred District, respectively,[627] while a lush landscape lies between them.[628] The building, whose name can also be seen from Senet's inscription (*sḥ n mww*), appears to be erected from light building materials. The floor plan of the building is depicted above the flat roof, under which an arch is stretched from wall to wall. In early examples, the plan shows a complicated spatial division, which soon gives way to a simplified representation. Settgast remarks that it is difficult to see the intention to present the ground plan of the hall of the *Mww* in these schematic drawings. Instead, he sees the symmetrical arrangement of the rooms as a conglomeration of the place and the adornment of the building facade.[629] In the tomb of Rekhmire (TT 100), this hall is labeled as *Mww*.[630] In seven of these thirteen examples, the *ḫbt*-dancers (who do the dance of the *Mww*) also appear near the Sacred District.[631] The *ḫbt*-dancers occur only twice in conjunctions with the *Mww* who welcome the deceased outside of their hall, so it would seem that including both of these micro-scenes was redundant (TT 17 and TT 41).

There are nine examples of the *Mww* standing outside their hall and wearing their conical headdress, welcoming the funeral cortege to the Sacred District. This is a common scene in the earliest examples of the Sacred District: Hery (TT 12), Tetiky (TT 15), Reneny (TC 7), and Ineni (TT 81), and this is possibly the result of its continuing employment from the Middle Kingdom, when it appeared in several tombs and on some stelae. Among the examples of the *Mww* that appear to connect the Old Kingdom examples with the New Kingdom examples are the tomb of Senet (TT 60), the twelfth dynasty tomb of Sehetepibre

620 Reeder 1995: 77–78.

621 The conical wickerwork headdress is indicative of the papyrus skiffs or floats used by the Delta boat people. This works well with the papyrus plants seen in another headdress the *Mww* wear. According to Reeder, this symbolism strengthens their association with Lower Egypt, as the papyrus is the symbolic plant of that region. Reeder bases his reading on *BD* chapter 99 and the *Papyrus of Ani* chapter 93 (1995: 83).

622 Reeder 1995: 76.

623 R. Wilkinson 1994: 194, fig. 144.

624 Ritner 1993: 227–229.

625 Reeder 1995: 77.

626 R. Wilkinson 1994: 207.

627 Settgast 1963: 49, note 1.

628 TT 127 and TT 39.

629 Settgast 1963: 50.

630 See register 9, scene 5.

631 The *ḫbt*-dancers occur in seventeen tombs included in this study.

at the Ramesseum,[632] the sixteenth dynasty tomb of Sobeknakht II at Elkab (TC 10),[633] and the stela of Abkaou (Louvre stela C 15).[634] In each of these examples the *Mww* greet the funeral cortege. Theban Tomb 17 has a unique preserved inscription for the *Mww* that reads: *ẖbt ḏfnw*. Karl Seyfried reads this as "the *ẖbt*-dancing of the ancestors (?)," following Säve-Söderbergh.[635]

The combination of the hall of the *Mww* and the *Mww* welcoming the deceased wearing their conical headdress occurs in only four tombs, three of which are included in the previous category representing the earliest tombs to include the Sacred District: Tetiky (TT 15), Reneny (TC 7), Ineni (TT 81), and Amenemope (TT 41). The first three tombs listed are the earliest New Kingdom tombs to display the Sacred District scene, while TT 41 is a post-Amarna tomb and an outlier in many respects.

After the emergence of the Sacred District scene, and thus after the experimental phase, one set of *Mww* becomes the norm. It is possible to interpret the *ẖbt*-dancers as replacements for the *Mww* who greet the deceased at the edge of the *tꜣ ḏsr* in the later tombs, as only TT 17 (from the reign of Amenhotep II) and TT 41 (post-Amarna period) display both examples. The *Mww* remain a popular episode from the reign of Thutmose III to that of Amenhotep III when the Sacred District loses momentum. Brunner-Traut summarizes the duration of the appearance of the *Mww* and ends with the tomb of Nebamun (TT 17), which dates to the reign of Amenhotep II.[636] However, some later examples of the *Mww* appear in the tombs of Amenemope (TT 41) and Setau (TC 4), among other Saite examples.

2. Pool with palms

One of the most characteristic aspects of the Sacred District is the pool with palm trees. This pool is usually surrounded by several palms and was one of the focal points of the Sacred District. The pool itself was the water source for the garden and clearly the cause of the garden's existence. This alone might account for the prominent position accorded to this micro-scene. As Egypt receives very little rainfall all gardens owe their creation to the manipulation of the Nile's inundation. This was a cyclical event that began every July, and the ancient Egyptians quickly learned to control the river water by collecting it in basins and using it as needed over a longer period of time. They channeled the water into their fields from their basins by cutting a small hole in the dike. Some illustrations of pools show an associated canal that would have fed water to the pool; however, this is not the case for the pool surrounded by palms in the Sacred District. This scene cannot be classified as an orchard because there are a limited number of trees depicted, and more specifically, the micro-scene represents trees growing only around the perimeter of the water source. These trees, which are usually palms, are planted in rows. The date palms are often missing their date bundles, so Christoffer Theis has suggested that the plants should be considered as belonging to the male sex.[637] In a few cases, as in the tomb of Rekhmire (TT 100), one finds sycamore trees also growing around a pool. Although popular in other scene types, the Sacred District does not show individual trees planted in pits with low retaining walls. These pits would have been used for watering, and the low walls surrounding them used to keep the water near the base of the tree. However, some of the illustrations of palms in the Sacred District suggest a bulkiness at the base of the tree. Most likely this is part of the plant itself, as seen in modern specimens of the same tree. There are also some illustrations of palms in the Sacred District that clearly show the excess foliage growing at the base. The pool nearby might account for the lack of pits.

There are sixteen examples of the pool and palms micro-scene. It begins to appear in the reign of Amenhotep I and is included regularly until the reigns of Hatshepsut and Thutmose III. It is also preserved in the post-Amarna tomb of Amenemope (TT 41). However, it is also probable that it once appeared in the Elkab tomb of Setau, as it does in the neighboring tomb of Paheri. The tombs that include this episode in the Sacred District are located in all sub-divisions of the Theban necropolis. Only four of the sixteen examples are illustrated in combination with the three pools, a separate micro-scene. Those four tombs are: TT 21, TT 81, TT 15, and TT 100. The first three tombs are among the earliest to include the Sacred District scene and the tomb of Rekhmire (TT 100) has the most complete funeral scene in the Theban necropolis. This pattern may suggest that the presence of one pool was usually sufficient, and that this redundancy decreased

[632] Downing and Parkinson 2016: 35–45.

[633] Tylor 1896: pl. III.

[634] Gayet 1889: 12, pl. LIV; Louvre Museum, "Abkaou stele."

[635] Seyfried 2003: 62, note 18; Säve-Söderbergh 1957: pl. XXV; *Wb* V, 572.

[636] Brunner-Traut 1938: 55.

[637] Theis 2011: 142. In Norman de Garis Davies' publication of the tomb of User (TT 21) he depicts the presence of date bundles on the palms around the pool (1913: plates xx–xxi).

as the scene was streamlined during the early part of the eighteenth dynasty.

As is the case with water sources, several tree varieties can also appear in the same Sacred District scene. It does not appear that the number of trees displayed in any given Sacred District mattered. There are twelve examples of the Sacred District scene that include both palm trees and sycamore trees. Eight of these examples also include garden plots for the production of more vegetation. Although several types of palm trees grow in Egypt today, it is the date palm that regularly appears surrounding the rectangular pool in the Sacred District. The date palm can grow quite tall, reaching heights of approximately forty meters. The stem is not divided but sometimes has off-shoots. The date palm grows a cylindrical, reddish-brown fruit with a pit inside. This tree flowers in February and March, its fruit ripens in August and September, and it needs artificial pollination to secure its production.[638] Many scholars assume the date palm originated in Africa, but the issue is controversial. The date was useful to the ancient Egyptians as it provided a good source of carbohydrates and protein, had medicinal purposes, and offered durable wood that could be used as building material and in furniture making.[639]

Another common type of palm found in Egypt today is the doum palm. In ancient Egyptian illustrations, the doum can be distinguished from the date palm by the split trunk that makes it appear as if it were two trees. This is exceptional within the palm family.[640] The doum palm grew spontaneously in ancient Egypt from at least Neolithic times, and today it is common in Upper Egypt, but rare elsewhere.[641] A. Lucas and J. R. Harris suggest that the doum palm never grew in Lower Egypt, even in ancient times.[642] Like the date palm, the doum palm was a useful tree. The fruit was eaten raw after being soaked in water and was also made into juice. The wood was also beneficial for building, and the leaves, stalks, and fibers were used in matting, basketwork, and funerary garlands. This type of palm is not the kind (usually) illustrated in the Sacred District.

According to Jürgen Settgast, the *Saisfahrt* from the Old Kingdom and the New Kingdom reveal two different perspectives of this area. He sees the pool with the palm trees as the New Kingdom reproduction of the archaic *wrt*-canal.[643] Echoing Settgast, Alix Wilkinson remarks that the pool among the palm trees is a characteristic feature of the predynastic cities in the Delta (Pe, Dep, and Djeba), which together equate with Buto.[644] However, this applies only to the date palm, as the trunks are not divided in the illustrations of the palms in the Sacred District, and the doum palm most likely did not grow in Lower Egypt in ancient times. Wilkinson also suggests that the pool with palms was interpreted as a significant locale because it was where the world began—where the sun god purified himself on the eastern horizon before he went on his daily journey across the sky.[645] Thus, the water of the garden pond has been considered to be the Nun by several scholars—the primordial water where life had originated—which evoked ideas of fertility and regeneration for the viewer. Moreover, several scholars have attempted to connect this micro-scene with earlier mortuary texts, namely *Pyramid Text* 519.[646] Accordingly, these scholars interpret the pool as the "Winding Waterway" that linked ancient Buto and Sais.[647]

There is a period of almost fifteen hundred years that passes between some of these references. In terms of the mortuary literature, many have argued that the different iterations over time represent an evolution of the same general "theology." However, Mark Smith asks, how much content must be the same to establish that different texts are indeed the same body of work? And how much content needs to be different to authenticate a "new" body of work?[648] I believe it is methodologically tricky to use texts from hundreds of years before the advent of the Sacred District scene to explain the symbolism in its micro-scenes. It is true that earlier texts may provide ideas and directions for study, but I do not think we can take older interpretations wholesale and apply them to

---

[638] Moens 1984: 30–31.

[639] Lucas and Harris 1999: 444.

[640] Lucas and Harris 1999: 444.

[641] Moens and A. Wilkinson contradict each other as to the location where the doum palm grows today. A. Wilkinson maintains that this tree grows only in Lower Egypt and the western oases (1998: 42) while Moens (1984: 331–2) asserts that it grows primarily in Upper Egypt.

[642] Lucas and Harris 1999: 444.

[643] Settgast 1963: 51.

[644] A. Wilkinson 1998: 16. This source offers no supporting documentation.

[645] A. Wilkinson 1994a: 391, 397, note 20.

[646] "*The King speaks:* I have bathed with Re in the Lake of Rushes. *The priest replies:* Horus will rub your flesh, O King, Thoth will rub your feet. O Shu, raise up the King; O Nut, give your hand to the King" (Faulkner 1998: 103). See also Grdseloff 1941: 35 and Kees 1956: 198. The king also purified himself according to *Pyramid Text* §§275 a-d, 525-9, 918a, 920b, 981-9, 1132-7, 1245b, 1247a, 1421.

[647] A. Wilkinson 1994a: 391, 396, note 21. See also Settgast 1963: 73.

[648] Smith 2017: 190–195.

more recent expressions of "spiritual" or "religious" thought.

3. *Two obelisks*

An obelisk is a tall, narrow stone shaft topped by a pyramidion. It is interpreted as an abstract exemplification of the *benben* stone of Heliopolis or as a petrified ray of light. The pyramid shaped topper is seen as the primeval mound, which symbolized eternity and repeated creation.[649] The ancient Egyptian word for obelisk was *tḫn.wy* and was usually written in the dual, as obelisks were erected in pairs.[650] There are two locations in ancient Egypt where obelisks were constructed: temples and tomb chapels.[651] As pairs of obelisks have solar symbolism, presumably those in the Sacred District scenes do as well.[652] Pairs of obelisks can appear in the Sacred District, typically close to the beginning (or on the far left when the scene appears on the left wall of the passage). The pair of obelisks inside the Sacred District is not to be confused with an adjacent scene which also includes two obelisks. In this scene, two men flank the pair and have one hand placed close to or against the tip. Perhaps these men are erecting the obelisks. These obelisks are usually slightly taller than the accompanying men.

During the fifth dynasty when interest in the cult of Re climaxes, pairs of small obelisks were erected at the entrance to private tombs. This type of obelisk is called a funerary obelisk and only one side was inscribed with the name and titles of the deceased.[653] Conventional temple obelisks begin to be erected in the sixth dynasty but only one survives. It is not until the eighteenth dynasty that obelisks begin to be raised regularly. Obelisks were usually erected at Heliopolis in Lower Egypt or at Thebes in Upper Egypt (Karnak Temple and Luxor Temple).

Jürgen Settgast includes the two obelisks in the Sacred District as part of his "Garden Pond" category and states that the significance of the obelisks is not apparent from the illustrations. However, he indicates that they are yet another place where rituals were performed in the Sacred District.[654] Since this architectural feature is indicative of the sun god Re, whose cult center was at Heliopolis, one of the ancient sacred Delta localities, Karl-J Seyfried has perceived the two-obelisk inclusion as representing the sacred Delta locality Heliopolis. He links them to the general theme of ritual journeys northward and understands them as a destination.[655]

Alix Wilkinson elaborates on the meaning behind the obelisks in the garden scenes and asserts that they belong to the western horizon and are associated with the cult of Re in Heliopolis.[656] She follows Leonard Lesko, who connects the western horizon with the Field of Hetep, the closest thing to paradise.[657] Using the work of K. Martin, A. Wilkinson furthers her point by noting that obelisks were a guarantee of life after death.[658] She points out that *Coffin Text* Spell 1011 provides evidence for the deceased praying to enter heaven between the two pillars of Re, "O you two pillars of Re, I go up and enter between you…I come and go between the two pillars of Re and the two *djed*-pillars of Geb."[659] This passage suggests their placement within the Sacred District is appropriate; however, it is rare for action to be associated with the obelisks. Moreover, there are never *djed*-pillars included in the Sacred District. Other than the obelisks as a symbol of a solar afterlife, there is not much evidence to provide a nuanced understanding of their inclusion here. Again, it is methodologically unsound to select random mortuary texts with mention of an obelisk and apply them indiscriminately to this scene.

There are five examples of a pair of obelisks found in the Sacred District scenes. They appear only in the earliest tombs (Theban Tombs 12, 15, 21, and 81 and TC 7). The episode that appears outside the Sacred District (but often nearby) and illustrates two men flanking the obelisks is more common, albeit unrelated. This micro-scene is found in Theban Tombs 179, 125, 53, 84, 96B, 41, 100, and 276.[660]

Since the pair of obelisks is a typical episode in only the earliest Sacred District scenes, this may indicate the solar cult's prominence in the early eighteenth dynasty in terms of funerary art (see chapter nine). However, it appears that as the eighteenth dynasty progresses, the solar symbolism decreases within the Sacred District scenes and the Osirian imagery intensifies.

---

649 Arnold 2003: 165.

650 Faulkner 1991: 301.

651 Van Siclen 2001: 561.

652 A. Wilkinson 1994a: 391, 396, note 19. Here she follows Junker and makes note of PT §1178, "…I am he who belongs to the two obelisks of Re which are on earth, and I belong to the two sphinxes of Re which are in the sky." (Faulkner 1998: 190.)

653 Van Siclen 2001: 561.

654 Settgast 1963: 51.

655 Seyfried 2003: 64.

656 A. Wilkinson 1994a: 391.

657 Lesko 1991: 120; Lesko 1971–72.

658 A. Wilkinson 1994a: 396, note 18.

659 Faulkner 2004: 110–111.

660 Settgast 1963: *Tafel* 10.

4. Garden plots

Square garden plots are commonly depicted in tomb scenes beginning in the Old Kingdom as a place where plants were cultivated.[661] The beds themselves are depicted in rectangular form but the plots are squared. In many cases a pool or canal is located near these plots and probably functioned as the water source, since rain was practically non-existent in ancient Egypt and farmers relied on the inundation cycle. Garden plots are commonly found in the Sacred District scene, as well as in many contemporary images of tomb gardens found in New Kingdom private tombs on the west bank of Thebes. There are also many references in the funerary literature that describe the deceased building a garden in conjunction with his tomb.[662]

Ancient examples have been rediscovered in modern excavations, specifically on the west bank of Thebes and Tell el-Amarna. In 2017, a Spanish archaeologist discovered a four-thousand-year-old funeral garden at Dra Abu el-Naga that resembles the garden plots depicted in the Sacred District scene.[663] It was unearthed in an open courtyard of a rock cut tomb of the Middle Kingdom, it measures three meters by two meters, and is divided into squares each measuring thirty centimeters. The initial assessment maintains that different kinds of plants and flowers grew in the garden, and there are two raised spots in the middle, possibly for a small tree or bush. José Galan of the Spanish mission has suggested that it played a role in the funerary rites. It is assumed that these small gardens in the Theban necropolis were intended to provide the deceased with food, water, and air. Everything that a garden meant to the living, it also meant to the deceased. Some tomb owners were happy with only a representation of a garden on their tomb wall, with the idea that the image would ensure shade, cool water, and substance in the next life. For example, the nearby tomb of Hery (TT 12) had a Sacred District scene illustrated on the wall inside. Thus far, this is one of only a few examples of a garden to be excavated at Thebes.[664] In Egypt today one can still see Egyptians gardening in a similar fashion, where they build up the edges of their garden plots to create a low dyke to trap the water inside (see Figure 20).

There are eight examples of garden plots appearing in the Sacred District scenes, this means they occur in approximately 20% of the examples. Three of the eight examples turn up in the earliest tombs: TC 7, TT 21, and TT 81. The other tombs that include scenes of garden plots all date to the reign of Thutmose III. Multiple forms of vegetation did not seem to create a redundancy like the appearance of multiple pools; therefore, garden plots appear in combination with palms and sycamore trees. And like the other vegetation depicted, it is likely that the garden plots symbolized fertility, abundance, and the presence of Osiris in his capacity as a god of fertility.

5. Two sycamore-fig trees

Two sycamore trees are a standard micro-scene within the Sacred District. They always appear in pairs and are commonly found adjacent to the pool with palms micro-scene. What is curious about the depictions of the sycamore is that they can be rendered in a variety of ways. Two very contrasting examples occur in the Elkab tombs of Reneny (TC 7) and Paheri (TC 3). In the tomb of Reneny, they are oval-like with a thin vertical line for a trunk, and they do not include any detail of the leaves. In the tomb of Paheri, the two sycamore trees appear broader, more umbrella-like, their trunks are thicker, and there is evidence for the depiction of inner branches (and possibly the leaves). In Reneny's tomb they appear side by side, while in Paheri's they occur one above the other. Therefore, we have two different perspectives on the same micro-scene in tombs situated very near to each other.

There are thirteen tombs where the sycamore trees appear as a micro-scene, including the four earliest tombs. This means that the sycamore trees should be considered an original episode of the Sacred District. At the same time, this is a micro-scene that persists into the Saite Period.

The sycamore tree was one of the most commonly depicted trees in ancient Egypt. However, the idealized illustrations of this tree sometimes make it difficult to recognize it in tomb and temple paintings.[665] The sycamore fig (*Ficus sycomorus* L.) does not produce seed in Egypt, North Africa, the Levant, or Cyprus, and has to be assisted.[666] The ancients created a technique to hurry ripening so that the fruit could be

[661] A. Wilkinson 1998: 21.

[662] PT Utterance 520.

[663] Galán, "4,000 Year Old Funerary Garden Discovered at Egyptian Tomb Entrance."

[664] American Research Center in Egypt, "Project Djehuty." For the Middle Kingdom garden in front of the tomb of Djari (TT 366), see Middle Kingdom Theban Project. "Tomb of Djari (TT 366)."

[665] Lucas and Harris 1999: 439.

[666] Harlan 1986: 11. M. F. Moens contradicts Harlan and suggests that in Egypt a wasp affects the fig, laying eggs in its ovaria and that the presence of this wasp seems to be a necessary condition for the development of the fig (1984: 29).

eaten before it was full of grubs. The fruit must be scraped or pierced, and special knives were probably employed in ancient Egypt for this purpose. The figs were artificially ripened, similar to a process that takes place with tomatoes in Florida today.[667] Depictions of the fruit in decorative scenes are always shown with a gash; this is how they are recognizable from the common fig; however, such detail is absent from most illustrations in the Sacred District. The sycamore tree has deep roots and can be found at the edge of the desert, often isolated and secluded. Moreover, this tree offers shade from the hot Egyptian sun because of its dense, wide-spreading foliage.[668] The durable wood had many purposes in ancient Egypt, as good wood was scarce.

Past scholarship has identified several early funerary texts as potentially explaining what is shown in the Sacred District scene. None of these texts is directly related to the private New Kingdom tomb scenes, but the content has been associated with it nonetheless. For example, James Henry Breasted, has highlighted *Pyramid Text* §699 as one that associates Osiris with the sycamore and vegetation in general. When Osiris is in his tomb a sycamore grows out of it and envelops his body; therefore, it should be interpreted as a visible symbol of the imperishable life of Osiris.[669] According to Alix Wilkinson, the two sycamores are located on the eastern horizon, and following Kees' suggestion, she points to *Pyramid Text* §§916 and 1433 and *Book of the Dead* chapter 149 for further explanation.[670] The relevant passages follow in their respective order:

> The High Mounds will pass me on to the Mounds of Seth, to yonder tall sycamore in the east of the sky, quivering (of leaves) (?), on which the gods sit...[671]

> This King has grasped for himself the two sycamores which are in yonder side of the sky: 'Ferry me over!' And they set him on yonder eastern side of the sky.[672]

> I know the gate in the middle of the Field of Reeds from which Re goes out into the east of the sky, of which the south is the Lake of Waterfowl and the north is the Waters of Geese, the place where Re navigates by wind or by rowing. I am the whip-master in the God's Ship, I row and never tire in the Bark of Re. I know those two trees of turquoise between which Re goes forth, and which have grown up at the Supports of Shu at that door of the Lord of the East from which Re goes forth. I know that Field of Reeds which belongs to Re...[673]

These passages indicate that the sycamore tree can have solar connections in the *Pyramid Texts* and the *Book of the Dead*. PT §1433 suggests that the two sycamore trees are on the other side of a body of water—so perhaps it is the *Mww* as ferrymen who help the deceased traverse the various waterways in the Sacred District? What might be problematic is that in the Sacred District Osiris sits at the end of the scene, while the *Pyramid Text* suggests the destination is the eastern horizon. Here the deceased travels toward the east in order to be reborn, after having died in the west, because following the path of the sun brings new life to the deceased. Contrastingly, this same author asserts that the sycamore is described in the *Coffin Texts* as the *goal* of the deceased's post-mortem journey. *Coffin Text* III, Spell 203 reads:

> Spell for power in the west, not to eat feces and not to walk upside down. O you who reject feces in On, be far from me, for I am the Bull whose throne is equipped. I have flown up as a swallow, I have cackled as a goose, I have alighted under the sycamore which nurses its *ḥknw*[674]

While the early excerpts attest to the solar aspirations of the dead, it is difficult to associate them concretely with what the artists are depicting in the private New Kingdom tombs. There was a lot of continuity in the funerary literature over the course of the different historic periods but there was a lot of change as well.

Several other funerary texts may offer additional information about the sycamore in the context of the Sacred District. One inscription from the sixth dynasty reads, "I went to the cemetery; I dug a pool one hundred cubits on each side and round it planted sycamores."[675] Another passage reads, "Build a domain in the west, dig pools and plant sycamores."[676] Both of these texts suggest the pool is in the west and it is surrounded by sycamore trees. These would suggest that what is depicted in the Sacred District

[667] Galil 1968: 178–190; Harlan 1986: 12.
[668] Harlan 1986: 12.
[669] Breasted also cites PT §§1285–7 (1959: 28).
[670] A. Wilkinson 1994a: 391, 396, note 15.
[671] Faulkner 1998: 159.
[672] Faulkner 1998: 222.
[673] Faulkner and Goelet 1994: 121.
[674] Faulkner 2004: 164–165, note 6.
[675] Vandier 1936: 36.
[676] CT II, 134, 144; VI, 171, 173.

would be a historically familiar image. In these cases, one understands the deceased as planting for eternity. Yet, there is never a tomb displayed in conjunction with the Sacred District. It is definitely possible that the pool was illustrated as a place for offerings to be made, however, there are never humans present in the Sacred District to make offerings, except for the *Mww* who do not interact with the pool.

A more local and contemporary text from Ineni's tomb (TT 81) offers an interesting treatise on the trees he planted in his garden by his tomb. He lists the trees in his garden and notes how they are economically useful. Among them, he mentions the sycamore tree and notes how it offers shade under the hot Egyptian sun. Furthermore, as the roots of the sycamore tree are deep and can reach the underground water, it is thought that this water could protect the dead from the fire in the hereafter, and that the sap could symbolize the milk of the goddess Nut.[677] Perhaps these texts provide some reasoning behind the inclusion of sycamore trees in the Sacred District scene.

6. Anubis shrine

The god Anubis is the patron of embalming and the protector of the necropolis. He is a jackal god who guides the deceased through the divine judgment before Osiris. Anubis is usually colored black, indicative of the afterlife, and usually appears in his composite form (especially during and after the New Kingdom), similar to other canine deities. Some of Anubis' most common epithets are, "He Who is before His Mountain," "Lord of the Sacred Land," "He Who is before the Divine Booth," "He Who is in the Mummy Wrappings," and "Undertaker."[678] One of Anubis' most popular roles is as weigher of the heart of the deceased; however, he does not appear in this capacity in the Sacred District scene.

There are five tombs that include the shrine of Anubis within the Sacred District. Each of these five decorative programs also includes the shrine of Osiris. This means that Anubis cannot stand alone as a primary deity within the Sacred District, nor can he act as a substitute for Osiris or the Goddess of the West. This pattern appears to confirm the dominant position that Osiris holds within the imagery of the Sacred District. Of the five examples of the Anubis shrine, two of them occur in the earliest tombs (TT 12 and TC 7). The earliest example of Anubis in his shrine appears in the tomb of Reneny (TC 7) at Elkab. Here, Anubis is in his composite form with animal head and human body. He stands facing to the right within a *ḫm*-chapel.[679] In his left hand, Anubis holds the *w3s*-scepter and in his left hand, which hangs by his side, he carries an *ankh* symbol. He dons a wide collar and a kilt, which both bear the remains of faint yellow paint. In Hery's tomb (TT 12), Anubis also appears with a human body and a jackal head, but he does not stand in a shrine. Although his image here is fragmentary, he faces to the left, has one leg forward, and carries the *w3s*-scepter.[680] And like Reneny's depiction, Anubis stands in front of Osiris, perhaps to lead Reneni toward the latter. As expected, Rekhmire's tomb (TT 100) also includes an example of Anubis in his shrine. In this example he is larger in size and appears bracketing several registers on the far right (the symbolic west). His positioning inside a shrine is comparable to Osiris and the Goddess of the West who perform the same function. He does not constitute an independent micro-scene as in Reneny's and Hery's tombs. What is similar with all three examples is that Anubis is positioned at the end of the Sacred District and appears in a comparable position to Osiris.

The other two examples of Anubis are found in Nebamun's tomb (TT 179), a tomb dating to the reign of Hatshepsut, and in the burial chamber of Sennefer (TT 96B). In TT 179, Anubis is shown in his most typical form of recumbent jackal on top of a shrine-shaped chest. He faces out of the tomb. His shrine sits inside another shrine with a *ḫkr*-frieze on top and two women kneel before it offering *nw*-jars. Anubis' shrine in TT 179 is similar to his shrine in TT 100 in that it is a rectangular shrine topped by the *ḫkr*-frieze. In Sennefer's burial chamber, Anubis appears on the right end of the left wall (west wall). This wall has four registers, now fragmentary, with the bottom register split into two sub-registers. Anubis, with perhaps Osiris behind him, faces left and is positioned just before a much larger image of Sennefer facing right. The Sacred District does not appear as a discreet unit in this decorative program, and instead the micro-scenes normally found in conjunction with the Sacred District are sporadically placed along the bottom two sub-registers—Anubis on a shrine-shaped chest is one of them.

Therefore, no chronological pattern emerges for the appearance of Anubis, but he should be considered subordinate to Osiris—the Anubis shrine cannot stand alone. However, when he does appear he is positioned

[677] Moens 1984: 48.

[678] Doxy 2001: 97.

[679] In the tomb of Reneny, the Sacred District scene appears on the right wall. This means that when Anubis faces to the right he is looking out of the tomb.

[680] Personal communication with José Galán.

as either standing with Osiris (sometimes in individual shrines) or in a comparable position to Osiris, in which cases he should be considered a complementary episode (TT 100, TT 179). The presence of Anubis in the Sacred District makes sense as he is a funerary deity and has responsibilities in terms of preparing the deceased for the afterlife.

7. Three pools

Another micro-scene within the Sacred District is the three pools, which appears in seven examples. This episode is usually portrayed as three rectangles stacked one on top of the other with a small space left in between. Often stacked vertically, they fit compactly within the framework of their allotted space. Most tombs show the pools empty except for the faint blue paint that indicates water. In the tomb of Tetiky (TT 15) the three pools are depicted within a shrine that is grouped with the open gods' shrines (see §8). This shrine is topped with the *ḫkr*-frieze and matches those around it.

The three pools are not a common episode within the Sacred District despite their appearance in the earliest examples. They appear predominately in early tombs at Thebes (TT 15, TT 81, TT 21, and TT 12), but not in the tomb of Reneny (TC 7) at Elkab. Three later examples appear in the tombs of Rekhmire (TT 100), Hekmaatrenakht (TT 222), and in the Saite tomb of Ibi (TT 36)—this last example represents a resurgence of traditional imagery.

The names of these pools remain visible in the tomb of Rekhmire: the pools of Kheper, Hekat, and Sokar. However, Jürgen Settgast notes that only two of the names are decipherable in the tomb of Hekmaatrenakht (TT 222): Kheper and Hekat. He is uncertain if a third pool was depicted at all since the wall is destroyed at this point.[681] He further remarks that these three pools are also found in the coffins of the early Middle Kingdom, but states that from all of the depictions of these pools it is still unclear as to what type of ritual was performed in them or what role they played in the funerary rituals.[682]

The three pools are always represented directly adjacent to the gods' shrines of the *ḥm* type. In Hery's tomb (TT 12) the three pools seem to be placed in between two gods' shrines.[683] In Tetiky's tomb (TT 15), the pools are actually inside the first shrine within a row of shrines. In User's tomb (TT 21) the three pools appear at the end of two rows of shrines with the bottom row extending directly below them. The upper row shows closed shrines, while the bottom row shows open ones. This arrangement has the three pools taking the spot of the last closed shrine at the end of the top row. In Ineni's tomb (TT 81) the three pools sit between the women's tent and the beginning of a row of open shrines. In Rekhmire's tomb (TT 100) there is a similar configuration, but instead of the women's tent the three pools sit between the guardians of the great gate and a row of open shrines. Even in Ibi's Saite tomb (TT 36), the three pools follow two sub-registers of shrines. This most likely indicates that these three pools should be interpreted as existing within the same area as the gods' shrines within the Sacred District.

Yet, the incorporation of the three pools into the series of the gods' shrines does not make their function any clearer. Settgast believes that it is only with the help of the pools' names that it is possible to interpret their importance in any meaningful way.[684] Through a comparison with several funerary texts that mention the names of the pools it is possible to flesh out some meaning behind their inclusion in the Sacred District scene. To begin, the pools of Kheper and Hekat are mentioned in the *Coffin Texts*, but the spell refers to four pools instead of three. *Coffin Text* Spell 234 reads as follows:

> To prepare an offering in the four basins of Khopri and Heket, the small, the medium and the large; to present the mooring-post, the bow-warp and the stern-warp; to turn over gifts(?) four times for N, virtuous and vindicated[685]

The problem with the translation of this passage is that it refers to four pools and not three pools, and the Sacred District displays only three pools. This presents an obstacle to better understanding the pools and makes what takes place at the three pools still indiscernible. Settgast states that *Coffin Text* 234 presents considerable difficulties, as only the first two names coincide with those in the inscription of

---

[681] Settgast 1963: 57, note 9. Settgast notes that this tomb is unpublished. Nina M. Davies describes some of the scenes in her 1946 article "An Unusual Depiction of Ramesside Funerary Rites," but it is short and does not comment on the three pools nor the accompanying inscriptions.

[682] Settgast 1963: 57.

[683] Menéndez 2005: 29–65.

[684] Settgast 1963: 57.

[685] Faulkner 2004: 184. Settgast points to the spells in G1T and A1C in his 1963 study but translates the passage differently. He does not acknowledge a "medium" pond and instead tries to assimilate this passage with the three pools that appear in TT 100 (1963: 58).

Figure 41: Line drawing of the rows of shrines in the tomb of Nakht (TT 161) from a page in Lepsius' notebook. After Manniche 1987: figure 92.

Rekhmire (TT 100).[686] In the tomb of Rekhmire, the third pool is assigned to the god Sokar. Following Faulkner's translation, this passage seems to have expanded the role of Heket in that there is a small, medium, and large pool associated with this deity. Following Settgast, if one instead assumes that this passage presents the name of the third pool, it is either a misinterpretation of this third pool, or that in addition to the *ḫpr*, *ḥḳt*, and *skry* pond, there was a *p3r.t wr.t* pool also.[687] However, the Sacred District displays only three pools in every example, and there is no known *p3r.t wr.t* deity who is analogous with *ḫpr* and *ḥḳt*. Furthermore, there is no corresponding determinative for a goddess written out in these inscriptions. To solve this problem, Settgast suggests that *p3r.t wr.t* should be read as *ḏr.t wr.t* "Greater Kite."[688]

It is curious that Spell 234 mentions only the ponds of *ḫpr* and *ḥḳt* and does not include the pool of Sokar. In Theban Tombs 55, 82, 112, and 125, only these two pools play a role in the course of the ritual. With reference to these textual passages, Settgast suggests that the three pools are connected to the dragging of the *tekenu*, and he adds that they can enhance the details of the ritual of the three pools.[689] There is no need to repeat this line of research here, as Settgast has aptly covered it in his own work, where he concludes that the three pools should be characterized as the place of action: the site of ritual movements, the center of which is the *tekenu*.[690] If Settgast's interpretation of connecting the pool of *ḥḳt* and the *tekenu* is accepted, then the *ḫpr* lake is the place where the *tekenu* rests. Settgast emphasizes that the captions are directly connected to the procession of the *tekenu*, from which a chronological sequence of the actions emerges.[691]

[686] Settgast 1963: 58.
[687] Settgast 1963: 58.
[688] Settgast 1963: 58.
[689] Settgast 1963: 38–47, 60. A Sokar pool has not yet been documented in the texts.
[690] Settgast 1963: 57–61.
[691] Settgast 1963: 61.

Alix Wilkinson agrees that these three pools, when they are represented as a group, indicate a progression from death to life.[692] The first pool is dedicated to Sokar, the falcon god of the dead, and signifies death; the second pool is dedicated to Kheper, the god of the rising sun, and symbolizes regeneration; and the third pool is dedicated to Hekat, the frog goddess, and represents new birth.[693]

8. Gods' shrines[694]

The gods' shrines are one of the most characteristic aspects of the Sacred District and often the rows of *ḥm*-chapels dominate the space allocated to this scene.[695] In fact, when room does not permit any other episode of the Sacred District to be included in a tomb's decorative program, it is these rows of shrines that appear. For example, in the tomb of Menna (TT 69) on the south wall where the funeral procession appears, there are two separate instances of *ḥm*-chapels. A row of open shrines appears in the bottom register and a row of closed shrines appear in the second to bottom register. Both of these registers are flanked by a large figure of the god Anubis. There are no other micro-scenes present that would typically appear in a Sacred District scene. The tomb of Nakht (TT 161) is another example of a similar decorative decision where only the shrines appear to represent the Sacred District (Figure 41).[696] When functioning as a lone marker of the Sacred District the shrines can be either open

[692] A. Wilkinson 1994a: 391, 397, note 24.
[693] A. Wilkinson 1994a: 391.
[694] There has been much confusion in the written material regarding the nature of the *ḥm*-structures in these tomb scenes. See Appendix I, §15 "*pr-nw* shrines with palms."
[695] See Gardiner's sign-list O 20 (1957: 495).
[696] Manniche 1986: 55–78. At the ARCE Annual Meeting in Oakland in 2010, Dr. Gay Robins presented a paper, entitled "The Decorative Program in Single-Roomed Pre-Amarna 18th Dynasty Tomb Chapels at Thebes" discussing the limited wall space for decoration and the importance of the scenes that were selected for the tomb chapels. She demonstrated that when wall space is at a premium the Sacred District scene does still appear in the repertoire of scenes.

or closed. These buildings, which are almost always represented in two registers, can be divided into two categories: open shrines with gods inside and closed shrines. The open shrines usually feature one god sitting inside, but on the rare occasion more than one god is depicted. There are nineteen examples of rows of open gods' shrines appearing in Sacred District scenes. Fifteen of these examples also include a row of closed shrines. These shrines appear in rows and can vary in number, but together constitute a group.

The *ḫm*-chapel is an upright rectangular chapel with a vaulted roof and extended corner posts. It was probably made of wood with a reed roof and mat hangings. The mat hangings or cover were represented by a crisscross pattern on the shrine. It is best to refer to these shrines as *ḫm*-chapels as this is a descriptive term for the architectural type. Barry Kemp describes it as an early tent shrine set within a paneled brick enclosure.[697] Alan Gardiner's O 20 sign is identical to the style of shrine shown in these rows, and he states that it is in the words *ḫm* "shrine," *pr-nw*, and *pr-nsr*. The latter two are the names for the pre-dynastic national sanctuary of Lower Egypt at Buto (Pe). Gardiner notes that this shrine can be a determinative for the pre-dynastic national sanctuary of Lower Egypt at Buto, so it may follow that the rows of shrines depicted in the Sacred District could be interpreted as rows of Lower Egyptian sanctuaries representing the gods of Lower Egypt.[698] The deities inside can be male, female, or zoomorphic, and include the Four Sons of Horus, Ptah, and an unknown deity named *šndt*.[699] In the case of Rekhmire (TT 100), there are four open shrines, and the inscriptions label the gods inside as Sokary, Sokaret, Ti (?), and *ʿttsḫt*—all anthropomorphic. Likewise, names of Delta sites can also appear as labels: *ḏbt*, *ḳdnw*, Pe and Dep, and some represent generic designations such as "the gods who are in their places."[700] The connection between the architecture of the shrines and Lower Egypt may have been used to emphasize the importance of the voyages to the sacred Delta localities during the New Kingdom for members of the elite.[701] However, it cannot be confirmed that these shrines are indeed of the *pr-nw* type. These gods typically face to the viewer's left, looking toward the entrance of the tomb. This means that they are imagined to be inhabiting the world beyond.

According to Dieter Arnold, the design of the *pr-nw* shrine was modeled on the shrine of the goddess Wadjet. He acknowledges that there is no physical evidence to support this claim, but he argues using peripheral evidence. He maintains that the *pr-nw* shrine acted as the Lower Egyptian counterpart to the *pr-wr*, the state shrine of Upper Egypt. Arnold also remarks on the shape of granite sarcophagi of the Middle Kingdom with their vaulted lids and raised walls as representing a *pr-nw* made of brick. Further evidence can be sought from the precinct of Djoser at Saqqara and the "House of the North" which is thought to represent the *pr-nw*.[702]

As noted, in addition to the open shrines, there are also closed shines within the Sacred District. There are two types of wall articulation that appear on the closed shrines. The first type of articulation is in the form of a rhombic grid with embedded points shown mainly in tombs with painted decoration. These show a variety of patterns within the series of shrines (TT 21, TT 81, and TT 82). The second type is in the form of vertical lines. This option appears in both tombs carved in relief and tombs decorated with paint (TT 100). Some tombs have a combination of both types of decorated shrine walls (TT 122). Additionally, some tombs have shrines with no internal design (TT 39 and TT 53). It is also possible that the decoration is either unfinished (TT 123) or the paint is no longer preserved (TT 39). These buildings are not empty shrines, but closed shrines.

Using the tomb of Rekhmire (TT 100) as an example, we can see that all fourteen closed shrines are labeled as gods' shrines. Unfortunately, there is no way to tell which god belongs to each shrine. The attempt to define the closed chapels is made more difficult by the fact that a uniform number of buildings cannot be determined, and for the shrines with gods, there is no equivalent number in all tombs. There is a tendency to distribute the shrines equally to gods and goddesses,[703] yet it is unknown what these pairs of gods might have represented. Only Rekhmire names his gods, where he adds to *skry* the apparently secondary feminine counterpart *skryt*.[704] However,

[697] Kemp 2018: 146–147.

[698] Gardiner 1957: 495.

[699] Diamond 2010a: 16–23.

[700] Settgast 1963: 53.

[701] Seyfried 2003: 63–65.

[702] Arnold 2003: 173. On the contrary, Settgast remarks that since the specific value of this chapel is fixed, it is unnecessary to call any building a *pr-nw*, and that one should revert to the neutral expression "*ḫm*-chapel" (1963: 52, note 2). For the sake of clarity, I have decided to employ *ḫm*-chapel for those that appear in rows.

[703] See Settgast's table 1963: 54.

[704] Settgast 1963: 55. Settgast notes that a *skrt* is unknown in Pharaonic times, but in the Ptolemaic period a *škr.t* appears in connection with Hathor.

other names do not appear complementary and some of the readings are suspect. Anubis is a common feature of the open shrines, where he either crouches or stands. The discussion on Anubis' shrine (§6 above) does not include examples of this god when he appears within an open shrine in the rows of *ḥm*-chapels.

In Settgast's study of these shrines, he remarks that the number of closed shrines always varies between six and ten. He suggests that nine shrines were intended and compares them to the nine shrines from the Old Kingdom tomb paintings.[705] Settgast supports his theory by noting that the external form of the shrines is consistent, and that in the tomb of Duauneheh (TT 125) and the tomb of Amenemhet (TT 123) there is another building directly following the shrines of the gods, namely the Sais shrine and the *pr-nw* shrine of Buto. However, this combination of shrines is less common and tends to appear primarily in the later tombs. Settgast also notes that post-Hatshepsut/Thutmose III only four shrines appear in the Sacred District. However, in this author's opinion there are not enough examples to determine a pattern. In several cases, the Sacred District is designated *only* by these rows of gods' shrines and the plethora of episodes that make up an actual Sacred District are missing. For example, this can be seen in the tomb of Menna (TT 69) which dates to the reign of Amenhotep II and in the tomb of Anen (TT 120) from the reign of Amenhotep III.

Osiris also appears in a shrine, but his shrine is not connected with the *ḥm*-chapels that appear in rows, just as Anubis in the larger shrine is also separate. It is conspicuous that Osiris is either standing under a canopy or inside a separate shrine but is never in a *ḥm*-chapel. Settgast correctly sees this separation of the shrines as the result of the Osirianization of the scene, and therefore Osiris as a secondary addition to an original composition.[706]

9. Women's tent

The women's tent is a light, wooden, open booth or shelter supported by an interior pole, inside which three women typically stand.[707] In most examples it has a simple plan (Theban Tombs 81, 82, 39, 53, 100[708]) but in one example it has a more stylized design. The women's tent begins to appear in the reign of Amenhotep I and continues until the time of Thutmose III. If one interprets the structure in the tomb of Hekmaatrenakht (TT 222) to also be a women's tent, then there is a Ramesside example as well.[709] There are nine examples of the women's tent (including TT 222) found in the tombs included in this study. They appear in Theban Tombs 21, 81, 82, 53, 39, 100, 123, 224, and 222. Seven of these examples occur in tombs located at Sheikh Abd el-Qurna, while the tomb of Puiemre (TT 39) is in Khôkha, and that of Hekmaatrenakht (TT 222) is in Qurnet Murai. Of the tombs that include the women's tent, two of these tombs are among the earliest tombs to include a Sacred District scene (TT 21 and TT 81), while six examples date to the reigns of Hatshepsut and Thutmose III. The tomb of Hekmaatrenakht (TT 222) dates to the Ramesside Period; however, the Sacred District scene most likely belongs to the original decorative program from the early eighteenth dynasty.

The tomb of User (TT 21) has a women's tent with a layout different from the others in that it has a plan that appears more complex and resembles the layout of the hall of the *Mww* more closely. Sometimes the tent appears wider (TT 39), but it can also appear more elongated as in the tomb of Ineni (TT 81). The reason for this change in shape may have to do with the number of women depicted inside the structure. For example, the tent in the tomb of Puiemre (TT 39) holds three women, while the tent in the tomb of Ineni (TT 81) holds only two. There is a post displayed in the center of each tent, but it does not fully divide the space. The tomb of Hekmaatrenakht (TT 222) displays a structure similar to the women's tent but there is only one woman inside facing to the right, and in front of her are two priests flanking a display of plants and offerings. This display surrounds what appears to be a statue of either the deceased or Osiris. Unfortunately, this illustration is no longer intact.[710]

The captions that refer to this area, of which there are at least four preserved examples, read *sḥ n ḥmwt* "women's tent." With the exception of the earliest illustration (TT 81), three women are in each tent, the first of which is on one side of the pole, with two on the other side and they face each other. All three women appear exactly the same, so there is no way to distinguish one from the other. However, in the depictions in the tombs of Rekhmire (TT 100) and Hekmaatrenakht

[705] Settgast 1963: 54–55.
[706] Settgast 1963: 55.
[707] Somewhat similar in shape to Gardiner's sign O 22 (1957: 495).
[708] One side of this enclosure appears to be at an angle but that is due to the angle of the ceiling of the tomb, which rises.
[709] A. Wilkinson 1998: 107, fig. 56. The tomb still retains some of its earlier decoration from before the time it was usurped by Hekmaatrenakht.
[710] N. M. Davies 1946: 69–70.

(TT 222), the third woman bears the label *nbt pr-wr* "Mistress of the per-wer," while the other two females remain without a title.[711] These women wear a collar around the neck and an ankle length sheath dress with one or two straps over the shoulders, and the woman in TT 222 wears a fillet around her head. As is the case with other episodes within the Sacred District these captions do not elucidate the ceremonies that took place inside the women's tent but simply name the participants and location. Jürgen Settgast suggests that it may be tempting to associate these women with the two *ḏryt*;[712] however, these women appear in threes, not as a pair.

In two of these examples the women's tent is positioned immediately after the rites before the mummy and before the pool with palms and two sycamore trees (TT 123 and TT 53). Continuing to the right stands the hall of the *Mww* in both cases. In the tomb of Puiemre (TT 39), the tent stands between the pool and palms with two sycamore trees and the guardians of the great gate. In the tomb of Ineni (TT 81) the tent is separated from the pool and palms by an additional pool and the garden plots. Perhaps the repetition of its placement next to the pool with trees implies it was imagined as sitting close to the entrance of the Sacred District. The women situated inside the tent do not perform any rituals in the Sacred District.[713]

10. Kneeling women before four basins

Another micro-scene in the Sacred District consists of two women kneeling before four rectangular basins of water that are connected by a simple channel system. Alternatively, four offering tables take the place of these basins in some scenes, for example, in the tomb of Paheri (TC 3) where these four pools look like offering tables with a rim around the edge. [714] It is in front of these four basins that one encounters the rare instance of ritualists performing a ceremonial act inside the Sacred District. The two women who kneel in front of the nameless basins offer *nw*-jars. In the various examples of this micro-scene, two sets of female titles are used as labels for these two women. The more common and better-understood titles read "Greater Kite and Lesser Kite," which are generally thought to refer to the goddesses Isis and Nephthys (TC 3 and TT 17). The other set is more enigmatic and reads "*dmḏyt*" and "*knwt*" (TT 82 and TT 100).[715]

There are fifteen examples of the four basins accompanied by kneeling women; however, most of these examples no longer retain their inscriptions (if there ever were any). Seven of the fifteen examples also have the rites to the mooring-post episode (§18). This is relevant because when there are extant labels these women bear similar titles, thus indicating a connection between the two episodes. The women kneeling before the four basins always occur within the Sacred District while the rites to the mooring-post appear to have been performed outside it. There are six examples of rites to the mooring-post in other tombs that do not include the four basins episode (Theban Tombs 125, 127, 53, 96B, 69, and 342). Of the original fifteen tombs noted above, two of them also include an episode with two kneeling women before the shrine of Anubis (TT 100 and TT 179). All fifteen examples occur during the reigns of Hatshepsut, Thutmose III, and Amenhotep II, with only three exceptions: Ineni (TT 81) and the tomb of Djehuty at Hierkonpolis as the earliest examples and Amenemope (TT 41) as the latest example.[716]

This scene begins to appear in the reign of Amenhotep I/Thutmose I (TT 81) and continues until the reign of Amenhotep II (TT 17). Ineni is one of the earliest tombs with this episode, and in his decorative program the four basins act as the last micro-scene before the offering bearers and separates the Sacred District from the surrounding scenes (as they do in Djehuty's tomb as well). The entire Sacred District is positioned behind the two kneeling women. Other early New Kingdom tombs, such as those of Reneny (TC 7) and Tetiky (TT 15), do not include this scene. Likewise, the tomb of Rekhmire (TT 100) shows this episode immediately before the large figure of Osiris flanking the registers, and as in the earlier examples, it appears within the Sacred District which is positioned

[711] Settgast 1963: 51. For the *pr-wr*, see Diamond 2010a: 17–18; Arnold 2003: 174.

[712] Settgast 1963: 51.

[713] Theis 2011: 142.

[714] A. Wilkinson identifies them as offering tables and makes note of the illustration in the tomb of Paheri at Elkab that portrays them more like tables (1994a: 396, note 7). However, in most cases the four structures appear to be basins, painted blue and employing a sort of drain. See also Tylor and Griffith 1894: pl. v.

[715] The example in TT 82 reads "*dmḏ(y)t*" and "*mnknwt*" (N. M. Davies and Gardiner 1915: pl. IX). See also Diamond 2008; *idem.* 2010a: 37–39; *idem.* 2015a; *idem.* 2017. Variations also occur in TT 222, TT 20 (not in this study) and in a fragmentary funerary liturgy published by Gardiner (1955: 9–17).

[716] The tomb of Amenemope (TT 41) is an outlier and there is a break in the appearance of this micro-scene between the reign of Amenhotep II and the end of the eighteenth dynasty.

behind it. This is also true for TT 122. In the tomb of Paheri (TC 3) the kneeling women appear as the second to last episode before Osiris. However, in the tomb of Amenemhet (TT 82) this episode has been isolated from the Sacred District and it appears as the last micro-scene after the ritual of the oars (which is not part of the Sacred District). The tomb of Nebamun (TT 17) includes a small Sacred District and shows the four basins wedged between the guardians of the great gate and a row of shrines on the left and the Goddess of the West on the right, who brackets the four registers. The basins appear next to the *Mww* in the tomb of Puiemre (TT 39), where they appear on a narrow sliver of wall to the right of the doorway. Thus, more often than not, the women who kneel before the four basins are positioned at the end of the Sacred District and close to Osiris.

In his 1963 study, Jürgen Settgast discusses this micro-scene. He corroborates that the four basins form the end of the Sacred District, and he interprets this scene through the titles attached to these two women.[717] He admits that the accompanying inscription in TT 82 "presentation to the desert" (translated by Alan Gardiner) seems odd. Instead, Settgast views this as a ritual carried out at the edge of the desert, a type of water libation, which he infers from the form of the vessels the women hold and the presence of the basins. He understands this ritual as intended for an area outside the Sacred District, namely the necropolis. He notes that it is the actual desert that is meant, and not its personification in the form of the Goddess of the West.[718] Using the tomb of Amenemhet (TT 82) as an example, Settgast views this as an attempt to establish a direct connection between the *smyt* "desert" and the *smyt imnt* "western desert."[719] These registers in TT 82 are enclosed by a large image of the Goddess of the West on the right, hence Settgast's distinction.[720] Accordingly, this example illustrates to Settgast that a change in the meaning of this scene is taking place, with the western goddess becoming the recipient of the water libation.

The illustration in the tomb of Rekhmire offers a label for these four basins, which reads *nṯrw š*, "pool of the gods." Settgast questions whether this inscription actually belongs to this scene since the two kites cannot be described as pool goddesses, even when the women giving the water libation are labeled as Isis and Nephthys.[721] He cannot conceive of any gods who could be appropriately attributed to these four basins. Therefore, Settgast thinks it should probably be transferred to the gods of the Three Pools.[722]

The titles associated with the females in this micro-scene have been studied elsewhere, so there is no need to reiterate the scholarship here.[723] Instead, a quick overview seems apposite. The ancient Egyptian word *dmḏ(y)t* occurs in several ancient sources: a funerary liturgy from the papyrus Ramesseum E, *Pyramid Texts* §2283, the decoration in the pyramid temple of Senwosret III at Dahshur, several New Kingdom private Theban Tombs (TT 20, TT 82, TT 100, and TT 222), and the seventh and eighth hours of the Book of the Amduat. Traditionally, this title had been grouped with a number of other female titles into a category of words for "a mourning woman." More recently, it has been determined that the word *dmḏ(y)t* has a very different meaning. In the cult drama, this woman (or women) was responsible for collecting the bones of the deceased in order for the body to become whole again in anticipation of its rebirth in the afterlife. Therefore, the title *dmḏ(y)t* may be translated as "bone or limb collector."[724]

It was initially thought by Gardiner, and followed by Faulkner, that the *dmḏ(y)t* was related to the *dmḏw*. The *dmḏw* is commonly translated as "crowd" and is far more common.[725] In his dictionary entry Faulkner cites examples of *dmḏ(y)t* only from a funerary text from the Ramesseum Papyri.[726] The entry for the word *dmḏ(y)t* in *Wb* V 462, 12 reads "*von der Flagfrau.*" The *Belegstellen* lists two references from the tomb of Amenemhet (TT 82) where the title refers to a single woman. In the former source, the funerary liturgy, this designation is used both in the singular, *dmḏ(y)t*, and the plural, *dmḏ(y)wt*. According to Gardiner, the word *dmḏ(y)t* also refers to a crowd and is "possibly identical with the collective *Wb* V 461, 12"—there transliterated *dmḏ.wt*.[727] Gardiner's assumption is based on the word's supposed connection with *dmḏw* and its reference to a crowd of people. With that, Gardiner points out that *Coffin Text* IV 371 features the "corresponding masculine word" (*dmḏw*) in "the

717 Settgast 1963: 64.
718 Settgast 1963: 65.
719 Settgast 1963: 65.
720 N. M. Davies and Gardiner 1915: pl. IX.

721 Settgast 1963: 65.
722 Settgast 1963: 65.
723 Diamond 2008; *idem.* 2010a: 37–39; *idem.* 2015a; *idem.* 2017.
724 Diamond 2008; *idem.* 2015a; *idem.* 2017.
725 *Wb* V 461, 12; Faulkner 1991: 313; Van der Molen 2000: 797.
726 Faulkner 1991: 313.
727 Gardiner 1955: 12, n. 2.

crowd at the burial of Osiris."[728]

In actuality, *dmḏ(y)t* and *dmḏw* ("crowd") are two different words with very different meanings that are derived from the same root. Therefore, it appears that when the singular form is used, it refers to a single woman; and when the plural form is used it refers to a group of women. The root of the two words is *dmḏw*, which in the Old Kingdom can mean "to collect or put together (the limbs of Osiris)."[729] This signification can be seen in the following *Pyramid Texts*:

> PT §318a: My limbs which were in concealment are **reunited**...[730]
> PT §617b: He has **put you together**.[731]
> PT §1036c-1037a: ...that you may **assemble** my bones and collect my members. May you **gather together** my bones...[732]
> PT §1514b: This King's bones shall be **reassembled**, his members shall be gathered together.
> PT §1890a: O Osiris the King, knit together [your] limbs, **reassemble** your members, set your heart in its place!

These passages demonstrate that in the Old Kingdom the root *dmḏ* is intimately connected to the revivification process of Osiris. The word *dmḏw* is a masculine passive participle that means "those who are collected/assembled," and thus form "a crowd" (at the burial of Osiris). The word *dmḏ(y)t* is a feminine active participle that means "she who collects/assembles" (the limbs of Osiris); the corresponding plural *dmḏ(y)wt* means "those (f.) who collect/assemble" (the limbs of Osiris). This is significant because the *dmḏ(y)t/dmḏ(y)wt* perform the rejuvenating rite of *ḥꜣi* at the funeral service in the funerary liturgy.[733]

Dmḏ(y)t is a term that designates a female ritualist and is also the name of a minor goddess. The situation is similar to that of the two females who impersonate Isis and Nephthys in the funeral scenes beginning in the late Old Kingdom in that both private women and Isis and Nephthys can be labeled "the Two Kites." Most examples of the *dmḏ(y)t* thus far discovered appear in an Osirian context—the funerary liturgy refers to the deceased as an Osiris, and the decoration in the private New Kingdom tombs encourages the deceased to participate in an Osirian afterlife. There are also attestations of the *dmḏ(y)t* that are devoid of a specifically Osirian context but are clearly funerary in nature, and therefore indirectly relate to Osiris.

There is the divine *dmḏ(y)t* who appears in the *Pyramid Texts*, the procession of the gods in the pyramid temple of Senwosret III, and in the Book of the Amduat.[734] *Pyramid Text* §2283 is the earliest *confirmed* attestation, and it demonstrates that the *Dmḏ(y)t* is a divinity, thus creating a tangible connection with Isis.[735] Admittedly, this passage is a little enigmatic and does not bear much resemblance to later attestations. The utterance reads, "Osiris Neith, accept Horus's eye, which Seth hid—THE HIDDEN VULTURE; which he joined—<u>THE JOINED VULTURE</u> (*Dmḏ(y)t*)."[736] This example is written with a vulture determinative (which is not the case with later examples) and may very well refer to a different goddess. The fact that avian motifs permeated ancient Egypt means that the presence of the vulture sign does not produce a clear association between this example in the *Pyramid Texts* and the goddess Isis, who takes many different bird forms. However, this Pyramid Text utterance does contain an early example of a deity named *Dmḏ(y)t.* This is significant when considering the later examples of *Dmḏ(y)t* in the pyramid temple of Senwosret III at Dahshur and the Book of the Amduat, all of which present her as a divine being.

In the square antechamber of Senwosret's temple, Adela Oppenheim suggests that the walls were configured so that three of them featured deities facing to the right, and one featured deities facing to the left.[737] One of the goddesses portrayed in the procession that faces toward the left, and is illustrated on the west wall, is probably *Dmḏ(y)t.* Here the east walls are associated with Lower Egypt and the west walls with Upper Egypt. If the proposed association with the south is correct, this might explain why

[728] Gardiner 1955: 12, n. 2. Faulkner (2004: 1.280) translates the passage entirely differently, namely "on that day when all the gods were clothed at the burial of Osiris."
[729] Hannig 1997: 979–981; *idem.* 2003: 1476–1478; *idem.* 2006: 2784–2790.
[730] Faulkner 1998: 69.
[731] Faulkner 1998: 119.
[732] Faulkner 1998: 173.
[733] Diamond 2010a: 37–39.

[734] Oppenheim 2008: 290–291; Hornung 1963a: 126, no. 518; 150, no. 612; Hornung 1963b: 134–150.
[735] There is an earlier enigmatic example found in *Pyramid Text* §2283 that does not bear much resemblance to later attestations in that it is written with a vulture determinative. However, this utterance does contain an early example of a deity named *Dmḏ(y)t,* thus prefacing the later examples of *Dmḏ(y)t* in the pyramid temple of Senwosret III at Dahshur and the Book of the Amduat which present her as divine.
[736] J. Allen 2005: 315. For an alternative translation, see Faulkner 1998: 317, "Which he has reassembled—a *dmḏyt*-vulture."
[737] Oppenheim 2008: 81, 236.

Dmḏ(y)t appears most frequently in the Theban area.

An early occurrence of the title *dmḏ(y)t* is found in the fragmentary funerary liturgy that was discovered by Quibell in a thirteenth dynasty tomb beneath the Ramesseum.[738] The word *dmḏ(y)t* occurs in columns 16, 20, 47, 65, and 117. In columns 47 and 117 the word is written as a plural. All of the examples are written with a female determinative. In columns 14a-16 the text reads, "second time [of circulating around] the mastaba; a summoning in (the) presence of the *dmḏ(y)t*, [they] *ḥꜣi*-ing."[739] Here the *dmḏ(y)t* is a single woman. In this example, the *dmḏ(y)t* is performing the ritual of *ḥꜣi* and calling to the deceased to revive in the form of a newly rejuvenated being.[740] According to Gardiner, this part of the text occurs in the first section of the liturgy, where he sees evidence for ritual action.[741] In column 20 the text is too fragmentary for a translation. Gardiner notes the occurrence of *ḏd mdw* twice and suggests that in the second occurrence it is the *dmḏ(y)t* who is speaking.[742] The next example of *dmḏ(y)t* is found in column 47 where the plural form occurs. According to Gardiner, the text suggests that the *dmḏ(y)wt* get involved, "...one time moving two ways (?), face to the north...."[743] The *dmḏ(y)wt* appear to be in motion, possibly moving simultaneously in opposite directions, and may still be performing the rite of *ḥꜣi* here (which is mentioned in column 44).[744] For column 65, Gardiner has managed to decipher the word *ḥꜣi* at the beginning of column 64 and the word *dmḏ(y)t*, again, in column 65. These columns are badly damaged.[745] Column 117 features the second example of the plural form *dmḏ(y)wt*. Here the liturgy ends with "the *dmḏ(y)wt* on their feet."[746]

From the funerary liturgy, the following conclusions can be made about the *dmḏ(y)wt* "the collectors of Osiris' limbs." First, the title *dmḏ(y)t* is one of the *dramatis personae* in the funerary cult drama. She is responsible for the ritual gathering of the deceased's bones or limbs, as demonstrated by the signification of the root word *dmḏ* and its usage in the *Pyramid Texts*. According to Jan Assmann, the concept of dismemberment reflected the idea of "redemption from death through collecting, joining, uniting, and knotting together."[747] The Osiris myth dramatized this circumstance with Isis being the collector of Osiris' limbs. The *dmḏ(y)wt* attend the service in the cemetery on the day of burial. They participate in the entire scripted cult rituals since they appear from beginning to end in the liturgy. The *dmḏ(y)wt* are participating in an important part of the funeral service, namely, a ritual purification that includes magical recitation.

In the New Kingdom the *dmḏ(y)wt* appear in the tombs of Mentuherkhepeshef (TT 20),[748] Amenemhet (TT 82),[749] Rekhmire (TT 100),[750] and Hekmaatrenakht (TT 222).[751] The *dmḏ(y)t* appears as a label for a female ritualist. The word functions as a title and appears in the same scenes in both TT 82 and TT 100, although one scene in TT 82 is damaged.[752] In the first scene is the four basins micro-scene of the Sacred District where two women—depicted one above the other—kneel before four basins of water in the *s(my)t*, "desert necropolis"[753] offering *nw*-jars.[754] They have their hair cut short and wear a fillet.[755] In TT 82 one woman is labeled *mnknw* and the other woman *dmḏ(y)t*. Gardiner suggests that *mnknw* is an epithet of Isis and *dmḏ(y)t* a name applied to Nephthys, based on the parallel scene in the tomb of Paheri but with different captions.

In TT 100 the women are dressed in a similar fashion, but they have switched positions with one another. One is labeled *dmḏ(y)t* and the other *knwt*. It can be assumed that the label *mnknw* (TT 82) and *knwt* (TT 100) refer to the same title. In the tomb of Rekhmire (TT 100), the second section of the western half of the south wall of the passage shows a man and woman at either end of a boat, tying it to two mooring-posts (see Rites to the Mooring-post below). The man is labeled *ḥry-wr*, the woman is labeled *knwt*, and *mnit* is written above the post.[756] Additionally, a *knwt* is represented twice sitting behind the *ḥry-wr* who is offering two *nw*-jars to the mooring-posts at

738 Gardiner 1955: 9–17.

739 Gardiner 1955: 12. In this article Gardiner translates *ḥꜣi* as "wailing." See Diamond 2007, 2008, 2010, and 2017.

740 It should be noted that the *dmḏ(y)t* regularly appears in conjunction with the ritual of *ḥꜣi* in the liturgy.

741 Gardiner 1955: 11.

742 Gardiner 1955: 12.

743 Gardiner 1955: 13.

744 Gardiner 1955: 13.

745 Gardiner 1955: 14.

746 Gardiner 1955: 16.

747 Assmann 2005: 26.

748 N. Davies 1913: pl. XIV.

749 N. M. Davies and Gardiner 1915: pls. X, XIII.

750 N. Davies 1973: pls. LXXXVIII, LXXIX.

751 Settgast 1963: 57.

752 N. M. Davies and Gardiner 1915: pl. XIII.

753 Faulkner 1991: 227.

754 N. M. Davies and Gardiner 1915: 52. Gardiner suggests that this ritual represents the fertilization of the barren desert to make it suitable for Osiris.

755 This same scene also appears in Theban Tombs 17, 21, 39, 81, and 123, although the labels are not the same. Settgast offers a brief discussion (1963: 64–65).

756 N. Davies 1973: pl. LXXXII.

the prow and the stern; she is labeled *ḥms(ỉ)t knwt*.[757] The *knwt* in these two scenes is depicted differently from the *knwt* who kneels with the *dmḏ(y)t* before the basins of water. It is possible that the label in TT 82 is attempting to combine the words *mnỉ* "to moor" and the title *knwt*; the title may actually be *knwt*, not *mnknw*.[758] Additionally, Settgast points out that a *knwt* also appears in column 13 of the above-mentioned funerary liturgy.[759] Since the text is broken and an "*n*" occurs before *knwt*, it is possible that the word is *mnknwt*. Gardiner, in his description of the text, was unable to recognize the title or make any sense out of it: "Col. 13 refers to a priestess or some other woman in a way which I do not understand."[760] There is also a third possibility. Hannig notes that *knỉ* means to do something in a weepy sort of way and states that *knwy* means "mourning women," and *knwt* "mourning woman."[761] Faulkner also suggests "be sullen(?); sullenness(?)."[762] It is also possible that the term *knwt* may also have something to do with complaining or lamenting, or that *knwt*, like *dmḏ(y)t*, has been grouped erroneously into this general category. Through personal communication, Lanny Bell suggested that the label may have read *mnk*, with the meaning of "one who cares for." His suggestion is based on a First Intermediate Period stela from Dra Abu el-Naga.[763] If this is the case, then the New Kingdom source has confused the words and misinterpreted the original meaning to have something to do with the *nw*-jars that the women are holding. It has also been suggested that *mnknw* may have a connection to the word "garden."[764]

As noted above, this same scene appears in several tombs, including the tomb of Paheri at Elkab, but the labels are different. In the tomb of Paheri, two women impersonate Isis and Nephthys illustrated by their respective titles: *ḏr(y)t wrt* and *ḏr(y)t nḏst*. The same titles appear in the tomb of Nebamun (TT 17). Even though there are several Sacred District scenes that include this micro-scene, only two tombs (still) contain the appellations *dmḏ(y)t* and *(mn)knwt*: the tomb of Amenemhet (TT 82) and the tomb of Rekhmire (TT 100).[765] Otherwise, when captions are still visible, they name the women as *ḏr(y)t wrt* and *ḏr(y)t nḏst*. The second scene in both TT 82 and TT 100 where the *dmḏ(y)t* and *(mn)knwt* appear is peripheral to the Sacred District. It shows the deceased being transferred to the west and a ceremony taking place with a female, or females, beside a shrine.[766] The third scene, the rites to the mooring-post, is discussed below.

To summarize, *dmḏ(y)t* does not refer to a crowd of females, or a mourning woman, but instead it is the title of a female ritual officiant for a funeral ceremony, whose identification was derived from the goddess *Dmḏ(y)t*. More research needs to be done on the appellation *knwt*. The job of the former (at least) was to collect and assemble the deceased's limbs, either literally or symbolically. By the Old Kingdom the root *dmḏ* was associated with the rebirth of Osiris, hence the presence of the *dmḏ(y)t* in the Sacred District enhances this location's Osirian character. The scenes of the Sacred District reiterate that the *dmḏ(y)t* and Isis are interchangeable. The *dmḏ(y)t* was the one who collected and assembled the deceased's limbs in the same way that Isis searched for Osiris' body parts and put them back together. In this respect, these two mythical characters could perform a similar ritual. Both goddesses also appear in funerary contexts and were considered protective deities. Why the *dmḏ(y)t* was utilized in the New Kingdom, albeit infrequently, when Isis was clearly the more popular alternative is unknown.[767]

If this episode is interpreted as standing at the edge, or end of the district, then this may be where the necropolis separates from the divine realm. The tomb of Amenemope (TT 41) displays this episode at the turn of the corner, and Assmann suggests that this marks the end of the "sacred" or divine scenes. The scene in Paheri places the basins adjacent to the hall of the *Mww,* which contradicts the supposition that the four basins feed water into a common canal that then provides water to the pool surrounded by palms. Action by ritualists in this area is exceedingly rare, therefore treating the two kneeling females as divine makes more sense—either as Isis and Nephthys or as *Dmḏyt* and *Knwt*. There is evidence to suggest these sets of goddesses were interchangeable, at least to some extent, as shown in the rites to the mooring-post episodes and in the decoration of the tombs of

[757] N. Davies 1973: pls. LXXX, LXXXI).
[758] Faulkner 1991: 107.
[759] Settgast 1963: 65.
[760] Gardiner 1955: 12.
[761] Hannig 1997: 884.
[762] Faulkner 1991: 286.
[763] Clère and Vandier 1948: 14, line 3.
[764] Tylor and Griffith 1894: 22; N. M. Davies and Gardiner 1915: 52.
[765] Settgast 1963: 64. See Appendix I, §18 "Rites to the Mooring-Post." There is an example in the tomb of Duanuneheh (TT 125) where a *ktnw* (read *knwt*) performs the rites to the mooring-post and an example in the tomb of Senemiah (TT 127) where Isis does the same.
[766] N. M. Davies and Gardiner 1915: pl. XIII; N. Davies 1973: pl. LXXXVIII; Settgast 1963: 87, *Tafel* 9.
[767] Diamond 2017: 59–61.

Amenemhet (TT 82) and Rekhmire (TT 100).

11. Guardians of the great gate

Close to the end of the Sacred District, there is a structure that stands out from the other installations, both by its external style and by its occupants. It is rectangular in form with a surrounding *ḫkr*-frieze and gives the impression of a fenced-in area whose central axis is emphasized by the symmetrical arrangement of the figures inside. The guardians of the great gate, labeled as such in the tomb of Rekhmire (TT 100), stand within this enclosed structure within the Sacred District. There are four guardians, the two on the left face to the right, and the two on the right face to the left. Sometimes they bend slightly forward at the waist (TT 53), but sometimes they stand upright (TT 39 and TT 17), and they do not have any arms. These figures are often painted black (TT 41) or a dark green or blue (TT 122) but they can also be painted yellow (TT 17).[768] They have their hair cropped and wear only kilts. An exception to this type of dress appears in the tomb of Tetiky (TT 15), where the two men on the left appear to be wrapped. It is difficult to interpret the meaning of this disparity as there are no parallels extant in the other scenes.

The rectangular structure in which the guardians stand comes in three styles. The first and most common version shows the gate from an aerial view surrounded by a *ḫkr*-frieze painted yellow (TC 3 and TT 17). In the tomb of Tetiky (TT 15), one of the earliest examples, the guardians of the great gate stand inside a *pr-nw* shrine among the other gods' shrines. In this case, the guardians are specifically identified as divine beings by being placed inside one of the shrines that stands in the rows of shrines that typically appear in the Sacred District. Their shrine is in the upper row of open shrines and is the last one before the large shrine of Osiris who flanks both registers. All of these shrines are topped with the *ḫkr*-frieze. The second style is less common and resembles a tent-like structure with a pitched roof. This version appears in the tomb of Amenemope (TT 41) and shows the guardians in an enclosure resembling Gardiner's O 22 sign. A third style in visible in the tomb of Amenhotep/Amenemhet (TT 122), where the guardians stand (bent forward) in a plain rectangular structure without decoration other than its yellow paint. In almost all examples, the gate is painted yellow (based on the colors that can be seen today). Yellow can be symbolic of eternity, the sun, or the flesh of the gods. The guardians in the tomb of User (TT 21) stand in a slightly larger structure with two dividing walls positioned between the pairs of men who face inward. However, other than the internal organization of the gate, it resembles others with the *ḫkr*-frieze. Jürgen Settgast suggests that this early illustration in TT 21 is evidence of an arrangement that explains the importance of the interposition—the interrupted boundary and the partition in the interior marks an entrance. Settgast further suggests that at the same time, this example shows that this zone is a fenced-in area within the district.[769] It is compelling to consider this rendition of the gate with that in the tomb of Tetiky (TT 15), where the gods appear inside an actual shrine. This corroborates the theory that the guardians stood inside an enclosed structure. The only other illustration of the guardians of the great gate that show any sort of interior separation is that of the tomb of Amenemope (TT 41), which appears to have each guardian segregated by a thin yellow line. The sequence of micro-scenes in this tomb is also unusual because the gate is placed in the second to top row beside the *Mww*. This means that the micro-scenes that typically begin and end the Sacred District are placed next to each other, leaving the internal features of the Sacred District to be positioned along the two registers out of sequence.

Inscriptions for the guardians of the great gate remain in only three tombs: TT 100, TT 112, and TT 222.[770] It is from these inscriptions that this scene's name has been determined. This is a relatively popular episode in the Sacred District. There are eighteen examples of this gate,[771] thirteen of which also include the shrine of Osiris immediately after it. Seven examples of the guardians of the great gate are located in the lowest register of the wall; six of these precede the shrine of Osiris. Seven of the eighteen examples occur on the second lowest register, five of which appear in conjunction with the shrine of Osiris. With this frequent combination, it is probable that the guardians are safeguarding the realm of Osiris, or possibly monitoring access to Osiris. The guardians of the great gate occur predominantly, but not exclusively, in the earliest tombs, such as TT 15, TT 81, TT 21, and TT 12 suggesting that when the Sacred District first began to appear as a complex this episode was paramount for conveying its meaning.

Settgast brings attention to *Coffin Text* 460 as a

[768] In TT 122 the guardians are painted three different colors: two dark green/blue, one brown, and one yellow.

[769] Settgast 1963: 52.

[770] Settgast 1963: 52.

[771] Settgast notes that TT 222 has the guardians of the great gate depicted, however, he does not illustrate it in his publication. The number eighteen includes TT 222.

possible reference to the guardians of the great gate. The relevant passage reads, "May he commend me to the door-keepers of the District of Silence, may they not oppose me…".[772] He suggests that the particularly peaceful ambiance portrayed in the Sacred District scene may be referred to as the District of Silence. Osiris was lord of silence and did not allow anyone to raise their voice in his vicinity.[773] Several chapters of the *Book of the Dead* may also be relevant for the interpretation of this scene, such as chapter 146 where the eleven portals of Osiris are listed and each mentions a guardian protecting Osiris.[774] Or, chapter 144 which reads, "O you gates, O you who keep the gates because of Osiris, O you who guard them and who report the affairs of the Two Lands to Osiris every day…."[775] Again, this micro-scene is left unexplained as far as the rituals that were performed here are concerned.

When discussing Osiris' "policemen," Jan Assmann points to the guardians who stand at the side of Osiris, warding off Seth and his band and all other threatening beings. These guardians act on the side of good and belong to Osiris. He points to *BD* chapter 127:

> O doormen, O doormen, who guard the gates,
> who gulp down bas and devour the bodies of the dead
> who pass by them, when they are condemned to the place of annihilation!
> Give good guidance to the *ba* of the excellent transfigure done,
> he being well protected in the places of the realm of the deceased,
> filled with *ba*-power like Re,
> praised like Osiris![776]

In light of the chapters referenced above and the regular position of the gate near Osiris, it is likely that the guardians inside it fortify and protect access to his realm. It may be significant that they are sometimes painted black or dark green/blue like Osiris, showing that they belong to him.

12. Osiris

Osiris was the most popular god of the afterlife. He is first attested in the fifth dynasty in the *Pyramid Texts* from the royal tombs and in the offering formulae of the private tombs. However, there is a late fourth dynasty offering formula in the tomb of queen Meresankh that lists Osiris' cult place Busiris before that of Abydos, so although there are early attestations of Osiris, he is not initially, nor always, associated with Abydos.[777] Osiris' cult becomes more prominent during the Middle Kingdom when it is both state sponsored and supported by private individuals. At this time, Abydos was his cult center, and it is here that recent excavations have revealed evidence for the popularity of his cult.[778] Osiris was originally a chthonic deity; however, he eventually inherited the celestial hereafter, possible in his identification with the Orion constellation. Osiris-Re, a syncretism of the gods Osiris and Re first appears in a royal context in the New Kingdom, but a belief in a solar afterlife first became popular for private individuals much earlier.[779]

In the majority of scenes, it is Osiris who presides over the scant rituals performed in the Sacred District, where he stands inside one of two types of shrines. The first one resembles the hieroglyph for "chapel" or "shrine" (*k3ri*) and brings to mind Gardiner's O 18 sign. This version of Osiris' shrine appears in the early scenes of the Sacred District. In the tomb of Tetiky (TT 15), this form of Osiris' shrine is simple and appears rickety and weak, so perhaps it was collapsible or temporary. It gives the impression of two (decorated?) poles upholding a light roof.[780] Dieter Arnold, in his work *The Encyclopedia of Ancient Egyptian Architecture*, suggests that this shrine may originally have been a king's tent that was made out of reed matting.[781] The illustration in Tetiky's tomb corroborates this assumption. The second structure depicts the façade of a shrine with a cavetto cornice and resembles Gardiner's O 21 sign. The cavetto is an important structural feature in Egyptian architecture and emerges out of a horizontal torus molding. Its origin, according to Arnold, can be traced to palm fronds planted in a row on the tops of walls. This is why its lower surface is decorated with an abstract form of red, blue, and green palm fronds and sometimes inlaid with colored faience tiles. Its symbolism is possibly related to the *sḥ nṯr* chapel.[782] Therefore, this shrine is a "divine booth" and should be interpreted more as a temple or chapel than as a tent

[772] Faulkner 2004: 88.
[773] Assmann 2005: 190.
[774] Faulkner and Goelet 1994: 121.
[775] Faulkner and Goelet 1994: 120.
[776] Assmann 2005: 148.
[777] Baines 2020: 187–88.
[778] See chapter three. For a comprehensive study of the god Osiris, see Mark Smith 2017.
[779] Smith 2017: 245–251.
[780] N. Davies 1925: pl. 5.
[781] Arnold 2003: 174.
[782] Arnold 2003: 46.

(as with the former). Examples of Osiris inside the divine booth are found in the tomb of Paheri at Elkab (TC 3), the tomb of Amenhotep/Amenemhet (TT 122), the tomb of Nebamun (TT 179), and the tomb of User (TT 21). There is also a unique example in the tomb of Amenemhet (TT 123) where Osiris seems to stand inside a rectangle. Perhaps this should be interpreted as a very simplified enclosure.

In many depictions of the Sacred District, Osiris appears in his shrine as one of the last micro-scenes (Theban Tombs 100, 15, 81, 21, 179, 224, 112, 122, 123, 53, A4, 96B, 12, 172, Tomb Chapels 3 and 7 at Elkab, and Djehuty at Hierakonpolis).[783] Of these seventeen examples the chronological breakdown is as follows. The six earliest tombs to include the Sacred District scene each have an Osiris shrine (TT 15, TC 7, TT 81, TT 21, TT 12, and Djehuty). Ten examples date to the reigns of Hatshepsut and Thutmose III, with two of these dating closer to the end of that period. The one exception is Sennefer's burial chamber (TT 96B), which is an anomaly in general. Geographically, the Osiris shrine appears as a micro-scene at Sheikh Abd el-Qurna (nine examples), Dra Abu el-Naga (three examples), Khôkha (two examples), Elkab (two examples), and Hierakonpolis (one example), and thus is not a product of one specific location. Osiris regularly faces to the left, toward the entrance of the tomb. However, his position varies depending on the tomb's architecture and where the artists have placed the Sacred District. His figure is intended to emerge from the land of the dead, and therefore he must face the figures who occupy the land of the living and enter into the tomb.[784] Contrastingly, in the tombs of Paheri (TC 3) and Amenhotep/Amenemhet (TT 122) he faces to the right and toward the interior of the tomb. As noted above, in several tombs the micro-scene of the guardians of the great gate appears adjacent to the shrine of Osiris (examples include TT 15, TT 21, TC 3, TT 122, TT 123).[785]

In the tomb of Paheri at Elkab (TC 3), and presumably that of Setau (TC 4) as well, the deceased is also shown kneeling in front of Osiris, having just traversed the Sacred District. Here, Osiris sits on his throne within his shrine at the far end of the left wall and brackets the bottom two registers that include the Sacred District scene (and a separate shrine of Osiris). In the tomb of Rekhmire (TT 100), an alternative version shows Osiris bracketing the three registers close to the top of the wall that contain several episodes of the Sacred District. Instead of sitting on his throne, here he stands on a small podium inside his divine booth in a mummiform pose with only his hands outside his garment, which hold a *w3s*-scepter and a flail (as noted above, this shrine resembles Gardiner's O 21 sign). It is common enough to show Osiris situated at the end of the left wall flanking several decorative registers, yet it is the Goddess of the West who stands at the end of the register most frequently (Theban Tombs 112, 17, 82, 39, 84, 69, 276, 260, 92, Djehuty at Hierakonpolis). Yet, she rarely appears in the earliest tombs, and she never figures as a micro-scene within the compendium of Sacred District episodes.

Figure 42: Pottery brazier from the tomb of Amenhotep (MMA 36.3.165). Accessed from the Metropolitan Museum of Art's website.

13. Braziers

This micro-scene consists of five to ten braziers placed alongside each other. They occur in a row and together represent a unit or episode. This micro-scene is relatively infrequent within the Sacred District and occurs in only eight decorative programs concentrated in the mid-eighteenth dynasty (Theban Tombs 21, 100, 224, 122, 123, 53, A4 and Paheri's tomb at Elkab). They are usually painted white (TT 122) or brown (TT 123).

[783] This list does not include Setau's tomb at Elkab (TC 4) even though it presumably included an Osiris shrine micro-scene like that of Paheri. There are remains of a large, seated image of Osiris at the end of the register.

[784] In the tomb of Reneny (TC 7) Osiris faces to the right because he is illustrated on the right wall of the chapel. He still faces toward the entrance of the tomb.

[785] In the tomb of Paheri (TC 3) and the tomb of Amenemhet (TT 123) the shrine of Osiris appears before the guardians of the great gate.

The tomb of User (TT 21) is the only early tomb to include this micro-scene, so the braziers do not appear to be an original part of the compendium of scenes. Braziers do not appear in Tetiky (TT 15), Reneny (TC 7), or Ineni (TT 81)—three of the earliest tombs. There are no late examples either. Rows of braziers often occur in conjunction with garden plots, appearing as though they are resting on top of them. In the tomb of User (TT 21) there are ten brown braziers set upon garden plots painted bright blue. In the tomb of Paheri (TC 3) there are six multi-colored braziers. The tomb of Amenemhet (TT 53) includes four braziers that alternate with another object, possibly a smaller pottery vessel, and appear to sit on top of a garden pool. In this case, the rectangular structure is not decorated with a grid and so it is unlikely to be a garden plot. The tomb of Rekhmire (TT 100) has both garden plots and braziers in combination as well. One of the best-preserved images of these braziers is in the tomb of Amenhotep/Amenemhet (TT 122), where they are colored white and delineated in brown. Here there are five braziers situated on top of a rectangular pool painted blue (similar to the image in TT 53). So, it appears that the row of braziers can be paired with a garden plot or a pool within the Sacred District.

Braziers were used for incense and burnt offerings during the funeral ceremonies and were usually made of pottery. There have been some discovered as burial goods in the Theban area. For example, there is a small brazier housed in the Metropolitan Museum of Art in New York that measures 22.5 cm in height (MMA 36.3.165). This brazier was found in the tomb of a boy named Amenhotep, Senenmut's younger brother, who lived sometime during the joint reign of Hatshepsut and Thutmose III (Figure 42).[786]

14. ḫbt-dancers

In previous scholarship the *ḫbt*-dancers have been frequently considered one form of the *Mww*. This is a fair assessment since they are described in the tomb inscriptions as doing the dance of the *Mww*. However, they should not be considered as strictly belonging to this group. I call them the *ḫbt*-dancers (for lack of a better term) because when they are accompanied by a label, the verb *ḫbỉ* is typically employed (TT 82, TT 125). The Egyptian language does not have a generic word for "dance" but instead has utilized two or three different words. The more common word for "dance" is *ỉbꜣ*, but *ḫbỉ* is also translated as "to dance," while *ḫbt* translates as "dance."[787]

The *ḫbt*-dancers are attested only during the first half of the eighteenth dynasty but not in the earliest group of tombs to contain the Sacred District scene. They tend to appear only in tombs dating to the reign of Hatshepsut and later. Sometimes they appear simultaneously with the *Mww* who wear the conical headdresses (discussed above in §1), but the *ḫbt*-dancers are always bare-headed. Unlike the *Mww*, the *ḫbt*-dancers appear in pairs and perform their dance in the same manner in each illustration—there is little variation. They raise a fist until their thumbs are almost touching and their other arm is bent across their chest with the hand in a fist.[788] They stand on one leg and cross the other one in front, bending that knee slightly (Figure 43). The partner is in opposite symmetry with the right limbs of one corresponding to the left limbs of the other. This must have been the most characteristic gesture of their particular dance.[789] The men wear their hair cropped short, often painted black, and they wear white kilts.

The illustration in the tomb of Senemiah (TT 127) has a slight variation of the aforementioned gesture in that the men's hands are configured differently: they are touching each other.[790] Likewise, the *ḫbt*-dancers in the tomb of Amenemhet (TT 53) show a variant in their leg poses. They have their back legs lifted slightly as if they are stepping with their heel against the ankle of their front leg. The most drastic anomaly appears in the Ramesside tomb of Amenemope (TT 41), where the men hold their arms in the *hnw*-gesture.[791] The front arm is bent at the elbow and is posed at a right angle with the hand in the air (not in a fist). The back arm is crossed over the chest.

There are seventeen examples of the *ḫbt*-dancers that appear in conjunction with the Sacred District. Two illustrations emerge as early as the reign of Hatshepsut and nine date to the time of Thutmose III. The instances of the *ḫbt*-dancers decline in the reign of Amenhotep II with only three examples. However, they do persist into the reign of his successor Thutmose IV with only one example. The latest two depictions appear in the Ramesside tombs of Amenemope (TT

[786] W. Hayes 1959: 208–209; Metropolitan Museum of Art, "Brazier from the Burial of Amenhotep."

[787] Meeks 2001: 356–360; Faulkner 1991: 15, 187.

[788] Lexová points out that pair dancing was common in ancient Egypt but that men danced with men and women with women (2000: 27). See also Spencer 2003: 115.

[789] Brigitte Dominicus classifies this arm gesture as one of worship (1994: 67–69).

[790] In the New Kingdom, dancers do not hold hands but instead clench their fists. These dancers touch each other only with their thumbs (Lexová 2000: 28).

[791] Dominicus 1994: 61–65.

Figure 43: *ḫbt*-dancers from the tomb of Duauneheh (TT 125). Photo by author.

41) and Setau (TC 4), but these are anomalies. The *ḫbt*-dancers are one of the more popular micro-scenes to occur in conjunction with the Sacred District. Yet, it must be noted that they do not occur within the Sacred District itself. This theory is corroborated by the pictorial evidence in the tomb of Amenmose (TT 42), a tomb that does not have the Sacred District scene but does feature the *ḫbt*-dancers. Here, the *ḫbt*-dancers appear in the funeral procession in the top register. They precede the dragging of the *tekenu* and they follow the passing of the oars. This demonstrates that the *ḫbt*-dancers are part of the funeral procession and are not directly tied to the Sacred District. This context is substantiated by the decoration in the tomb of Nebamun (TT 179) where the background of the registers characterizes the realm in which the activities take place. The beige background signifies activities in this world, i.e., during the funeral, and the bluish-gray background characterizes events in the next realm. The *ḫbt*-dancers appear in the former while the Sacred District appears in the latter.

The *ḫbt*-dancers mingle with the members of the funeral procession and can appear in several different places along the cortege. Yet, they never precede it. They commonly appear juxtaposed with the Delta shrines (Theban Tombs 100, 125, 127, 17, and Tomb Chapels 3 and 4), which has led modern scholars to associate them with the Butic burial.[792] For example, in the tomb of Rekhmire (TT 100), the *ḫbt*-dancers appear in the third register from the bottom in the scenes representing the journey to Sais.[793] However, they appear just as frequently dispersed among the funerary personnel (Theban Tombs 179, 82, 96B, 53, 41, 42).

As in the case of the actual *Mww*, the *ḫbt*-dancers have also been a controversial topic. Greg Reeder asserts that these men perform a ferryman's dance ("His-face-in-front-His-face-behind") and are associated with the people of Pe. He correctly remarks that they are not the *Mww* themselves, but they do the dance of the *Mww*. Therefore, the dance they do is about ferrymen, and they perform their dance on the day of burial during the funeral ceremony.[794] The well-known passage from *The Story of Sinuhe* recounts the procession from the embalming workshop to the tomb and the activities of the *ḫbt*-dancers on the day of burial:

> The procession's following is made for you on the day of interment,
> the mummy-case of gold, with head of lapis-lazuli,
> the sky above as you lie on the bier,
> oxen drawing you, chanters in front of you.
> Funerary dances (*ḫbb nnyw*) are done for you at your tomb's mouth,[795]

[792] Wild 1963: 97–98. See Appendix I, §§15–17.

[793] Dominicus 1994: 74.

[794] Reeder 1995: 77.

[795] Allen's literal translation for this line is "dance of the inert ones" and he states that in this ritual the performers

the offering-list is recited for you,
and slaughter is done for you at the mouth of your offering-slabs[796]

The *ḫbt*-dancers are not part of the Sacred District, but instead have been regularly associated with it by modern scholars because of their role in the funeral procession and their positioning adjacent to the combined Delta shrines that have been interpreted as part of the Butic Burial.

15. pr-nw *shrines with palms*[797]

Past scholarship on the *pr-nw* shrines with alternating palm tree has been confused and contradictory, with researchers offering many differing opinions as to their significance.[798] As noted above, there are rows of both open and closed *ḫm*-chapels that appear within the Sacred District (§8 above). This is the same style of shrine that occurs in this micro-scene, *pr-nw* shrines with palms, but only two shrines appear and each one is coupled with a palm tree—thus, a shrine and a palm alternate. In the tombs that depict a Sacred District scene, these two micro-scenes (the *ḫm*-chapels and the *pr-nw* shrines, as I refer to them in this work) are separate, with only the rows of *ḫm*-chapels appearing inside said area. However, in the Old Kingdom rows of *pr-nw* shrines juxtaposed with other stylized shrines were illustrated in several tombs, which has contributed to scholarly uncertainty about the meaning of these shrines in New Kingdom tomb decoration. When the pair of *pr-nw* shrine and palm tree is illustrated in tomb scenes of the New Kingdom, this episode is placed next to the Saite shrine and an unnamed structure. These three different shrines typically appear together. It is this combination of shrines that has a connection to the Delta and thus also with the "Butic Burial." To reiterate, these three shrines appear together *outside* the Sacred District. Strictly speaking, these shrines are not part of the Sacred District scene, however, they almost always appear adjacent to it.[799] When the Sacred District scene has been explored in previous scholarship, these three shrines are usually included in the discussions. For these reasons, I have included them in this appendix.

This section explores the coupling of the *pr-nw* shrine and palm and their relationship to the Sacred District, while the Saite shrine and unnamed structure are discussed in §§16 and 17 below. The type of shrine displayed in both the rows of gods' shrines and the alternating shrine and palm tree resemble Gardiner's O 20 sign. This sign can be used as a determinative in many words, such as *itrt* "row of sanctuaries," *ḫm* "shrine," *pr-nw* or *pr-nsr* (the names of the predynastic national sanctuaries of Lower Egypt at Buto), and *itrt mḥt* (the row of Lower Egyptian sanctuaries and a collective term for the gods of Lower Egypt).[800] Our understanding of the origins of this shrine is murky. In his work on ancient Egyptian architecture, Dieter Arnold points out that our knowledge of the form of the *pr-nw* shrine is based on the hieroglyph which shows an upright rectangular chapel with a vaulted roof and extended corner posts (Figure 44). He presumes it was made of wood with a reed roof and mat hangings.[801] Pictorial evidence for this style of shrine can be traced back to the Early Dynastic period. The Scorpion mace head shows a seasonal agricultural ritual performed on a flat band of water with a winding waterway branching off below it. The setting shows papyrus marshes and an aquatic setting which is not easily located in Upper Egypt where the artifact was discovered. John Baines, in his article on watery landscapes and the rituals performed therein, suggests that this location is better compared to the wider northern valley, specifically the Delta. There are two reed buildings depicted on the mace head which he discerns as shrines.[802] However, it is uncertain which shrine is actually depicted. Examples of this same shrine style appear in the Old Kingdom, where the *Mww* perform in the vicinity of the rows of *ḫm*-chapels (possibly to be identified as *pr-nw* shrines) and the Saite shrine. In fact, these two episodes, which are distinguishable in the New Kingdom, seem to have been conflated at an earlier date. Evidence for this can be seen in the Old Kingdom mastaba of Ptahhotep I

represent the ancestors of the deceased who welcome the arrival of the procession. He claims that the term *nnyw* is a reinterpretation of the original designation of the dancers—*mww* (of unknown meaning). Allen suggests it may be a plural nisbe of *mww* (water), citing Altenmüller (J. Allen 2015: 122; Altenmüller 1975b).

796 B192–196 (J. Allen 2015: 120).

797 For more information on the *ḫm*-shrines see Gods' Shrines above (§8).

798 Junker 1940; Vandier 1944; Settgast 1963; Seyfried 2003; Kemp 2018: 97–107.

799 It may be correct to speak of the Saite shrine and the unnamed structure as one micro-scene, except the unnamed structure does not appear in the tomb of Amenemhet (TT 82) while the Saite shrine does. It may also be correct to group together the two *pr-nw* shrines with alternating palm, the Saite shrine, and the unnamed structure since they typically appear as a cohesive unit. I have separated them here for clarity's sake.

800 Gardiner 1957: 495.

801 Arnold 2003: 173.

802 Baines 2020: 181.

Figure 44: Reconstruction of the *pr-nw* shrine after Arnold 2003: 173. Illustration by Roman Reed.

and Ihi and in the mastaba of Idwt, where there are rows of *ḥm*-chapels with a stylized palm tree between each one.[803]

Scholars have acknowledged that the holy cities in the Delta were pilgrimage sites, but there has been some uncertainty expressed in the research in terms of origin and significance. Hermann Junker has suggested that pilgrimage to the holy cities should be linked, not to the Osirian legend, but to the ancient funeral ritual of the kings of Buto. Accordingly, the funeral procession left from Buto, the capital of the kingdom, and visited the main sanctuaries at Sais and Heliopolis, and then returned to the necropolis of Buto where the deceased king was welcomed by the *Mww*. Following Junker's 1940 work "Der Tanz der Mww und das Butische Begräbnis im Alten Reich," the *pr-nw* structures beside the palm trees symbolize Buto. Junker employs Kurt Sethe's theory that the *pr-nw* structure was not for a sanctuary in the beginning, but the royal palace of Lower Egypt—a theory which he adopted and then developed.[804] Junker uses the archaic relief from the Late Period Palace of Apries at Memphis to provide evidence for this identification. This relief features an inscription giving the old name for Buto (*ḏb῾wt*).[805] To Junker, one of the significant factors in identification is that the number of structures illustrated can fluctuate in the representations, the oldest example showing up to six structures, if not more. What is problematic about using Junker's work for the New Kingdom depictions is that he fuses the two micro-scenes together and thus some of his conclusions about the rows of *ḥm*-chapels is applied to the pair of *pr-nw* shrines with alternating palm tree, and vice versa. For example, to evaluate the function of the *pr-nw* structure, Junker asks which buildings could stand under palm trees and occur in such great a number side by side. This is a great question, but in the Sacred District the only shrine that stands under a palm is the *pr-nw,* while the rows of *ḥm*-chapels do not. In the case of the two *pr-nw* shrines juxtaposed with the two palm trees, there is never a reference to divinity, as there is with the rows of open *ḥm*-chapels (§8). In addition, Junker rightly believes that there would not have been this many sanctuaries in Buto, and so he concludes that these structures are not temples or chapels. Yet, in the Sacred District gods sit inside many of them. Furthermore, he concludes that these buildings cannot be a collection of royal palaces because this is illogical.[806]

As concerns the origin of the *pr-nw* structure, Junker remarks that in the beginning *ḥm* denoted the royal palace of Lower Egypt, not a chapel. Since the dwelling of the god is often imitated by the dwelling-places of the people, and especially the king, it is not surprising that one encounters the same form in temples, chapels, and shrines as well.[807] The Lower Egyptian palace has also been the model for other buildings, especially for the royal tomb. Later, the form of the coffin also imitated the tomb structure and the palace of the king, even long after the tomb had assumed different forms. Junker points to some of the limestone work from the Old Kingdom, now in the Egyptian Museum in Cairo, to illustrate these connections. He clarifies his point by noting the similarity between the hieroglyphic sign for the *pr-nw* palace and that of the coffin and adds that the fundamental difference is only the width-to-height ratio.[808] Junker's conclusion that the buildings in the Old Kingdom tomb scenes depict the royal cemetery of Buto has been influential and is still reiterated more than eighty years later. One issue that arises is how do we reconcile the rows of *ḥm*-chapels that have divine affiliations, even if their number cannot be easily

[803] Vandier 1944: figs. 3–4. The palm trees do not create a pattern with the rows of gods' shrines in the New Kingdom. Therefore, it is necessary to separate these two micro-scenes in association with the Sacred District scene, which earlier scholars have not always done.

[804] Sethe 1930: 130.

[805] According to Junker, a more detailed explanation of the exact locality has not been attempted, but perhaps it could still be determined which district of the capital is meant by the designation *ḏb῾wt* (1940: 17). This was the case in 1940 and still today there is much confusion surrounding the depictions of these shrines. See Baines 2013: 135–136; Baines 2020: 183.

[806] Junker 1940: 20.

[807] Junker 1940: 17.

[808] Junker 1940: 18.

explained. In this case, Junker rightly asserts that if they are sanctuaries, the gods should not be omitted. A better argument can be made for the pair of shrines with palm trees as tombs (the micro-scene discussed in this section). Thus, the most acceptable solution is that the royal cemetery of Buto is to be interpreted in the image of the two *pr-nw* shrines coupled with the palms. Here the number of buildings is irrelevant, and the palm trees make sense since trees are a well-known phenomenon at the tomb in ancient Egypt.[809] A good example is found in the archaeological record at the site of Avaris from the thirteenth dynasty. Here, the Austrian expedition has uncovered two strata of gardens just south of a palace. Manfred Bietak, in his publication *Avaris, The Capital of the Hyksos: Recent Excavations at Tell el-Dab'a* notes that the older gardens consisted of squares lined by trees with an unfinished pool in the center. Afterward, these gardens were used as a cemetery for the palace functionaries. In all, six tombs were discovered with parallel tree-pits located about nine meters to the east.[810] In his publication, these tombs are reconstructed with a vaulted roof and Bietak suggests that they preserve an ancient Lower Egyptian tradition.[811]

Citing the illustration in the tomb of Rekhmire (TT 100), Junker points to the fourteen *ḫm*-chapels bounded by a falcon on a high stage. He associates this sign with the heron that appears in plate 6 of Sir William Flinders Petrie's publication of the palace of Apries (mentioned above).[812] Apries' depiction shows two rows of two *pr-nw* shrines each alternating with a palm tree with a path between them indicated by the hieroglyph for "road," but marked with the internal detail of water.[813] This locale is presented as *ḏb'wt*. Junker suggests that the two images are displaying the same location—the royal cemetery at Buto, and that the same significance should also be derived from the *pr-nw* structures in other illustrations that are reproduced without the palm trees (*ḫm*-chapels) and without the water. The problem is that in the New Kingdom contexts the *ḫm*-chapels are open and show deities crouching inside. Moreover, the fourteen *ḫm*-chapels in the upper portion of the left wall (south wall) in the tomb of Rekhmire (TT 100) have divine designations, even though they do not display gods inside.[814] This indicates that even when the *ḫm*-chapels are closed, they should still be interpreted as gods' shrines. There is no doubt that the symbol of the falcon on a platform that brackets the scene is indicative of the necropolis, yet this may be a rendition of the superimposition of the divine realm onto the necropolis.[815]

Jürgen Settgast relies heavily on Junker's work and reiterates several of his points but disagrees with others. The *pr-nw* shrines in the tomb of Rekhmire, which Junker cites as proof for the royal cemetery of Buto, Settgast interprets as gods' shrines.[816] Settgast does not see evidence for Junker's theory and presents a lengthy exposé on the variability of this style of chapel. Accordingly, he interprets the structure as a shrine of the gods and, since it is transported on a ship in some cases (not in the Sacred District scene), it must be made of lighter building materials. In this connection, it must also be remembered that at the end of the eighteenth dynasty similar chapels are frequently carried along during the burial procession.[817]

These Lower Egyptian traditions were eventually Osirianized, and thus the pilgrimages were represented differently depending on the date of the tomb in which they appear. In the tombs of the Middle and New Kingdoms, the Osirian religion—then in full triumph—tends to absorb all the funerary rites, even those which originally had no connection with it. J. Gwyn Griffiths, in his book *The Origins of Osiris and His Cult,* states that this god's cult is of Upper Egyptian origin but as time has continued it has been infiltrated by various Lower Egyptian elements. Here he makes note of the ritual voyage to Buto, Sais, and Heliopolis illustrated in the tomb scenes of private individuals during the Old Kingdom.[818] In Griffiths' opinion, this voyage is strictly of Lower Egyptian origin and should not be connected to the cult of Osiris during the Old Kingdom (echoing Junker). He further explains why particular traditions would not have been popular under the kings of the Old Kingdom, as

[809] Junker 1940: 20.

[810] Bietak 1996: figs. 18–19.

[811] Bietak 1996, 25.

[812] Junker 1940: 17, Abb. 9; Petrie 1909: pl. 6. See also Baines 2013: 135–136.

[813] Petrie 1909: pl. 6; Junker 1940: Abb. 9; Baines 2020: 183.

[814] In the scene in Rekhmire, the inscriptions cite the Four Sons of Horus, who Junker equates with the Souls of Buto and Hierakonpolis, and the deceased kings, the gods Ptah, Sendet, Herer, Her-sen, and Menkeret of Pe and Dep (N. Davies 1973: pl. 24). See also Kemp 2018: 83.

[815] H. Hayes 2013: 173.

[816] Settgast 1963: 56; Junker 1940: 177–20.

[817] His argument includes the following points. There are *pr-nw* and *pr-nsr* shrines already mentioned in the Palermo stone inscription and he notes that Wadjet is represented by both buildings. He insists that the function of *pr-nw* and *pr-nsr* structures must be documented from the entire historical period of Egypt in order for this to be a valid method of comparison (Settgast 1963: 53–57).

[818] Griffiths 1980: 59–60.

they represented a regime from the south, who would not be anxious to follower Lower Egyptian traditions. Their funerary cult originated in Abydos, and this is made clear in the *Pyramid Texts*, despite the solar over-tones in the utterances.[819] Griffiths suggests that at a later date, when the cult of Osiris was firmly established, the Butic elements reappear after having been absorbed by the Upper Egyptian cult. In the New Kingdom, these voyages are Osirian in nature and the deceased who makes these trips aspired to follow Osiris.[820]

As the Butic shrine and the Saite shrine occur in combination with each other, all of what is stated here also applies to the Saite shrine described below. Karl-J Seyfried has suggested that the Sais/Buto/ Heliopolis cycle is represented in the Sacred District by the appearance of a specific piece of architecture indicative of that area. For example, the pair of obelisks represents the ancient city of Heliopolis, one of the sacred Delta localities, the Saite Shrine represents Sais, and the *pr-nw* shrine represents Buto. What is now evident is that the pair of *pr-nw* shrines with alternating palm tree is depicted outside the Sacred District, as are the Saite shrine, the unnamed structure, and the pair of obelisks accompanied by two men.[821]

There are nine tombs that include the two *pr-nw* shrines with alternating palm tree adjacent to the Sacred District scene (Theban Tombs 100, 125, 127, 112, A4, 17, 342, 82, and TC 3). All these tombs date to the reigns of Thutmose III and Amenhotep II, except for the tomb of Duauneheh (TT 125) which dates to the reign of Hatshepsut. These tombs were erected at Sheikh Abd el-Qurna, Dra Abu el-Naga, and Elkab. As well as being associated with the Saite shrine and the unnamed structure, this micro-scene is typically accompanied by the *ḫbt*-dancers. Five of these tombs also include rows of open or closed *ḫm*-chapels within the Sacred District (§8 Gods' shrines) (TT 100, TT 125, TT A4, TT 342, TC 3). Only four tombs include both the *pr-nw* shrines with alternating palm tree and the shrine of Osiris (TT 100, TT 112, TT A4, TC 3), and they are also from Sheikh Abd el-Qurna, Dra Abu el-Naga, and Elkab. Therefore, this micro-scene was popular at a specific time, but its iterations do not seem to be connected to a particular location. It was not typically included in the earliest tombs to include the Sacred District scene, nor the latest ones.

16. Saite shrine

This shrine is a representation of the archaic shrine of Neith, the patron deity of the Delta site of Sais and is the second of three shrine-types that appear as a unit of micro-scenes outside the Sacred District. Of the tombs included in this study, nine of them show the Saite shrine (Theban Tombs 100, 125, 127, 112, A4, 17, 342, 82, and TC 3). When the Saite shrine appears, it is almost always shown in conjunction with the *pr-nw* with alternating palm and an unnamed structure (one exception is TT 82 where the unnamed structure does not appear). All these tombs date to the reigns of Thutmose III and Amenhotep II, with the except of the tomb of Duauneheh (TT 125) that is slightly earlier. Therefore, this collection of shrines becomes a popular micro-scene during the reign of Thutmose III. It does not occur in the earlier tombs, nor does it appear in the latest decorative programs. The tomb of Amenemhet (TT 123) may have two additional shrines depicted between the rows of open and closed *ḫm*-chapels and the two women kneeling before the four basins, but the fragmentary nature of the tomb relief obscures the style of these buildings.[822] In each of the ten tombs where a version of the Delta shrine unit occurs, the *ḫbt*-dancers also appear; however, the *ḫbt*-dancers can occur independently of the Delta shrines.

By the Middle Kingdom, the Saite shrine is represented as a *front*-elevation, and so in the New Kingdom tomb scenes it is always shown from the perspective of its gateway. The façade is thus used as the symbol for the shrine. Most likely, this shrine consisted of a rectangular reed structure enclosed by a wattle fence and marked on its two front corners with two primitive cloth pennants.[823] These flags later came to symbolize the god (*nṯr*). Likewise, the poles with pennants are pushed together in the New Kingdom and result in a new building with a gabled façade. At the back of the enclosure was a hut with four corner posts, a side (or back) door, and a vaulted roof. The standard with the emblem of the deity would have been erected in the center of the court. However, this emblem is not shown in any of the depictions of the Saite shrine included in this study. In actuality, these flags would probably have been present in all Lower Egyptian shrines whether they were dedicated to Neith, Khnum, Sobek, Thoth, *etc*., and would have been erected in many northern localities.

[819] Griffiths 1980: 60.

[820] Griffiths 1980: 60, note 98. Here Griffiths uses the scenes in TT 82 as an example of the new Osirianized art in the Sacred District.

[821] In the early New Kingdom tombs, the micro-scene of the two obelisks does not include human intervention and it appears inside the Sacred District.

[822] Pellini 2022b: fig. 2.

[823] Badawy 1990: 34, fig. 22.

Archaeological evidence attests to a journey to Sais from an early age. A tag from the reign of king Aha of the first dynasty shows a royal visit to this site. This journey was probably initiated at the royal residence in the area of Memphis. On this tag there are two ships above the shrine, which John Baines suggests might represent the outward and return journey of the king.[824] The Saite shrine also occurs on a twenty-sixth dynasty statue, thus attesting to its longevity.[825] Following the work of Jürgen Settgast, there are two depictions of boat trips, each forming the center of different scenes, that he summarizes under the heading *Saisfahrt*. He documents only two tombs that display the course of events as a complete group, namely Theban Tombs 100 and 17. However, he suggests that a combination of both journeys was intended in the decoration of TT 127, TT 112, and Paheri's tomb (TC 3) at Elkab, although these scenes are extremely abbreviated.[826] The first section of this journey (also not considered to be part of the Sacred District) begins with a recitation by a *ḫry-ḥbt* priest standing in front of a building with an *ḫkr*-frieze. This recitation is connected with the description of the action that belongs to the boat trip. In the following scene, a papyrus skiff is towed by priests, in which an object in the form of a small canopy is placed mid-ship and flanked by the Greater and Lesser Kites.The inscriptions present key information for this scene group: "Accompanying N.N. with bread and beer, cattle and poultry, and any kind of nice sacrifice. Landing in Sais, the place where the great god dwells."[827] The general expression *r bw nṯr nfr im*, which frequently replaces a precise location, is preceded here by the mention of the landing in Sais.

17. Unnamed structure

Like the *pr-nw* and Saite shrines above, an unnamed structure is the third to appear as a gateway design used symbolically for the building itself. The unnamed structure takes the form of a vertical rectangle with two smaller rectangles outlined inside, interpreted by Settgast as windows.[828] On top of the rectangle there are four poles (or battlements?) erected, which Vandier has described as four *ḫkrs*.[829] This structure always appears in conjunction with the two shrines mentioned above; however, the configuration of the elements within the group can differ. As noted above, Settgast interprets this scene as a landing site marked by two buildings—the façade of the Saite shrine, above which two palm trees and two chapels are depicted in alternating order, and then the unnamed structure. There is continuity in the reproduction of this group of structures, with only a couple of anomalies. In the scene in the tomb of Paheri (TC 3), the *pr-nw* shrines continue from the top of the Saite shrine onto the top of the unnamed building. In most examples, the four poles reach to the top of the register and measure at about one third the height of the structure. In the tombs of Rekhmire (TT 100) and Menkheperreseneb (TT 112), this second structure appears to sit on a small podium.

There are nine examples of the unnamed structure (Theban Tombs 100, 125, 127, 112, 123, A4, 17, 342, and TC 3). However, the decoration in the tomb of Amenemhet (TT 82) does not include this unnamed structure, and the tomb of another Amenemhet (TT 123) does not include the Saite shrine—all other examples have both. All these tombs date to the reigns of Thutmose III and Amenhotep II, with the exception of the tomb of Duauneheh (TT 125) that is slightly earlier. Therefore, this collection of Delta shrines became a popular micro-scene during the reign of Thutmose III.

This unit of Delta shrines is depicted outside of the Sacred District but is addressed here because their characterization as "Butic" has seeped into modern descriptions of the Sacred District as a whole. The *Saisfahrt* is a hold-over from at least as early as the Old Kingdom, as it was displayed in several Old Kingdom private tombs. There are changes in some of the details after it re-emerges in the decoration of the New Kingdom private tombs. In both cases, the starting point of the procession is a building decorated with a *ḫkr*-frieze, but in the former the procession takes place on the "winding canal" while in the latter it occurs on a straight watercourse. This straight water way was typical and exclusively used in the New Kingdom. Settgast confirms that one and the same event is meant by the various groups of scenes passed down from different periods.[830] At the same time, however, he asserts that this comparison over time makes clear that the actions portrayed in the New Kingdom tomb decoration could no longer have been carried out at the time of its pictorial reproduction. The lector priest, who does not recite at the point when the boat with the coffin leaves the building with the *ḫkr*-frieze, but rather he directs his recitation to the chapel standing in front of him—a scene that is often depicted separately

[824] Baines 2020: fig. 9.2.

[825] Baines 1991: 35–36.

[826] Settgast 1963: 99.

[827] After Settgast (1963: 100).

[828] Settgast 1963: 100.

[829] Vandier 1944: 41.

[830] Settgast 1963: 99–101.

from the procession.[831] Even though the object under the canopy is reminiscent of the form of the canopy in the Old Kingdom, it cannot possibly be explained as a coffin in the New Kingdom representations.

18. Rites to the mooring-post

Although the rites to the mooring-post have often been associated with the Sacred District in modern scholarship, they are not performed in it. The appearance of this micro-scene could be considered comparable to the appearance of the *ḫbt*-dancers in that they are both often juxtaposed with the Sacred District but are not part of it. Some explanation of this scene appears above under §10. The primary association between the rites to the mooring-post scene and that of the four basins is the interchangeability of the participants.

The principal scene in the rites to the mooring-post shows a woman and a man facing toward each other and flanking a mooring-post. In most examples, of which there are fourteen included in this study, the woman and the man can be seen tying a boat to the post. Examples of this micro-scene occur in Theban Tombs 100, 179, 125, 127, 112, 122, 53, A4, 96B, 17, 69, 41, 342, and in Djehuty's tomb at Hierakonpolis. This episode does not appear in those tombs from Elkab included in this study. The tombs in which this micro-scene appears date from the reign of Hatshepsut to that of Thutmose IV, with an early exception in the tomb of Djehuty at Hierakonpolis that dates to the reign of Thutmose I and a late exception in the tomb of Amenemope (TT 41). Most of these tombs are located at Sheikh Abd el-Qurna, with two instances at Dra Abu el-Naga (TT A4 and TT 17) and one at Hierakonpolis.

This scene shows the mooring of a boat and describes the rites that center around the two mooring-posts. Jürgen Settgast has articulated the actions that took place before and after this ceremony, utilizing primarily the material presented in the tomb of Rekhmire (TT 100). Accordingly, three scenes show the laying down of the thighs at the mooring-posts, the bringing of the sacrificial pieces, and the slaughter. However, this sequence of scenes is probably incorrect because the slaughtering had to precede the laying down of the thighs. Settgast suggests reading the scenes backward to get the correct order: slaughter, offering bearer, and sacrifice. Unfortunately, the accompanying inscriptions are intended as recitations because of their introduction with *ḏd-mdw* and do not supply ample information about what is actually transpiring in the scenes. This sequence is discussed in detail by Settgast so there is no need to repeat it in full here.[832]

The central scene of the rites to the mooring-post, in which the boat is fastened, is attested in numerous tombs. These representations show that the mooring of the boat is the main scene of the group of scenes. Using the decoration in the tomb of Rekhmire as an example, the action begins with the incense of a *sm*-priest, in the presence of a *ẖry-ḥbt* priest, and continues in a ceremony before an offering table heaped with offerings in front of which a *ḥry-wr* kneels. A *ẖry-ḥbt* monitors the action in the gesture of recitation. This is followed by the actual mooring of a boat which, with the exception of Rekhmire, appears to be a simple papyrus boat. In the boat rests a coffin-like container with a groove and niche structure on a lion-shaped bier. An unnamed male figure squats in the bow and stern of the barge. The boat is tied to the mooring-post by a *ḥry-wr* and a *knwt*. The captions *ḏd mdw ỉn ktnw* (TT 125) and *ḏd mdw ỉn knwt* (TT 100) show that the process was accompanied by recitations, the wording of which is unknown.[833] Only the tomb of Rekhmire presents the conclusion of the rites to the mooring-post. The action is performed by the same characters as in the previous sections. A *ẖry-ḥbt* priest, in the gesture of recitation, watches over the *ḥry-wr* who kneels and hands two *nw*-jars to the mooring-posts, while a *knwt* squats behind him. Again, the inscriptions are not very informative: "Offering for the mooring-post of the bow and stern rope." Most likely this scene was no longer understood when it was being copied from papyrus onto the tomb walls, thus accounting for the erroneous order of the various episodes, the lack of cohesiveness, and the misspellings in the captions.

As noted previously, the female ritualists who moor the boat in the tombs of Rekhmire (TT100) and Duauneheh (TT 125) bear the title *knwt* (Figure 45). This female appellation is also applied to one of the two women who kneels before the four basins of water in the tombs of Amenemhet (TT 82) and Rekhmire (TT 100) (see §10 above). In fact, it may be only the repetition of this female ritualist that make the rites to the mooring-post relevant to a study about the Sacred District. To summarize Settgast's research, the label *knwt* identifies the female figure in the scene and acts as a "director's note." The parallel scene of the Opening of the Mouth ritual represents the *ḏr.t wr.t,* so he concludes that *knwt* is a pseudonym of *ḏr.t wr.t* used only in the burial ritual. He also notes that Eberhard Otto has already drawn attention to the

[831] Settgast 1963: 100.

[832] Settgast 1963: 105–111.

[833] The word is written *ktnw* but should be read *knwt*.

similarity of this scene with the scenes of the Opening of the Mouth ritual but does not use the evidence to equate these characters. Instead, he confines himself to the statement: "Here the woman is called *ḏr.t*, 'kite', without qualifying addition."[834] Settgast further notes that the female figure involved in mooring the boat in the tomb of Nebamun (TT 17) is called Dr.t wr.t, while she is named knwt in TT 100 and TT 125. In TT 127 she is named as Isis.. This same interchangeability between the kites and *knwt* (and also the kites and *dmdyt*) appears in the collection of scenes showing the two women kneeling before the four basins.[835]

Mooring one's boat is a euphemism of death. The goddesses Isis and Nephthys typically accompany the coffin to the burial area in tomb scenes, and this procession often involves crossing over water to the west. As far back as the *Pyramid Texts*, both goddesses bear the related epithets of "the moorer" and "the mooring-post."[836] These titles are related to the mooring of the boats and paradoxically can mean "to make firm the deceased" at the end point of their journey to the west, in that the deceased is referred to as the "moored one"—a euphemism for the one who has died. According to Susan Tower Hollis in her book on the early evidence for five goddesses, these titles are interchangeable and neither goddess consistently carries one or the other title. The mooring-post refers to the actual place where the boat is tied and suggests the support and stabilization of the deceased. The *Pyramid Texts* also suggests that Isis handles the bow line and Nephthys the stern line and that both goddesses would have been responsible for tying up the funerary boat.[837]

19. Slaughtering area

The slaughtering area is one of the largest episodes in the Sacred District scene but not a particularly common one, as it appears in only eleven of the studied tombs (Theban Tombs 100, 81, 21, 179, 82, 127, 112, 69, 36, 389, and on a fragment from A4). Its appearance is random chronologically, in that it appears in some of the earliest tombs, some tombs that date to the reigns of Hatshepsut and Thutmose III, and in two Saite tombs. Live cattle occur in combination with the slaughtering scene in only one instance: the tomb of User (TT 21). This area is typically depicted with a pond at its center, for example in Theban Tombs 21, 81, 82, 36, 100, and 389. While the pond is usually surrounded

Figure 45: Rites to the mooring-post in the tomb of Duauneheh (TT 125). Photo by author.

by sycamore trees, the pond in Theban Tombs 21 and 81 do not have any trees. The appearance of a pond within the slaughtering area begins with the tomb of User (TT 21) in the time of Amenhotep I, while Ibi's (TT 36) and Basa's Saite tombs have the latest examples of a slaughtering area with a pond. Jürgen Settgast points out that the tombs he categorizes as the "Middle Group" (TT 53, TT 123, TT 125) did not incorporate the slaughtering area into their depictions of the Sacred District.[838] In the examples that include a pond, eight bovines encircle it (Theban Tombs 21, 82, 36, 100, 389). It seems that these are male animals that, with the exception of the four standing bulls in TT 21, have already been presented to Osiris, and might already be slaughtered.

There are two tombs whose inscriptions are useful for further understanding what is going on in the slaughtering scene: TT 82 and TT 100. In TT 82 there are two short inscriptions, but both are quite fragmentary. In TT 100 there is one longer inscription that appears to combine the two short inscriptions from TT 82:

> *ḏd mdw in imy-ḫnt r k3w 8 in ḫry-ḥb sʿḥw rdit r wnḫ k3w ʿnḫw m šmt*
>
> *Words said by the Chamberlain concerning the eight bulls, [words said] by the lector priest for the sʿḥw, giving signs to bind the living bulls walking* (?).[839]

In Rekhmire's tomb (TT 100), the second inscription is directly connected to the preceding one, so that both

[834] Settgast 1963: 106, note 7.
[835] Diamond 2010a: 38–39; *idem*. 2017: 52, 57–58.
[836] Hollis 2020: 101, notes 66 and 67; J. Allen 2015: 361.
[837] Hollis 2020: 101. See PT 548, §1347b.
[838] Settgast 1963: 61.
[839] Settgast 1963: 62.

texts together form a column to the left of six officials who flank the slaughtering area. Settgast suggests that because of the presence of the infinitive form of the verb this would not have actually been recited, despite the writing of *ḏd mdw in imy-ḫnt*.[840] Thus, the *ḏd mdw* at the top of the vertical line should also be seen as the introduction to the second part of the inscription, "[Words said] by the lector priest for the blessed dead, giving a sign[841] in order to bind the living bulls." Settgast suggests that the text should be viewed as twofold, the recitation on the part of the lector priest, whose wording is not present, and the description of the action which is performed during this recitation.[842]

In Amenemhet's tomb (TT 82), the earlier of the two, the first caption above the slaughtering scene can be reconstructed as follows: *ḏd mdw in imy-ḫnt r [k3w 8]*, "Words said by the Chamberlain concerning [eight bulls]."[843] This inscription is fragmentary as portions of the wall are not preserved well in this area; however, since the inscription in TT 100 is very similar, it has been used to reconstruct the missing portions. In TT 82 this inscription is placed above the bound oxen which surround a pool with sycamore trees. To the right of the slaughtering scene are two men who face one another. Although the wall is broken at this spot as well, it seems as though a third man once stood behind the man on the right and was facing in his same direction. Above these men, in four short columns, the second inscription has been reconstructed by Alan Gardiner to read as follows: "Recitation. Placing the hand; binding(?) living oxen at the going of…."[844] Clearly these inscriptions are not overly informative as to the nature of this scene. Settgast reaches the following conclusions: First, the *ḫry-ḥb* is the benefactor of the ceremony; second, the *sꜥḥw* is the receiver and the doer of his order; and third, the bulls are the objects on which the action is carried out.[845] If the representation is compared to the text, then it can be determined that it was the moment of this command that was selected for the representation.[846] The question that remains is, who are to be understood as the generic *sꜥḥw*?[847] Rekhmire's scene presents six men turned back-to-back and standing in pairs in three registers to the left of the pond and slaughtering area. Settgast views three of these men as devoted to the slaughtering area, and three for the *ḫry-ḥb*. It appears that they may be officiating the ritual.

What is conspicuously absent from both tomb illustrations is any indication of the actual slaughtering of the animals. Although the process of binding the animals is not documented, there is a depiction that is reminiscent of the latter part of the inscription. In the case of User (TT 21), four bulls are depicted running free, while four others are already tied to the ground. All of the other Sacred District scenes show the animals captured and, with the exception of the two "young bulls" in Rekhmire (TT 100), already slaughtered. Thus, the course of action in the slaughtering area has been reconstructed by Settgast as follows: The slaughter of the tied bulls must have been preceded by the signal the *ḫry-ḥb* gave the *sꜥḥw*—the sign to tie the eight bulls that are shown encircling the pond. When this was finished, the *imy-ḫnt* took over and continued the ritual. Again, while reciting, he gave the signal for the slaughtering of the animals. Settgast infers from this course of action that the two texts were reproduced in reversed order when they were inscribed on the tomb walls.[848] Furthermore, the representations in Theban Tombs 82 and 100 are restricted to the beginning and the end of the ritual but these episodes were intended to be symbolic of the full ritual.

20. Cattle

The tomb of User (TT 21) is unique in its depiction of live cattle within the Sacred District. This micro-scene may preface the slaughter scene when the live cattle were brought to slaughter. If one follows Settgast's account of the ritual slaughtering of animals, then this scene may only be a precursor to it, and thus its inclusion was not essential.

840 Settgast 1963: 61.
841 Possibly a hand(?).
842 Settgast 1963: 62.
843 Settgast 1963: 61.
844 N. M. Davies and Gardiner 1915: 54.
845 Settgast 1963: 62–63.
846 Settgast 1963: 63.
847 Settgast translates this term as "nobles" or "dignitaries," but "the blessed dead" may be more appropriate.
848 Settgast 1963: 64.

APPENDIX TWO: CATALOGUE OF TOMBS INCLUDED IN THIS STUDY[849]

Tomb of Hery (TT 12)

Hery was the overseer of the granary of the king's mother and royal wife Ahhotep, and he lived during the reigns of Ahmose and Amenhotep I. He was buried in the central area of Dra Abu el-Naga in the Theban necropolis.[850] Through his mother Ahmose he might have been related to the royal family.[851] The decoration is rather fragmentary and therefore parallels from other tombs have been used to reconstruct the images here.[852] In fact, many relief fragments were detached from the wall and found on the ground both inside and outside the tomb. The west wall of the corridor was decorated with the funerary scenes, including the Sacred District, and divided into three registers. Gemma Menéndez sees the nearby tomb of Senet (TT 60) as a clear precedent for some of the artistic motifs found in TT 12, and she also compares the images found on some of these fragments to scenes in the tomb of Tetiky (TT 15) and the tomb of User (TT 21).[853]

One fragment of a mourning woman shows the remains of a tip of an obelisk from the register below, suggesting that the two obelisks were part of this Sacred District. There is also a row of open *ḥm*-chapels, the three pools, and the guardians of the great gate, followed by both Anubis and Osiris. These two deities appear at the end of the first register in a similar manner to how they appear in the tomb of Reneny (TC 7), that is as micro-scenes, not bracketing the registers. The *Mww* appear in the top register wearing their conical headdresses, where perhaps this narrative starts. These *Mww* are not in their hall but instead greet the funeral procession as it arrives at the *tꜣ ḏsr*, as in the tomb of Senet (TT 60) and Reneny (TC 7). The *Mww* have their index fingers pointing at the ground in front of them as they appear to step forward.

Tomb of Tetiky (TT 15)

Tetiky was the mayor of Thebes during the reign of Ahmose at the beginning of the eighteenth dynasty. He was the son of Rahotep, the overseer of the harem of the lake, and Sensoneb. His tomb is located at Dra Abu el-Naga.[854] The tomb of Tetiky was recorded by George Herbert Carnarvon and Howard Carter from 1907–1911 and published in 1912; however, it has been severely damaged, probably beyond repair. This family tomb features a brick vaulted chamber, typical of the type found at Deir el-Medina. Two of the chambers were painted, with the Sacred District illustrated on the southern wall of the room called "painted vaulted chamber"—a rectangular chapel with barrel-vaulted roof.[855] This is also the only place to feature an extant inscription. The scenes run from left to right and are topped by a *ḫkr*-frieze. Below the *ḫkr*-frieze there is a line of text. The transcription of the hieroglyphic inscriptions appears in the 1912 publication by Legrain, which he based on his visit to the tomb in 1909 during Carnarvon's excavations and on photographs taken by Carter. The decoration is painted on stucco mixed with straw, and it appears as though the tomb was reused in antiquity and had some of the scenes covered up.

The south wall depicts Tetiky's funeral procession and the arrival of the deceased in the realm of Osiris. This wall is divided by the entrance door, which separates the scenes. Here, the funeral procession is met by three *Mww* who wear the typical conical headdress. They come forward to meet the cortege and "dance before it."[856] The mummy is then shown upright under a canopy and a priest presents a censer. Moving from left to right, the scene presents two *Mww* standing in their hall and facing to the right, two (red granite?) obelisks, two trees (covered with fruit?), a row of shrines with gods and goddesses and the guardians of the great gate inside (see Figure 30). In the sub-register below, also to the immediate right of the hall of the *Mww*, is a rectangular pool with three palms followed by a row of open *ḥm*-chapels. The first one illustrates the three pools, and the others have a standing god or goddess inside. It is unusual to show both the three pools and the guardians of the great gate inside a *ḥm*-chapel. In other illustrations of the Sacred District, they are stand-alone episodes and not part of the row(s) of gods' shrines. Here, the Sacred District ends with a larger image of Osiris in a lightly built structure that brackets both sub-registers. He has his arms crossed, carries the crook and flail, and faces to the left. Farther to the right, the wall is mostly

[849] The tombs are presented in numerical order by Theban Tomb number with the tombs from Elkab and Hierakonpolis at the end.

[850] Galán 2007: 777–787; *idem*. 2014: 3–8.

[851] Galán and Jiménez-Higueras 2015: 101; Galán 2020: 42.

[852] Menéndez 2005: 29–65.

[853] Menéndez 2005: 29–65.

[854] Hofmann 2011: 42–55.

[855] Carnarvon and Carter 1912: 12.

[856] This is how Legrain describes the scene (Carnarvon and Carter 1912: 17; pl. VIII).

destroyed. The inscription in this tomb is significant for identifying the name of this district as the *t3 ḏsr*.

Tomb of Nebamun (TT 17)

Nebamun was a chief physician during the reign of Amenhotep II and his tomb lies at the site of Dra Abu el-Naga.[857] The Sacred District scene is located on the south wall (left wall) in the bottom two registers among the funerary scenes. The bottom register shows the funeral cortege pulling various sleds toward the *Mww*, who greet the procession with their arms out in front of them, palms facing upward. These *Mww* wear the typical conical headdress and are perhaps labeled as *ḫbt ḏft*(?). The remaining micro-scenes of the Sacred District form a unit at the right end of the bottom two registers. All four registers are bracketed by the Goddess of the West.

Immediately above the *Mww*, from left to right, are the guardians of the great gate, and below the guardians are four closed *ḫm*-chapels. To their right are two women holding *nw*-jars and kneeling before four basins. They are labeled as the Greater and Lesser Kites. The shrines of the sacred Delta localities and the *ḫbt*-dancers (who do not bear this label here), are located side by side in the third register from the bottom. Between the dragging of two boats, the fragmentary remains of a *pr-nw* shrine with a palm tree on top is possibly coupled with a Saite shrine (no longer visible). To its right is an unnamed structure. This micro-scene most likely resembled originally the one in the tomb of Senemiah (TT 127). This is a good example of the Delta shrines illustrated separately from the episodes of the Sacred District, which leads to the interpretation that the Delta shrines are a separate scene entirely. The rites to the mooring-post, also separate from the main Sacred District scene, appear on the left end of the bottom register. Here they show a ceremony connected with a landing-pole and performed by the "Greater Kite" and a *smr*.

In total, there are eight relevant micro-scenes in this tomb, the core of them situated immediately in front of the Goddess of the West and comprising the Sacred District proper. This Sacred District is smaller and includes fewer micro-scenes than most. It is also one of the later examples. It should also be noted that in the second register from the bottom the voyage to and from Abydos is shown prefacing the Sacred District.

Tomb of User (TT 21)

User was the scribe and steward of Thutmose I. His tomb is located in Sheikh Abd el-Qurna.[858] User's tomb is considered one of the earlier tombs to include the Sacred District scene. Here, this scene is found in the bottom two registers of the south wall (left wall of the passage). Unfortunately, there are no inscriptions remaining on the left wall and most of the decoration on the wall above this scene has not been preserved.

Beginning in the bottom register on the left side after the purification of the mummy there are two sub-registers with seven shrines each. The bottom sub-register displays seven open shrines with anthropomorphic deities sitting inside. The top sub-register displays seven closed shrines with a cross-hatching design. The closed shrines are slightly narrower than the open shrines below, thus allowing for the addition of the three pools micro-scene to be placed above the last open shrine. Immediately to the upper right of the three pools is a garden plot with ten braziers surmounting it. The garden plot with braziers takes up a small portion of the space that is occupied by the slaughtering area. There is a small pool (or pond) in the middle of the scene with four tied calves spaced around it, one on each side. They are flanked by two bulls facing outward on each side. The last micro-scene on the bottom register that belongs to the Sacred District is the two women kneeling before four basins. In this instance, the water is shown flowing into a trough that runs before the two women. Moving toward the right (into the tomb) and up one register, two men with the typical headdresses stand in the hall of the *Mww* and face to the right. In front of them stand the two obelisks on small platforms and then the garden pool and three large palms. These palms have date bundles.[859] Next the register divides into two sub-registers, on the top are two sycamore trees and, on the bottom, stand the guardians of the great gate. These sycamore trees are of the more leafy, realistic variety. User's gate for the guardians is the largest example and includes two poles representing an entrance way. This gate is often painted yellow, but because the background color of all the scenes is yellow, this gate is white. Continuing toward the right, Osiris stands inside his shrine which is also painted white. The last visible micro-scene is the remains of the women's tent. Only the upper portion remains where the heads of two women appear facing each other. The remnants of two interior poles can also be seen, thus this tent appears similar to the gate of the guardians in its style

[857] Säve-Söderbergh 1957: 30–31; pls. XXIV, XXV; Shirley 2007: 381–401.

[858] N. Davies 1913: 20–27.

[859] *contra* Theis 2011: 142.

and structure.

Tomb of Ibi (TT 36)

Ibi was chief steward of Nitocris I, the Divine Adoratrice, during the reign of Psamtik I in the twenty-sixth dynasty. Ibi's tomb, located in the Asasif, contains one of the few known Saite examples of the Sacred District scene. It is located on the left part of the north wall in the upper registers of the third room of his tomb. It has been placed below and to the left of the funeral scenes.

Beginning at the top left corner and moving to the right there are the fragmentary remains of a garden plot topped with five braziers, two sycamore trees, and four *ḫm*-chapels. Below the garden plot the wall is destroyed, but the excavators have reconstructed the scene to show two *Mww* standing in their hall and facing to the right toward the district. The pool with palms has also been reconstructed to the right of this hall. Following, there are five *ḫm*-chapels which correspond to the four *ḫm*-chapels directly above them. These two rows are bracketed by the three pools at the right end. Below this is the slaughtering area where eight bulls with tied legs lie around a pool with a *ḫkr*-frieze. There is a lector priest to the left of the scene and on the right side two men face each other. The man on the far right has his right arm across his chest.[860]

Tomb of Puiemre (TT 39)

The tomb of Puiemre was constructed in the sub-division of Khôkha. Both the location and the plan of the tomb of Puiemre are unusual, and therefore the Sacred District appears in an unusual fashion. It was produced in the right, or north chapel, which was the largest of three. This is the chamber that lies nearest to the west, so it was appropriate for the funeral scenes to be shown here. The Goddess of the West stands on the right sidewall, which is the western wall of the western chapel.[861]

This wall is divided into three registers and the Sacred District is located in the bottom one. From right to left, the viewer sees the pool with palms and two sycamores, the women's tent with three women inside, and the guardians of the great gate who stand in a square enclosure surrounded by the *ḫkr*-frieze. The only intervening scene between the district and the goddess is Puiemre kneeling before a tale of offerings and facing the goddess. The Sacred District is also illustrated on the entrance wall. From inside the chapel facing the doorway, in the second register from the bottom the *Mww* stand in their hall and face the right, probably in anticipation of the funeral procession which starts on the east wall. In front of the *Mww* are the two women holding *nw*-jars and kneeling before four basins. It is unusual to have these two micro-scenes adjacent to one another.

To the left of the doorway, in the bottom register, there are two rows of *ḫm*-chapels. The bottom row has seven *ḫm*-chapels, the first five of which are open and the last two are decorated with a series of vertical lines. In the upper row there are eight closed shrines. In total there are seven separate micro-scenes illustrated in this Sacred District, including two sycamore trees that are among the palm trees near the pool.

Tomb of Amenemope (TT 41)

Theban Tomb 41 belongs to Amenemope, the chief steward of Amun in the Southern City, whose tomb dates to the transitional period between the eighteenth and nineteenth dynasties. It has been variously dated from the reign of Horemheb to the reign of Ramesses II.[862] What this tomb has in common with many of the other tombs that include the Sacred District scene is that it is located at Sheikh Abd el-Qurna, otherwise Theban Tomb 41 is an outlier in that it post-dates the majority of Sacred District scenes and has a triple depiction of the funerary procession.

It is the funerary scenes on the south and west walls at the far-left end of the pillared transverse hall that is of concern here. In this tomb, the Sacred Districts scene rounds the corner, beginning on the south wall and ending on the west wall. The series of micro-scenes that make up the Sacred District appear in the top two registers. Jan Assmann has written extensively about this tomb and uses it to support his principle of bipartition or tripartition wall decoration, where the wall is divided into two or three horizontal sections and adapted from the principle of stela decoration to create a vertical axis within the space of the tomb. He maintains that this vertical axis is related to the construction of sacred space and that the upper section is dedicated to sacred scenes involving representations of gods while the lower sections represent the funerary cult.[863]

In the top register on the south wall one of the scenes that prefaces the Sacred District is that of the erecting of two obelisks. These obelisks are accompanied by two men who each have one arm raised with the palm of the hand close to the top of one obelisk. This micro-

[860] Kuhlmann and Schenkel 1983: *Tafeln* 65 and 128.

[861] N. Davies 1923: plates 46–47; Lythgoe 1923: 186–188.

[862] Assmann 1991; Assmann 2003: 49.

[863] Assmann 2003: 49.

scene often appears in conjunction with the Sacred District, but it is not the one that sometimes appears within the Sacred District. Following the obelisks are the *ḫbt*-dancers and two closed *ḥm*-chapels placed one above the other and painted blue. It is unique that there are only two shrines here.[864] Next, the two women kneel before the four basins of water (see Figure 25). However, the wall ends between the women and the basins so that the women are shown on the south wall while the basins are on the west wall. On the west wall, the first micro-scene is the basins, but instead of draining the water into a channel in front of the women as is typical, the water is shown draining into a channel on the other side (west wall). Following this scene is the pool with palms. Perhaps the water is shown feeding this pool. At this point there is a break in the micro-scenes that make up the Sacred District and four men carry the coffin. The Sacred District scene in TT 41 is not shown as a discreet unit as it is in many other renditions. Before the row of gods' shrines appears, the carrying of the coffin and a priest with two small braziers who stands before a small shrine intervene. Finally, the last episode of the Sacred District is shown—three open gods' shrines (the third one is damaged). The god inside the first (right) shrine is a falcon god and the god in the middle shrine is canine-headed.

Returning to the south wall and to the second register from the top, the relevant scenes begin with two *Mww* wearing the conical headdresses. These *Mww* face to the right and appear in their typical stance as if stepping forward. They do not meet the funeral procession as is usual and based on the orientation of the figures on this and the west wall, they appear to be facing in the wrong direction. The *Mww* face toward a single *ḥm*-chapel painted blue. The last micro-scene before the south wall ends is the guardians of the great gate. They are painted a dark bluish-black color and wear yellow kilts. There is nothing particularly unusual about the way they are depicted other than the style of the structure in which they stand, which appears as a tent-like structure, not the typical gate surrounded by the *ḫkr*-frieze. Thus ends the south wall. On the west wall, again there are intervening scenes that are not part of the Sacred District that include two boat scenes. Directly below the man carrying the braziers in the top register a man kneels before a shrine and offers a haunch of meat. To the right of this shrine is another row of open gods' shrines that is placed directly below the open gods' shrines in the top register, thus making a precise unit of shrines. From left to right, these shrines display a baboon-headed god, a canine-headed god, and an anthropomorphic god. Although the numbering is not right, these gods may represent the Four Sons of Horus: Qebehsenuef, Hapi, Imsety, and Duamutef.[865]

According to Assmann, the funeral procession fills the western part of the south wall and continues on the west wall, with the corner marking the border between what is happening at the tomb and what is happening beyond the tomb, in the hereafter. This supposition is problematic since the women kneeling before the four basins is one scene, not two. Since the tomb of Amenemope (TT 41) dates to the transitional period between the eighteenth and nineteenth dynasties, the older wall-filling tableau had already been abandoned, but the new principle of dividing the wall into superimposed horizontal sections had not yet been developed.[866]

The manner in which this tomb is decorated emphasizes that the Sacred District scene was utilized as a transitional scene for the deceased's passing from this world to the next, and that its placement was purposeful. This is reiterated by the positioning of the sloping passage that leads to the burial chamber immediately in front of the Sacred District scene in the southwest corner of the pillared transverse hall.

Tomb of Amenemhet (TT 53)

Theban Tomb 53 belongs to a man named Amenemhet who was an agent of Amun during the reign of Thutmose III. His tomb style is typical for the period, and it is situated in the area of Sheikh Abd el-Qurna. The Sacred District scene appears on the southwest, or left wall, which is decorated with four registers of carved and painted scenes. The Sacred District scene appears in the bottom register. This tomb is well preserved and finely executed; unfortunately, there are no inscriptions to aid this assessment. The decoration begins in three registers but eventually splits into four registers. The order of episodes seen here is similar to that presented in Theban Tomb 123 (see below); however, TT 53 has two pool and palm scenes, no Saite shrine and unnamed structure, and at the end of the Sacred District the two kneeling women with the four basins is missing. Instead, the *ḫbt*-dancers precede the deceased's coffin which is carried by two men with two mourners underneath it.

As in other examples, the first scene of the Sacred

[864] Perhaps the artist was confused by the juxtaposition of the rows of *ḥm*-chapels and the two *pr-nw* shrines with alternating palm and conflated the two, producing two *ḥm*-chapels instead.

[865] Settgast 1963: 53, note 1.

[866] Assmann 2003: 49.

District is positioned after the rites before the mummy and features the women's tent. As is typical, there are three women inside the tent, with one on the right side of the pole and two on the left. The women on each side face inward. The next micro-scene shows two sycamore trees in the abstract style, one above the other. This is followed by an empty pool and four palm trees with fruit bundles.[867] Usually, the basin is painted blue to indicate that it is filled with water, but here the basin is empty. There may be a drainpipe protruding from the short end of the basin on the right. Next, there are two more sycamore trees. This garden scene is followed by the hall of the *Mww* in which two men wearing the conical headdress face to the left and overlook the garden. At this point, still moving from left to right, there is another pair of sycamore trees placed one above the other. Following, is the more typical pond with four palm trees all situated on the same ground line. The pool is shown behind two trunks and in front of the other two trunks. Above the pool with palms, but within the same register, is an image that is reminiscent of Gardiner's M 8 sign, what he terms the pool with lotus flowers. This micro-scene is less certain as there is no remaining blue paint in the pool. Also, at first glance the episode appears similar to the garden plot with accompanying braziers but there are no grid lines for the garden plots. Another difference here is that there is another item alternating with what might be brown braziers. They appear as small, green shrubs (hence the comparison with Gardiner's M 8 sign). After this micro-scene are the guardians of the great gate, a gap in the wall, and two rows of shrines. In the upper sub-register, there are seven closed shrines remaining (with possibly one missing from the beginning of the row) and in the lower sub-register there are three open shrines remaining. Of the three that remain, there appear to be anthropomorphic deities inside the first two and a canine god in the third. This is where the Sacred District ends.

The episode immediately following the Sacred District is the *ḫbt*-dancers. Closer to the interior of the tomb, and in the same register, is the micro-scene of the two obelisks. This example includes the two men; thus, it is not part of the Sacred District. The rites to the mooring-post are displayed in the second register from the bottom, immediately above the guardians of the great gate.

Tomb of Menna (TT 69)

Menna is the owner of Theban Tomb 69. He was a scribe of the fields of the Lord of the Two Lands of Upper and Lower Egypt and the overseer of fields of Amun.[868] His tomb is located at Sheikh Abd el-Qurna and has been traditionally dated to the reign of Thutmose IV. More recently, the date of the tomb's decoration has been adjusted to the reign of Amenhotep III.[869] Menna's tomb is a simple T-shaped tomb with the funerary scenes on the southeast wall, or the left wall of the passage. The Sacred District appears in an abbreviated version, as it does in several other small tombs of this time period (see Figure 41) (TT 120, TT 161).

The tomb of Menna has the left wall of the passage decorated with the funeral procession. There are four registers of decoration that end in two large figures of the Goddess of the West and Anubis flanking two registers each. After that, closer to the interior of the tomb, the deceased stands before the weighing of the heart scene and Osiris sitting in his shrine facing outward. The micro-scenes that belong to the Sacred District appear in the bottom two registers. In the bottom register stand five open gods' shrines featuring one canine god and four anthropomorphic gods. The shrines are brightly colored, and the interior of the shrines alternates from white to yellow. In the register above the open shrines, and slightly to the left, stand six closed shrines.. All of these shrines are of the *ḥm*-chapel type. Aside from the open and closed shrines of the gods, there are no other micro-scenes from the Sacre District portrayed. This may be due to the tomb's small size, or it might be a contemporary convention. Other elite tombs from approximately the same period exhibit a similar abbreviated Sacred District. What seems apparent is when a tomb owner wanted to depict the Sacred District but did not have the space, it was the rows of shrines that were chosen as symbolic of this area. Likewise, when space is at a premium, the Sacred District is an important enough scene to warrant inclusion. During the reign of Amenhotep III, the Sacred District was decreasing in frequency; however, when it was depicted, it was typically shown in its shortened (or emblematic) form.

The rites to the mooring-post also decorate this tomb, and these rites too have been abbreviated because of the available space. The rites to the mooring-post appear in the bottom register several scenes to the left of the open gods' shrines.

Tomb of Senenmut (TT 71)

Senenmut was the chief steward of Amun during

[867] The palms in TT 123 also feature fruit bundles.

[868] Hartwig 2013: 16.

[869] Hartwig 2013: 19.

the reign of Hatshepsut. Unfortunately, there is nothing left in the tomb of Senenmut (TT 71), but early archaeologists noted that several elements of the Sacred District scene were present in this tomb. Accordingly, any relevant scenes would originally have been placed on the south wall of the axial corridor (passage), with the east part displaying the pilgrimage to Abydos and the west part showing the funerary rituals.[870] Plaster fragments have been used to reconstruct the scene content for the Abydos pilgrimage, including pictorial excerpts from the boat trip from Abydos (frag. H), a woman following the funeral cortege (frag. I), a foreleg offered at the tomb façade (frag. J), and a caption from above the head of a priest (text 10).[871] The boat journey most likely shows the homeward voyage proceeding to the viewer's left with the sail raised on the towing vessel, as this is typical for contemporary scenes.[872] If there are two registers, then the return journey is shown on the upper level. Moving into the interior of the tomb, the funerary scenes were most likely shown on the far right of the south wall. The discovered fragments also shed some light on these scenes. They attest to the carrying of effigies in the procession (frag. F), goods being brought to the tomb (frag. E), the lower part of a standing female figure (frag. I), and the foreleg and heart of a cow offered at the door of the tomb (frag. J). It is estimated that there were three, or perhaps four, registers of decoration here. Peter Dorman has suggested that this scene might have been similar to those of Amenemhet (TT 82) and Rekhmire (TT 100).[873] Unfortunately, this tomb does not offer any new information about the Sacred District, and it might be argued that there is insufficient evidence for this tomb to be included in this study. This tomb's location and its date suggest that it was a good candidate for the inclusion of a Sacred District in its decoration, as does the fact that Senenmut's predecessor Ineni (TT 81) had a Sacred District illustrated in his tomb.

Due to the style of the architecture of this tomb, it has been the subject of several studies on Butic rituals. The arrangement of the ceilings in the broad hall may be reminiscent of the roof forms of some of the shrines of the sacred Delta localities, according to Karl-J Seyfried.[874] He interprets the broad hall (transverse hall) as having a *qȝr*-shaped roof and he can find four roof forms (flat/straight, vaulted/concave, pointed gable, *qȝr* -shaped) within the interior space of this one tomb. Dorman has also suggested previously that there is a link between the architecture of this tomb and specifically that of the *pr-wr* or *pr-nsr* shrines.[875]

Tomb of Ineni (TT 81)

The tomb of Ineni (TT 81) is located in Sheikh Abd el-Qurna and dates to the early eighteenth dynasty. Despite the fact that Ineni's biographical inscription makes note of several events from the reign of Amenhotep I to that of Thutmose III, there has been much debate over the date of this tomb.[876] The inscription remarks on Ineni's role in the construction of Thutmose I's tomb in the Valley of the Kings and the accession of Thutmose III with Hatshepsut. Ineni's titles include overseer of the granary in the domain of Amun, overseer of all seal-bearers in the temple of Amun, and scribe.

The Sacred District scene is located on the southwest wall, or the left wall of the passage. There are a total of four registers of decoration of which the Sacred District occupies the second register from the bottom.[877] In the bottom register below the Sacred District the funeral procession meets three *Mww*. These *Mww* face to the left and toward the lead funerary priest and subsequent procession as it arrives. They wear their typical conical headdresses and have one foot raised as if stepping forward, and they hold their fingers in their standard hand gesture with one or two outstretched fingers.[878]

The first episode on the left is the hall of the *Mww*, which begins the register. Unfortunately, this micro-scene is damaged, and the men are no longer visible. However, their feet still remain and suggest that the *Mww* faced to the left. In other early tomb scenes, such as those in the tombs of Reneny (TC 7) and Tetiky (TT 15), the hall of the *Mww* is positioned so that they can look out over the garden district, but here the *Mww* appear to face nothing. Perhaps their positioning has something to do with the three *Mww* who greet the procession in the register below, in that all five *Mww* would have faced in the same direction and these episodes should be considered as continuing. After the hall of the *Mww*, the register splits into two sub-registers with the two obelisks followed by two sycamore trees positioned in the upper sub-register and the pool and palms positioned below them.

[870] Dorman 1991: 38–39.

[871] Dorman 1991: 45; pl. 24a.

[872] Säve-Söderbergh 1958: 288, fig. 6.

[873] Dorman 1991: 46.

[874] Seyfried 2003: 65–66.

[875] Dorman 1991: 27, fig. 2.

[876] Dziobek shows that Ineni reused a tomb originally cut in the Middle Kingdom (1992: 77–81). See Baines 2013: 77.

[877] For a discussion of this scene, see Baines 2013: 76–79.

[878] Reeder 1995: 76–77.

Following the sycamore trees in the upper sub-register are five, or perhaps six closed shrines with thatched decoration. It is difficult to tell if the sixth shrine is open or closed, but the length of its base suggests that it might be closed.[879] After the closed shrines, there are at least three open shrines, but the space allows for more. There is a break in the decoration here. It is possible that the row of open shrines is followed by the guardians of the great gate and then by the shrine of Osiris. The remains of a *ḫkr*-frieze can be seen, as can Osiris' elbow—the remains of an episode of Osiris standing inside his shrine. This ends the upper sub-register. In the lower sub-register following the pool and palms, there are garden plots above a blue, rectangular pool. Something was depicted to the right of the pool, but nothing remains other than some ochre paint. Next is the women's tent with only two women inside facing one another, the three pools, and three open shrines with anthropomorphic deities inside. The final scene of the Sacred District is the two women kneeling before four basins of water, and this micro-scene spans both sub-registers.

Tomb of Amenemhet (TT 82)

Amenemhet (TT 82) was a counter of grain of Amun and the steward of the vizier. He was considered a lower-level official and a subordinate of Aametju who owned TT 83.[880] His tomb is located in Sheikh Abd el-Qurna and dates to the reign of Thutmose III.[881] His Sacred District scene decorates the southwest, or left wall of the passage and is placed amongst the funerary scenes. The decoration on the left wall consists of five registers with micro-scenes belonging to the Sacred District that primarily occupy the bottom two registers. However, the two women who kneel before the four basins of water are found in the top register as the last scene before a large figure of the Goddess of the West. The placement of this last micro-scene is an anomaly, as it is typically within the Sacred District and often acts as the last scene. Unfortunately, there are three substantial gaps in the decoration of the left wall of the passage, thus obscuring large portions of the Sacred District. The Sacred District in TT 82 does not reflect a temenos garden as other examples of this scene do. Beginning in the bottom lefthand corner remains of the women's tent is visible, followed by two rows of closed shrines. It is difficult to discern how many shrines originally stood here, but the remains of four are still visible. Above these shrines, in the second register from the bottom, are the Saite shrine with two *pr-nw* shrines alternating with two palms. The gap to the right obscures the subsequent events in both registers. After the break, in the second register from the bottom the remains of a slaughtering area with a pool in the middle can be seen. Also noteworthy are the *ḫbt*-dancers in the second register from the top, who have been separated from the Saite shrine and *pr-nw* shrine with alternating palm tree.

The scene with the two kneeling women before four basins does have its captions preserved in this tomb.[882] This is one of two tombs where inscriptions help identify these female ritualists—the other being that of Rekhmire (TT 100). In this scene, two women (depicted one above the other) kneel before four basins of water in the *s(my)t*, "desert necropolis," offering *nw*-jars.[883] The woman above is labeled *mnknw* (what appears to be a variant spelling of the archaic word *knwt*) and the woman below is labeled *dmḏ(y)t*.[884] Gardiner suggests that *mnknw* is an epithet of Isis and *dmḏ(y)t* a name applied to Nephthys.[885] He bases his interpretation on a parallel scene in the tomb of Paheri where these two women are assumed to impersonate Isis and Nephthys because of their respective titles: *ḏr(y)t wrt* and *ḏr(y)t nḏst*, "Greater Kite" and "Lesser Kite."[886] Kites are one of their many bird forms.[887]

Tomb of Amunedjeh (TT 84)

Theban Tomb 84 belongs to the prince, chief royal herald, and steward of the palace, Amunedjeh, who lived during the time of Thutmose III. His tomb is situated in Shiekh Abd el-Qurna and the relevant scenes are on the south, or left wall of the passage. This T-shaped tomb was almost completely decorated in its original form but suffered damage in its reuse by Mery in the reign of Amenhotep II.[888]

The left wall of the passage is very damaged and large portions of the bottom part of the wall have fallen away. There were probably five registers of decoration originally. Remains of the Sacred District can be detected in the third register on the first half of the south wall. The far-left part of the south wall of

[879] Open shrines tend to be wider.

[880] Dorman 2003: 37.

[881] Porter and Moss 1970: 163.

[882] Diamond 2017: 51; N. M. Davies and Gardiner 1915: plates X and XIII.

[883] For *s(my)t,* see Faulkner 1991: 227.

[884] It is unclear as to whether "*mn*" belongs to the title or if it should be regarded as independent; I prefer the latter option.

[885] N. M. Davies and Gardiner 1915: 52.

[886] Tylor and Griffith 1894: pl. V. See Theban Tomb 17 for similar labels.

[887] Diamond 2015b: 2–4.

[888] University of Basel. "Tomb TT84."

the passage is completely destroyed. Remains of the following micro-scenes are still visible: at least five open gods' shrines, the three pools, and the guardians of the great gate. The top three registers end with a large image of the Goddess of the West.

Tomb of Suemniwet (TT 92)

Suemniwet was a royal butler and cupbearer of the king during the time of Amenhotep II, and his tomb is located at Sheikh Abd el-Qurna. His tomb was created and decorated in the earlier years of this king whose prenomen remains in his tomb.[889] Unfortunately, the paintings in this tomb were largely unfinished. The only micro-scene that connects this tomb to this study is that of the five open shrines with gods inside. They appear in the top register of the southern passage. They face to the right and are of the same orientation as the offering bearers in the funeral procession. The shrines are painted blue and four of the gods are anthropomorphic while one is canine-headed. Likewise, the *ḫbt*-dancers appear, but they have been shown to be an auxiliary scene and not part of the district itself. The Sacred District scene in this tomb resembles others of the same approximate date.

Tomb of Sennefer (TT 96B)

The tomb of Sennefer (or more properly, his burial chamber) does not include a proper Sacred District. There are elements in the tomb scenes, like in the tomb of Suemniwet, that have historically been connected to the Sacred District. Sennefer was mayor of the Southern City and lived sometime between the reigns of Thutmose III and Thutmose IV.[890] His tomb is located at Sheikh Abd el-Qurna. As the eighteenth dynasty progresses, fewer and fewer remnants of the Sacred District appear in tombs. Perhaps the existing micro-scenes associated with the Sacred District can be attributed to the fact that his father Ahmose, called Humay (TT 224), had a Sacred District displayed in his tomb. The associated scenes can be found on the northwest wall of Sennefer's pillared burial chamber.

The left wall is badly preserved, but it is here that some associated micro-scenes remain. On the far left of the wall, Sennefer strides toward the beautiful west and goes into his tomb as he follows the transport of his coffin.[891] The funeral procession is shown in three registers in front of the tomb owner. In the top register are four oxen that once towed the sarcophagus. The tow rope was attached to the sarcophagus and is still seen wound around the oxen's horns. Traces of the hands of the mourners are visible behind them. The men with offerings walk in front. In the second register from the top, Sennefer and his wife travel on a boat to the necropolis. In front of them are sleds with divine figures and a canopic shrine. On the far right are four sacrificial cattle and some offerings. This micro-scene could arguably be equated with the slaughtering area as it appears in examples of the Sacred District. The reason this tomb is included in this study is because the scenes in the bottom register (actually two sub-registers) have been interpreted as Butic in nature.[892] Those episodes include the *ḫbt*-dancers, the rites to the mooring-post, and the erection of two obelisks accompanied by two men. Through this study, it has been determined that none of these micro-scenes actually occur inside the Sacred District but instead are scenes that often occur adjacent to the Sacred District. Due to the date of Sennefer's tomb it is not surprising that a proper Sacred District is not present.

Tomb of Rekhmire (TT 100)

This tomb has the most elaborate Sacred District scene of all the private Theban tombs. The left wall of the passage is divided into eleven registers and shows the Sacred District embedded within the funerary scenes. The top register shows two rows of *ḥm*-chapels, three on the top and eleven on the bottom, all of them are closed. Moving from top to bottom, the next three registers are bracketed by Osiris on the right. Immediately in front of Osiris are the pool with palms, sycamore trees, garden plots, offering stands, kneeling women before four basins, and then the division between the top two registers dissolves and there is a large slaughtering scene with eight tied bulls surrounding another pool with sycamore trees encircling it. On the other side of the slaughter scene, and intermixed with various unique and enigmatic rituals, are the hall of the *Mww,* the rites to the mooring-post, and the women's tent. In the fifth row from the top, still in front of Osiris, are the two obelisks. The next three registers are bracketed by Anubis. In the sixth register from the top, four open shrines with gods inside sit directly in front of Anubis and face out of the tomb. The three pools and the guardians of the great gate follow. The rest of the register is filled with performances of ritual. There are no micro-scenes from the Sacred District in the remaining two registers laid out in front of Anubis. The lowest three registers

[889] Bryan 2001: 63.

[890] Seyfried dates this tomb to the time of Thutmose III and Amenhotep II (2003: 66), while Assmann pushes it forward to the time of Thutmose IV (2003: 48).

[891] Hodel-Hoenes 2000: 120–121.

[892] Hodel-Hoenes 2000: 122.

are flanked by the Goddess of the West, and in the third register from the bottom the *ḥbt*-dancers and the shrines of the sacred Delta localities appear. As noted previously, these micro-scenes do not occur within the Sacred District proper, but adjacent to it. They have been connected to the Sacred District in discussions in previous scholarship, which is why they are mentioned in this study.

Rekhmire's tomb depicts the most elaborate version of an ancient Egyptian funeral, and as such some of the Sacred District's micro-scenes have been separated by other rituals. The only part that actually resembles a "district" are the micro-scenes that are displayed in the upper right corner of the wall in front of Osiris. There are also several episodes in the top register of those bracketed by Anubis, which is one register below those before Osiris. The Delta shrines and the *ḥbt*-dancers are illustrated farther away in the third register from the bottom, thus corroborating the distinct nature of these episodes.

The voyage to Abydos is depicted in the bottom two registers on the left. The journey to the tomb begins in these same registers on the right. Reading from bottom to top, the three registers above (in front of Anubis) are dedicated to the journey to Sais and the trip to the embalming workshop. The remaining six registers above show the necropolis. This is the area that exhibits the Sacred District.

Tomb of Djehuty (TT 110)

The tomb of Djehuty, located at the northern end of the lower slop at Sheikh Abd el-Qurna, has recently been cleared and recorded by the American Research Center in Egypt.[893] Djehuty was the royal butler for Hatshepsut and royal herald under Thutmose III. What remains of the Sacred District scene in this small T-shaped tomb is found on the south, or left wall of the passage. This tomb's decoration is blackened from later use of it as living space. According to Norman de Garis Davies, who published his notes and line drawings in a short article, the left wall of the passage contained the usual burial rites in four registers with Osiris standing at the end, swathed, and holding his crook and flail. There is a table of food before Osiris with an image of Djehuty facing him.[894] During a visit to this tomb on January 26, 2009, I was able to discern the following micro-scenes: pool with four palms followed on the right by two rows of open gods' shrines, perhaps containing two shrines in each row, and possibly the remains of the gate for the guardians of the great gate.[895] Estimating that what remains of the Sacred District is at waist height, I suggest the micro-scenes occur in either the bottom or second to bottom register.[896] It may also be possible to see the remains for four closed *ḥm*-chapels in the upper register, but the wall decoration is too concealed to confirm this.[897]

Tomb of Menkheperreseneb (TT 112)

Theban Tomb 112 belongs to Menkheperreseneb (II), the high priest of Amun during the reign of Thutmose III. His tomb is located at Sheikh Abd el-Qurna. There is some controversy regarding the relationship between the owner of this tomb and that of TT 86, which does not feature a Sacred District scene. It is unclear if the owners are one and the same.[898] Both tombs are T-shaped and separated spatially from each other. Theban Tomb 112 was decorated originally in the eighteenth dynasty but was then usurped in Ramesside times by Ashefytemwaset who ruined the first five feet of scenes on the left end of the south wall of the passage. Here, the area was lime washed and a kiosk of gods adored by the new tomb owner's family was added. Otherwise, he just added his name in captions and added text at the far end.[899] This tomb was also substantially fired, rendering large portions of the decoration illegible, including most of the passage.

The south wall of the passage is decorated in four registers with the Sacred District appearing in the bottom register. The relevant episodes begin with the rites to the mooring-post on the left, which commonly appears adjacent to the Sacred District. To the right of this micro-scene is a boat carrying the coffin flanked by two crouching figures facing outward. Next are the guardians of the great and Osiris in his shrine facing to the left. The last episode is the two women holding *nw*-jars and kneeling before four basins of water (Figure 4). This is a fairly typical selection of micro-scenes

[893] American Research Center in Egypt, "Theban Tomb 110 Epigraphy and Research Field School"; Bednarski 2013: 1, 3–9.

[894] N. Davies 1932: 290; Google Arts and Culture, "TT 110: A Private Tomb with Royal Depictions."

[895] Diamond 2009.

[896] I would like to thank JJ Shirly for sharing photos of this section of the south wall of the passage.

[897] I would like to thank ARCE for allowing me to visit this tomb while they were conducting their conservation work.

[898] Dorman 1995: 153–154. Dorman thinks there are two different Menkheperresenebs, an uncle and a nephew, both men having been high priests of Amun under Thutmose III. The younger Menkheperreseneb (the nephew) was the owner of TT 112. Menkheperreseneb "the younger" may have held his title into the reign of Amenhotep II, but this king's name does not appear in his tomb.

[899] N. Davies 1933: 18–28.

for a Sacred District of this date. The temenos-style district is waning and only select micro-scenes are chosen for inclusion, but it is not yet at the point when only a group of gods' shrines comes to symbolize the Sacred District. The *ḥbt*-dancers also appear in the second register from the bottom on the far left before the coffin being transferred on a boat.

Tomb of Anen (TT 120)

Anen was the second prophet of Amun and the brother of Queen Tiye (and thus the brother-in-law of king Amenhotep III). His tomb is located at Sheikh Abd el-Qurna and includes what might be the remains of a Sacred District scene on the north, or right wall of the inner room of the chapel. His is a typical T-shaped tomb for this period, but unfortunately it has been badly damaged. Three registers with the remains of the funeral procession and "rites in the garden" were reported on the far-right wall of the inner room (north wall).[900] More recent excavations have revealed that these scenes are no longer visible except for the possible remains of (moving from right to left) the guardians of the great gate, Osiris standing in his shrine, and a row of open or closed gods' shrines.[901]

Tomb of Amenhotep (with Amenemhet) (TT 122)

Theban Tomb 122 is an unusual tomb in its style and in its positioning of the Sacred District scene in a side chapel.[902] This tomb was used by two different, but almost contemporary, men. One man was named Amenhotep (or Neferhotep) and was a member of the family of the mid-eighteenth dynasty vizier Ahmose-Aametu (TT 83). The owner of the side chapels is Amenemhet, overseer of the granary of Amun, wab-priest, and scribe of divine offerings. Both men held the title overseer of the granary of Amun.

TT 122 is a special form of type IVa—a corridor and rear hall often with a niche—but could also be of type IIIa.[903] Side chapels are not a common feature in eighteenth dynasty tomb constructions, but here there are three small chapels that open off the corridor's south wall. The Sacred District appears on the west wall of the third chapel—a chapel that was most likely part of the tomb's original architectural design.[904] The decoration in the third chapel and the corridor confirm that this tomb was decorated sometime during the reigns of Hatshepsut and Thutmose III. JJ Shirley has shown in her study of this tomb that despite the decoration of the side chambers displaying early characteristics, the inscriptions reveal that the chapels were finished slightly later, probably closer to the end of Thutmose III's reign.[905]

On the west wall of the third chapel there are four decorated registers displaying the funeral rites, but no inscriptions were ever made. The top two registers are oriented from right to left and the bottom two registers from left to right—an unusual arrangement. In the second to bottom register several colorful micro-scenes of the Sacred District can be seen running from the outside edge of the chapel toward the main corridor of the tomb. This tomb exhibits another temenos-style, or compact Sacred District. With the advent of the Sacred District at the far-left end, the register splits into two sub-registers. The first micro-scene is the two sycamore trees placed one above the other. This is the more abstract version of the tree, not the leafy variety shown in some tombs. Following the sycamore trees in the upper sub-register is the pool with palms. This episode is fragmentary. Below this, the garden plots are shown painted blue with five white braziers above them. In the upper sub-register and to the right are two women facing to the right and wearing white sheath dresses and perhaps three closed shrines and three open shrines. This scene is also fragmentary. Below the two women is the first closed shrine in a row of at least five closed shrines that give way to several open shrines. There is a missing patch in the center of the row of shrines making their number difficult to determine. In both sub-registers the decoration of the closed shrines alternates between a typical *ḥm*-chapel painted blue and a *ḥm*-chapel with white background and red cross-hatching. Continuing to the right, the guardians of the great gate are shown after the last open shrine in the upper sub-register (see Figure 27). Below, are the three pools. The shrines in the two sub-registers do not end uniformly, instead the last open shrine in the lower sub-register sits below the guardians. The gate the guardians stand in is painted brown and is of the simple type, not the *ḫkr*-frieze style nor the tent style. The guardians themselves are of two types—the outer two armless men have reddish-brown skin, dark blue hair, and wear white kilts, while the inner two armless men have dark blue skin, reddish-brown hair,

[900] Porter and Moss 1970: 232, 234.

[901] Personal communication with Lyla Pinch-Brock and Ted Brock. I would like to thank Lyla Pinch-Brock for sharing her photographs with me. For the publication of this tomb see American Research Center in Egypt, "Conservation of the Tomb of Anen (TT120)."

[902] Shirley 2010: 271.

[903] Shirley 2010: 272; Polz 1990: 318.

[904] Shirley 2010: 278.

[905] Shirley 2010: 280.

and wear yellow kilts. All four men bend inward at the waist toward the center of the gate. At this point, the sub-registers end with the shrine of Osiris that fills the whole register. Osiris stands in a shrine with a cavetto cornice that resembles Gardiner's O 21 sign, and it is painted white. His skin in painted dark blue, his tight-fitting garment is white, and he holds the crook and flail. What is peculiar is that he faces to the right. Logic should have him occupying the next world and facing toward the living, i.e., the left. Perhaps it is the unusual orientation of the figures in the four registers on this wall that is to blame. However, this same unusual orientation is also seen in the figure of Osiris in the tomb of Paheri at Elkab (TC 3), which is actually quite similar in its selection of micro-scenes for the Sacred District when compared to TT 122. The last micro-scene here is the two women kneeling before four basins of water. As has been noted, this scene is often the last scene of the district (Theban Tombs 179, 123, 112, and TC 3 at Elkab). These basins are more square than other examples, but they too are linked to a trough that runs in front of the two women. As a final note, the rites to the mooring-post appear in the bottom register directly under the first closed shrine.

Tomb of Amenemhet (TT 123)

Theban Tomb 123 belongs to a man named Amenemhet who was a scribe during the reign of Thutmose III. His tomb is located at Sheikh Abd el-Qurna next to Theban Tombs 55 and 56. The carved decoration in this tomb has some paint preserved, but for the most part the walls are very fragmentary. Unfortunately, there are no inscriptions preserved. The Sacred District was displayed on the south wall or the left side of the passage. The far side of the left wall (toward the interior of the tomb) is severely damaged, but fortunately the Sacred District seems to be preserved. As in several other tombs, the Sacred District begins after the rites before the mummy and ends before the micro-scene of the *ḫbt*-dancers. In the tomb of Amenemhet, the Sacred District has been placed in the bottom register, as it has in many other tombs.[906]

The first episode to appear here is the women's tent. It is not altogether unusual for this to be the first scene of the Sacred District (see TT 53), although the hall of the *Mww* is more common (for example in TT 15 and TT 81). The women's tent is followed by the pool with four palms, two above the drawing of the pool and two below it, and two sycamore trees, one in each corner. It appears that the palm trees have fruit bundles, as in TT 53 (Figure 46).[907] Moving from left to right, we come to the hall of the *Mww*, in which stand two men with the conical headdresses who face to the left. They are looking back onto the pool and trees. Next is the shrine of Osiris who stands inside and faces to the left. He is followed by the guardians of the great gate of which one still has some brown paint remaining. At this point, the bottom register splits into two sub-registers. On the upper sub-register there is a garden plot with possibly eleven brown braziers above it. Immediately to the right of this scene the wall is broken. What appears in the lower sub-register, below the garden plot, is unrecognizable. Next are two sub-registers of shrines. The closed shrines appear in the upper sub-register and the open shrines appear in the lower sub-register. There may be eight or nine closed shrines above five or six open shrines. The last shrine in the lower sub-register appears to be the Saite shrine, or a gateway similar in style to the Saite shrine with a smaller shrine inside.[908] To the right of this shrine is the unnamed structure (Appendix I, §17).[909] The next, and last, micro-scene of the Sacred District is the two women kneeling before the four basins of water. This episode officially terminates the Sacred District, but it is followed by the *ḫbt*-dancers.

Tomb of Duauneheh (TT 125)

Theban Tomb 125 is located in the sub-division of Sheikh Abd el-Qurna. Duauneheh was the first herald and overseer of the estate of Amun in the time of Hatshepsut. The Sacred District scene is preserved on the southwest wall of his tomb on the left side of the passage where five registers of decoration remain. The decoration is beautifully carved with inscriptions intact. Unfortunately, at certain points large chunks of carved relief have crumbled to the floor.

The Sacred District begins in the bottom register on the left with two rows of gods' shrines. The upper row has nine closed shrines with slight remains of brown paint, and the bottom row has five open shrines, these ones each being substantially wider than the closed shrines. Inside the open shrines sit four anthropomorphic deities followed by one canine-headed god. The gods in the first shrine and the third shrine have beards. To the right of the two rows of shrines is the Saite shrine surmounted by the alternating *pr-nw* shrine and palm tree. As is usual, these shrines are followed by an unnamed structure

[906] Pellini 2022b: 166–168.

[907] *contra* Theis 2011: 142.

[908] Pellini 2022b: figs. 2–3.

[909] The details of this part of the wall are unclear. See Pellini's work (2022b: 168 and fig. 2).

Figure 46: The Sacred District scene in the tomb of Amenemhet (TT 53). Photo by author.

with the remains of blue paint and four brown poles protruding from the roof. The last micro-scene before a substantial break in the wall shows the *ḫbt*-dancers accompanied by the inscription, *ḫbt Mww* (see Figure 43). It is not known which other micro-scenes from the Sacred District originally stood to the left of the rows of gods' shrines. There is evidence of a tall, thin line that perhaps makes up one side of Osiris's shrine or the women's tent. Due to this tomb's location and date, it is likely that some of the more traditional micro-scenes appeared originally at the beginning of the left wall but are now lost.

In the third register from the bottom (middle register), the rites to the mooring-post appear. They are given a rather central location on the wall and the accompanying inscription is preserved. Immediately above the mooring-post the caption reads *ḏd mdw in ktnw*. This tomb offers an additional example of the female ritualist, the *knwt* (see also TT 82 and TT 100) (see Figure 45).

Tomb of Senemiah (TT 127)

The tomb of Senemiah (TT 127), a royal scribe and overseer of all that grows, was originally decorated during the time of Hatshepsut and Thutmose III, but it was subsequently reused by Piay and and his son Pairy in the Ramesside period.[910] Today the walls and ceiling are blackened from human occupation, but parts of the walls have been cleaned. Unfortunately, there is no paint residue left. On the southwest wall, or left wall of the passage, there are five registers of decoration in raised relief. In the bottom register on the far right is the hall of the *Mww*. This episode is preceded by men on a skiff and an oar ritual before a shrine (see TT 82 for a parallel scene). Inside the structure, two *Mww* stand and face to the right wearing their usual conical headdresses. In most other tombs where the hall of the *Mww* appears the micro-scenes of the Sacred District are spread out in front of them as if they are watching over the area. Unfortunately, the wall immediately to their right has been left uncleaned and thus the few remaining inches of carved wall are illegible (Figure 47). In the Ramesside period, most likely in conjunction with the reuse of the tomb, someone cut an opening in the wall to create an annex, thus breaking off the scene.

Moving up one register, in the second register from the bottom the unit of Delta shrines is followed by the *ḫbt*-dancers. Beginning in the bottom left is what appears to be the remains of the Saite shrine and to its right is the unnamed structure with four poles. Above the Saite shrine are two *pr-nw* shrines with alternating palms. These *pr-nw* shrines are raised above the ground line and they hover in the spaces between the palm fronds. Moving up one more register into the third register, the rites to the mooring-post are displayed.

The layout of the scenes is not altogether unusual in that the Delta shrines, *ḫbt*-dancers, and rites to the mooring-post have all been positioned in the general vicinity of the Sacred District, with the *ḫbt*-dancers appearing immediately to the rite of the Delta shrines. It is disappointing not to be able to determine which micro-scenes used to lay to the right of the hall of the *Mww*. The Sacred District's placement at the far end

[910] Polz 1990: 312.

Figure 47: The Hall of the *Mww* in the tomb of Senemiah (TT 127). Left wall of the passage. Photo by author.

of the passage is commonplace as it was a transition scene for the deceased before he reached the hereafter.

Tomb of Nakht (TT 161)

Theban Tomb 161 belongs to Nakht, the bearer of the floral offerings of Amun, and may date to the time of Amenhotep III.[911] Others have dated this tomb as early as the reign of Thutmose III.[912] It is located at Dra Abu el-Naga and considered to be a small tomb. There are four registers that contain the funeral scenes on the right wall of the rectangular chamber (see Figure 41). This tomb shows only the row of shrines in the upper register, much like the scene in Menna's tomb (TT 69). A page from Lepsius' notebook referring to TT 161 shows a man with a haunch in his hands kneeling before a shrine façade. Following to the left (because the episodes are on the right wall) are two sub-registers each with four *ḥm*-chapels. Next, the deceased and his wife stand with their arms in a gesture of adoration before Osiris in his shrine.[913]

As the Sacred District is reduced to one symbolic episode, it also appears to have migrated from the left wall to the right wall sometime around the beginning of the reign of Amenhotep III (see TT 120 for a parallel). Melinda Hartwig has traced one style of painting in TT 120, TT 69, and TT 161, which may help account for this coherence.[914] Another reason for the abbreviation of the scene could be that the size of the tombs in which it is found are on the smaller side and do not have room for the full series of micro-scenes. This may indicate that even when space was at a premium, this was a scene worth including.

Tomb of Mentiywiy (TT 172)

Mentiywiy's titles include royal butler and a child of the nursery, and he lived during the time of Thutmose III and possibly into the reign of Amenhotep II. His tomb is located in the sub-division of Khôkha. According to Porter and Moss, the Sacred District scene is found on the left wall of the passage where the decoration is divided into three registers.[915] In the middle register after the dragging of the *tekenu*, are two *Mww* wearing headdresses and facing to the left, and two kneeling women immediately on their right. These women have short hair and wear a fillet and a dress with one strap. There are only three basins in front of them, not four. This is the only example I know of where only three basins appear before the kneeling women. Lastly, Osiris is seated in his shrine and faces toward the left. In front of him are offerings. In the top register and to the left of Osiris there are four *ḥm*-chapels shrines with gods inside. In the bottom register and to the left of Osiris there are two *ḥm*-chapels with gods inside. Unfortunately, I was not able to enter this tomb.

[911] Hartwig 2004: 14; Quirke 1986: 79–90.
[912] Kampp-Seyfried 1996: 712.
[913] Manniche 1987: 114, fig. 92.
[914] Hartwig 2004: 31.

[915] Porter and Moss 1970: 279–280; MMA photos 3079–82. See also Settgast 1963: 119.

Tomb of Nebamun (TT 179)

Theban Tomb 179 belongs to Nebamun, the scribe and counter of grain in the granary of divine offerings of Amun during the time of Hatshepsut. His tomb is a small rectangular one without a transverse hall and it is located in Khôkha. The painted Sacred District appears on the west/southwest wall, or on the left when you enter the tomb. There are six registers of decoration in total, with the Sacred District appearing in the second register from the bottom.

The background of this register is painted a light blueish gray, as opposed to the more neutral colored background of the four registers above it. Unfortunately, the micro-scenes on the far-left side of the wall have not been preserved and it is likely that this part of the wall originally displayed more of the Sacred District. Moving from left to right, the Sacred District shows the guardians of the great gate, Osiris standing in his shrine and facing to the left, and two women kneeling before four basins of water. These women are shown kneeling side by side, not one above the other as in other examples. This micro-scene of the women kneeling before the four basins of water ends the Sacred District and immediately to the right are the rites to the mooring-post. The register in which the Sacred District appears ends with a large image of the deceased and his wife sitting before a table of offerings and facing to the left. This image shares a baseline with the Sacred District.

The episodes that often appear in conjunction with the Sacred District (but are not part of it) are here dispersed throughout the six registers. For example, in the second register from the top the *ḫbt*-dancers appear before the Goddess of the West who flanks the top two registers. The third register from the bottom shows two men with a pair of obelisks (note: this micro-scene is different from the two obelisks that appear in some examples of the Sacred District as there is human activity). In this same register, but closer to the interior of the tomb, there are two women kneeling with *nw*-pots before the shrine of Anubis. This scene is reminiscent of the micro-scene with the two women kneeling before the four basins of water that regularly appears inside the Sacred District. The women before the Anubis shrine are not part of the Sacred District, but perhaps the same ritualists participate in both performances. There are no inscriptions to either confirm or refute this interpretation

Tomb of Hekmaatrenakht, called Turo (TT 222)

Theban Tomb 222 belongs to Hekmaatrenakht, the first prophet of Montu, Lord of Thebes, who lived during the time of Ramesses III and IV. His tomb is located in the sub-division of Qurnet Murai on the west bank of Thebes. This tomb is an anomaly for a couple of reasons: first, there are not many tombs in this area that include a Sacred District scene as part of their decorative program, and second, this is one of the latest tombs to include this scene (along with Setau at Elkab). However, Nina M. Davies notes that this tomb was usurped by Hekmaatrenakht in the twentieth dynasty as parts of the burial scenes in the upper registers on the north wall of the passage are reminiscent of the eighteenth dynasty. It is these reminiscences that exhibit the Sacred District. Hekmaatrenakht's tomb has not been thoroughly published, but details of the scenes can be found in Davies' brief publication of the tomb and in Jürgen Settgast's 1963 study of funerary rituals. Settgast also notes that the Sacred District scene is found in the upper registers on the right wall of the passage (north wall).[916] Unfortunately, this tomb is described by Davies as a "much damaged and burnt tomb" with large portions of the decoration having been cut out by thieves.[917]

Settgast remarks that the women's tent is noted in one of the partially preserved inscriptions in TT 222. Here, one woman bears the title "mistress of the *pr-wr*," while her two companions remain unnamed.[918] Regrettably, there are no accompanying illustrations in Settgast's publication, and in Davies' work only one woman appears in a tent-like structure on an island, and this is probably part of the later decoration anyhow. An inscription mentioning the guardians of the great gate is also noted by Settgast for this tomb, of which *nṯr.w ꜥ3.w…r.w* remains.[919] The three pools are a third micro-scene mentioned in captions in this tomb. Of the three pools, only the first two are named: *š.w ḫpr* and *š.w ḥkt*.[920] Whether there was a third pond cannot be determined, as the wall at this point has been destroyed. This is one of only two tombs that have inscriptions for these pools.

Tomb of Ahmose (TT 224)

Ahmose, called Humay, became the overseer of the queen's harem and tutor of princes sometime during the reigns of Hatshepsut and Thutmose III. His other titles include overseer of the estate of the god's wife

[916] N. M. Davies 1946: 69–70; Settgast 1963: 50–52, 57, 120.

[917] N. M. Davies 1946: 70.

[918] Settgast 1963: 50–51.

[919] Settgast 1963: 52. See also Menéndez 2005: 29–65.

[920] Settgast 1963: 57, note 9.

and overseer of the double granaries of the god's wife Ahmose-Nefertari. He and his wife Nub were Sennefer's (TT 96B) parents.[921] Ahmose's tomb is located at the foot of Sheikh Abd el-Qurna and is of Kampp-Seyfried's type IVa. This tomb is carved with little to no paint remaining, and it is unfortunately quite blackened and fragmentary.

The Sacred District scene is located on the northeast wall, or the left wall immediately upon entering the tomb. There are four registers of decoration with the relevant scene depicted in the second register from the bottom. The bottom register shows the opening of the mouth ritual and the register above the Sacred District shows the funeral procession. As in other contemporary tombs, the Sacred District begins immediately after the rites before the mummy (TT 21 and TT 123), at which point the register is split into two sub-registers. In the upper sub-register is the women's tent with one woman on the left-side facing right and two women on the right-side facing left. This micro-scene can sometimes begin the Sacred District (TT 53 and TT 123). In the lower sub-register is the pool with palms; the pool is shown in an aerial view raised off the ground line between several palm trees placed in front and behind it. Continuing in the upper sub-register, the women's tent is possibly followed by a bound bull and a row of braziers, but this part is extremely fragmentary. Following this, the remains of a *Mww* wearing the typical headdress can be seen facing to the left and standing inside a structure. Usually, these figures appear in pairs. The lower sub-register shows the remains of an enclosure, which probably held the four armless guardians of the great gate, but only two are visible. This is followed by one and a half gods' shrines (*ḫm*-chapels). Next, Osiris stands in his shrine facing left and he spans both sub-registers. After this micro-scene, the register splits again with at least five closed shrines in the upper sub-register and at least four open shrines in the bottom sub-register. There is a large break in the wall at this point spanning at least two feet.

Tomb of User (TT 260)

Theban Tomb 260 belongs to User, the scribe, weigher of Amun, and overseer of fields of Amun, and is located at the lowest eastern slope of the hill of Dra Abu el-Naga.[922] It dates to the reign of Thutmose III and consists of a single chamber with a niche at the back.[923] The Sacred District scene is found on the left or southern wall of the tomb which was likely divided into five registers of decoration. In the third register from the top, User's funeral procession is met by two *Mww* who wear the typical conical headdress and step east toward the approaching cortege.[924] Their headdresses are outlined in white paint. The Goddess of the West flanks two of the registers (registers 2 and 3 if counting down from the top). The lower registers are badly damaged.

Perhaps it is no coincidence that two of the earliest tombs to include the Sacred District scene (TT 12 and TT 15) are situated nearby, and that Tetiky (TT 15) features a similar procession that is greeted by the *Mww*. This may have prompted the inclusion of the scene of the *Mww* in Theban Tomb 260. Perhaps, as in other one room tombs, one micro-scene alluding to the Sacred District was sufficient. The closest parallels to this scene are in the tombs of Senet (TT 60) and Sobeknakht II at Elkab (TC 10) where only the *Mww* occur. There are also some similarities with the tomb of Nebamun (TT 17), where in the bottom register the procession is greeted by two *Mww* and the Goddess of the West flanks the registers immediately after. Perhaps more episodes of the Sacred District were depicted in one of the lower registers which are now damaged.

Tomb of Sobekmose (TT 275)

Theban tomb 275 is unpublished but is recorded briefly in Porter and Moss.[925] It is located in the sub-division of Qurnet Murai; however, it is unclear when it was constructed. Sobekmose was the head purification priest and divine father in the temples of Amenhotep III and Sokari. Most likely this tomb dates to sometime after the Amarna Period, perhaps during the reigns of Tutankhamun or Horemheb.[926] Today this tomb is badly preserved and has a lot of smoke damage. Its location at Qurnet Murai is definitely unusual, as very few tombs that include a Sacred District scene are found in this sub-division (ex. TT 222).

What remains of the Sacred District scene is found on the far end of the left wall (south wall) of the passage of the T-shaped tomb, but it is difficult to discern. In the upper register, there are four closed gods' shrines, two above two. In the register below, and slightly to

---

921 Hodel-Hoenes 2000: 112.

922 See also Brussels Photos M VI, 33–34.

923 Nasr 1993: 176.

924 Lüddeckens 1943: 73; Settgast 1963: *Tafel* 4; Nasr 1993: 183, *Tafel* 3.

925 Porter and Moss 1970: 352.

926 Kampp-Seyfried 1996: 546–547. Luc Gabolde suggests a date of Amenhotep III citing the destruction of the name Sobek from the Amarna Period (1995: 159). Porter and Moss list it as Ramesside (1970: 352).

the right (toward the interior of the tomb), is a basin outlined in blue (not colored-in) and surrounded by four palm trees. The trees' trunks are brown, and their palms are green, and each one is situated at one of the four corners of the basin. Immediately to the right are four open gods' shrines, two sitting above the other two, with the arched roofs painted white. In the top left shrine, there is an anthropomorphic god with black hair wearing a brown garment. In the shrine to its right the god wears a white garment, but I cannot make out the head of the deity. There is a small space between these shrines and what might be a larger figure of the deceased facing out of the tomb and flanking the registers. I cannot discern what appears in this space. The background color changes from a blue gray to a brownish tone behind the deceased, reminiscent of the background colors seen in TT 179.

Even though only two micro-scenes are visible, there is enough to indicate that a full Sacred District scene was illustrated here. The late date of this tomb is unusual as several other tombs from the reigns of Thutmose IV to Amenhotep III have only gods' shrines depicted. The pool with palm trees is usually found in tombs dating to the reign of Thutmose III or earlier, as it is one of the earliest micro-scenes to be included in the Sacred District. The one exception to this is the tomb of Amenemope (TT 41) from Sheikh Abd el-Qurna. Perhaps the location of the Sacred District in the upper portion of the wall is indicative of this tomb's late date.[927]

Tomb of Amenemopet (TT 276)

Theban Tomb 276 dates to the reigns of Thutmose IV and is located at Qurnet Murai.[928] This tomb belongs to Amenemopet, the overseer of the treasury of gold and silver, judge, and overseer of the cabinet. This tomb was brought to my attention by Settgast's 1963 study, but it illustrates only the unnamed structure and neighboring scenes.[929] Among these scenes is that of the two obelisks. However, these obelisks are accompanied by two men, and thus this episode is different than the pair of obelisks that appear in the tomb of Ineni (TT 81) or Tetiky (TT 15). The micro-scene with a man standing on both sides of the pair of obelisks is not part of the compendium of Sacred District episodes. It can now be determined that there is no Sacred District scene in this tomb's decorative program.

Tomb of Djehutymose (TT 342)

Djehutymose was a hereditary prince and royal herald during the reign of Thutmose III. His tomb is located in the sub-division of Sheikh Abd el-Qurna but is now mostly destroyed. On the left wall of the passage are the remains of two registers depicting the funeral procession, where Porter and Moss describe the scene as including "gods in shrines."[930] This tomb remains unpublished, but according to Jürgen Settgast it displays the Saite shrine with alternating *pr-nw* shrine and palm above it and the unnamed structure. This unit of shrines is indicative of the sacred Delta localities, not the Sacred District. Predictably, these micro-scenes are followed by the *ḫbt*-dancers.[931] The rites to the mooring-post are also recorded for this tomb, but like the sacred Delta localities, this micro-scene is shown adjacent to the Sacred District, not within it. Other than Porter and Moss's mention of gods shrines, there is no other evidence to suggest that Theban Tomb 342 has a Sacred District scene. However, it would make a likely candidate as it fits the criteria for having a Sacred District in terms of its location at Sheikh Abd el-Qurna, its date in the reign of Thutmose III, and the status of its owner.

Tomb of Basa (TT 389)

Basa was a *smꜣti*-priest, chamberlain of Min, *ḥsk*-priest, and mayor of the Southern City during the twenty-sixth dynasty. His tomb is quite small and is located in the Asasif, an area that acquired new importance in the late Period. Basa's tomb continues a tradition of tomb building from the twenty-fifth dynasty and it located to the east. Ibi's tomb (TT 36) is also located in this area (in the southeast next to the tomb of Petamenope). The choice of this location may have something to do with returning to where it all began—the Asasif is the oldest Theban necropolis of supra-regional importance.[932]

The remaining relevant scene depicts the sycamore pond in the slaughtering area. In the tomb scenes that are typologically close to Basa—Rekhmire (TT 100), Amenemhet (TT 82), and the Saite tomb of Ibi (TT 36)—such a pond forms the center of the slaughtering area and is surrounded by bound bulls lying on the ground. As with Rekhmire's image (TT 100), the pond is supplemented with four sycamores on the long sides and two on the narrow sides. It has been suggested

[927] This supposition in made is reference to Jan Assmann's theory that sacred scenes are illustrated in the upper registers of the wall in post-Amarna tombs (2003: 49).

[928] Porter and Moss 1970: 352.

[929] Settgast 1963: 120, *Tafel* 10.

[930] Porter and Moss 1970: 409–410.

[931] Settgast 1963: 120, *Tafel* 11.

[932] Assmann 1973: 11.

that the slaughtering area in Ibi's tomb (TT 36) is directly connected to the crossing to the Anubis tent, so it is possible that Basa had the same order. Perhaps the model used for these earlier tombs was also used for Basa's tomb decoration, particularly for scenes 42–45.[933]

Tomb of Unknown Official (TT 392)

Theban Tomb 392 does not have an identified owner and is unpublished. It dates approximately to the Saite Period (seventh to sixth century BCE) and is situated in the sub-division of Khôkha, but has unfortunately collapsed.[934] Friederike Kampp-Seyfried suggests that this tomb was reused from the New Kingdom.[935] Bertha Porter and Rosalind Moss describes the hall of Theban Tomb 392 as having "Three registers, I–III, funeral procession, with mourners and shrine containing mummy in I, and rites in garden in III."[936] According to their map, these image were displayed on the southeast wall of the transverse hall to the right of the main entrance.[937] The placement of the Sacred District here does not correspond to what would be expected if these images were left over from an original early New Kingdom decorative program—before its reuse. The description of the remains of Osiris and a goddess on the left wall of the inner chamber *is* more in-line with the scene's expected placement.

Tomb of Wensu (TT A4)

Theban Tomb A4 has been identified from early modern records, but unfortunately its exact location is no longer known.[938] In 1801 W. Hamilton was the first traveler to describe this tomb.[939] It was probably located in the sub-division of Dra Abu el-Naga but today portions of its decoration are housed in the Louvre Museum in Paris. Robert Hay sketched the plan and indicated its measurements, so its T-shape is known. The scenes that remained in good condition on the walls of the passage showed the burial of the deceased and the funerary episodes on the left side. Evidence for these scenes include a sketch by Hay and descriptions and detailed sketches by James Burton. Interestingly, Lise Manniche includes among the sources for TT A4 the following item: "for comparison a wall depicting similar scenes in the tomb of Paheri. The individual groups in this tomb are to a large extent identical with those in TT A4, judging from the available drawings of the latter. Portions missing from the tomb of Paheri may be restored from the contemporary tomb of Rekhmirē."[940] What she seems to mean is that there are parallel micro-scenes in the two tombs, but their layout is different. Considering the Sacred District was a well-used tomb scene consisting of many different combinations of micro-scenes, it is misguided to suggest that the tomb of Paheri and TT A4 have almost identical scenes without also describing the other thirty-odd tombs that include a Sacred District as also almost identical.

In her book *Lost Tombs: A Study of Certain Eighteenth Dynasty Monuments*, Manniche has reconstructed the funerary scenes which include the Sacred District.[941] Her reconstruction consists of five registers of decoration with the figures moving from left to right. In all registers except the second from the top, there are episodes belonging to the Sacred District. Moving from left to right and beginning in the top register, Manniche has reconstructed a series of micro-scenes similar to what occurs in the tomb of Amenemhet (TT 82), where the ritual of the oars is followed by two kneeling women in front of four basins of water (Appendix I, §10). As in Theban Tomb 82, the two women before the basins has been isolated from the rest of the Sacred District. The fragmentary inscription in front of these women suggests that they may have been labelled *ḏryt nḏst* and *ḏryt wrt*.[942] The rites to the mooring-post appear farther to the right on the same register, but there is a break in the scene between the two visible series of scenes. The rites to the mooring-post often appear adjacent to the Sacred District. In the next register down there are no micro-scenes belonging to the Sacred District proper, but at the far right end the *ḫbt*-dancers appear and are labelled with the caption *ḫbt Mww*. In this case, they are not placed beside the sacred Delta localities. In the third, or middle register, the rituals end at the necropolis on the far right. Here, there are four closed shrines (two above and two below), a space, and then four open shrines with gods sitting inside. Three of the gods are anthropomorphic, but the god in the shrine in the upper right corner is canine-headed. All shrines are of the *ḥm*-chapel type. It is in the second register from the

933 Assmann 1973, *Abb*. 48.

934 Personal communication with Supreme Council of Antiquities, Luxor, January 2009.

935 Kampp-Seyfried 1996: 604, 657–658. Theis notes it as anonymous tomb Nr. 256 (2011: 297).

936 Porter and Moss 1970: 442.

937 Porter and Moss 1970: 438.

938 Hay MSS 29824, 19; Burton MSS 25638, 48; Porter and Moss 1970: 447–448. See Manniche 1988: 62.

939 Manniche 1998: 64.

940 Manniche 1998: 74.

941 Manniche 1988: fig. 31.

942 Manniche 1988: fig. 25.

bottom that the majority of the micro-scenes belonging to the Sacred District have been reconstructed by Manniche. The procession drags the coffin to the right (presumably to the west), and it encounters a lector priest standing in front of a building façade. To the right of this, two *Mww* stand inside their hall and face to the right. They wear the typical conical headdresses and watch over the Sacred District which is situated to the right. The next micro-scene is the pool with three palm trees; one small tree stands in front of the pool and two taller palms stand behind it. Next, the register splits in two and in the upper portion there is a single row of garden plots surmounted by seven braziers, and in the lower portion there are two sycamore trees of the leafy variety. This is followed by four closed *ḥm*-chapels sitting two above two. Osiris terminates the registers, where he is depicted standing in his shrine and facing to the left toward the world of the living. In the bottom register, Manniche has situated the Saite shrine and the unnamed structure almost at the halfway point, but the alternating *pr-nw* shrine with palm is absent. At the far-right end, the slaughtering area and the guardians of the great gate are found. The slaughtering scene has a pool with trees reconstructed in the middle of it—the so-called sycamore pond.

According to Hay, the figures situated at the end of the register were larger in size than the preceding five registers, where a kneeling figure (of the deceased?) is positioned before "the green god" (presumably Osiris) with a table of offerings. Behind Osiris stands the Goddess of the West who would normally stand in a separate register. Perhaps the priest offering to the couple was positioned below the gods.[943]

In reference to the supposed connection between Wensu and Paheri, it is prudent to consider that Paheri, as scribe of the grain, may have had the Theban area in his jurisdiction. However, there is no conclusive evidence to suggest that there was a family relation or acquaintance between the two men—and their tombs were 83 kilometers apart. Manniche purports that the two tombs were decorated at the same time because they are similar in style. Paheri's tomb was decorated at the beginning of the reign of Thutmose III, and so possibly was Wensu's.

Tomb of Reneny at Elkab (TC 7)

Reneny held the titles mayor and overseer of prophets, and his tomb dates to the time of Amenhotep I, the earliest of the three tombs to include a Sacred District scene at Elkab. It is located on the same terrace as the tombs of Paheri (TC 3) and Setau (TC 4), on the far left or west side. The primary difference between the chapel of Reneny and the other two is that the artist placed the funerary scenes on the right, or east wall of the chapel instead of on the left, or west wall as in the others. The funeral scenes occupy a rather large portion of the right wall, indicating the importance of these images.

In the tomb of Reneny the funeral procession travels from right to left because of the placement of the scenes on the right wall. The orientation of the figures shows that those who inhabit the world of the living face left and proceed to the symbolic west, the world of the dead. Those who inhabit the other world, like Anubis and Osiris face right toward the living.

What has been restored in the tomb chapel of Reneny consists of three large registers (see Figure 37). The top register illustrates the dragging of the coffin to the tomb and the entourage. The Goddess of the West waits at the far end of the register for the deceased to arrive. The sequence of participants consists of the following: two men, a man dragging the *tekenu* on a sledge, and two men carrying a lion bier surmounted by the canopic chest with a *ḏryt* standing underneath. Placed in the middle of the procession are three *Mww* who receive the funeral cortege as it approaches. They mark the beginning of the Sacred District.[944] The *Mww* wear their typical conical headdress and short white kilt, and each one holds his left leg forward in the air. Immediately in front of the *Mww* is the sledge with the coffin. This part of the scene is very fragmentary. It is in the middle register that the Sacred District is found.

The first micro-scene within the Sacred District of Reneny is the hall of the *Mww*, with two *Mww* dancers standing inside facing to the left and watching over the area. The tomb of Reneny features two variations of the *Mww*: the greeters and the guardians. It is clear in the tomb of Reneny that the first appearance of the *Mww* as greeters occurs in this world on the day of burial.[945] The second time the *Mww* appear, they are in the Sacred District in the world of the gods. The tomb of Reneny represents both of these *Mww* as the Sacred District characterizes the superimposition of the mythical realm on the necropolis.[946] After the hall of the *Mww*, the register splits into two sub-registers: in the upper section there are two obelisks and two sycamore trees. In the bottom register there is a long, rectangular pool bordered by seven palm trees and followed by garden plots. The trees in the tomb of Reneny are stylistically different from those appearing

943 Manniche 1998: 76–77.

944 Seyfried 2003: 62.

945 Reeder 1995: 69–83.

946 Diamond 2010b: 41; *idem*. 2011: 42.

in the nearby tomb of Paheri.

In the bottom register, and outside of the Sacred District, going from right to left, there is a line of priests facing to the left followed by a large gap, another group of mourning women, two men carrying a chest accompanied by two mourning women, one walking beside them and the other in front. It appears that they are walking toward a slaughtering area where two men work. This slaughtering area is spatially distinct from the Sacred District in this tomb.

Tomb of Paheri at Elkab (TC 3)

The second tomb from Elkab belongs to Paheri, the mayor of Nekheb (Elkab) and of Inyt (Esna), which dates to the early eighteenth dynasty (possibly to the reign of Thutmose III).[947] It is by far the best preserved of the three chapels with the Sacred District at this site. In this tomb the Sacred District scene appears at the north end of the left side, or west wall of the rectangular chapel. The funerary scenes occupy all five registers of the northernmost portion of the west wall. The Sacred District scene has been placed in the bottom two registers with a large scene of the deceased kneeling before Osiris enthroned in his shrine (see Figure 28). The logical progression of the funerary scenes involves the participants traveling from left to right, from the top down. Consequently, those who lead the procession are to be found down in the fourth register approaching the Sacred District. The upper three registers show the funeral procession of Paheri, including the coffin being dragged, the visit to the sacred Delta localities and Abydos, the dragging of the *tekenu*, and the bearing of papyrus stems. The beginning of the fourth register shows the funeral procession arriving at the Sacred District. The first thing the cortege encounters is a series of garden plots surmounted by a row of braziers and a pool surrounded by three palm trees. This sequence of events is uncommon because most typically the funeral procession encounters the *Mww* who greet the entourage. After the garden plots, braziers, and pool with palms, there are two sycamore trees, one above the other, and two rows of five shrines each. The last three shrines in the bottom row have gods sitting inside them, whereas all of the other shrines are closed. The first two have human-headed gods that resemble very closely the hieroglyphic determinative for god. The third shrine contains a canine-headed deity.

Continuing in the fifth and final register one finds the guardians of the great gate. Although unlabeled in the tomb of Paheri, this scene is so captioned in the tomb of Rekhmire at Thebes (TT 100). The paint color of the guardians' skin is not well preserved but may have been black or dark blue/green. The yellow paint of their kilts is more visible. Following the great gate there is the shrine of Osiris containing the label *Wsỉr nṯr ʿ3*. Osiris stands in his typical tight-fitted garment with his arms crossed holding the crook and flail. Faint green paint remains on his skin, and his garment and headdress are white. In many other examples of this micro-scene Osiris is situated as though he inhabits the land of the dead, the west, and is looking out toward the living who approach him. Here, Osiris unexpectedly faces to the right. Following the shrine of Osiris are two women facing to the right toward the symbolic west who kneel before four basins of water. The caption above their heads identifies them as *ḏryt nḏst* and *ḏryt wrt*. Variant captions for these women appear in Theban Tombs 82 and 100, where the two appellations used to identify the women are *dmḏyt* and *mnknwt/knwt*.[948] The last scene of the Sacred District is the hall of the *Mww*. In the case of Paheri, the *Mww* stand inside their hall and face toward the symbolic west. It is more common to see the *Mww* watching over the district, not turned away from it. If the hall were positioned earlier in the scene then the direction the *Mww* face would be typical. Since they are situated at the end of the Sacred District and facing to the right, they are unable to monitor it, as per their customary positioning.

In addition to the shrine of Osiris noted above, there is another image of this god on the far right end of the left wall of the chapel. It is not standard practice to have two shrines of Osiris, so perhaps some discussion is in order. Osiris typically appears as a micro-scene inside the Sacred District or as a large figure bracketing several registers. In the nearby and earlier tomb of Reneny, the shrine of Osiris is the last micro-scene of the Sacred District and functions as the destination of the procession. Perhaps the artists of Paheri's tomb used Reneny's design as an inspiration but then added the larger seated figure of Osiris with the deceased kneeling before him. This latter image may have been inspired by the large images of Osiris,

[947] Ex. Porter and Moss (1962: 177) places this tomb in the eighteenth dynasty. Tylor and Griffith classify this tomb as mid-eighteenth dynasty in their 1894 study of the tomb (Tylor and Griffith 1894: v). Manniche suggests that the Sacred District scene from the tomb of Paheri resembles the decoration from TT 100 and from TT A4, noting that they must all be of a similar date. Manniche dates TT A4 (that of Wensu) to the reign of Thutmose III (1988: 62–87). See also Lichtheim 1976: 15; BBenderitter, "Pahery"; Devillers 2018.

[948] Diamond 2008; *idem*. 2015a; *idem*. 2017.

Anubis, and the Goddess of the West that often bracket the registers that display the funerary scenes in the contemporary Theban decorative programs.[949]

The tomb of Paheri has one of the first appearances of the *ḫbt*-dancers, the two men who face one another and do the dance of the *Mww*.[950] In this example, each man has a bare head with one arm across his chest with this hand in a fist and his thumb protruding, and his other arm out-stretched in front of him with his hand in a fist with his thumb protruding. The decoration in the tomb of Paheri also reiterates that the voyages to the sacred Delta localities is a distinct scene and not part of the Sacred District proper.

Tomb of Setau at Elkab (TC 4)

The third example of a Sacred District scene from Elkab is in the tomb chapel of Setau, the first prophet of Nekhbet, which dates to the time of Ramesses III-IX.[951] This tomb is located to the west of the tomb of Paheri (TC 3). Unfortunately, the Sacred District scene in this tomb is badly damaged and it has been possible to restore only a couple of fragments to the wall (see Figure 39).[952] The shape of the tomb chapel is reminiscent of that of Paheri with one auxiliary room protruding out from the northwest end and two extending out from the east wall.[953] The main chapel is rectangular just like those of Paheri and Reneny. Due to this, there are many similarities between the tombs of Paheri and Setau with regard to the placement and composition of the Sacred District scene.

Despite the fact that almost the entire left wall of the chapel of Setau is now devoid of decoration, it is still possible to see the remains of the Sacred District scene there. The Sacred District scene was placed at the very end of the left wall among the funerary scenes, just as in the tomb of Paheri. In the upper register the remains of the dragging scene appear where the men hold their arms in the A 28 pose. The second register is extremely fragmentary, but at the far right one can see the carrying of the canopic chest. The third register is almost entirely absent except for a man oriented to the right and bearing a papyrus stem in procession at the far right of the register. All of these scenes are identical to those in the tomb of Paheri. The funerary scenes extant in the tomb of Setau appear to be exact replicas of those preserved in the tomb of Paheri next door. It is therefore logical to assume that what once appeared in the lower registers in the tomb of Setau is the same as what is currently preserved in the tomb of Paheri.

There are several factors that indicate the existence of the Sacred District scene in the lower two registers. First and foremost, one can see the figure of Osiris enthroned in his shrine with his back to the symbolic west and facing out toward the world of the living. His figure equals the height of two registers. In front of him there is a pile of offerings and the deceased Setau is visible kneeling before him. Again, this is exactly what one sees in the tomb of Paheri. Additionally, the legs of the *Mww* who stand inside their hall can be detected faintly. Unfortunately, the rest of the Sacred District scene is lost. This is a rather late example of the Sacred District and there are no Ramesside tombs confirmed to include this scene in their decorative program.[954]

Tomb of Djehuty at Hierakonpolis

The tomb of Djehuty, the overseer of the stone masons, is the one tomb from Hierakonpolis to include the Sacred District in its decorative program.[955] It dates to the reign of Thutmose I and thus is also one of the earliest examples.[956] This tomb is located well into the desert at the edge of the main wadi that bisects the

[949] See Tomb of Wensu (TT A4) above.

[950] Reeder 1995: 70. The *ḫbt*-dancers also appear in contemporary tombs: TT 179, TT 125, TT 100, TT A4, TT 127, TT 112, TT 123, TT 82, TT 53. Perhaps the decoration in the tombs of Nebamun (TT 179) and Duauneheh (TT 125) predate Paheri.

[951] Porter and Moss 1962: 181. See also Limme 2008: 26; Kruchten and Delvaux 2010.

[952] Kruchten and Delvaux 2010: 352–353.

[953] Kruchten and Delvaux 2010: 322.

[954] There are tombs, such as TT 127, that were reused in Ramesside times, but the inclusion of the Sacred District scene dates to the original decorative programs from the early eighteenth dynasty (Polz 1990: 312). Another late example is TT 41, which Assmann dates as early as the reign of Horemheb but Kampp-Seyfried dates to sometime between Horemheb and Sety I (Assmann 1991; *idem*. 2003: 46–52; Kampp-Seyfried 1996: 235). Assmann also points to this tomb as the last one to display "Butic elements." This later date is supported in Porter and Moss (1970: 78) who date TT 41 to the time of Ramesses I-Sety I. Another late tomb that also contains the Sacred District is TT 222, which was reused during the reigns of Ramesses III-IV (Porter and Moss 1970: 323; Kampp-Seyfried 1996: 496), but the decoration in question relates to the original owner of the tomb. TT 275 is another late tomb that includes the Sacred District; however, there is some debate regarding its date. It may date as early as the reign of Amenhotep III according to Gabolde (1995: 159, note 27), to the time of Tutankhamun or Horemheb according to Kampp-Seyfried (1996: 546–547), or as late as the Ramesside Period (Porter and Moss 1970: 352).

[955] Hierakonpolis Expedition. "The Upper Tombs."

[956] R. Friedman 2001: 106–112.

site. It is carved into the upper terrace of the round-topped knoll known as the Burg el-Hammam, "Pigeon Hill." It is possible that this tomb is the earliest one in this cluster of tombs as it is located on the far right.[957] Djehuty's tomb is rectangular in shape and quite similar to the tombs situated across the river at the site of Elkab.

The western half of the south wall comprises three registers of decoration showing the funerary scenes, which move toward the west. This wall is damaged, and the decoration is fragmentary due to a broad fissure running through the tomb at the middle of each of the registers. The lower two registers are bracketed at the end by the Goddess of the West. These scenes are similar to those appearing in the tomb of Reneny (TC 7) across the river at Elkab and those in the tombs of User (TT 21) and Ineni (TT 81) at Thebes.

The Sacred District is found in the top register and the preserved portion begins with *ḫm*-chapels set in two rows. The upper row may have had at least three slightly narrower closed shrines followed by four open shrines with gods inside. In the lower row, there are the three pools followed by four shrines, possibly containing female occupants. Moving toward the Goddess of the West, the next episode is the guardians of the great gate who are painted blue and stand in a rectangular enclosure bordered by the *ḫkr*-frieze on three sides. This is followed by the Anubis shrine, also painted blue, and then the shrine of Osiris. Finally, the district ends with the two women offering *nw*-jars and kneeling before four basins of water. Here, the *nw*-jars and the basins are painted blue. Along with Ineni's tomb (TT 81), this is the earliest example of this micro-scene. Unfortunately, the remaining band of text is too fragmentary to read. Overall, there are six separate micro-scenes that are shown within Djehuty's Sacred District.[958]

---

[957] R. Friedman 2001: fig. 2.
[958] R. Friedman 2001: pls. 36, 2–3.

Bibliography

Ali, Osman. "The Argun Palm, *Medemia Argun*, in the Eastern Desert of Sudan." *Palms* 60.3 (2016): 145–153.

Allen, James P. *The Ancient Egyptian Pyramid Texts*. Atlanta: Society of Biblical Literature, 2005.

———. *Middle Egyptian Literature: Eight Literary Works of the Middle Kingdom.* Cambridge: Cambridge University Press, 2015.

Allen, T. George. Review of *Totenglauben und Jenseitsvorstellungen der alten Ägypter. Grundlagenund Entwicklung bis zum Ende des Mittleren Reiches,* by Herman Kees. *JNES* 17 (1985): 148–149.

Altenmüller, Hartwig. *Die Texte zum Begräbnisritual in den Pyramiden des Alten Reiches.* Wiesbaden: Otto Harrassowitz, 1972.

———. "Bestattungsritual." *Lexikon der Ägyptologie.* Band I, 745–765. Wiesbaden: Otto Harrassowitz, 1975a.

———."Zur Frage Der Mww." *Studien zur Altägyptischen Kultur* 2 (1975b): 1–37.

———. "Muu," *Lexikon der Ägyptologie.* Band IV, 271–272. Wiesbaden: Otto Harrassowitz, 1980.

American Research Center in Egypt. "Conservation of the Tomb of Anen (TT120)." ARCE Projects. Accessed 30 July 2022. https://www.arce.org/project/conservation-tomb-anen-tt120.

American Research Center in Egypt. "Project Djehuty." Antiquities Endowment Fund Projects. Accessed 10 May 2023. https://arce.org/project/djehuty-project/.

American Research Center in Egypt. "Theban Tomb 110 Epigraphy and Research Field School." Antiquities Endowment Fund Projects. Accessed 10 May 2023. https://arce.org/project/theban-tomb-110-epigraphy-research-field-school/.

Angenot, Valérie. "Semiotics and Hermeneutics." In *A Companion to Ancient Egyptian Art*, edited by Melinda Hartwig, 98–119. Malden: Wiley-Blackwell, 2014.

Arnold, Dieter. *The Encyclopedia of Ancient Egyptian Architecture.* Princeton: Princeton University Press, 2003.

Ashmore, Wendy and A. Bernard Knapp. "Archaeological Landscapes: Constructed, Conceptualized, Ideational." In *Archaeologies of Landscape: Contemporary Perspectives,* edited by W. Ashmore and A. B. Knapp, 1–32. Malden: Blackwell Publishers, 1999.

Assmann, Jan. *Das Grab des Basa (Nr. 389) in der thebanischen Nekropole. Grabung im Asasif 1963–1970, Bd. 2.* Mainz am Rhein: P. von Zabern, 1973.

———. *Das Grab des Amenemope (TT 41),* Theben, Bd. 3. Mainz am Rhein: P. von Zabern, 1991.

———. "The Ramesside Tomb and the Construction of Sacred Space." In *The Theban Necropolis: Past, Present and Future*, edited by Nigel Strudwick and John H. Taylor, 46–52. London: British Museum Press, 2003.

———. *Death and Salvation in Ancient Egypt*. Ithaca: Cornell University Press, 2005.

Badawy, Alexander. *A History of Egyptian Architecture: From the Earliest Times to the End of the Old Kingdom*. London: Histories & Mysteries of Man Ltd., 1990.

Baines, John. "On the Symbolic Context of the Principal Hieroglyph for 'God.'" In *Religion and Philosophy im alten Ägypten: Festgabe für Philippe Derchain zu seinem 65. Geburtstag,* OLA 39, edited by U. Verhoeven and E. Graefe, 29–46. Leuven: Peeters, 1991.

———. *High Culture and Experience in Ancient Egypt.* Sheffield/Bristol: Equinox Publishing Ltd., 2013.

———."Watery Egyptian landscapes and performances within them." In *Ritual Landscape and Performance: Proceedings of the International Conference on Ritual Landscape and Performance, Yale University, September 23–24, 2016,* Yale Egyptological Studies 13, edited by Christina Geisen, 177–203. Atlanta: Lockwood Press, 2020.

Baines, John and Jaromir Málek. *Atlas of Ancient Egypt.* New York: Facts on File Publications, 1980.

Bakir, Abd-el-Mohsen. "Remarks on Some Aspects of Egyptian Art." *JEA* 53 (1967): 159–161.

Barrie, Thomas. *Spiritual Path, Sacred Place: Myth, Ritual, and Meaning in Architecture*. Boston: Shambhala Publications, 1996.

Bednarski, Andrew. "ARCE's Excavation of the Tomb of Djehuty (TT 110)." *Bulletin of the American Research Center in Egypt* 203 (2013): 1, 3–9.

Bell, David. "Spirituality and Scholarship: Sacred Acts a Sacred Spaces." In *Loci Sacri: Understanding Sacred Places*, edited by Thomas Coomans, *et al.*, 13–27. KADOC Studies on Religion, Culture and Society. Leuven: Leuven University Press, 2012.

Benderitter, Thierry. "Pahery." Osirinet: Tombs of Ancient Egypt. Accessed 23 May 2023. http://www.osirisnet.net/tombes/el_kab/pahery/e_pahery1.htm.

Bennett, C. J. "A Genealogical Chronology of the Seventeen Dynasty." *JARCE* 39 (2002): 123–155.

Bestock, Laurel. *The Development of Royal Funerary Cult at Abydos: Two Funerary Enclosures from the Reign of Aha*. Wiesbaden: Harrassowitz Verlag, 2009.

Bietak, Manfred. "Zu den Heiligen Bezirken mit Palmen in Buto und Sais – ein Archäologischer Befund aus dem Mittleren Reich." In *Zwischen den beiden Ewigkeiten. Festschrift Gertrud Thausing*, edited by M. Bietak, *et al*., 1–18. Vienna: Im Eigenverlag des Institutes für *Ägyptologie der Universität Wien*, 1994.

———. *Avaris: The Capital of the Hyksos. Recent Excavations at Tell el-Dab`a*. London: British Museum Press, 1996.

Bircher, Warda. *The Date Palm—A Friend and Companion of Man*. Cairo: Elias Modern Publishing House, 1995.

Bolshakov, Audrey. "The Old Kingdom Representations of Funeral Procession." *GM* 121 (1991): 31–54.

———. *Man and his Double in Egyptian Ideology of the Old Kingdom*, Ägypten und Altes Testament 37. Wiesbaden: Harrassowitz Verlag, 1997.

Borchardt, Ludwig. *Das Grabdenkmal des königs Ne-User-Re*. Wissenschaftliche Veröffentlichungen der Orient-Gesellschaft 7. Leipzig: J. C. Hinrichs, 1907.

Breasted, James Henry. *Development of Religion and Thought in Ancient Egypt*. Philadelphia: University of Pennsylvania Press, 1959. Orig. pub. 1912.

———. *Ancient Records of Egypt, Volume 2: The Eighteenth Dynasty*. Chicago: University of Illinois Press, 2001.

Brovarski, Edward. "The Doors of Heaven." *Orientalia* 46 (1977): 107–115.

Brunner-Traut, Emma. *Der Tanz im Alten Ägypten nach bildlichen und inschriftlichen Zeugnissen*. Glückstadt: J. J. Augustin, 1938.

Bryan, Betsy. "Painting Techniques and Artisan Organization in the Tomb of Suemniwet, Theban Tomb 92." In *Colour and Painting in Ancient Egypt*, edited by W. V Davies, 63–72. London: British Museum Press, 2001.

———. "Administration in the Reign of Thutmose III." In *Thutmose III: A New Biography*, edited by

Cline, Eric H. and David O'Connor, 69–122. Ann Arbor: University of Michigan Press, 2006.

———. "Pharaonic Painting." In *A Companion to Ancient Egypt*, edited by A. B. Lloyd, 990–1007. Oxford: Blackwell Publishing Ltd., 2010.

Butzer, Karl. *Early Hydraulic Civilization in Egypt*. Chicago: University of Chicago Press, 1976.

Carnarvon, G. E. S. M. H. and H. Carter. *Five Years' Explorations at Thebes: A Record of Work Done 1907–1911*. London: Frowde, 1912.

Chassinat, E. *Le Mystère d'Osiris au mois de Khoiak*. Cairo: IFAO, 1966.

Clère, J. J. and J. Vandier. *Textes de première période intermédiaire et de XIème dynastie*. Bibliotheca Aegyptiaca 10. Bruxelles: Foundation Égyptologique Reine Élisabeth, 1948.

Collier, Mark and Bill Manley. *How to Read Egyptian Hieroglyphs*. London: British Museum Press, 2002.

Coomans, Thomas, *et al*., (eds). *Loci Sacri: Understanding Sacred Places*. KADOC Studies on Religion, Culture and Society. Leuven: Leuven University Press, 2012.

Coones, Paul. "One landscape or many? A geographical perspective." *Landscape History* 7 (1985): 5–12.

Daines, Alison. "Egyptian Gardens." *Studia Antiqua* 6.1 (2008): 15–25.

Davies, Nina M. "An Unusual Depiction of Ramesside Funerary Rites." *JEA* 32 (1946): 69–70.

Davies, Nina M. and Alan H. Gardiner. *The Tomb of Amenemhet (No. 82)*. The Theban Tombs Series 1. London: Egyptian Exploration Fund, 1915.

Davies, Norman de Garis. *Five Theban Tombs (being those of Mentuherkhepeshef, User, Daga, Nehemaway and Tati)*, Archaeological Survey of Egypt, 21st Memoir. London: Egyptian Exploration Fund, 1913.

———. *The Tomb of Puyemrê at Thebes*, 2 vols. New York: Metropolitan Museum of Art, 1923.

———. "The Tomb of Tetiky at Thebes (No. 15)." *JEA* 11 (1925): 10–18.

———. "Tehuti: Owner of tomb 110 at Thebes." In *Studies Presented to F. Ll. Griffith*, edited by S. R. K. Glanville, 279–290. London: Egypt Exploration Society, 1932.

———. *The Tombs of Menkheperrasonb, Amenmose, and Another*. Theban Tomb Series V. London: Egyptian Exploration Society, 1933.

———. *Tomb of Rekh-mi-re at Thebes*. Metropolitan Museum of Art. Egyptian Expedition Publications, Reprint Edition 11. New York: Arno Press, 1973.

Davies, Norman de Garis, Nina M. Davies, and Alan H. Gardiner. *The Tomb of Antefoker, Vizier of Sesostris I, and his wife, Senet (No. 60)*. London: EES, 1920.

Davies, W. V. "The Dynastic Tombs at Hierakonpolis: The Lower Group and the Artist Sedjemnetjeru." In *Colour and Painting in Ancient Egypt*, edited by W. V. Davies, 113–125. London: British Museum

Press, 2001.

———. "The tomb of Ahmose son-of-Ibana at Elkab. Documenting the family and the other observations." In *Elkab and Beyond. Studies in Honour of Luc Limme,* edited by W. Claes, H. De Meulenaere and S. Hendrickx, 139–175. Louvain/ Paris/Bristol: Peeters, 2009.

———. "Renseneb and Sobeknakht of Elkab: The Genealogical Data." In *The Second Intermediate Period: Current Research, Future Prospects,* OLA 192, edited by Marcel Marée, 223–240. Leuven: Peeters Press, 2010.

———. "A Tomb of a Governor of Elkab of the Second Intermediate Period." In *The World of Middle Kingdom Egypt (2000–1550 BC),* Vol 2., edited by Gianluca Miniaci and Wolfram Grajetzki, 71–83. London: Golden House Publications, 2016.

Dawson, Warren R. "Mummy as a Drug." *Proceedings of Royal Society of Medicine* 21.1 (1927): 34–39.

Den Doncker, Alexis. "Theban Tomb Graffiti during the New Kingdom. Research on the Reception of Ancient Egyptian Images by Ancient Egyptians." In *Art and Society. Ancient and Modern Contexts of Egyptian Art*, edited by Katalin Anna Kóthay, 23–34. Budapest: Museum of Fine Arts, 2012.

———. "Identifying copies in the private Theban necropolis: Tradition as reception under the influence of self-fashioning processes." In *(Re) productive Traditions in Ancient Egypt* edited by Todd Gillen, 333–370. Liège: Presses Universitaires de Liège, 2017.

Devillers, Alisee. "The Artistic Copying Network Around the Tomb of Pahery in Elkab (EK3): A New Kingdom case study." In *The Arts of Making in Ancient Egypt: Voices, Images, and Objects of Material Producers 2000–1550 BC*, edited by Gianluca Miniaci, *et al.*, 31–48. Leiden: Sidestone Press, 2018.

Diamond, Kelly-Anne. Ancient Egyptian Funerary Ritual: The Term *ḥꜣi*. Ph.D. dissertation. Brown University, 2007.

———. "*dmḏ(y)t*: The 'Bone Collector.'" *GM* 218 (2008):17–32.

———. "An Investigation into the Sacred District as Depicted in New Kingdom Private Tombs." *ARCE Bulletin* 195 (2009): 23–27.

———. *Transporting the Deceased to Eternity: The Ancient Egyptian Term ḥꜣi.* BAR International Series 2179. Oxford: Archaeopress, 2010a.

———. "Depictions of the Sacred District in Private New Kingdom Tomb Scenes." Abstract, *The 61st Annual Meeting of the American Research Center in Egypt, April 23–25, 2010* (San Antonio, 2010b): 41.

———. "The Sacred District and the Term *tꜣ ḏsr*." Abstract, *The 62nd Annual Meeting of the American Research Center in Egypt, April 1–3, 2011* (San Antonio, 2011): 42.

———. "The Sacred District Scene in Rectangular Tombs at Elkab." *JARCE* 48 (2012): 97–110.

———. "The Function and Structure of the *dmḏ(y)t* 'Myth.'" *JARCE* 51 (2015a): 225–234.

———. "The Goddess Isis: She who Makes Shade with her Feathers." *ARCE-PA Newsletter* (2015b): 2–4.

———. "The *dmḏ(y)t*: A Prototype for Isis?" *JSSEA* 43 (2017): 45–67.

———. "Mapping the Sacred District Scene in the Theban Necropolis and at Elkab." Seshat's Apprentice. Accessed 11 May 2023. https://kellyannediamond.wordpress.com/mapping-the-sacred-district-scene-in-the-theban- necropolis-and-at-elkab/?frame-nonce=cee38777a7.

———. "Some Preliminary Notes on the Female Appellation *knwt*." *In progress.*

Dominicus, Brigitte. *Gesten und Gebärden in Darstellungen des Alten und Mittleren Reiches.* Studien zur Archäologie und Geschichte Altägyptens, Band 10. Heidelberg: Heidelberger Orientverlag, 1994.

Dorman, Peter. *The Tombs of Senenmut.* PMMA 24. New York: Metropolitan Museum of Art, 1991.

———. "Two Tombs and One Owner." In *Thebanische Beamtennekropolen. Neue Perspecktiven archäologischer Forschung Internationales Symposion Heidelberg 9.–13.6. 1993,* edited by J. Assmann, *et al.*, 141–154. Studien zur Archäologie und Geschichte Altägyptens, Band 12. Heidelberg: Heidelberger Orientverlag, 1995.

———. "Family Burial and Commemoration in the Theban Necropolis." In *The Theban Necropolis:Past, Present and Future,* edited by N. Strudwick and J. Taylor, 30–41. London: British Museum Press, 2003.

Downing, Melissa and R. B. Parkinson. "The Tomb of the Ramesseum Papyri in the Newberry Papers, The Griffith Institute Oxford," British Museum Studies in Ancient Egypt and Sudan 23 (2016): 35–45.

Doxy, Denise. "Anubis." In *The Oxford Encyclopedia of Ancient Egypt*, edited by Donald Redford, 97–98. Oxford: Oxford University Press, 2001.

Dziobek, Eberhard. *Das Grab des Ineni: Theben Nr. 81.* Mainz am Rhein: Philipp von Zabern, 1992.

Engelmann-von Carnap, Barbara. "Unconventional Versions: The Theban Tomb of Puiemra, Second

Prophet of Amun under Hatshepsut." In *Creativity and Innovation in the Reign of Hatshepsut*, SAOC 69, edited by José Galán, *et al.*, 337–359. Chicago: The Oriental Institute, 2014.

EurekaAlert. "Djehuty Project discovers significant evidence of the 17th Dynasty of Ancient Egypt." Public Release by CSIC, 5-Apr-2013. Accessed 24 May 2023. https://www.eurekalert.org/news-releases/495225.

Fakhry, Ahmed. *The Monuments of Sneferu at Dahshur*, Vol. 2, Part 1. Cairo: General Organization for General Printing Offices, 1961.

Faulkner, R. O. "Spells 38–40 of the Coffin Texts." *JEA* 48 (1962): 36–44.

———. *A Concise Dictionary of Middle Egyptian*. 2nd ed. Oxford: Griffith Institute, 1991.

———. *The Ancient Egyptian Pyramid Texts.* Oxford: Oxford University Press, 1998.

———. *The Ancient Egyptian Coffin Texts.* Oxford: Aris & Phillips, 2004. Orig. pub. 1973.

Faulkner, R. O. and O. Goelet. *The Egyptian Book of the Dead: The Book of Going Forth by Day.* San Francisco: Chronicle Books, 1994.

Fischer, Henry George. "Representations of Dryt-Mourners in the Old Kingdom." In *Egyptian Studies I: Varia*, edited by Henry G. Fischer, 39–50. New York: Metropolitan Museum of Art, 1976.

Fox, Michael V. *The Song of Songs and the Ancient Egyptian Love Songs.* Madison: The Universityof Wisconsin Press, 1985.

Friedman, Florence Dunn. "The Underground Relief Panels of King Djoser at the Step Pyramid Complex." *JARCE* 32 (1995): 1–42.

Friedman, Renée. "The dynastic tombs at Hierakonpolis: painted tombs of the early Eighteenth Dynasty." In *Colour and Painting in Ancient Egypt,* edited by W. V. Davies, 106–112. London: British Museum Press, 2001.

Gabolde, Luc. "Autour de la tombe 276: Pourquoi va-t-on se faire enterer à Gournet Mourai au début du Nouvel Empire?" In *Thebanisch Beamtennekropolen. Neue Perspecktiven archäologischer Forschung Internationales Symposion Heidelberg 9.–13.6. 1993*, edited by J. Assmann, *et al.* 155–165. Studien zur Archäologie und Geschichte Altägyptens, Band 12. Heidelberg: Heidelberger Orientverlag. 1995.

Galán, José. "The Tombs of Djehuty and Hery (TT 11–12) at Dra Abu el-Naga." In *Proceedings of the Ninth International Congress of Egyptologists,* OLA 150, edited by Jean-Claude Goyon and Christine Cardin, 777–787. Leuven: Peeters Press, 2007.

———. "The rock-cut tomb-chapels of Hery and Djehuty on the west bank of Luxor: History, environment and conservation." In *The Conservation of Subterranean Cultural Heritage*, edited by C. Saiz-Jimenez, 3–16. Leiden: CRC Press, 2014.

———. "4,000 Year Old Funerary Garden Discovered at Egyptian Tomb Entrance." News Network Archaeology. May 4, 2017. https://archaeonewsnet.com/2017/05/4000-year-old-funerary-garden.html

———. "Discovering a Twelfth Dynasty Funerary Garden in Thebes." *Scribe* 6 (2020): 40–47.

Galán, José and David Garcia. "Twelfth Dynasty Funerary Gardens in Thebes." *Egyptian Archaeology* 54 (2019): 4–8.

Galán, José and Ángeles Jiménez-Higueras. "Three Burials of the Seventeenth Dynasty in Dra Abu el-Naga." In *The World of Middle Kingdom Egypt (2000–1550 BC),* Vol 2., edited by Gianluca Miniaci and Wolfram Grajetzki, 101–119. London: Golden House Publications, 2015.

Galil, J. "An Ancient Technique for Ripening Sycamore Fruit in East-Mediterranean Countries." *Economic Botany* 22 (1968): 178–190.

Gamer-Wallert, Ingrid. *Die Palmen im alten Ägypten: eine Untersuchungen ihrer praktischen, symbolischen und religiösen Bedeutung.* Berlin: B. Hessling, 1962.

Gardiner, Alan H. "A Unique Funerary Liturgy." *JEA* 41 (1955): 9–17.

———. *Egyptian Grammar.* Oxford: Griffith Institute, 1957.

Gayet, A. J. *Stèles de la XIIe Dynastie.* Bibliothèque de l'École des Hautes Études publiée sous les auspices du ministère de l'instruction publique 68. Paris: Musée du Louvre, 1889.

Gee, John Laurence. The Requirements of Ritual Purity in Ancient Egypt. Ph.D. dissertation. Yale University, 1998.

Gessler-Löhr, B. *Die heiligen Seen ägyptischer Tempel. Ein Betrag zur Deutung sakaler Baukunst im alten Ägypten.* Hildesheim: Gerstenberg, 1983.

Google Arts and Culture. "TT 110: A Private Tomb with Royal Depictions." Accessed 9 May 2023. https://artsandculture.google.com/story/tt110-a-private-tomb-with-royal-depictions-american-research-center-in-egypt/yQVxqjPTy_ycBw?hl=en.

Grajetzki, Wolfram. *Court Officials of the Egyptian Middle Kingdom.* London: Duckworth, 2009.

Griffiths, J. Gwyn. "The Tekenu, the Nubians and the Butic Burial." *Kush* 6 (1958): 106–120.

———. *The Origins of Osiris and his Cult.* Leiden: Brill, 1980.

Grdseloff, Bernard. *Das agyptische Reinigungszelt: archaeologische Untersuchung.* Cairo: IFAO, 1941.

Hannig, Rainer. *Die Sprache der Pharaonen. Großes Handwörterbuch: Ägyptisch-Deutsch*, 2nd ed., Mainz: Zabern, 1997.

———. *Ägyptisches Wörterbuch I: Altes Reich und Erste Zwischenzeit.* Mainz: Zabern, 2003.

———. *Ägyptisches Wörterbuch II: Mittleres Reich und Zweite Zwischenzeit.* Mainz: Zabern, 2006.

Harlan, Jack. "Lettuce and the Sycomore: Sex and Romance in Ancient Egypt." *Economic Botany* 40, No. 1 (1986): 4–15.

Harpur, Yvonne. *Decoration in Egyptian Tombs of the Old Kingdom: Studies in Orientation and Scene Content.* London: Kegan Paul International, 1987.

Hartung, Ulrich. "Constructions of the Early Dynastic Period at Tell el-Faraʿin/Buto." In *Egypt at its Origins* 5. *Proceedings of the Fifth International Conference "Origin of State. Predynastic and Early Dynastic Egypt," Cairo, 13th-18th April 2004.* OLA 260, edited by B. Midant-Reynes, *et al.*, 63–80. Leuven: Peeters, 2017.

Hartwig, Melinda. *Tomb Painting and Identity in Ancient Thebes, 1419–1372 BCE.* Monumenta Aegyptiaca X, Série Imago No. 2. Turnhout: Brepols Publishers, 2004.

———. *The Tomb Chapel of Menna (TT 69). The Art, Culture, and Science of Painting in an Egyptian Tomb.* Cairo: The American University in Cairo Press, 2013.

Harvey, Stephen Phillip. *The Cults of King Ahmose at Abydos.* ProQuest Dissertations Publishing, 1998.

Hassan, Selim. *Excavations at Giza 1932–1933*, Vol. IV. Cairo: Government Press, 1943.

Hayes, Harold. "The End of Rites of Passage and a Start with Ritual Syntax in Ancient Egypt," *Revista Studi Orientali Supplemento* 2 (2013): 165–186.

Hayes, William C. *Scepter of Egypt II. A Background Study for the Study of Egyptian Antiquities in the Metropolitan Museum of Art: The Hyksos Period and the New Kingdom (1675–1080 B.C.).* Cambridge: Metropolitan Museum of Art, 1959.

———. "A Selection of Tuthmoside Ostraca from Dēr el-Bahri." *JEA* 46 (1960): 29–52.

Heynickx, Rajesh, *et al.* "Introduction." In *Loci Sacri: Understanding Sacred Places*, edited by Thomas Coomans, *et al.*, 13–27. KADOC Studies on Religion, Culture and Society. Leuven: Leuven University Press, 2012.

Hierakonpolis Expedition. "The Upper Tombs." Hierakonpolis: City of the Hawk." Accessed 10 May 2023. http://www.hierakonpolis-online.org/index.php/explore-dynastic-tombs/the-upper-tombs.

Hodel-Hoenes, Sigrid. *Life and Death in Ancient Egypt.* Ithaca: Cornell University Press, 2000.

Hofmann, Eva. "Zwischen den Zeiten–Das thebanische Grab des 'Konigsohns' Tetiki (TT 15)." *Imago Aegypti* 3 (2011): 42–55.

Hoffmeier, James K. "The Possible Origins of the Tent of Purification in the Egyptian Funerary Cult." *SAK* 9 (1981): 167–177.

———. Sacred *in the Vocabulary of Ancient Egypt: The Term* ḏsr, *with special Reference to Dynasties I-XX.* Freiburg: Universitätsverlag Freiburg Schweiz Vandernhoeck & Ruprecht Göttingen, 1985.

Hollis, Susan Tower. *Five Egyptian Goddesses: Their Possible Beginnings, Actions, and Relationships in the third Millennium BCE.* London: Bloomsbury Publishing, 2020.

Hornung, Erik. *Das Amduat: Die Schrift des Verborgenen Raumes*, vol. 1. Wiesbaden: HarrassowitzVerlag, 1963a.

———. *Das Amduat: Die Schrift des Verborgenen Raumes*, vol. 2. Wiesbaden: Harrassowitz Verlag, 1963b.

Houlihan, Patrick, F. *The Animal World of the Pharaohs.* London: Thames and Hudson, 1996.

Ingold, Tim. "The Temporality of the Landscape." *World Archaeology* 25.2 (1993): 152–174.

James, T. G. H. (ed.). *Excavating in Egypt: The Egypt Exploration Society 1882–1982.* London: British Museum, 1982.

Junker, H. "Der Tanz der Mww und das Butische Begräbnis im Alten Reich." *MDAIK* 9 (1940): 1–39.

Kaiser, Werner. "Die dekorierte Torfassade des spätzeitlichen Palastbezirkes von Memphis." *MDAIK* 43 (1987): 123–154.

Kampp-Seyfried, Friederike. *Die Thebeniche Nekropole: zum Wandel des Grabgedankens von der XVIII. zur XX. Dynastie,* Theben Bd. 13. Mainz am Rhein: Verlag Philipp von Zabern, 1996.

———. "The Theban Necropolis: An Overview of Topography and Tomb Development from the Middle Kingdom to the Ramesside Period." In *The Theban Necropolis: Past, Present and Future*, edited by Nigel Strudwick and John H. Taylor, 2–10. London: British Museum Press, 2003.

Kamrin, Janice. *The Cosmos of Khnumhotep II at Beni Hasan.* London/New York: Kegan Paul International, 1999.

Kantor, Helene J. "Narration in Egyptian Art." *AJA* 61, 1 (1957): 44–54.

Kees, Hermann. *Totenglauben und Jenseitsvorstellungen der alten Ägypter: Grundlagen und Entwicklung bis zum Ende des Mittleren Reiches.* Berlin: Akademie-Verlag, 1956.

———. *Ancient Egypt: A Cultural Topography.* Chicago: University of Chicago Press, 1961.

Kemp, Barry. "Abydos." *Lexikon der Ägyptologie.* Band I, 28–41. Wiesbaden: Otto Harrassowitz, 1975.

———. *Ancient Egypt: Anatomy of a Civilization.* London/New York: Routledge, 2018.

Köhler, E. "The Orientation of Cult Niches and Burial Chambers in Early Dynastic Tombs at Helwan," In *Ancient Memphis 'Enduring is the Perfection,'* edited by L. Evans, 279–297. Leuven/Paris/Walpole: Peeters Publishers, 2012.

Kruchten, Jean Marie and Luc Delvaux. *Elkab VIII. La tombe de Sétaou.* Brussels/Turnhout: Brepols, 2010.

Kuhlmann, Klaus P. and Wolgang Schenkel. *Das Grab des Ibi, Obergutsverwalters der Gottesgemahlin des Amun (Thebanisches Grab Nr. 36).* Band 1: Beschreibung der unterirdischen Kult-und Bestattungsanlage. Mainz am Rhein: Verlag Philipp von Zabern, 1983.

Laboury, Dimitri. "Tracking Ancient Egyptian Artists, a Problem of Methodology. The Case of the Painters of Private Tombs in the Theban Necropolis during the Eighteenth Dynasty." In *Art and Society: Ancient and Modern Contexts of Egyptian* Art, edited by Katalin Anna Kóthay, 199–208. Budapest: Museum of Fine Arts, 2012.

———. "Tradition and Creativity: Toward a Study of Intericonicity in Ancient Egyptian Art." In *(Re)productive Traditions in Ancient Egypt: Proceedings of the conference held at the University of Liège, 6th–8th February 2013,* Ægyptiaca Leodiensia 10, edited by Todd Gillen, 229–258. Liège: Presses Universitaires de Liège, 2017.

Leahy, Anthony. "Death by Fire in Ancient Egypt." *JESHO* 27, No. 2 (1984): 199–206.

———. "A Protective Measure at Abydos in the Thirteenth Dynasty." *JEA* 75 (1989): 42–60.

Lesko, Leonard. "The Field of Hetep in Egyptian Coffin Texts." *JARCE* 9 (1971–72): 89–101.

———. "Ancient Egyptian Cosmogonies and Cosmology." In *Religion in Ancient Egypt*, edited by Byron E. Shafer, 88–122. Ithaca and London: Cornell University Press, 1991.

Lexová, Irena. *Ancient Egyptian Dances.* New York: Dover Publications, 2000. Orig. pub. 1935.

Lichtheim, Miriam. *Ancient Egyptian Literature: The Old and Middle Kingdoms.* Vol. 1. Berkeley/Los Angeles/London: University of California Press, 1975.

———. *Ancient Egyptian Literature: The New Kingdom.* Vol. 2. Berkeley/Los Angeles/London: University of California Press, 1976.

———. *Ancient Egyptian Autobiographies Chiefly of the Middle Kingdom.* Orbis Biblicus et Orientalis 84. Freiburg: Göttingen, 1988.

———. *Maat in Egyptian Autobiographies and Related Studies.* Orbis Biblicus et Orientalis 120. Freiburg Schweiz: Universitätsverlag /Göttingen: Vandenhoeck & Ruprecht, 1992.

Limme, Luc. "Elkab, 1937–2007: Seventy years of Belgian archaeological research." *BMSAES* 9 (2008): 15–50. Archived on 1 August 2019. http://www.britishmuseum.org/pdf/Limme.pdf.

Loeben, Christian E. and Sven Kappel. *Die Pflanzen im ältagyptischen Garten.* Rahden: Verlag Marie Leidorf GmbH, 2009.

Louvre Museum. "Abkaou stele." Collections. Accessed 11 May 2023. https://collections.louvre.fr/en/ark:/53355/cl010037481.

Lucas A. and J. R. Harris. *Ancient Egyptian Materials and Industries.* Mineola: Dover Publications, 1999.

Lüddeckens, Eric. *Untersuchungen über religiösen Gehalt, Sprache und Form der ägyptischen Totenklagen.* Vols 11–12. Mitteilungen des Deutschen Institutes für Ägyptische Altertumskunde in Kairo. Berlin: Reichsverlagsamt, 1943.

Lythgoe, Albert M. "The Tomb of Puyemrê at Thebes." *The Metropolitan Museum of Art Bulletin* 18,no. 8 (1923): 186–188.

Macramallah, R. *Le Mastaba d'Idout.* Cairo: IFAO, 1935.

Manassa Darnell, Colleen. "Self-Presentation in the Ramesside Period." In *Living Forever: Self-Presentation in Ancient Egypt*, edited by Hussein Bassir, 159–176. Cairo: American University Cairo Press, 2019.

Manniche, Lise. "The Tomb of Nakht, the Gardener, at Thebes (No. 161) as Copied by Robert Hay."*JEA* 72 (1986): 55–72.

———. *City of the Dead: Thebes in Egypt.* Chicago: University of Chicago Press, 1987.

———. *Lost Tombs: A Study of Certain Eighteenth Dynasty Monuments in the Theban Necropolis.* London: Kegan Paul International, 1988.

Mariette, Auguste. *Abydos, Description de fouille execute sur l'emplacement de cette ville.* Vol. II. Paris: Imprimerie nationale, 1880.

Mathieu, B. "Mais qui est donc Osiris? Ou la politique sous le linceul de la religion," *ENiM* 3 (2010): 77–107.

Meeks, Dimitri. "Dance." In *The Oxford Encyclopedia of Ancient Egypt*, edited by Donald Redford, 356–360. Oxford: Oxford University Press, 2001.

Menéndez, Gemma. "La Procesión Funeraria de la tomba de Hery (TT 12)." *Boletín de la Asociación Española de Egiptología* 15 (2005): 29–65.

Merzeban, R. "À propos de quelques analogies inconographiques dans les tombes privées." *BIFAO* 114 (2014): 339–361.

Metropolitan Museum of Art. "Brazier from the Burial of Amenhotep." Egyptian Art. Accessed 20 May 2022. https://www.metmuseum.org/art/collection/search/548873.

Middle Kingdom Theban Project. "Tomb of Djari (TT 366)." Accessed 8 January 2023. https://thebanproject.com/en/tomb-of-djari/#:~:text=The%20tomb%20of%20Djari%20(TT,overseer%20of%20the%20king's%20harem%E2%80%9D.

Moens, M. F. "The Ancient Garden in the New Kingdom. A Study of Representations." *Orientalia Lovaniensia Periodica* 15 (1984): 11–53.

Mogensen, Maria. *La Collection Egyptienne, La Glyptothèque Ny Carlsberg.* Copenhagen: Fr. Bagge, 1930.

Morenz, Siegfried. *Egyptian Religion.* Ithaca: Cornell University Press, 1973

Muhammed, M. Abdul-Qader. *The development of the funerary beliefs and practices displayed in the private tombs of the New Kingdom at Thebes.* Cairo: General Organization for Government Print Offices, 1966.

Nasr, Mohammed W. "The Theban Tomb 260 of User." *SAK* 20 (1993): 173–202.

O'Connor, David. *Abydos: Egypt's First Pharaohs and the Cult of Osiris.* London: Thames & Hudson, 2009.

Oppenheim, Adela. Aspects of the Pyramid Temple of Senwosret III at Dahshur: The Pharaoh and Deities. Ph.D. dissertation. New York University, 2008.

Pellini, J. R. Encounters, Affects and Intra-actions: Difracting the Theban Tomb 123. *Archaeologies: Journal of the World Archaeological Congress* 18 (2022a): 338–369. https://doi.org/10.1007/s11759-022-09451-4.

———. "Crossing the gates of tA-Dsr. The Sacred District scenes in TT 123: Affecting and Being Affected." *JARCE* 58.1 (2022b): 163–170. https://doi.org/10.5913/jarce.58.2022.a009.

Petrie, William M. Flinders. *The Royal Tombs of the Earliest Dynasties. Part II.* London: EEF, 1901.

———. *The Palace of Apris (Memphis II).* London: EEF, 1909.

Piankoff, Alexandre and Natacha Rambova. *Mythological Papyri: Texts and Plates.* Bollingen Series XL, 3 vols. New York: Pantheon Books, 1957.

Polz, D. "Bemerkungen zur Grabbenutzung in der thebanischen Nekropole." *MDAIK* 46 (1990): 301–336.

Porter, B and R. Moss. *The Topographical Bibliography of Ancient Egyptian Hieroglyphic Texts, Reliefs, and Paintings. The Theban Necropolis: Private Tombs.* I.i. Oxford: Griffith Institute, 1970. Orig. pub. 1960. Accessed 24 May 2023. http://www.griffith.ox.ac.uk/topbib.HTML.

———. *The Topographical Bibliography of Ancient Egyptian Hieroglyphic Texts, Reliefs, and Paintings. Upper Egypt: Sites.* V. Oxford: Griffith Institute, 1962. Orig. pub. 1937.

———. *The Topographical Bibliography of Ancient Egyptian Hieroglyphic Texts, Reliefs, and Paintings. Memphis: Saqqâra to Dahsûr.* III.ii. Oxford: Griffith Institute, 1981.

Quirke, Stephen. "The Hieratic Texts in the Tomb of the Nakht the Gardener, at Thebes (No. 161) as Copied by Robert Hay." *JEA* 72 (1986): 79–90.

Randall-MacIver, D., Francis Llewellyn Griffith, and Arthur C. Mace. *El Amrah and Abydos, 1899–1901.* London: Egyptian Exploration Fund. 1902.

Redford, Donald. *Pharaonic King-Lists, Annals and Day-Books: A Contribution to the Study of the Egyptian Sense of History.* Toronto: Benben Publications, 1986.

Reeder, Greg. "The Mysterious Muu and the Dance They Do." *KMT* 6, No. 3 (1995): 69–83.

Richards, Janet. "Conceptual Landscapes in the Egyptian Nile Valley." In *Archaeologies of Landscape: Contemporary Perspectives*, edited by Wendy Ashmore and A. Bernard Knapp, 83–100. Malden: Blackwell Publishing, 1999.

———. *Society and Death in Ancient Egypt: Mortuary Landscapes of the Middle Kingdom.* Cambridge: Cambridge University Press, 2005.

Ritner, Robert Kriech. *The Mechanics of Ancient Egyptian Magical Practice*, SAOC 54. Chicago: Oriental Institute of the University of Chicago, 1993.

Robins, Gay. "Some Principles of Compositional Dominance and Gender Hierarchy in Egyptian Art." *JARCE* 31 (1994): 33–40.

———. *The Art of Ancient Egypt: Revised Edition.* Cambridge: Harvard University Press, 2008.

———. "The Decorative Program in Single-Roomed Pre-Amarna 18th Dynasty Tomb Chapels at Thebes," Abstract, *The 61st Annual Meeting of the*

American Research Center in Egypt, April 23–25, 2010 (San Antonio, 2010): 78–79.

Robinson, Peter. The Cognitive Geographies of the Ancient Egyptians: An Introduction. Ph.D. dissertation. University of Manchester, 1996.

———. "Ritual Landscapes in the Coffin Texts — A cognitive mapping approach." In *Current Research in Egyptology 2004: Proceedings of the Fifth Annual Symposium,* edited by R. Dann, 118–132. Oxbow: Oxford, 2005.

Ryholt, Kim S. B. *The Political Situation in Egypt during the Second Intermediate Period, c. 1800–1550 B.C.* CNI Publications 20. Copenhagen: Museum Tuscalanum Press, 1997.

Säve-Söderbergh, Torgny. *Four Eighteenth Dynasty Tombs*. Private Tombs at Thebes 1. Oxford: Oxford University Press, 1957.

———. "Eine Gastmahlsszene im Grabe des Schatzhausvorstehers Djehuti." *MDAIK* 16 (1958): 280–291.

Scamuzzi, Ernesto. *Egyptian Art in the Egyptian Museum of Turin.* New York: Harry N. Abrams, 1965.

Scharff, Alexander. *Die Altertümer der Vor- und Frühzeit Ägyptens*, Vol. II. Berlin: Staatliches Museum zu Berlin, 1929–1931.

Serrano, José Miguel. "Djehuty, 'Commissioner of Hierakompolis.'" Proyecto Djehuty. 2003. Accessed 20 May 2023. https://proyectodjehuty.com/djehuty-comisionado-de-hierakompolis/.

Sethe, Kurt. *Urgeschichte und Älteste Religion der Ägypter.* Leipzig: Deutsche Morgenlaendische Gesellschaft, 1930.

Settgast, Jürgan. *Untersuchungen zu altägyptischen bestattungsdarstellungen.* Glückstadt-Hamburg-New York: Verlag J.J. Augustin, 1963.

Seyfried, Karl-J. "Reminiscences of the 'Butic Burial' in Theban Tombs of the New Kingdom." In *The Theban Necropolis: Past, Present and Future*, edited by Nigel Strudwick and John H. Taylor, 61–68. London: British Museum Press, 2003.

Shirley, JJ. "The Life and Career of Nebamun, the Physician of the King in Thebes." In *The Archaeology and Art of Ancient Egypt: Essays in Honor of David B. O'Connor*, edited by

Hawass, Zahi A. and Janet Richards, 381–401. Cairo: Supreme Council of Antiquities, 2007.

———. "One Tomb, Two Owners: Theban Tomb 122—Re-Use or Planned Family Tomb?" In

Millions of Jubilees: Studies in Honor of David P. Silverman, Vol. 2, edited by Zahi A. Hawass and Jennifer Houser Wegner, 271–301. Cairo: Supreme Council of Antiquities, 2010.

———. "Crisis and Restructuring of the State: From the Second Intermediate Period to the Advent of the Ramesses." In *Ancient Egyptian Administration,* edited by Juan Carlos Moreno Garcia, 521–606. Leiden/Boston: Brill, 2013.

Simpson, William Kelly. *The Terrace of the Great God at Abydos: The Offering Chapels of Dynasties 12 and 13.* Philadelphia: Eastern Press, 1974.

——— (ed.). *The Literature of Ancient Egypt.* New Haven/London: Yale University Press. 2003.

Smith, Grafton Elliot and Warren R. Dawson. *Egyptian Mummies.* London: Routledge, 2002.

Smith, Mark. *Following Osiris: Perspectives on the Osirian Afterlife from Four Millenia.* Oxford: Oxford University Press, 2017.

Spencer, Patricia. "Dance in Ancient Egypt." *Near Eastern Archaeology* 66.3 (2003): 111–121.

Spiegel, J. *Die Götter von Abydos.* Wiesbaden: Harrassowitz, 1973.

Springuel, Irina. *The Desert Garden: A Practical Guide.* Cairo: The American University in Cairo Press, 2006.

Stevenson Smith, William. *The Art and Architecture of Ancient Egypt.* New Haven/London: Yale University Press, 1998.

Taylor, John. *Death and the Afterlife in Ancient Egypt.* Chicago: University of Chicago Press, 2001.

Theis, Christoffer. *Deine Seele zum Himmel, dein Leichnam zur Erde: zur idealtypischen Rekonstruktion eines altägyptischen Bestattungsrituals,* SAK Beiheft 12. Hamburg: Helmut Buske Verlag, 2011.

Tilley, Christopher. *A Phenomenology of Landscape: Places, Paths and Monuments.* Berg: Oxford/Providence, 1994.

———. "Introduction: Identity, Place, Landscape and Heritage." *Journal of Material Culture* 11 (1/2) (2006): 7–32.

Toonen, Willem H. J., Angus Graham, Benjamin T. Pennington, *et al*. "Holocene fluvial history of the Nile's west bank at ancient Thebes, Luxor, Egypt, and its relation with cultural dynamics and basin-wide hydroclimatic variability." *Geoarchaeology* 33.3 (2018): 273–290. https://doi.org/10.1002/gea.21631

Tylor, Joseph, J. *Wall Drawings and Monuments of El Kab: The Tomb of Sobeknekht.* London: B. Quaritch, 1896.

Tylor, Joseph J. and Francis Llewellyn Griffith. *Wall Drawings and Monuments of El Kab: The Tomb of Paheri*. London: Egypt Exploration Fund, 1894.

———. *Wall Drawings and Monuments of El Kab: The Tomb of Renni.* London: B. Quaritch,

1900.

University of Basel. "Tomb TT84." Life Histories of Theban Tombs. Accessed 3 July 2022.https://lhtt.philhist.unibas.ch/sheikh-abd-el-qurna/tt84/.

Van der Molen, Rami. *A Hieroglyphic Dictionary of Egyptian Coffin Texts.* Leiden: Brill, 2000.

Van Siclen, Charles C. "Obelisk." In *The Oxford Encyclopedia of Ancient Egypt,* edited by Donald Redford, 561–564. Oxford: Oxford University Press, 2001.

Vandier, Jacques. "Une tombe inédite de la Vie dynastie," *ASAE* 36 (1936): 33–44.

———. "Quelques remarques sur les scènes de pèlerinage aux villes saintes dans les tombes de la XVIIIe dynastie." *Chronique d'Égypte* 37 (1944): 35–60.

Vivas Sáinz, Inmaculada. "The Artist in his Context: New Tendencies on the Research of Ancient Egyptian Art." *TdE* 7 (2016): 203–220. http://doi.org/10.25145/j.TdE.2016.07.11

———. "Egyptian artists in the New Kingdom: Travelling artists and travelling ideas?" In *Current Research in Egyptology 2016: Proceedings of the Seventeenth Annual Symposium,* edited by Julia M. Chyla, *et al.*, 107–120. Oxbow Books, 2017.

Weeks, Kent (ed.). *Egyptology and Social Sciences: Five Studies.* Cairo: American University in Cairo Press, 1979.

Wegner, Mary-Ann Pouls. The cult of Osiris at Abydos: An archaeological investigation of the development of an ancient Egyptian sacred center during the Eighteenth Dynasty. Ph.D. dissertation. University of Pennsylvania, 2002.

Wente, Edward. "Some Graffiti from the Reign of Hatshepsut." *JNES* 43 (1984): 47–54.

Whale, Sheila. *The Family in the Eighteenth Dynasty of Egypt: A Study of the Representation of the Family in Private Tombs.* Sydney: The Australian Centre for Egyptology, 1989.

White, Richard. "What is Spatial History?" Stanford University Spatial History Lab. (2010): 1–6.

Wild, Henri. *Les danses sacrées de l'Égypte ancienne.* In *Les danses sacrées: Sources Orientales*, vol. 6, edited by Jean Cazeneuve, 33–117. Paris: Editions du Seuil, 1963.

Wilkinson, Alix. "Landscapes for Funeral Rituals in Dynastic Times." In *The Unbroken Reed: Studies in the Culture and Heritage of Ancient Egypt, in Honour of A. F. Shore,* edited by Christopher Eyre, Anthony Leahy and Lisa Montagno Leahy, 391–401. London: Egypt Exploration Society, 1994a.

———. "Symbolism and Design in Ancient Egyptian Gardens." *Garden History* 22, 1 (1994b): 1–17.

———. *The Garden in Ancient Egypt.* London: Rubicon Press, 1998.

Wilkinson, Richard H. *Symbol and Magic in Egyptian Art.* London: Thames and Hudson, 1994.

Wilkinson, T. *Early Dynastic Egypt.* London/New York: Routledge, 1999.

Index

A

B

C

D

E

F

G

H

S

T

U

W